5000

THE BOOK OF ACTS IN ITS FIRST CENTURY SETTING

I. The Book of Acts in Its Ancient Literary Setting
II. The Book of Acts in Its Graeco-Roman Setting
III. The Book of Acts and Paul in Roman Custody
IV. The Book of Acts in Its Palestinian Setting
V. The Book of Acts in Its Diaspora Setting
VI. The Book of Acts in Its Theological Setting

Bruce W. Winter

Series Editor

I. Howard Marshall • David W. J. Gill

Consulting Editors

THE BOOK OF ACTS IN ITS FIRST CENTURY SETTING

VOLUME 5

The Book of Acts in Its Diaspora Setting

by

Irina Levinskaya

WILLIAM B. EERDMANS PUBLISHING COMPANY
GRAND RAPIDS, MICHIGAN

THE PATERNOSTER PRESS
CARLISLE

© 1996 Wm. B. Eerdmans Publishing Company
255 Jefferson Ave. S.E., Grand Rapids, Michigan 49503

First published 1996 jointly
in the United States by
Wm. B. Eerdmans Publishing Company
and in the U.K. by
The Paternoster Press,
P.O. Box 300, Carlisle, Cumbria CA3 0QS

Printed in the United States of America

00 99 98 97 96   7 6 5 4 3 2 1

Library of Congress Cataloging-in-Publication Data

Levinskaya, Irina.
The book of Acts in its diaspora setting / by Irina Levinskaya
(The book of Acts in its first century setting; v. 5)
p.   cm.
Includes bibliographical references and indexes.
ISBN 0-8028-2437-4 (cloth: alk. paper)
1. Bible. N.T. Acts — Criticism, interpretation, etc.
2. Jewish diaspora. 3. Proselytes and proselyting, Jewish.
4. Rome — Religion. I. Title. II. Series.
BS2625.2.L47 1996
226.6'067 — dc21   96-46659
CIP

Paternoster ISBN 0-85364-567-1

CONTENTS

Preface   vii
Acknowledgements   xi
Abbreviations   xv

Diaspora Jews, Proselytes and God-fearers

CHAPTER 1: Diaspora Jews in the Book of Acts   1
    I. Jewish Identity and the Jewish Tax:
      The Religious Boundary   2
    II. Jewish Identity and the Circumcision of Timothy:
      The Ethnic Boundary   12

CHAPTER 2: Proselytes: Non-Christian Evidence   19
    I. Epigraphic Evidence   25
    II. Literary Sources   26

CHAPTER 3: Proselytes: Christian Evidence   35
    I. The Proselytes of Matthew 23:15   36
    II. Later Christian Evidence   40
    III. The Proselytes in Acts   46

CHAPTER 4: God-fearers: Epigraphic Evidence   51
    I. Introduction   52
    II. Evidence for God-fearers   59
    III. Indirect Epigraphic Evidence for God-fearers   81

CHAPTER 5: God-fearers and the Cult of the Most High God   83
    I. Pagan Background   84
    II. Jewish Background   95
    III. The Most High God in Acts: Pagan or Jewish?   98

CHAPTER 6: God-Fearers: The Bosporan Kingdom: 105
    A Case Study

CHAPTER 7: God-Fearers : The Literary Evidence   117
    I. Non-Christian Literary Evidence   118
    II. God-fearers in the Book of Acts   120

Jewish Diaspora Communities

CHAPTER 8:   Antioch   127

CHAPTER 9:   Asia Minor   137
                   I. Introduction   138
                   II. Ephesus   143
                   III. Miletus   148
                   IV. Pisidian Antioch   150
                   V. Iconium   150

CHAPTER 10:   Macedonia and Achaia   153
                   I. Thessalonica   154
                   II. Beroea   157
                   III. Athens   158
                   IV. Corinth   162

CHAPTER 11:   Rome   167
                   I. Literary Evidence   168
                   II. Epigraphic Evidence   182

CHAPTER 12:   Conclusion   195

APPENDIX 1:   Syncretism- The Term and the Phenomenon   197

APPENDIX 2:   The Meaning of 'Proseuche'   207
                   I. Criteria for distinguishing Jewish Inscriptions 208
                   II. The Meaning of 'Proseuche'   213

APPENDIX 3:   Inscriptions from the Bosporan Kingdom   227
                   I. Dedications   229
                   II. Manumissions   231
                   III. Religious Associations   242

Bibliography   247
Index of Greek Inscriptions in Appendix 3   263
Index of Biblical References   267
Index of Ancient Authors   269
Index of Modern Authors   273
Index of Subjects   279

PREFACE

This book is written by an ancient historian who, during the last ten years, has become more and more absorbed by New Testament studies through research into the book of Acts. When I was a student in the Department of Classics of St. Petersburg university (which was called then by another name which I do not like to remember), on one occasion our professor asked us, as first year undergraduates, what particular field each of us was interested in. I immediately and rather naively said 'New Testament' and got the answer 'It is out of the question, at least on these premises'. The expression on my teacher's face prompted me never to bring up this subject with him again. Later I realised that his response was out of concern for a young and inex-perienced person—he had spent ten years of his life in one of Stalin's camp and ten years in exile. Such an experience teaches one to be especially careful. I therefore studied classical literature and for some time my hero became Herodotus. I was enchanted by his breath-taking ability to combine history with story-telling. The fascinating process of looking for the historical core of the stories captured me completely and, under the influence of these studies, my interests changed. I defected from philology to ancient history.

When I was looking for a subject for my doctoral dissertation I suddenly realised that, though I could not work in the field of New Testament, I could at least move nearer. I chose the subject of the cult of the Most High God—paganism was *religio licita* under the communists and this cult was usually viewed as a pagan one! In the course of investigating the sources and secondary literature, I came to the conclusion that this cult in the Bosporan Kingdom was a manifestation of Jewish influence, and that the most interesting parallels are provided by the book of Acts. This was the beginning of my intense interest in Acts.

But the more I read of the scholarly literature on Acts the more I was surprised by approaches to the book: it could be viewed either as a purely theological scheme or, in the minds of some, as a second-rate combination of contradictory sources and legends about the beginnings of the Christian church. The few exceptions have not changed the general trend. My impression from the book of Acts was quite different. The studies of Herodotus taught me that a novelistic genre and a strong theological framework (in the case of Herodotus that of the envy of the gods—φθόνος θεῶν) can go hand in hand with first-rate social, cultural, ethnographical and historical information. There is no reason whatsoever to treat Acts any differently from other first century writings. The almost universally accepted dichotomy for studying Acts is somewhat surprising for an ancient historian. In my perception, the book of Acts, though it has a notable theological conception, was both a valuable historical work and an important source of background material for the first century AD. My further studies have confirmed and strengthened this perception.

Not surprisingly, I was delighted by the invitation to participate in a project on the background to the book of Acts. Since this volume forms part of a series, *The Book of Acts in its First Century Setting*, the series editor gave a very specific brief— to gather the evidence we possess on the Diaspora in the first century in order to provide the background for our on-going discussion of Acts in relation to the Diaspora.

As an ancient historian interested in the building material out of which edifices are constructed, I have devoted this book to the discussion of the detailed evidence that we possess on the Diaspora at this present moment. It is extremely important to note at the very beginning of this work that, compared with those subsequent centuries, the sources for Jewish life in the Diaspora in the first century are very limited indeed. All regions mentioned in the Acts of the Apostles are known to have had a substantial Jewish population long before the first century AD. Archaeological discoveries, mainly in the second half of the twentieth century, have supplied us with rich Jewish material which confirms the wide dissemination of Jews all around the Mediterranean world. The problems arise when we start to distribute material chronologically. The overwhelming majority of inscriptions, which are our main and the most important source, belong to the period from the end of the second century AD and later. The first century is extremely poorly represented by epigraphic evidence and among excavated synagogues only one belongs to this period. There is only one district outside Egypt, (which is beyond the scope of this book), that yielded a whole series of Jewish, or Jewish related, inscriptions—the Bosporan kingdom, situated in a remote part of the Mediterranean world, on the northern coast of the Black Sea. I consider this evidence so important for understanding certain aspects of Jewish-Gentile relations that, despite the fact that the Bosporan kingdom was outside the world of the book of Acts, I decided to discuss it at length in a separate chapter. The selection of inscriptions from the Bosporan kingdom is presented in Appendix 3 to this book as well as the photographs of the inscriptions—some of which have not been published before.

The same deficiency for the first century Jewish Diaspora outside Egypt also exists among literary sources. The greater part of the extant Jewish literature was written either before or after the first century and mostly in Egypt. Though in the first century we have two great Jewish writers, Philo and Josephus, the information one can obtain from the writings of the former is relevant mostly to Egypt, and from those of the latter, to Judea, with the exception of a few episodes associated with the contemporary Jews in the Diaspora. Some aspects of Jewish life, mostly in Rome, are reflected in Greek and Roman literature, but usually as occasional references which are sometimes not easy to interpret.[1] All this makes Luke's evidence for the first century western Diaspora, which is the main scene of Acts, especially valuable. The problem is: how can we check his information? Given the situation with the contemporary sources the attraction of the material from a later period seems to be unavoidable. This creates a methodical challenge: what kind of later sources can possibly be used for comparison with Acts?

As a result of the great archaeological achievements in the field of the Jewish Diaspora, a new and sometimes unexpected picture of Jewish life had emerged[2] and many of the old assumptions have been rightly questioned—among them the

---

[1] Cf., for instance, notoriously puzzling reference in Horace *Sat.* I.9.69 (= Stern, *GLAJJ* I, No. 129) to the *tricensima sabbata* (thirtieth Sabbath); for the latest interpretation see L.H. Feldman, 'The Enigma of Horace's Thirtieth Sabbath', *SCI* 10 (1989-1990), 87-112.

[2] About the difficulties which are immanent in the very nature of archaeological evidence, first of all inscriptions, and its limitations for the reconstruction of cultural and religious life see P. Trebilco, *Jewish Communiies in Asia Minor* (Cambridge: CUP, 1991), 2f..

possibility of using rabbinic texts to understand Jewish life in the Diaspora and of applying rabbinic norms for the pre-rabbinic period. This cautious approach seems to be justified. Rabbinic norms were produced in a different milieu and reflect different stage of religious development. Even at the synchronous level we need to be cautious when using Palestinian material for the Diaspora. On the other hand, there was no impassable border between Palestine and the Diaspora and we may expect to find in rabbinic writings the reflection of problems which were posed by life in the Diaspora.[3]

But on the whole it seems that we are on safer ground with inscriptions originating from the same region though dated a century or two later. The reconstruction of an earlier period based entirely on later sources is always unreliable (as well as the reverse situation: the forward reconstruction). But if we have an earlier source (for example, the book of Acts) whose information is supported by later evidence we have a chance of recovering reliable data. It is better if it can also be supported by an earlier source. The case when the later inscriptional evidence does not support the earlier source, or even conflicts with it, is more complicated, because it can mean a new development which happened after the earlier one was produced.

The second part of this work deals with a detailed description of the evidence of the Jewish Diaspora communities in Antioch, Asia Minor, Macedonia, Achaia and Rome in the first centuries AD.

The first part addresses the Jewish world in the Diaspora as it was described by Luke. This world consisted of Jews, proselytes and sympathetic Gentiles—God-fearers, as they are usually called in scholarly literature. I shall commence with the first group.

---

[3]Cf. L.V. Rutgers, *The Jews in Late Ancient Rome: Evidence of Cultural Interaction in the Roman Diaspora* (Leiden, New York, Köln, 1995, Religions in the Graeco-Roman World, 126), 206: 'to contrast a supposedly full-fledged, orthodox rabbinic Judaism of Palestine with a consciously un-rabbinic Judaism of Diaspora is to impose categorizations on the evidence that are far too rigid'.

ACKNOWLEDGEMENTS

This work would never come into being without the most generous help and encouragement of the series editor, Bruce Winter. Not only did he honour me with the invitation to join the project on the background studies of the book of Acts but was a most kind, helpful and understanding editor. The book was written mostly in Tyndale House, Cambridge, with the help of a postdoctoral fellowship granted by its Academic Committee. I am much indebted to the friendly atmosphere of this place, and the expertise of the scholarly community in Tyndale House.

While I was working in Cambridge I had the great privilege of staying in the home of the leading British epigraphist, Joyce Reynolds, and enjoying both her amazing hospitality and her generous professional advice. I owe a tremendous debt of gratitude to her for her invaluable editorial assistance on many aspects of this book.

Then my thanks go to other people who have given their time and energy to edit the book and make the English language—foreign to me—sound more natural than anything I could produce, especially those who took pains to read the first draft and put right anything that I had put wrongly (first of all definite and indefinite articles—for the outsider, the insoluble enigma of the English language). Gerald Bray read through much of the book and suggested helpful changes. Myles Burnyeat for a short while came down from the heights of Plato and Aristotle to look through the texts of the humble Christian writers. He edited some of my translations and Appendix 2. And then Janet Fairweather, who sacrificed hours of hard-won vacation time in valiant attempts to give this Russian's English a more British flavour.

Despite the efforts of this wonderful team of native speakers, I am sure that errors inevitably remain, and the responsibility for these, needless to say, lies with me alone.

I should also like to thank the St. Petersburg Branch of the Institute of History of the Russian Academy of Sciences for permission to publish photographs of the Bosporan inscriptions and for graciously tolerating my absence for extended periods.

My thanks with help with materials go to: Elena Vlasova, the curator of the Hermitage collection of the inscriptions, Irina Tunkina from the Archive of the Russian Academy of Sciences and Dmitry Danshin from the Institute of Archaeology. My appreciation also goes to John Barclay for sending me the manuscript of his useful and important book before its publication.

I am especially grateful to my mother and to my husband who showed much patience and accepted with understanding my physical absence from St. Petersburg for long periods, and then my spiritual absence despite my physical presence in St. Petersburg, while I was writing this book.

To the blessed memory of my father
Alexey Levinsky
and my teachers
Aristid Dovatur and Jacobus Borovskij

List of Abbreviations

AEM	Anuario de estudios medievales
AJ	Archaeological Journal
AJA	American Journal of Archaeology
ANRW	Aufstieg und Niedergang der römischen Welt
BASOR	Bulletin of the American Schools of Oriental Research
BC	*The Beginnings of Christianity*, Foakes Jackson and Kirsopp Lake
BE	Bulletin Épigraphique
CBQ	Catholic Biblical Quarterly
CIG	Corpus Inscriptionum Graecarum (1828-77)
CIJ	Corpus Inscriptionum Iudaicarum (I, 1936; II, 1952)
CIL	Corpus Inscriptionum Latinarum (I, 1863-1909)
CIRB	*Corpus Inscriptionum Regni Bosporani*, I. Struve, 1965
CRINT	*Compendia Rerum Iudaicarum ad Novum Testamentum*
ET	English Translation
Expt	Expository Times
GLAJJ	*Greek and Latin Authors on Jews and Judaism*, M. Stern,3 vols. Jerusalem : Israel Academy of Sciences and Humanities, 1976, 1980, 1984
GRBS	Greek, Roman and Byzantine Studies
HTR	Harvard Theological Review
IG	Inscriptiones Graecae
IM	Mitteilungen des deutschen Archäologischen Instituts, Istanbuler Abteilung
IPE	Inscriptiones orae septentrionalis Ponti Euxini, B. Latyshev, vols. I-IV, I2 (St Petersburg, 1885-1901, 1916)
JAC	Jahrbuch für Antike und Christentum
JBL	Journal of Biblical Literature
JIGRE	*Jewish Inscriptions of Graeco-Roman Egypt*, W. Horbury and D. Noy
JIWE	*Jewish Inscriptions of Western Europe*, vols. 1 & 2, D. Noy
JJS	Journal of Jewish Studies
JÖAI	Jahreshefte des östereichischen archäologischen Instituts
JQR	Jewish Quarterly Review
JRA	Journal of Religion in Africa
JSJ	Journal for the Study of Judaism
JSNT	Journal for the Study of the New Testament
JSS	Jewish Social Studies
JThSt	Journal of Theological Studies
LCL	Loeb Classical Library
NewDocs	*New Documents illustrating Early Christianity*, Macquarie University (1982-)
NIS	*Nouvelle inscriptions de Sardes* , L. Robert, (Paris: Librairie d'Amérique et d'Orient, 1964)
Or	Orientalia. Roma
REJ	Revue des études juives
ResQ	Restoration Quarterly
RHR	Revue d'histoire et des religions
SEG	Supplementum Epigraphicum Graecum
TDNT	*Theological Dictionary of the New Testament*
TynB	Tyndale Bulletin
TZ	Theologische Zeitschrift
ZAW	Zeitschrift für Aszese und Mystik
ZNW	Zeitschrift für die neuetestamentliche Wissenschaft
ZPE	Zeitschrift für Papyrologie und Epigraphik

CHAPTER 1

DIASPORA JEWS
IN THE BOOK OF ACTS

This chapter discusses the problems of Jewish religious and ethnic identity. It was recently proposed that until the very end of the first century Jews were unconcerned about who of the sympathetic Gentiles were to be considered as Jews and who as outsiders. A clear sense of Jewish identity was obtained once this issue was clarified by the Roman state in the course of repudiating Domitian's abuses in collecting the Jewish tax. This theory is contested and it is argued that the extant sources are in harmony with the picture drawn by Luke in Acts. It shows that Jews were well aware of the divide that existed between them and friendly Gentiles. Apart from the religious boundary, there was the ethnic one which was of great significance for Diaspora Jews who lived in a Gentile milieu. The episode concerning the circumcision of Timothy (Acts 16:1-3) provides the earliest reference for the matrilineal principle of pedigree which became a norm in later rabbinic legislation.

1

I. Jewish Identity and the Jewish Tax (*Fiscus Iudaicus*): the Religious Boundary

In recent years the problem of Jewish identity has become the centre of a lively debate. However, the important evidence provided by Acts for this discussion is either underestimated or sceptically dismissed. M. Goodman sums up the prevailing attitude when he says that Acts 'should be treated as a work of theology rather than history' and this approach 'for better or worse, is now fairly standard among specialists in the study of New Testament'.[1] On the whole the use of Acts as evidence for the first century is rather inconsistent. On the one hand, its narrative is widely used for locating Jewish communities in the first century: such places as, for instance, Iconium or Philippi appeared on the map of the first century Jewish Diaspora exclusively from the pages of Acts. On the other, the veracity of Acts' evidence for Jewish life and, in particular, for relations with surrounding Gentiles, is often questioned.

No one would deny that Luke's theological ideas influenced his choice of material and his evaluation of this material. Every historian ancient or modern is influenced by some kind of ideology—Tacitus' claim to write *sine ira et studio* is an expression of impracticable *desiderata*: to write *sine ira* is within human power but *sine studio* is not. No one historian, if he is trying to reconstruct what he believes has actually happened and is not just producing tables of events and dates, can escape selectivity with respect to his material, and either implicit or explicit judgements. Of course, Luke had his own views on the development of the Christian mission and the early church, and arranged his material in accordance with them. But his historical outlook and the reliability of the background material are different issues. Some scholars have argued to defend the credibility of Luke as an historian and especially the accurate presentation in Acts of the stage on which the events took place and suggest that a writer who is careful to get background right may be expected to tell a reliable story as well. Unfortunately these things do not necessarily go together. An historical novel can be dressed in a garment very appropriate for its period. However, no substantial historical work can be produced without knowledge of the background material. The previous volume in this series, *The Book of Acts in its Palestinian Setting*, shows that Luke displays a good knowledge of Palestinian background.[2] Let us test his Diaspora data and if

---

[1] M. Goodman, 'Who was a Jew?', (Oxford: The Oxford Centre for Postgraduate Hebrew Studies, 1989), 10.

they can be shown to resonate with what we know elsewhere, see how they may affect the course of our discussion on Jewish identity.

One of the most important contributions to this discussion has been made by M. Goodman. In a number of articles, and in his recent book[3], he argues that till the very end of the first century and, even more precisely, before AD 96, the year of the reform of the exaction of the Jewish tax *(fiscus Iudaicus)* by Nerva, there was no clarity about Jewish status; Jews were unconcerned about who of the Jewish sympathizers among the Gentiles were in fact to be considered as Jews, and who were just friendly outsiders. Nerva stopped a witch-hunt for Jewish tax-evaders and commemorated this act by minting coins with the legend: *fisci Iudaici calumnia sublata*—'the wrongful accusations with regard to the Jewish tax are suppressed'.[4] Goodman suggests that the main point of Nerva's action was a new Roman definition of a Jew, not by race as before, but by religion. One of the results was that the Roman state became aware of the Jewish concept of a proselyte, since Romans started to desert the traditional Roman gods in favour of the Jewish God. Another result of his move was the clarification for Jews of their attitude towards friendly Gentiles.[5]

It seems to me doubtful in the extreme that the Roman state had no knowledge of the concept of a proselyte at the time of the Jewish war against Rome of AD 66-70 when the Adiabeneans, whose ruling dynasty was converted to Judaism in the middle of the first century AD, took part on the Jewish side. The existence of such a phenomenon as Jewish sympathizers was well known to the Roman authorities. This is well attested by a variety of pieces of evidence, including the expulsions of Jews from Rome.[6]

---

[2]Cf. for instance, *The Book of Acts in its Palestinian Setting,* (Carlisle, Grand Rapids; Paternoster, Eerdmans, 1994), 174-177 (S. Mason), 209 (R. Riesner), 355-356 (B. Capper), 263-265 (W. Reinhardt), 27, 77-78 (M. Hengel), .

[3]M. Goodman, 'Nerva, The *Fiscus Judaicus* and Jewish Identity', *JRS* 79 (1989), 40-44; 'Who was a Jew?', 1-19; 'Proselytising in Rabbinic Judaism', *JJS* 38 (1989), 175-185; 'Diaspora Reactions to the Destruction of the Temple', *Jews and Christians: The Parting of the Ways AD 70 to 135,* ed. J.D.G. Dunn (Tübingen: Mohr, 1992), 27-38; *Mission and Conversion: Proselytizing in the Religious History of the Roman Empire* (Oxford: Clarendon Press, 1994), 121-126.

[4]H. Mattingly, *Coins of the Roman Empire in the British Museum* III *Nerva to Hadrian* (London: The Trustees of the British Museum, 1936), No. 88, 98, 105, 106; *The Roman Imperial Coinage,* ed. H. Mattingly and E.A. Sydenham, II (London: 1926), No. 58, 72, 82.

[5]Goodman, 'Who was a Jew?', 15f.

The precise nature of Nerva's reform is not known.[7] It has been reconstructed on the basis of a combination of the account of abuses in collecting the Jewish tax under Domitian given by Suetonius, on the one hand, and from the evidence of Cassius Dio, on the other. Dio reports that some members of the Roman upper class were executed by Domitian on charges of Jewish 'atheism', and that Nerva prohibited accusations from being brought against the Jewish way of life.

According to Suetonius, under Domitian the Jewish tax was exacted with particular vigour (*acerbissime*) and

> *ad quem deferebantur qui vel[ut] inprofessi Iudaicam viverent vitam vel dissimulata origine imposita genti tributa non pependissent*[8]

those were prosecuted who, without publicly acknowledging that faith, yet lived as Jews, as well as those who concealed their origin and did not pay the tribute levied upon their people.

(trans. J.C. Rolfe, *LCL*)

After this statement Suetonius referred to his own recollection of an old man of ninety being stripped before the procurator and a crowded court to see whether he was circumcised.[9] This passage is usually interpreted to mean that two groups of people were considered to be

---

[6]See pp. 28-32, 171-77. This does not mean that the Roman state scrupulously distinguished between these categories. What the Roman authorities were well aware of was that in some cases the enthusiasm for Judaism that penetrated into the highest echelons of Roman society (and was regarded as atheistic) could go too far—the example of Adiabene was a serious warning.

[7]What M. Sordi means when she writes that Nerva 'suppressed the Jewish tax' which should not 'be confused with *fiscus Iudaicus*' is beyond my understanding. M. Sordi,*The Christians and the Roman Empire*, ET (London and New York: Routledge, 1994), 48.

[8]*Domitianus*, 12:2 = Stern, *GLAJJ* II No. 320.

[9]The story about the investigation of the ninety year old man seems to contradict the traditional assumption that in accordance with the documents from Egypt the upper age limit of taxation was sixty or sixty two years old. But on the other hand, the notion that Jews were exempted from tax at this age is based on general consideration and analogy with the *laographia* (poll tax)(Stern, *GLAJJ* II, 131). For the exemption of women at this age there exists documentary evidence, though with obscure wording, but whether it was applied also to men is not certain. E.M. Smallwood, *The Jews under Roman Rule. From Pompey to Diocletian* (Leiden: E.J. Brill, 1976[2], SLLA 20), 373. It cannot be ruled out completely that among Domitian's abuses was the abolition of the upper limit (I.A.F. Bruce, 'Nerva and the *Fiscus Iudaicus*', *PEQ* 96 (1964), 40f.; C.J. Hemer, 'The Edfu *Ostraka* and the Jewish Tax', *PEQ*, 104-105 (1972-1973), 7, n. 10).

evading the tax and were subject to punishment for this: those who were not ethnic Jews but adherants of Judaism[10] and those who were Jews by origin but gave up their way of life and concealed their origin.[11] The collection of the Jewish tax from these groups is generally viewed as Domitian's innovation.[12] Cassius Dio records:

> The same year (AD 95) Domitian slew, along with many others, Flavius Clemens the consul, although he was a cousin and had to wife Flavia Domitilla, who was also a relative of the emperor's. The charge brought against them both was that of atheism (ἔγκλημα ἀθεό-τητος), a charge on which many others who drifted into Jewish ways (ἐς τὰ Ἰουδαίων ἤθη ἐξοκέλλοντες) were condemned. Some of these were put to death, and the rest were at least deprived of their property.[13]

(trans. E. Cary, *LCL*)

> Nerva also released all who were on trial for treason *maiestas* (ἀσέβεια) and restored the exiles . . . and no persons were permitted to accuse anybody of *maiestas* or of adopting the Jewish mode of life (Ἰουδαικὸς βίος).[14]

(trans. E. Cary, *LCL*)

---

[10]Under what heading can they be listed? Here opinions vary, see references in M.H. Williams, 'Domitian, the Jews and the 'Judaizers'— a Simple Matter of Cupiditas and Maiestas?', Historia, 34:2 (1990), 198, n. 9. See also list of literature in Hemer, 'The Edfu *Ostraka*', 6, n. 3. Bruce, 'Nerva', 41-45, suggested that the innovations of Domitian concerned ethnic Jews from Italy who were previously exempted from the tax, but it contradicts Josephus' evidence in *BJ* 7.218, (Williams, 'Domitian', 198, n. 9). Sordi's argument on the basis of Dio's testimony (see below), that *improfessi* were exposed to the death penalty while those who admitted their 'Jewish ways' only had to pay tax and enjoyed freedom of *religio licita*, and that thus the stubbornness of the Roman aristocrats who preferred to be executed rather than to proclaim themselves openly as adherents of Judaism (*The Christians*, 48f.) can only be explained if they were Christians, is in conflict with the clear statement of Suetonius that *improfessi* had to pay tax.

[11]Cf., for instance, Stern, *GLAJJ* II No. 130.

[12]But see Williams, 'Domitian', 198ff., who denies any fiscal initiative by Domitian. She refers to the same opinion of H.J. Leon, *The Jews of Ancient Rome*, (Philadelphia: The Jewish Publication Society of America, 1960) 33. Leon, however, considers those who *improfessi Iudaicam viverent vitam* to be proselytes who, though they were obliged to pay, failed to register on the tax rolls, while she views them as Judaizers.

[13]*Dio Cassius*, 67.14, 1-3 = Stern, *GLAJJ* II No. 435. The major part of Dio's history devoted to the reign of Domitian, including this passage, is preserved only in the abridgement by Xiphilinus (eleventh century).

[14]*Dio Cassius*, 68.1, 2 (cited by Xiphilinus) = Stern, *GLAJJ* II No. 437.

Comparison of Suetonius' passage with the first one by Dio leads Goodman to conclude that, since Gentiles could not be both taxed and executed for the same offence, Suetonius was referring only to ethnic Jews, 'who had given up public identification with their religion either by hiding their continued Jewish practices or by pretending that their customs had nothing to do with their Jewish ethnic origin which they dissimulated'.[15] Thus in Goodman's view the reform of Nerva concerned only abuses towards Jews, which were treated as an extremely serious matter, as is shown by the coins. The Roman state not only stopped them, but worked out a new approach to the 'Jewish question'.

Such an interpretation does not seem convincing. Judaism was a *religio licita*.[16] Roman citizens could not be prosecuted just for adding another exotic god to their pantheon, with the proviso, of course, that they did not abandon their civil duties and testified their loyalty by worshipping state gods[17] which in this period included worship of the emperor. The refusal to do so under the Principate could be treated as treason (*maiestas*) and the Roman treason law had a very wide range of application.

> It was *maiestas* to conspire against the State . . . but it was also *maiestas* to lose a battle; . . . to lay false claim to Roman citizenship; to visit a brothel in an official capacity; to hold court while intoxicated, or dressed in woman's clothes; to publish defamatory pamphlets, and to commit adultery with the emperor's daughter.[18]

Under the Principate, apart from the ordinary categories for the law dealing with state security (sedition, treachery in the field, conspiracies against the magistrates of the state, misconduct in public affairs, etc.), which are attributed to a *lex Julia maiestatis* and went back to the Republican period it was expanded to support the charges in verbal or real injuries to the emperor. Acts of impiety offensive to the gods became capable of being dealt with as treason. Through the rulings in fa-

---

[15]M. Goodman, 'Nerva', 41, cf. also 'Who was a Jew?', 15.

[16]The term stepped into the pages of scholarly works from Tertullian's description of Judaism in *Apol.* 21,1: . . . *quasi sub umbraculo insignissimae religionis, certae licitae.*

[17]For the actions taken in the Republican period to secure the worship only of true Roman gods, see R.A. Bauman, 'Tertullian and the Crime of *Sacrilegium*', *The Journal of Religious History*, 4 (1966-1967), 181f., who argues that nevertheless all these actions were taken outside the scope of the public criminal law.

[18]R.A. Bauman, *The Crimen Maiestatis in the Roman Republic and Augustan Principate* (Johannesburg: Witwatersrand University Press, 1967), VII.

vour of *Divus Augustus* the category of *impietas* towards the deified emperor was incorporated into the *lex maiestatis*. Under Caligula *divina maiestas* of the emperor began to be expressed in terms of *crimen maiestatis*. The refusal to offer sacrifices for the emperor was regarded as such a crime.[19]

The term 'atheism' which was used by Dio is not a legal one.[20] What legal accusations could possibly stand behind Dio's wording?[21] It could not be *crimen laesae religionis*, since offences against religion had never been part of the Roman criminal law[22] and it was only under the Severan dynasty that refusal to worship the gods was prosecuted as a *crimen*. Suetonius, who was a contemporary witness of the events, did not mention any charges of atheism. He briefly reported that Flavius Clemens, whose sons were officially recognised as Domitian's heirs, was suddenly put to death on the merest suspicion: *repente ex tenuissima suspicione*.[23] It is evident from Suetonius' account that he considered the real reason for this execution to have been Domitian's suspicion that Clemens was plotting against his life to clear the way to power for his sons. It is also evident that he did not believe that Clemens was involved in such a plot—hence his characterization of Clem-

---

[19]R.A. Bauman, *Impietas in Principem: A Study of Treason against Roman Emperors with Special Reference to the First Century A.D.* (Munich: C.H. Beck, 1974, Münchener Beiträge zur Papyrforschung und Antiken Rechtgeschichte, 67), 1-24.

[20]An explicit accusation of Jews as atheists was mentioned by Josephus in his account of Apollonius Molon's anti-Jewish attacks (*apud c. App.* 2.148 = Stern, *GLAJJ* I No. 49). Apart from Dio, the direct references to Jewish 'atheism' can be found in Julian, *Contra Galilaeos* 43B = Stern, *GLAJJ* II 513, No. 481, cf. also Ptolemy, *Apotelesmatica* II, 3.66 (31) = Stern, *GLAJJ* II No. 336a and Porphyry, *Adv. Christianos* I.3 *ap.* Eus. *Praep. Ev.*= Stern, *GLAJJ* II No. 458. For the examples of the implicit accusations of atheism, see Smallwood, 'The Jews', 379, n. 8. The concept of 'atheism' is not found in Latin usage before the beginning of the fourth century and not among the jurists, H. Conzelmann, *Gentiles –Jews –Christians: Polemics and Apologetics in the Greco-Roman Era*, ET (Minneapolis: Fortress Press, 1992), 246.

[21]Cf. Bauman, *Impietas*, 4f. on the inability of Dio and Greek authors on the whole to come to terms with Latin juridical terminology.

[22]Cf. the episode in the reign of Tiberius, which was recounted by Tacitus, *Ann.* 1.73.2ff.: when a complaint was lodged against a certain Rubrius, that he had sworn falsely by the *numen* of Augustus, Tiberius refused to punish him on the grounds that *deorum iniurias dis curae* ('injuries to the gods are the business of the gods'). Bauman, 'Tertullian', 182. When Tacitus reports in *Ann.* 3.24.2f. that Augustus charged the two Julias and their lovers with a (*crimen*) *laesarum religionum ac violatae maiestatis*, it is important that '*laesarum religionum* did not stand alone as the basis of the charge with which Augustus was concerned, for he added the words *ac violatae maiestatis*,' Bauman, 'Tertullian', 180.

[23]*Domitianus*, 15,1.

ens as a man of 'most contemptible laziness' (*contemptissimae
inertiae*).[24] Suetonius said nothing about official charges against Clemens. But taking into consideration his rank, the punishment and 'an active period of the *lex maiestatis*' at the latter part of Domitian's reign,[25]
it is almost an inevitable conclusion that he was charged with treason.
If Dio's information is correct, which, given his special interest in the
phenomenon of Jewish proselytism,[26] may well be the case, then the
accusation of atheism, which could give rise to the *crimen maiestatis*,
was used as a pretext for Clemens' execution. During the period of terror at the end of Domitian's reign,[27] this could happen despite the fact
that being the *consul ordinarius* for AD 95, Clemens as a supreme magistrate inevitably participated in official rituals. It looks as if for Dio the
fact that *atheotes* was treated by Domitian in terms of treason was self-
evident. It was not by accident that he mentioned the *maiestas* accusations and charges against the Jewish manner of life side by side in the
second passage.[28]

It is difficult to say, however, how well-grounded such charges
were. On the one hand, given Domitian's claims to divinity[29] any reservations about such claims could have been reckoned sufficient basis
for accusing someone of rejecting state gods and, since such reservations were traditionally connected with Jews, of Jewish atheism. On
the other hand, Judaism had become rather fashionable among the Roman upper classes.[30] It is quite possible that Clemens was actually a
Jewish sympathizer. It is also difficult to define how many victims of
Domitian's terror were slaughtered on the charge of Jewish 'atheism'.

---

[24]Cf. E.T. Merrill, *Essays in Early Christian History* (London: Macmillan, 1924), 149f.,
who suggested for *inertia* the following interpretations 'lack of energy' or 'lack of
activity', or 'want of reasonable ambition', or 'absence of interest in public affairs',
or 'leading a retired life'. The word was treated by some as a hint to Clemens'
Judaizing practices, such as Sabbath observance, which the Romans scornfully
stigmatized as a laziness, Williams, 'Domitian', 208, n. 89, or to his Christianity,
see, e.g. Sordi, *The Christians*, 52.
[25]Bauman, *Impietas*, 159.
[26]Stern, *GLAJJ* II, 348.
[27]It is quite possible that there was a period of abeyance of the *lex maiestatis* in the
early years of Domitian's reign; Bauman, *Impietas*, 169.
[28]See p. 5.
[29]Roman apotheosis was always posthumous (see in detail E.Bickerman, 'Conse-
cratio', *Le culte des souverains dans l'Empire romain* (Vandoevres-Genève: Fondation
Hardt, 1973, Entretiens sur l'Antiquité classique, XIX), 9-25. Domitian's demands
to be addressed as *dominus et deus noster* (Suetonius, *Domit.* 13.2) were extraordinary indeed and can only be compared with Caligula's bizarre behaviour.
[30]See pp. 65-66, 131.

Though Dio talked about 'many' victims, were there actually many other cases of alleged atheism besides those which he mentioned? As E.T. Merrill put it,

> neither in Suetonius, nor in Dio, nor in any other of the pagan writers who touch upon the subject, is there the slightest intimation that Domitian's bloody jealousy was directed against any but the leading aristocrats whom he supposed he had reason to fear, or that it ravaged at all outside the narrow circle of the Court and the Parliament. There is no indication of its extension into the provinces, or among the commonality even in Rome. And if there had been such extension, it is altogether probable that some echo of it would be heard. There is absolute silence.[31]

In view of all that has been said above, it seems reasonable to suppose that normally those who were suspected of Judaizing were forced to pay tax, but when it suited imperial purposes it was treated as atheism and punished accordingly.[32] Domitian started the witch-hunt for Jewish tax-evaders quite probably out of fiscal considerations—Suetonius discussed it in the context of his *cupiditas*. The great number of Judaizers, including those who belonged to the best families, must have been exposed at times when denunciations were profitable and delators were encouraged. This could have suggested to Domitian that Jewish atheism was a very convenient charge to bring against those who were politically dangerous. It was the importance of aristocratic names involved in cases, connected in popular thought with the denunciations of Jewish tax-evaders, that made Nerva mint a coin repudiating Domitian's *calumnia*.

The tax continued to be collected after Domitian's abuses were abolished. Our sources give no evidence for any kind of changes in exacting the Jewish tax.[33] It is reasonable to suppose that Nerva simply restored the normal routine which existed before Domitian's intervention and that the tax was exacted from the same category of people who had been liable before. But how was the liability to pay determined by the Roman authorities before Domitian's intervention?

---

[31]Merrill, 'Essays', 157f. Similar observations can be found in Williams, 'Domitian', 208f., who explains the accusation of 'Jewish life' in the cases of Roman aristocracy under Domitian by his aversion to Judaism.
[32]Cf. Williams, 'Domitian', 207ff.
[33]We have no Edfu *ostraka* for Nerva's reign, but the documents from Trajan's time are very close in form to those of Domitian; Hemer, 'The Edfu *Ostraka*', 9.

According to Josephus, Vespasian 'imposed a tax on the Jews, whatever their place of residence, requiring each person to pay two *drachmae* annually to the Capitoline temple, just as they had previously paid this amount to the Temple of Jerusalem.'[34] Since the Temple tax was paid by proselytes as well as by ethnic Jews,[35] the Josephus' passage implies that proselytes were liable to *fiscus Iudaicus*. Dio supplements Josephus' evidence:

κaὶ ἀπ᾿ ἐκείνου δίδραχμον ἐτάχθη τοὺς τὰ πάτρια αὐτῶν ἔθη περιστέλλοντας τῷ Καπιτωλίῳ Διὶ κατ᾿ ἔτος ἀποφέρειν.[36]

From that time (the day of the destruction of Jerusalem) forth it was ordered that the Jews who continued to observe their ancestral customs should pay an annual tribute of two *denarii* to Jupiter Capitolinus.

(trans. E. Cary, *LCL*).

This passage implies that the imposition of this tax was determined by religion and only practising Jews were liable. The wording of the phrase suggests that in Dio's view those who abandoned their 'ancestral customs' were exempted from the lists of payers.[37] Such Jewish apostates, exemplified by Tiberius Julius Alexander, a nephew of Philo who had an outstanding career (governor of Judaea, prefect of Egypt),[38] were among targets of Domitian's tax innovations.

The comparison of Dio's testimony with the passage in Josephus shows that, since the Roman state determined Jewishness by religion from the very beginning of the collection of the Jewish tax, and since the tax was paid by the households who had paid the Temple tax, the religious boundary of the Jewish communities was established long before the destruction of the Temple. As Cohen argues, adding a Jewish religious self-definition to an ethnic self-definition and establishing a dual identity in Palestine, goes back to the Maccabean period:

. . . in the third and second centuries BCE . . . common blood remained important, common language became much less important, and com-

---

[34]*BJ* 7.218, (trans. H.St.J. Thackeray, *LCL*.)
[35]Bruce, 'Nerva and the *Fiscus Iudaicus*', 41; Smallwood, 'The Edfu *Ostraka*', 376; Thompson, 'Domitian', 333.
[36]Dio 65.7,2 (*apud Xiphilinum*)
[37]Bruce, 'Nerva and the *Fiscus Iudaicus* ', 36; Thompson, 'Domitian', 333.
[38]Tacitus, *Ann.* 15.28.3.

mon mode of worship and common way of life became much more
important, in the new definition of *Ioudaios*.[39]

It seems that this observation is also relevant to the first century Jewish
Diaspora. By this time Jews were well aware both of their religious
identity and of the status of friendly Gentiles.

The question which still remains is to what extent we can rely on
Dio who is known to colour 'his history by his own views and experience' and not 'lose sight of contemporary situations and implications'.[40] Could the contemporary situation affect his report of the past
events?[41] It seems that Acts can help answer this question.

The picture which emerges from the pages of Acts shows that
there was no way that Jews as they were depicted by Luke would have
any uncertainty about who were Jews and who were Gentiles, for the
boundary between them was fixed. This boundary for men was circumcision.[42] Luke like Paul uses οἱ ἐκ περιτομῆς ('they of the circumcision') as a synonym for 'Jews'.[43] Even the model God-fearer
Cornelius, who feared God with all his house, was a benefactor of the
Jewish community, prayed to God non-stop and gained a good reputation among the whole Jewish nation, was nevertheless, in Jewish
eyes undoubtedly a Gentile.[44]

Acts also shows that there were no doubts about the Gentile status of sympathetic women. A purple-seller, Lydia from Thyatira, who
was a God-fearer, invited Paul and his companions to stay with her after being baptized with her household (Acts16:15). Even Paul, who at
this stage of the mission had to think about Jewish reaction to his shar-
ing a house with a Gentile, did not feel able to accept her invitation
readily. Lydia had to 'constrain' them (παρεβιάσατο is an expressive
word with the root 'force'), using powerful arguments which Luke
found necessary to cite: 'If you have judged me to be faithful to the

---

[39]S.J.D. Cohen, 'Religion, Ethnicity, and "Hellenism" in the Emergence of Jewish
Identity in Maccabean Palestine', *Religion and Religious Practice in the Seleucid
Kingdom*, eds. P. Bilde, T. Engberg-Pedersen, L. Hannestad, J. Zahle (Aarhus
University Press, 1990, Studies in Hellenistic Civilization, 1), 220; cf. also 204.
[40]Stern, *GLAJJ*, II, 347.
[41]So Goodman, *Mission and Conversion*, 123.
[42]*Contra* N.J. McEleney's theory that proselytes had not necessarily been uncircumcised ('Conversion, Circumcision and the Law', *NTS* 20 (1974), 319-341) see
the exhaustive arguments by J. Nolland, 'Uncircumcised Proselytes?', *JSJ* 12:2,
(1981), 173-194.
[43]Acts 10:45; 11:2; Gal. 2:12; Col. 4:11; Tit. 1:10.
[44]Acts 10:2, 22, 45. See in more detail pp. 120-21.

Lord, come into my house and abide there'. Later in Corinth Paul moved to the house of a Gentile, the God-fearer Justus, after he met strong opposition in the local synagogue. It was a gesture of great symbolic importance and expressed in very strong words: τὰ αἶμα ὑμῶν ἐπὶ τὴν κεφαλὴν ὑμῶν· καθαρὸς ἐγὼ ἀπὸ τοῦ νῦν εἰς τὰ ἔθνη πορεύσομαι—'your blood be upon your own heads, I am clean: from henceforth I will go to the Gentiles' (Acts 18:16).

One can argue that while the divide between Jews and sympathetic Gentiles was fixed in Palestine which predetermined the position of the Jerusalem church towards circumcision, Diaspora Jews were much less strict in this respect and were actually unaware of 'which friendly Gentiles were Jewish.'[45] This contradicts, however, Luke's account of the episodes with Lydia. It is beyond doubt that in the Diaspora, Jewish relations with the surrounding Gentile world were much closer than in Palestine. At the same time the danger of being absorbed by this world made the issue of Jewish identity more urgent. Apart from religious self-definition, common blood, i.e. ethnic self-definition, given the fact that mixed marriages were practically inevitable, retained its significance among Diaspora Jews. And Acts supplies us with evidence for this facet of Jewish identity as well.

II. Jewish Identity and the Circumcision of Timothy: the Ethnic Boundary

In Acts 16:1-3 Luke records that Paul did what no one would have expected him to do—he circumcised a disciple. The whole story and Luke's explanation of Paul's extraordinary action reads as follows:

> And he came also to Derbe and Lystra. And, behold, a certain disciple was there, named Timothy, the son of a Jewish woman, who was a believer, and a Greek father. He was well reported of by the brethren at Lystra and Iconium. Paul wanted Timothy to accompany him; and he took him and circumcised him because of the Jews that were in those places, for they all knew that his father was a Greek.

This act of Paul seems to be in striking contradiction with Galatians 2:3-4. There Paul tells about his visit to Jerusalem to discuss with the Jerusalem leaders his mission to the Gentiles, one of whom, an uncircumcised Greek, Titus, accompanied him. The appearance of Titus occasioned a fierce debate, but in the end Paul won his case and Titus

---

[45]Goodman, 'Nerva', 42.

was not forced to submit to circumcision at least by the leaders (οἱ δοκοῦντες and οἱ δοκοῦντες στύλοι εἶναι, as Paul calls them) of the church
in Jerusalem: ἀλλ᾽ οὐδὲ Τίτος ὁ σὺν ἐμοί, Ἕλλην ὤν, ἠναγκάσθη περιτμ-
ηθῆναι.[46] Thus the circumcision of Timothy seems not only to have
been against Paul's teaching but also not to have been demanded by
the chief apostles in Jerusalem whose position was far from being as
radical as Paul's. The easiest way to solve this contradiction seems to
be through the difference in the ethnicity of Titus and Timothy[47]—the
former was a Greek and thus was exempted from circumcision while
the latter was a Jew and thus was not.[48] Such an interpretation would
be in harmony with the previous chapter of Acts in which an account
of the Jerusalem conference[49] is given and its ruling is quoted which related only to Christians of Gentile origin. The decision, exempting
Gentile Christians from circumcision, was revolutionary and marked
a significant victory for Paul, but, of course, it implied that children
born into Jewish Christian families were obliged to be circumcised.

However, this simple explanation has seemed to many scholars
to be unsatisfactory, or at least insufficient. The radicalism of Paul's

---

[46]The next phrase (Gal 2:4) is notoriously difficult. For discussion of what it limits,
i.e. what it was that was done because of the false brothers (διὰ δὲ τοὺς παρ-
εισάκτους ψευδαδέλφους, see E. Burton, *Galatians* (Edinburgh: T. & T. Clark, 1921,
The International Critical Commentary), 77-82; the grammatical options are also
discussed in detail by H. Ljungvik, 'Aus der Sprache des Neuen Testaments',
Eranos 66 (1968), 30-34; B. Orchard, 'The Ellipsis between Gal 2,3 and 2,4', *Bib* 54
(1973), 469-481; M. Blommerde, 'Is There an Ellipsis between Gal 2,3 and 2,4?', *Bib*
56 (1975), 100-102. The interpretation according to which ἠναγκάσθη was used
emphatic and implied that Titus was in the long run circumcised on his own initiative (or on Paul's) is artificial and should be rejected, see H.D. Betz *Galatians*
Hermeneia, (Philadelphia: Fortress Press, 1979,), 89. n. 298.

[47]W.O. Walker, 'The Timothy Titus problem Reconsidered', *ExpT* 92 (1980/81),
231-234) proposed an interpretation according to which Luke *consciously* substituted Timothy for Titus. Walker views it as a development of Lake and Cadbury's
careful suggestion (*BC* IV, 184) that an account of Timothy's circumcision could be
'a confused and perhaps erroneous memory of the story of Titus'. This seems to
me to be implausible in the extreme.

[48]This explanation is accepted by many modern scholars usually with reference to
the corresponding passages from the Talmud (m.Qidd. 3-12; m.Yebam. 7:5), or
simply to rabbinic law; see e.g. F.F. Bruce: 'By Jewish law Timothy was a Jew,
because he was the son of a Jewish mother . . . .Timothy's situation was quite
different from that of the Gentile Titus.' (*The Acts of the Apostles*, 352). See the list of
those who consider Timothy to be a Jew in S.J.D.Cohen, 'Was Timothy Jewish
(Acts 16:1-3)? Patristic Exegesis, Rabbinic Law, and Matrilineal Descent', *JBL* 105:2
(1986), 262, n. 34.

[49]It is generally assumed that both Acts 15:4-29 and Gal 2:4-8 retell the same event.

position and contradiction of this action to his basic teaching (1 Cor. 7:18; Gal. 5:6; 6:15 and especially Gal. 5:2-4—'if you be circumcised, Christ shall profit you nothing', cf. also Rom. 2:25-29) make them emphasize the difference between Paul as we know him from his epistles and the Lucan vision of the apostle. An extreme solution has been to declare Timothy's circumcision a fiction, as those who belonged to the Tübingen school did,[50] or in a slightly milder way to treat Luke as the 'victim of an unreliable tradition'.[51] Many of those who trusted Luke's account nevertheless considered that a simple reference to a different ethnic setting was not enough. They sought to find additional explanations for this contradiction, referring to a practical reason for Paul's action: a wish to shield the mission from troubles.[52]

The problem of Timothy's ethnicity is discussed in full in an important article by Cohen.[53] He reasonably suggests that it involves two specific questions: first, did Luke himself regard Timothy as a Jew or a Gentile, and second, how was Timothy regarded by the first-century Jews and Paul? Cohen gives one and the same answer to both of these questions—Timothy was viewed as a Gentile. Lüdemann approaches the problem in similar way. He also distinguishes between Luke's understanding of the situation and the Jewish attitude. But his answer is different. He considers Timothy in Luke's view to be a Gentile and claims that he does not reflect the matter correctly: as the son of a Jewish woman Timothy in Jewish eyes must have been a Jew.[54] Both answers, in my view, can be challenged.

Let us commence with the first question: whose circumcision—that of a Jew or a Gentile—did Luke think he was recounting? Our understanding of Luke's text, apart from an analysis of the specific passage (Acts 16:1-3), very much depends upon whether we admit that

---

[50]Cf. W. Gasque, *A History of the Criticism of the Acts of the Apostles* (Tübingen: Mohr-Siebeck, 1975), 66: '. . . the circumcision of Timothy was considered to be the most flagrant contradiction to Pauline doctrine. The Paul of the epistles could *never* have agreed to such action; of this the Tübingen critics were certain'.

[51]E. Haenchen, *The Acts of the Apostles*: A Commentary, ET, (Oxford: Basil Blackwell, 1971), 482.

[52]Cf., for instance, M. Hengel, *Acts and the History of Early Christianity*, ET (Philadelphia: Fortress, 1979), 64. The similar explanation that Paul acted against his own principles in order to benefit the spreading of Christianity had already been suggested by Tertullian, Clement of Alexandria, Origen and Jerome, sometimes with a reference to 1 Cor. 9:20; Cohen, 'Was Timothy Jewish?', 255ff.

[53]Cohen, 'Was Timothy Jewish?', 251-268.

[54]*Early Christianity according to the Tradition in Acts: A Commentary*, ET (London: SCM Press, 1989), 173ff.

Luke's narrative has a certain logic, or whether we should view it as a combination of different sources not always well coordinated. The latter supposition gives licence to any kind of interpretation which ignores the broader context. But if we allow that Luke's account has a narrative logic (an assumption which any writer deserves before he is shown to have been an illogical eclectic), then his explanation of Paul's action must be viewed against the background of the Jerusalem conference and its decisions.

The position of Jews and Jewish Christians on circumcision was the same: it was a sign of Covenant, a feature which divided the people of God from the surrounding pagan world. Jewish Christians persuaded by Paul changed their position and agreed not to lay upon Gentile Christians the burden (βάρος) of circumcision. Circumcision thereby ceased to be a characteristic which distinguished Christians from the pagan world, but it retained its importance for Jews.

Paul, as Luke explains, circumcised Timothy because of the Jews who knew that his father was a Gentile. From the Christian position which had just been formulated in Jerusalem and had been discussed in detail by Luke in a previous chapter, this was an unnecessary action unless Timothy was a Jew. This seems to imply that Luke considered him to be Jewish in accordance with a matrilineal lineage of pedigree. But in this case it looks, at first glance, as though logically it would be better if Luke referred to his mother and not to his father, as Conzelmann suggested, 'a reference to the mother—instead of the father—would have been better. . . . Apparently Luke does not have precise understanding of Jewish law.'[55] But what if he had this understanding (I shall leave aside for some time the problem of the existence of this law in the first century) and for him the Jewishness of Timothy was self-evident after he had mentioned the ethnicity of his mother? That Timothy was not circumcised was not self-evident from the fact that his father was a Greek. That is why it was necessary to refer to his father for a second time: the Jews in that vicinity knew that he was not circumcised (which was improper) because of his father.

According to 2 Tim. 3:15, Timothy had been instructed in the Holy Scriptures from childhood: ἀπὸ βρέφους τὰ ἱερὰ γράμματα οἶδας. I doubt very much that Timothy was a teenager at the time when Paul decided to take him as a travelling companion. In this case it seems reasonable to suppose that his mother brought him up as a Jew and did not break with the Jewish community after her marriage. This made

---

[55]H. Conzelmann, *Acts of the Apostles*, (Philadelphia: Fortress, 1987), 125.

the status of Timothy among Jews, which was ambiguous as it stands, even more confusing. He was at the same time Jewish because of his mother (an ethnic definition of Jewishness) and non-Jewish because he was not circumcised (a religious definition). These two principles of Jewish self-identification were in conflict in the person of Timothy.

Cohen argues that 'the phrase "because of the Jews in that vicinity" implies that, were it not for them, Paul would have left Timothy uncircumcised'. He stresses that 'this implication confirms the charge that the Lucan Paul tries to deny in Acts 21:21', i.e. the charge of teaching Jews not to circumcise their children'. He considers both passages to be consistent only if Luke viewed Timothy as a Gentile.[56] I do not think that there is a contradiction between these passages if, for Luke, Timothy was Jewish. Paul would not have circumcised Timothy were it not for the local Jews, because for 'the Lucan Paul', as well as for the Paul of the epistles, circumcision had no relation to salvation. For him 'circumcision is nothing and uncircumcision is nothing' (I Cor 7:19). But this indifference does not imply active teaching against the circumcision of Jews, which was an accusation recorded in Acts 21:21. 'Is any man called being circumcised? Let him not become uncircumcised' (I Cor 7:18). Circumcision is an act symbolic of becoming a part of the chosen people, a sign of Jewishness. Timothy was called formally uncircumcised, but if he was Jewish in Luke's eyes, then the circumcision only confirms the status which he had before as a son of a Jewish mother. This act was not impossible for the Paul of Acts, with his respect for the law. What was absolutely impossible was to circumcise a Gentile.

This answer to the first question—Luke believed Timothy to be Jewish—in fact predetermines the answer to the second. If the matrilineal principle did not exist in the first century how could Luke know about it? It can hardly be a possible coincidence. Cohen points out that this law is not registered by any premishnaic text with 'the only possible exception of Acts 16:1-3'.[57] It is a quite common thing, unfortunately, that in the field of ancient history, Christianity included, certain information appears only in one isolated source. We know only from Acts that Paul was a Roman citizen. It is only from Cassius Dio that we know that Roman soldiers who took part in the siege of Jerusalem, suspecting that the city was impregnable, defected to the Jewish side.[58] We know only from Josephus the details of conversion of the royal

---

[56]Cohen,'Was Timothy Jewish?', 254.
[57]Cohen,'Was Timothy Jewish?', 267.
[58]Dio Cassius, 66.5.4 = Stern, *GLAJJ* II No. 430.

house of Adiabene. But if Luke's evidence for the acknowledgement of the matrilineal principle is supported by later rabbinic law, then in accordance with the routine practice of ancient historians, we have to treat it as a *terminus post quem*.

Cohen does not exclude completely the possibility that the matrilineal principle was of first century origin, but claims that, even if it 'existed in the proto-rabbinic circles of the first-century Palestine, we cannot assume that it reached and won the acceptance of the Jews of Asia Minor'.[59] I wholly agree that rabbinic (or proto-rabbinic) legislation was not in operation in the first century Diaspora. But in this particular case I think that the movement was the other way round. Rabbinic legislation did not come out of the blue nor from purely theoretical discussions of unimportant issues. Though it mostly reflects the Palestinian agenda, Palestinian Jews were not separated by an iron curtain from the Diaspora world. Rabbinic laws absorbed what was gradually developing in the Jewish world and gave answers to the questions that had already been posed by life.

The problems of intermarriage and the status of the offspring of such marriages were for the most part Diaspora issues where Jews lived in a Gentile milieu. It is reasonable to suppose that it was in the Diaspora that the matrilineal principle first emerged and became widespread, probably not without some influence from Roman legislation. According to Roman law, children follow the status of the mother in case of marriage between a citizen and noncitizen, a marriage which was treated as valid but not legal.[60] This principle of defining ethnic Jewish identity along matrilineal lines was registered by Luke in his story of Timothy's circumcision.

---

[59]Cohen, 'Was Timothy Jewish?', 267.
[60]Cf. the comparison between the Roman law of persons and rabbinic law (Qidd. 3:12) in Cohen, 'Was Timothy Jewish?', 263ff.

CHAPTER 2

PROSELYTES:
NON-CHRISTIAN EVIDENCE

This chapter contributes to the debate on whether Judaism was a missionary religion. It does so by assessing the known epigraphic and literary sources and concludes that while Gentiles might have been attracted to Judaism, they were not the objects of an active missionary strategy. While it may be tempting for some to conclude that the growth of Judaism in the Diaspora was the result of aggressive proselytising, the evidence does not necessarily support this view. If it had been the case that such a mission existed it is somewhat surprising, given Luke's theological concept of Christianity as a missionary religion, that the Book of Acts gives no such hint of a Jewish mission.

As Marcel Simon noted, 'in the history of Judaism around the beginning of the Christian era there is no more controversial question than that of proselytism'.[1] Starting from the turn of the century, the most hotly debated issue was whether, or to what extent, Judaism in the Second Temple Period was a missionary religion. For many scholars the primary interest lay in the field of Christianity. They were searching for an explanation for the unprecedented missionary activity of early Christianity, which, as many believed, 'had been prepared by a Jewish missionary impulse, so that it did not have to begin from scratch'.[2] Unfortunately, some could not avoid a battlefield mentality when discussing this issue. They saw the replacement of 'Jewish mission' by Christianity as another proof of the superiority of the Christian religion. By the 1950s a general consensus had been reached. Most scholars treated Judaism of the Second Temple period as a missionary religion.[3] The only difference of opinion among them was over determining the time when this mission disappeared. A majority held the view that the crucial dates were the crises of AD 70

---

[1]M. Simon, *Verus Israel*, ET, (Oxford: OUP,1986), 271. The most influentual works in this field are: A. Bertholet, *Die Stellung der Israeliten und der Juden zu den Fremden* (Freiburg, Leipzig: J.C.B. Mohr, 1896); A. von Harnack, *The Mission and Expansion of Christianity in the First Three Centuries.* 2 vols. (ET: London: Williams & Norgate, 1904-5); S. Bialoblocki, *Die Beziehungen des Judentums zu Proselyten.* Vortrag gehalten bei dem wissenschaftlichen Kursus der Rabbiner der suddeutschen Landesverbande in Mainz am 17.XII.1929 (Berlin: n. p., 1930); B.J. Bamberger, *Proselytism in the Talmudic Period,* (New York: Ktav, 1968); P. Dalbert, *Die Theologie der hellenistisch-judischen Missionsliteratur unter Aussluss von Philo und Josephus* (Hamburg-Volksdorf: Herbert Reich, 1954); K.G. Kuhn, προσήλυτος, *TDNT;* 6 (1968), 727-744. J. Jeremias, *Jesus' Promise to the Nations,* ET, (London: SCM, 1958); D. Georgi, *The Opponents of Paul in Second Corinthians* (Philadelphia: Fortress Press, 1986); K.G. Kuhn and H. Stegemann, 'Proselyten', in *RE,* Suppl. vol. 9 (1962); K. Lake, 'Proselytes and God-fearers', *BC,* vol. 5, 74-96; W.G. Braude, *Proselytizing in the First Five Centuries of the Common Era, the Age of Tannaim and Amoraim* (Providence: Brown University Press, 1940); E. Schürer, *The History of the Jewish People in the Age of Jesus Christ,* A New English Version Revised and Edited by G. Vermes, F. Millar, M. Goodman, Edinburgh: T.&T. Clark, 1986, (hereafter referred to as Schürer, Vermes, Millar, Goodman), vol. 3, 1, 150-177; M. Simon, 'Sur les débuts du prosélytisme juif', *Hommages à André Dupont-Sommer,* eds. A. Caquot & M. Philonenko (Paris: Librairie d'Amérique et d'Orient Adrien-Maisonneuve, 1971), 509-520).
[2]S. Sandmel, *The First Christian Century in Judaism and Christianity. Certainties and Uncertainties* (New York: Oxford University Press,1969), 234.
[3]See list in n. 1. An exemplary formulation of this general attitude was given by D. Bruner, *Matthew, The Churchbook, Matthew 13-28,* vol. 2, (Dallas; Word Publishing, 1990), 821: 'Palestinian Judaism under Pharisaic leadership prosecuted a vigorous missionary program in Jesus' time'.

and 135. Others considered that proselytizing survived for a long time afterwards. Simon proposed that within the Roman Empire a proselytizing movement existed until the disappearance in AD 425 of the Jewish Patriarchate and even longer in some Eastern regions, especially in the environs of Palestine and in the area on both sides of the Red Sea.[4]

As quite often happens, as soon as a consensus is reached it is immediately contested. In this case the role of *enfant terrible* was played by A.T. Kraabel. In a challenging article he mentions Jewish 'missionary zeal' among six traditionally held assumptions about ancient Judaism.[5] The others were: (i) that the Jewish Mediterranean Diaspora was syncretistic; (ii) that Jews outside Palestine knew themselves to be aliens in the Roman world and strove to make Jews out of some Gentiles; that there were, as a result, plenty of Jewish sympathizers like the God-Fearers of Acts; (iii) that both Diaspora Jews and proselytes belonged to the lower classes; (iv) that Diaspora Jewry was monolithic and even directly controlled from Palestine; (v) and that all evidence about the Jews must be interpreted in the context of religion. He came to the conclusion that no true picture of Diaspora Judaism could emerge until scholars abandoned these assumptions. Kraabel was joined by S. McKnight, who aimed 'to establish Kraabel's criticism' of the missionary nature of Judaism.[6] The same sceptical attitude towards a Jewish mission can be found in the works of S.J.D. Cohen[7] and M. Goodman.[8] Little by little 'a new consensus is beginning to emerge according to which . . . Diaspora Judaism was not a missionary religion'.[9] This position was epitomized in the title of the

---

[4]Simon, *Verus Israel*, 304-305.

[5]A.T. Kraabel, 'The Roman Diaspora: Six Questionable Assumptions', *JJS* 33 (1982), 450-456; cf. also *id*. 'Synagoga Caeca: Systematic Distortion in Gentile Interpretations of Evidence for Judaism in the Early Christian Period', *'To See Ourselves as Others See Us'*: *Christians, Jews, 'Others' in Late Antiquity*, eds. J. Neusner & E.S. Frerichs (Chico: Scholars Press, 1985), 219; both articles were reprinted in *Diaspora Jews and Judaism: Essays in Honor of, and in Dialogue with, A.Thomas Kraabel* (University of South Florida, 1992, South Florida Studies in the History of Judaism, 41).

[6]Scott McKnight, *A Light Among Gentiles: Jewish Missionary Activity in the Second Temple Period* (Minneapolis: Fortress Press, 1991), 4.

[7]S.J.D. Cohen, 'Adolf Harnack's "The Mission and Expansion of Judaism"': Christianity Succeeds where Judaism Fails', *The Future of Early Christianity: Essays in Honour of Helmut Koester*, eds. B.A. Pearson, A.T. Kraabel, G.W.E. Nikelsburg and N.R. Peterson (Minneapolis: Fortress, 1991), 163-169; *id.*, 'Was Judaism in Antiquity a Missionary Religion?', *Jewish Assimilation, Acculturation and Accomodation: Past Traditions Current Issues and Future Prospects*, ed. M.Mor (Lanham, New York, London: University Press of America, 1992), 14-23.

book by E. Will and C. Orrieux, *'Prosélytisme juif'? Histoire d'une erreur*.[10] Nevertheless, L. Feldman holds to the traditional view of Jewish mission which he strongly advocates.[11] Thus, at the present time the proselytism problem fluctuates between two extremes—on the one hand, a complete negation of Jewish proselytism ('une erreur') and on the other, full acceptance of 'a lively Jewish mission'.

In modern languages the term 'proselyte' and its derivative with an active meaning—'proselytism', 'to proselytize'[12] are used to denote a non-Jewish adherent of Judaism and the practice of making proselytes. This word is a transliteration of the Greek προσήλυτος which in turn was coined in a Jewish milieu to render the Hebrew גֵּר. In the OT the word denoted a class of resident aliens (who were distinguished from נֵכָר, foreigners who were present in the country only for some time such as, for instance, travellers), and so described a social reality. But gradually, due to the fact that the resident aliens had certain religious obligations (cf. Deut. 5:14, 16:10, 16:13, 16:9-14) and became integrated into the community of Israel, the concept acquired religious connotations. The date of this change is uncertain[13] but it is usually assumed that by the first century AD προσήλυτος meant

---

[8]M. Goodman, 'Jewish Proselytizing in the First Century', *The Jews among Pagans and Christians in the Roman Empire*, eds. J. Lieu, J. North and T. Rajak (London and New York: Routledge, 1992), 53-78; *id. Mission and Conversion*.

[9] Cohen, 'Harnack's "Mission"', 166.

[10]Paris: Les Belles Lettres, 1992.

[11]L.H. Feldman, 'Jewish Proselytism', *Eusebius, Christianity and Judaism*, eds. H.W. Attridge, G. Hata (Detroit: Wayne State University Press, 1992), 372-408; *id.*, 'Proselytism by Jews in the Third, Fourth, and Fifth Centuries', *JSJ* 24,1 (1993), 372-408. All his work in this field was summarized in his book *Jew and Gentile in the Ancient World* (Princeton: Princeton University Press, 1993).

[12]E. Will and C. Orrieux consider a shift from the intransitive sense, which the word had in the ancient world, to the transitive sense, which it acquired in modern languages, to be 'grammatically illegitimate' (the expression was used in a very useful review by F. Millar, 299-304). They seek explanation in modern European history: 'On peut donc tenir pour presque assuré que cette mutation sémantique dont nous étions partis, de l'intransitif "prosélyte" au transitif-causatif "prosélytisme", s'est faite dans les milieux anglicans qui se sentaient menacés par les succès des prédications sectaires dirigées contre la théologie, le ritualisme sacramentaliste, la hiérarchie et les privilèges sociaux et politiques de l'Establishment' (p. 44).

[13]Bertholet, *Die Stellung*, 178; G.F. Moore, *Judaism in the First Centuries of the Christian Era: The Age of the Tannaism*, vol. 1, (Cambridge, Mass.: 1927), 328f.; W.C. Allen, 'On the Meaning of προσήλυτος in the Septuagint', *Expositor*, IV, 10 (1894), 264-275; Th.J. Meek, 'The translation of Ger in the Hexateuch and Its Bearing on the Documentary Hypothesis', *JBL* 49(1930), 172-180. See also S. McKnight, *A Light Among Gentiles*, 131, n. 5.

'proselyte'.[14] The starting point for those who see Judaism of the Second Temple Period in terms of a mission, is a demographic shift—dramatic population changes among the Jews in Palestine and the Diaspora are attributed partially to the great number of proselytes'.[15] Harnack counted as many as four to four and a half million Jews within the Roman Empire.[16] Juster's estimation was even higher—about six or seven million.[17] Baron's figure for the middle of the first century A.D. was eight million, one-eighth of the whole population of the Roman Empire, as he thought.[18] Nevertheless it seems that one must be cautious rather than confident in dealing with demographic calculations of this sort until more primary archaeological information becomes available and a more secure methodology is established.[19] But though these high estimates of the Jewish population must be treated with caution, there is no doubt that the size of the Jewish Diaspora was substantial and there was a certain growth in population. This is confirmed by both literary evidence and archaeological data.[20] Logically it is quite possible (and very tempting) to attribute this growth to the proselytizing movement. But we need stronger evidence in favour of the Jewish mission than a logical

---

[14]See, however, McKnight, *A Light Among Gentiles*, 131, n. 5 who considers that in Qumran literature the term was used with both meanings, and does not exclude the possibility that the old one was intended in Acts 13:43. See also Goodman 'Jewish Proselytizing', 62, who supposes that in the first century προσήλυτος was becoming a technical term for a converted Gentile, but that its meaning was not yet confined to this sense alone. This is discussed in more detail in the next chapter.

[15]J.R. Rosenbloom, *Conversion to Judaism: From the Biblical Period to the Present* (Cincinatti: Hebrew Union College Press, 1978), 38.

[16]von Harnack, *The Mission*, vol. 1, 8.

[17]J. Juster, *Les Juifs dans l'empire romain*, vol.1, (Paris: Geuthner,1914), 209-212.

[18]S.W. Baron, *A Social and Religious History of the Jews* (New York: Columbia University Press, 1952,[2]), vol. 1, 167-179.

[19]McKnight, *A Light Among Gentiles*, 33 and 133, n. 20. For modern methods in demographic studies on ancient cities in which consideration of the density of population assumed importance, see W. Reinhardt, Chapter 8: The Population Size of Jerusalem and the Numerical Growth of the Jerusalem Church, *The Book of Acts in Its First Century Setting, vol. 4: Palestinian Setting* (Grand Rapids, Carlisle: Eerdmans, Paternoster, 1995), 237-265. Reinhardt's own figure for Jewish population is about five million. Cf. also L.V. Rutgers, 'Attitudes to Judaism in the Greco-Roman Period: Reflections on Feldman's, *Jew and Gentile in the Ancient World*', *JQR* 85: 3-4 (1995), 364: 'The study of Jewish demography in the Hellenistic and Roman periods is beset by the same difficulties that face research into the demographic structure of the non-Jewish population: (1) a lack of primary data; (2) our inability to determine the reliability of the little evidence that is available; and (3) our incapacity to interpret the available evidence properly'.

probability for this to be regarded as historical fact. If we are not dazzled by the enormous figures and just assume that there was a substantial increase in the Jewish population, explanations such as Jewish fertility, opposition to abortion, infanticide, contraception, and the concept of charity are just as valid.[21] Apart from the demographic factor, what other evidence supports the existence of Jewish proselytizing activity?

Before starting to discuss sources which were interpreted in this way, mostly from the first century (as this period is our focus of attention here), it is necessary to clarify certain points. No one working in the field of first-century Judaism would dream of denying the existence of Jewish proselytes at this time. The real question, as mentioned at the beginning of this chapter, is whether the Jews were actively searching for proselytes or whether, though they welcomed and sometimes even encouraged Gentile converts, they did not see this as their religious duty. As Goodman has succinctly stated,

> the desire to encourage admiration of the Jewish way of life or respect
> for the Jewish God, or to inculcate general ethical behaviour in other
> peoples, or such pious hope for the future, should be clearly distin-
> guished from an impulse to draw non-Jews into Judaism.[22]

The particular task of this chapter is to compare the evidence of non-Christian first-century sources with the picture given by the book of Acts, which is the only New Testament book apart from Matthew where proselytes are mentioned. Acts shows no trace of a Jewish mission. This is especially remarkable considering that this book by Luke has as its central aim, the portrayal of the beginnings of Christianity as a mission. The existence of a Jewish precedent would have given a different slant to his theological reflection.

---

[20]Literary *loci classici* on this matter are: Or. Sib. III 271; I Macc. 15:23-4; Strabo *apud*: Josephus, *AJ* 14. 115; *BJ* 2. 398; 7.43; Philo, *In Flaccum* 45-6; *Legatio* 281-2; Acts 2:9-11. On archaeological and epigraphic evidence see Schürer, Vermes, Millar, Goodman, *The History of the Jewish People*, 3, 1, 1-86.

[21]M. Goodman, *The Ruling Class of Judaea. The Origins of the Jewish Revolt against Rome A.D. 66-70* (Cambridge: CUP, 1987), 61; *id.* 'Jewish proselytizing', 55.

[22]Goodman, 'Jewish Proselytizing', 53.

I. Epigraphic Evidence

Before turning to the literary sources let us examine the epigraphic evidence. The number of proselyte inscriptions is very small.

Until recently only sixteen of them in all were known— mostly epitaphs.[23] Subsequently an Aphrodisias inscription has added three more proselytes to the harvest.[24] This number, according to P.W. van der Horst, represents no more than one per cent of all Jewish inscriptions.[25] It is impossible to date them precisely, but they belong roughly to a period from the first century BC to the fifth AD. Half of the epigraphical proselytes are women (in Rome, five out of seven or eight), which is a rather high percentage when compared with the representation of women in inscriptions. One of these women, who died at the age of eighty-six years and six months, had been converted at the age of seventy.[26] She was honoured with the title of the mother of two synagogues, which shows her high status in the Jewish community.[27] The youngest proselyte died at the age of three years

---

[23]*CIJ* I² 21, 68, 202, 222, 256, 462, 523 (Rome) = Noy, *Jewish Inscriptions of Western Europe*. Vol. 2: *The City of Rome* (Cambridge: CUP, 1995) (henceforth Noy, *JIWE*, 2), 489, 491 (in Latin), 392, 224 (in Latin), 218 (in Latin), 62 (in Latin), 577 (in Latin); *CIJ* I² 576 (Venosa) = D. Noy, Jewish Inscriptions of Western Europe. Vol. 1. Italy (excluding the City of Rome), Spain and Gaul (Cambridge: CUP, 1993). (Henceforth *JIWE*, 1), 52; *CIJ* II 1385, 1390 (Jerusalem, the last is in Aramaic); P.B. Bagatti-J.T. Milik, *Gli scavi del Dominus Flevit (Monte Oliveto - Gerusalemme)* I (Jerusalem: Franciscan Press,1958) No. 13, 21, 31 (Jerusalem, the last one in Aramaic, with the form *gerit* used instead of a more common *gioret*), B. Lifshitz, *Inscriptions Greque de Césaré en Palestine (Caesarea Palaestinae)*, RB 68 (1961) 115 No. 2; G. Lüderitz, *Corpus judischer Zeugnisse aus der Cyrenaika mit einem Anhang von Joyce M.Reynolds* (Wiesbaden: Dr. Ludwig Reichert Verlag, 1983), N12 (Cyrenaica); J. Naveh, *On Stone and Mosaic: The Aramaic and Hebrew inscriptions from Ancient Syngogues* (Tel Aviv, 1978) No. 88 (Dura Europos, *in Aramaic*). All these inscriptions (with exception of the one from Caesarea) are published together with some commentaries in: P. Figueras, 'Epigraphic Evidence for Proselytism in Ancient Judaism', *Immanuel* 24/25 (1990), 196-201.

[24]J. Reynolds & R. Tannenbaum, *Jews and God-fearers at Aphrodisias* (Cambridge: The Cambridge Philological Society, 1987, Proceedings of the Cambridge Philological Society, Supplementary Volume 12), 5.

[25]P.W. van der Horst, *Ancient Jewish Epitaphs: An Introductory Survey of a Millenium of Jewish Funerary Epigraphy (300 BCE - 700 CE)* (Kampen: Kok Pharos Publishing House, 1991), 72.

[26]*CIJ* I 523

[27]About the meaning of the title see B.J. Brooten, *Women Leaders in the Ancient Synagogue: Inscriptional Evidence and Background Issues* (Chico: Scholars Press, 1982, BJS, 36), 64-72.

and seven months.[28] It looks as if two of the Roman proselytes, one man and one woman, were freed slaves, as the inscriptions were set up by their patrons.[29] Sarra from Cyrene, a proselyte buried with a Jewish family, seems to have been a slave or an adopted child.[30] We should not press the modest number of proselytes in inscriptions too far as an argument against mass conversions. Our sources have plenty of lacunae and we know nothing about whether it was obligatory, or only desirable from a Jewish point of view, to mention proselyte-status in the epitaphs. Besides, the Roman laws from Hadrian onwards, which treated the conversion of a Gentile as a capital crime, 'certainly did not encourage people to divulge such a conversion, not even on a tombstone',[31] probably because of the possibility of implication by association.[32]

II. Literary Sources

As to the literary sources for proselytes of the first century, I shall discuss only those which are interpreted as evidence for aggressive proselytizing, putting aside those which indicate a favourable attitude toward proselytism, divested of any missionary zeal. They can be divided into three groups: Gentile, Jewish and Christian. The first two groups will be discussed in this chapter and the last in the following chapter.

---

[28]*CIJ* I 21. Figueras ('Epigraphic Evidence', 199) argues that the girl was probably born before her parents were converted and thus was considered to be a proselyte and recalls in this connection the fact, that the Mishnah had special regulations regarding a female who became a proselyte before the age of three years and one day (*op. cit. 199*). See the discussion of different possible interpretations of this inscription in: R.S. Kraemer, 'On the Meaning of the Term "Jew" in Graeco-Roman Inscriptions', *HTR* 82.1 (1989), 39 (reprinted in: *Diaspora Jews and Judaism*, 311-329); cf. also Noy, *JIWE* 2, 489, 391.

[29]*CIJ* I^2 256, 462; Leon, *The Jews*, 254.

[30]Lüderitz, *Corpus*, 27.

[31]van der Horst, *Ancient Jewish Epitaphs*, 72.

[32]Contrary to Cohen, 'Crossing the Boundary', 29f., who, trying to show that the proselytes had an ambiguous status in the Jewish community, strongly exaggarates the number of proselytes in inscriptions, 'Many epitaphs and synagogue inscriptions attach the label 'proselyte' after the name of the person being commemorated', and argues that 'the proselyte felt obliged (was obliged?) to call attention to this fact'. If it was so and all the proselytes had to register their status in the inscriptions, we should consider this category, which could be traced only in sixteen inscriptions, virtually non-existent in real life.

1) Gentile sources

The most famous Roman evidence used to support the theory of 'the missionary zeal of the Jews' is undoubtedly Horace, Sat.1.4.142-3 ac veluti te / Iudaei cogemus in hanc concedere turbam,[33] which was translated in LCL as 'and we, like the Jews, will compel you to make one of our throng' (trans. H. Rushton Fairclough).[34] Though these lines are slightly earlier than the period under discussion, it is important to mention them because of the significance which has been attached to them. Those who treat Horace's words in terms of Jewish proselytizing understand his comparison as an indication that Jews forced other people to join their community. J. Nolland on the contrary, analysing the broader context of the satire and its structure, has very convincingly argued that the main emphasis in the last part of the satire is in the opposition between force and reason. The comparison with Jews is made not with reference to the pressure that they applied in order to make anyone part of their throng but with reference to their practice of applying pressure on others in extra-religious contexts. Nolland's conclusion, to which I subscribe, is:

> Certainly Horace knows of the Jews pushing their point of view for-ward—but it is in the realm of politics and personal advantage that Horace sees this occurring, not in the realm of the propagation of re-ligious ideas.[35]

The classical text for the first century AD is Seneca *De superstitione* (cited in Augustinus, *De Civitate Dei* VI, 11):

> *Cum interim usque eo sceleratissimae gentis consuetudo convaluit, ut per omnes iam terras recepta sit; victi victoribus leges dederunt ... Illi tamen cau-sas ritus sui noverunt; maior pars populi facit, quod cur faciat ignorat.*

> Meanwhile the customs of this accursed race have gained such influ-ence that they are now received throughout all the world. The van-quished have given laws to their victors. . . . The Jews, however, are

---

[33]So Stern, *GLAJJ* I, 321. Cf. also J. Nolland, 'Proselytism or Politics in Horace *Satires* I, 4, 138-143?', *VC* 33 (1979) 347, who asserts, that these words 'are claimed as the earliest reference in Roman literature to the prozelytizing zeal of the Jews'.
[34]Other English translations of this verse, and the problem of understanding the verb *concedere* in line 140 and in line 143, are discussed in Nolland, 'Proselytism or Politics', 347ff.
[35]Nolland, 'Proselytism or Politics', 353.

aware of the origin and meaning of their rites. The greater part of the people go through a ritual not knowing why they do so.

(trans. W.M. Green, *LCL*)

The text is considered to have been written in the last years of Seneca's life, i.e. in the 60s or twenty years earlier,[36] and is interpreted as a recognition on the part of the author of the success of Jewish missionary activity.[37] Nevertheless it seems that nothing in this text supports such an understanding. Seneca detested and opposed the spread of Oriental cults and Oriental rites in Rome. Judaism was just another foreign superstition which became fashionable. He worried that the Jewish practice of resting on the Sabbath, which he considered to be inexpedient—'by introducing one day of rest in every seven they lose in idleness almost a seventh of their life, and by failing to act in times of urgency they often suffer loss'—was finding advocates. He suggested that the lighting of the Sabbath lamps should be prohibited as well as any other kind of ceremonial worship, because they all attracted human ambitions and had nothing to do with the real worship of God (*Epistulae Morales* XCV.47). He definitely did not suggest that Jewish rites should be prohibited for Jews; he did not care about Jews. It was the Romans who were his concern. He credited the Jews with only one thing—they, unlike others, at least knew the meaning of their rituals.[38] The only reliable information yielded from this fragment of Seneca is that Jewish rituals, and especially the celebration of the Sabbath, had some attraction for the Gentiles.[39] The famous phrase *victi victoribus leges dederunt* must not be taken too seriously. It is a rhetorical commonplace,[40] which demonstrates the extent of Seneca's irritation with foreign cults *per se*.

It would seem that information about the Jewish mission must be looked for elsewhere, for instance, in the reports about the

---

[36]See references in Stern, *GLAJJ* I 429, n. 2.
[37]See, for instance, Stern, *GLAJJ* I 429, who wrote that the work was composed 'at the height of the Jewish proselytizing movement'.
[38]Seneca's statements on Jews in *De Superstitione* are separated from each other by Augustine's commentary. It is impossible to say how much of Seneca's argument Augustine omitted. But in the context of Augustine's discussion it seems obvious that the implied contrast is between the Jews *(illi)* and non-Jews who picked up their customs. The only possible alternative, to my mind, is to treat this statement as a more general one: Jews are better educated concerning their religious ceremonies than Gentiles concerning theirs. The interpretation revived by Turcan, namely that Seneca contrasted Jewish priests who knew what they were doing, and the rest of Jews who did not, was rightly rejected by Stern, *GLAJJ* I, 432.

expulsion of Jews from Rome. We know of at least three—139 BC, 19 AD and under Claudius, mentioned in Acts (18:2). It was assumed that in the first two cases the reason was Jewish proselytizing activity.[41]

The first report is preserved only in two Byzantine epitomes of Valerius Maximus, who lived at the beginning of the first century AD and possibly used Livy as his source.[42] In one of the epitomes it is stated that Jews were expelled by the *praetor peregrinus*, Cn. Cornelius Hispalus, (the correct name of the *praetor* was Cn. Cornelius Scipio Hispanus) for the attempt to spoil Roman mores by introducing the cult of Sabazius Jupiter. This comment became one of the foundation stones of the theory of Judaeo-pagan syncretism.[43] The careful study of manuscript tradition by E.N. Lane showed that the idea of Jews as propagandists of the cult of Sabazius Jupiter appeared as a result of the confusion of the three acts of Cornelius Hispanus, *viz*. the expulsion of the Chaldaeans, the Sabazius-worshippers, and the Jews, which were mentioned in the original text of Valerius Maximus.[44] What then was the reason for this expulsion? According to the second epitome Jews were punished for an attempt to transmit to Romans *sacra sua*. Their private altars were removed from public places (*arasque privatas e publicis locis abiecit*). The key issue in this story is the mention of altars. I agree with Goodman that it is difficult to imagine Jews installing

---

[39]Cf. Josephus *contra Apion*. 2.282 (with quite understandible exaggeration): οὐ μὴν ἀλλὰ καὶ πλήθεσιν ἤδη πολὺς ζῆλος γέγονεν ἐκ μακροῦ τῆς ἡμετέρας εὐσεβείας, οὐδ᾽ ἔστιν οὐ πόλις Ἑλλήνων οὐδ᾽ ἡτισοῦν οὐδὲ βάρβαρος, οὐδὲ ἓν ἔθνος, ἔνθα μὴ τὸ τῆς ἑβδομάδος, ἣν ἀργοῦμεν ἡμεῖς, ἔθος διαπεφοίτηκεν, καὶ αἱ νηστεῖαι καὶ λύχνων ἀνακαύσεις καὶ πολλὰ τῶν εἰς βρῶσιν ἡμῖν οὐ νενομισμένων παρατετήρηται.
'The masses have long since shown a keen desire to adopt our religious observances; and there is not one city, Greek or barbarian, nor a single nation, to which our custom of abstaining from work on the seventh day has not spread, and where the fasts and lightening of lamps and many of our prohibitions in the matter of food are not observed.' (trans. H.St.J. Thackeray, *LCL*)
[40]Cf. Plinius, *Naturalis Historia, XXIV, 5 vincendoque victi sumus* and other examples collected by Stern, *GLAJJ* I, 432.
[41]The third expulsion during the reign of Claudius, which was mentioned by Suetonius, Claudius 25,4 and by Luke (Acts 18:2), was nowhere explained as a punishment for proselytizing and is usually treated within another context; see pp. 171-179.
[42]Val. Max. 1.3.3. = Stern, *GLAJJ* I, 357.
[43]F. Cumont, 'Les mystères de Sabazius et le judaisme', *CRAIBL* (1905) 63-79. Cf. critical examination and repudiation of his theory in S.E. Johnson, 'The Present State of Sabazios Research', *ANRW* II 17,3, 1583-1613.
[44]E.N. Lane, 'Sabazius and the Jews in Valerius Maximus: a Re-examination', *JRS* 69 (1979) 37.

altars all over Rome or encouraging newly-converted Romans to pay tribute to God in such a manner. This is more suitable for Jewish sympathizers, who 'impressed by Jews, chose to express their admiration in conventional Roman fashion by the setting up of altars within the city'.[45]

The second expulsion is reported by Tacitus, Suetonius, Josephus and also by Dio Cassius in a fragment of his history which was preserved by the seventh-century writer John of Antioch.[46] It is only in the last text that the expulsion is explained as a punishment for the conversion of the Gentiles:

> τῶν τε Ἰουδαίων πολλῶν ἐς τὴν Ῥώμην συνελθόντων καὶ συχνοὺς τῶν ἐπιχωρίων ἐς τὰ σφέτερα ἔθη μεθιστάντων, τοὺς πλείονας ἐξήλασεν.[47]

As the Jews flocked to Rome in great numbers and were converting many of the natives to their ways, he banished most of them.

(trans. E. Cary, *LCL*)

Dio Cassius, although he is a valuable source of information, in relating the past often reflects the situation of his own time, that is, the end of the second and the beginning of the third century AD.[48] That was a period when Christian mission was fully in operation and had changed the religious atmosphere dramatically. This consideration makes it necessary to regard Dio's explanation of the cause of the expulsion as unreliable, given especially that it is not supported by earlier historians and is preserved only in quotation.

Nevertheless all other sources demonstrate that a religious issue was involved. Josephus explains the expulsion of all the Jews as a punishment for the misbehaviour of four Jewish imposters from Palestine. They persuaded a noble and wealthy Roman lady, Fulvia, who had been converted to Judaism (νομίμοις προσεληλυθυῖαν τοῖς Ἰουδαϊκοῖς), to send valuable gifts to the Temple, and then they misappropriated the gifts. When their fraud became known to

---

[45]Goodman, *Mission and Conversion*, 83. The right of the Gentiles to make altars to God was authorized by the Jewish side: E.Bickerman, 'The Altars of Gentiles: A Note on the Jewish 'ius sacrum'', *id. Studies in Jewish and Christian History* II (Leiden: Brill, 1980), 324-326.

[46]For the connection of anti-Jewish policy which Philo ascribes to Sejanus (*Legatio* 159-161, also in Eusebius, *HE* II, 5, 6-7) with the expulsion of AD 19, see E.M. Smallwood, 'Some Notes on the Jews under Tiberius', *Latomus* 15 (1956), 324-329.

[47]Dio Cassius, 57.18.5a=Stern, *GLAJJ* II No. 419.

[48]Stern, *GLAJJ* II, 347.

Tiberius, all the Jews were expelled from Rome. Four thousand of them were drafted for military service and sent to the island of Sardinia. Many of the Jews refused, for fear of breaking the Law, and were penalized by the Roman authority. Thus, Josephus sums up, because of the wickedness of four men, the whole Jewish community had to leave Rome: οἱ μὲν δὴ διὰ κακίαν τεσσάρων ἀνδρῶν ἠλαύνοντο τῆς πόλεως.[49]

The account of Tacitus differs from that of Josephus. According to the Roman historian not only Jewish but also Egyptian rites were banished and a *senatus consultum* directed that four thousand freedmen of suitable age who were infected by Jewish superstition (*quattuor milia libertini generis ea superstitione infecta*) were to be sent to Sardinia to reinforce police units fighting against local brigands. 'If they succumbed to the pestilential climate, it was a cheap loss', commented Tacitus. Jews also had to leave Italy if they did not abandon their rites by a given date.[50]

According to Suetonius, Jewish young men were assigned to serve in the army in provinces which had a severe climate, and both Jews and Gentiles who adopted Jewish beliefs were banished from the city on pain of perpetual slavery (which therefore precluded the possibility of manumission) for those who did not obey: *reliquos gentis eiusdem vel similia sectantes urbe summovit, sub poena perpetuae servitutis nisi obtemperassent.*[51]

The combined evidence of these sources makes a very strong case in favour of Jewish proselytizing and therefore cannot be dismissed as summarily as it is by Goodman.[52] Despite differences in detail, these sources show that Tiberius' expulsion was aimed not against Jews as an ethnic group, but against their religion, because it had won adherents among the Gentiles. But is Jewish missionary activity the only possible explanation?

According to Tacitus Egyptian rites were also disqualified from being celebrated in Rome. No one explains this as a result of particular missionary zeal on the part of Egyptian preachers. The Roman authorities were mainly concerned with the preservation of traditional Roman virtues and beliefs and took measures to protect Roman society from the unwanted influence of oriental cults. Expulsions of representatives of the cults which had become fashionable in different

---

[49]Josephus, *AJ* 18. 81-84.
[50]Tacitus, *Annales* 2.85,4 = Stern, *GLAJJ* II No. 284.
[51]Suetonius, *Tib.* 36.1 = Stern, *GLAJJ* II No. 419.
[52]Goodman, *Mission and Conversion*, 68.

periods (for different reasons),[53] were, from the Roman point of view, among the most obvious measures to take. Judaism did become fashionable in Rome, as the evidence in the next chapter will show, but the majority of those who were attracted to Judaism did not become proselytes.[54] Besides the painful operation of circumcision which men had to undergo, it involved isolation from traditional public ceremonies and from a traditional way of life. But to become an adherent of an exciting oriental cult, whether it was of Isis or of Mithra, of Sabazius or of the Jewish God, without changing their Roman identity was quite in accordance with Roman ways. They were looking for 'supplements' and not for 'substitutes',[55] and therefore the Romans did not need any large scale mission as a means of attracting them.

2) Jewish sources

Before the revolutionary article by V. Tcherikover,[56] it was generally accepted that Jewish literature in the Greek language was mainly apologetic and was written with a purpose in mind, i.e. to win proselytes. This literature was scrutinized in order to learn about methods of Jewish propaganda. Tcherikover however, argued that 'the so-called "Apologetic Literature" . . . was directed inwards and not outwards'.[57] The main proof which demonstrates the correctness

---

[53]Cf. how Livy described the spread of the rites of the Bacchanalia in Rome and explained the reason of this disaster 39.8.5: *Initia erant, quae primo paucis tradita sunt: deinde vulgari coepta sunt per viros mulieresque. additae voluptatis religioni vini et epularum, quo primum animi inlicerentur.* 'There were initiatory rites which at first were imparted to a few, then began to be generally known among men and women. To the religious element in them were added the delights of wine and feasts that the minds of a larger number might be attracted' (trans. E.T. Sage *LCL*). A little further on (39.15), Livy cites the speech of a consul who described the adherents of Bacchanalia as many thousands in number and explained that this misfortune was started by women: *primum igitur mulierum magna pars est, et is fons mali huiusce fuit.* It looks as if Romans quite often followed one and the same pattern in adopting foreign cults, with women being more active than men. Cf. also the comment by Goodman, *Mission and Conversion*, 29, 'In any case neither the episode nor Livy's description of it in themselves constitute good evidence of a proselytizing mission by worshippers of Dionysus'.
[54]So Smallwood, *The Jews* But she does not doubt that judaizers came into being as a result of active Jewish proselytizing.
[55]A.D. Nock, *Conversion* (Oxford: Clarendon Press, 1933, reprinted 1972), 6.
[56]'Jewish Apologetic Literature Reconsidered', Eos 48, 3 (1956), 169-193.

of his approach lies in a startling lack of knowledge of the Septuagint by the Gentile public.[58] The defence of Judaism and polemics against polytheists which are definitely present in this Jewish literature, are something markedly different from signs of missionary zeal. Simple comparison with Christian literature shows the difference of approach.

Both Philo and Josephus were acquainted with the concept of proselytism and, on the whole, show a favourable attitude towards proselytes. However, there is no hint in their writings of the existence of concerted Jewish missionary activity. The term 'proselyte' was never used by Josephus. The closest reference is the paraphrase of the term in the story of the deception of Fulvia: καὶ νομίμοις προσεληθυῖαν τοῖς Ἰουδαϊκοῖς.[59] Philo used the word προσήλυτος, only when quoting the Septuagint where it was used.[60] The conversion of the royal house of Adiabene is described by Josephus in terms which do not suggest missionary zeal as a motivation of the Jewish merchant Anania.[61] Rather the reason for this conversion was political, with the strategic aim of gaining a dominant position in the region and, in the event of a Jewish victory in the war against Rome, probably even of inheriting the throne of Jerusalem.[62]

---

[57]'Jewish Apologetic Literature Reconsidered', Eos 48, 3 (1956), 183.

[58]A. Momigliano, *Alien Wisdom: The Limits of Hellenization* (Cambridge: CUP, 1976), 92: 'The LXX remained an exclusive Jewish possession until the Christians took it over'.

[59]*AJ* 18. 8

[60]*De somniis* II, 273; *De cherubim* 108, 119; *De specialibus legibus* I, 51, 308. The biblical passages are: Deut. 10:18-19; Lev. 19:33-34, 25:23.

[61]*AJ* 20. 34-48. Cf. Goodman, *Mission and Conversion*, 84.

[62]J. Neusner, 'The Conversion of Adiabene to Judaism', *JBL* 83:1 (1964), 63-66. Feldman rejects Neusner's inference that the royal house of Adiabene cherished a hope of winning the throne of Jerusalem, arguing that according to Deut. 17:15 only a native Jew can be a king, *Jew and Gentile*, 331. But such considerations were never taken too seriously in political games when power was at stake, and an impediment could be overcome, as in the case of that half-Jew, the Idumaean, Herod the Great.

CHAPTER 3

PROSELYTES:
CHRISTIAN EVIDENCE

Matthew 23:15 is examined in detail since it has been cited as the clearest evidence of aggressive Jewish proselytising. However, recently M. Goodman has cogently argued a new interpretation of this passage, based on a suggestion by J. Munck that the term προσήλυτος could also be applied to Jews who were converted to Pharisaism. The possibility of this wider application of the word is here supported by later Christian examples. They demonstrate that the word, due to its obvious connection with προσέρχομαι, was capable of being extended beyond its traditional use with reference to Gentile converts to Judaism. It was applied by Christian authors to converts to Christianity. It is proposed that Acts 13:43 is the first example of this meaning of the word προσήλυτος.

I. The Proselytes of Matthew 23:15

Proselytes are mentioned four times in the New Testament: once in Matthew (23:15), and three times in Acts (2:10, 6:5, 13:43). The passage in Matthew is probably the most famous and the most widely used argument in favour of aggressive Jewish proselitizing:

Οὐαὶ ὑμῖν, γραμματεῖς καὶ Φαρισαῖοι ὑποκριταί, ὅτι περιάγετε τὴν θά-λασσαν καὶ τὴν ξηρὰν ποιῆσαι ἕνα προσήλυτον, καὶ ὅταν γένηται ποιεῖτε αὐτὸν υἱὸν γεέννης διπλότερον ὑμῶν.

Woe to you Scribes and Pharisees, hypocrites, for you compass sea and land to make one proselyte; and when he is become so, you make him twofold more a son of Gehenna than yourselves.

One's position in the discussion about this *locus classicus* quite often, though not necessarily, depends upon the position one takes in the general discussion on Jewish proselytism. Some scholars, who deny the existence of the Jewish mission, and sometimes a favourable attitude of the Rabbis to the converts as well, consider this verse to be a misrepresentation of the Pharisaic position.[1] Others, in attempts to overcome the obscurity of the passage, see in it a reference either to a unique event, such as the conversion of Flavius Clemens[2] or that of Izates,[3] or to matrimonial alliances of the Herod family,[4] or even to the custom of making a single proselyte each year.[5]

---

[1]See the classical formulation of this position in: J. Derenbourg, *Essai sur l'Histoire et la Geographie de la Palestine* (Paris: 1867): republished (Westmead: Gregg International Publishers Limited, 1971), 227f.

[2]H. Graetz, *Die jüdischen Proselyten im Römerreiche unter den Kaisern Domitian, Nerva, Trajan, und Hadrian* (Breslau, 1884), 27f.; id, 'Der Vers in Matthäus-Evangelium: einen Proselyten Machen', *Monatsschrift*, 28 (1869), 169f.

[3]M. Friedlaender, *Die religiösen Bewegungen innerhalb des Judentums im Zeitalter Jesu* (Berlin, 1905), 31ff. Cf. also R.H. Gundry *Matthew. A Commentary on his Literary and Theological Art* (Grand Rapids: Eerdmans, 1982), 461 who rejects this interpretation as geographically incorrect: 'The failure of the journey from Galilee to Adiabene to meet the requirements of Matthew's expression "You go about the sea and the dry land" rules out a particular reference to the historical incident described by Josephus'.

[4]J. Munck, *Paul and the Salvation of Mankind* (London: SCM, 1959), 266f. His interpretation was rejected by Jeremias, *Jesus' Promise to the Nations*, 18, n. 1, on the same grounds of geographical incongruity.

[5]This rather eccentric interpretation was suggested by A. Jellinek (*non vidi*): Bamberger, *Proselytism*, 268.

Those who take this text on face value, i.e. as a record of factual Jewish proselytizing zeal, have suggested a number of interpretations, although they sometimes deny the genuineness of this utterance and view it as a polemic of the early Christian community against Pharisaic Judaism.[6]

K.G. Kuhn, for example, who does not question the very fact of the existence of the Jewish mission, distinguished between the missionary activity of Judaism in the Diaspora and that in Palestine. The first was satisfied with 'the loose adherence of Gentiles as σεβόμενοι τὸν θεόν', the second demanded acceptance of the whole Jewish law. In his view Matthew's Jesus raises his voice against the Pharisees' attempts to make proselytes members of their party, i.e. 'to keep the Law as they themselves do'.[7]

S. McKnight came to a similar conclusion though from a different starting point—denial of a Jewish mission. He compared Matthew's passage with Paul's polemics in Galatians and Romans and concluded that both authors describe similar situations. In Galatia Paul contended with 'Jewish-Christian advocates of Torah piety' who most probably belonged to the Pharisaic party and tried to turn 'partial converts' (perhaps 'God-fearers') into 'total converts' (proselytes). Jesus as portrayed in Matthew's gospel, criticized not Jewish missionary activity as such, but 'Torah proselytization', i.e. the concern of the Pharisees to make the Gentile God-fearers, who had already been attracted to Judaism, go the whole way and 'assume the yoke of Torah'.[8] Both Kuhn and McKnight consider that the Pharisees imposed their understanding of the law on Gentiles and speak about partly converted Gentiles becoming adherents of Pharisaism.

A slightly different line of interpretation was suggested by A. Plummer[9] and W.C. Allen.[10] They both admitted the success of Jewish proselytizing, but assumed that Pharisees had no share in this successful enterprise. The Pharisees tried to repair this omission and made extraordinary efforts to achieve this aim and to make converts to

---

[6]Bamberger, *Proselytism*, 271; A.J. Saldarini, *Matthew's Christian-Jewish Community*, (Chicago and London: The University of Chicago Press, 1994), 46. For another position see McKnight, *A Light among Gentiles*, 106f.: 'The saying ought to be given serious consideration as being an authentic word of Jesus'.

[7]*TDNT* 6, 742.

[8]McKnight, *A Light among Gentiles*, 104ff.

[9]A. Plummer, *An Exegetical Commentary on the Gospel according to St. Matthew*, (New York, 1909), 317f.

[10]W.C. Allen, *A Critical and Exegetical Commentary on the Gospel according to St. Matthew*, (New York, 1907), 246.

Pharisaism. Thus Jesus objected, not to conversion to Judaism, but to conversion to Pharisaic doctrine.

All these scholars, though they differ in details of interpretation, speak about the conversion of Gentiles. The basic meaning of προσή-λυτος as a *Gentile* convert to Judaism remains unshaken. The very idea of regarding προσήλυτος as a designation of a Jewish convert to Phar-isaism was rejected in passing without serious consideration: 'We should not think of converts to Pharisaism from among the Jews, for the term 'proselyte' connotes Gentiles'.[11]

However it was exactly this interpretation that was introduced by Munck. He argues that, if the *logion* was pronounced by Jesus, it 'may refer only to *Pharisaic* proselytes within the Jewish connection, i.e. the Jews who are won for Pharisaism by the work of the Pharisaic scribes'.[12] And recently Goodman has suggested a number of argu-ments in favour of this interpretation.[13] He treats Matthew's *logion* as a polemic against the conversion of *Jews* to Pharisaism. Pharisees, who believed themselves to be the only ones to interpret the Torah correct-ly, argues Goodman, might wish as many Jews as possible to follow Pharisaic *halakhah*. The most obvious objection to such an interpreta-tion is the meaning 'convert to Judaism' attributed to the word προση-´λυτος, which seems to be established by the first century. Goodman puts forward the following arguments to confirm the linguistic possi-bility of Munck's interpretation: (1) the term is very rare in the first century with the exception of quotations from the Septuagint; (2) it was hardly used by Philo and never used by Josephus; (3) the term is mentioned only four times in the whole of the New Testament; (4) Phi-lo pointed to the etymology of the word in *De Specialibus Legibus* I 9 (51), which suggests that προσήλυτος comes to (προσέρχεσθαι) a new godly constitution (καινῇ καὶ φιλοθέῳ πολιτείᾳ) from a different one; (5) this sense of the verb προσέρχεσθαι as the approach to something

---

[11]Gundry, *Matthew*, 461. The same attitude was expressed by H.J. Flowers, 'Matthew XXIII. 15', *ExpT 73 (1961)*, 67-69, who wrongly attributed such an under-standing of the term to Allen.

[12]Munck, *Paul*, 267. The same idea of not using the word προσήλυτος technically is indeed implied by F.W. Beare, *The Gospel According to Matthew, A Commentary* (Oxford: Basil Blackwell, 1981), 454. He supposes that this saying is 'an outburst of Matthew's exasperation at the attempts of the leaders of the Jewish communities to win over those who had been converted to Christianity', i.e. Jewish Christians.

[13]M. Goodman, 'Jewish Proselytizing in the First Century', *The Jews among Pagans and Christians in the Roman Empire*, eds. J. Lieu, J. North, and T. Rajak (London, New York: Routledge, 1992); the article is reprinted with some modifications in *Mission and Conversion*.

sacred can be traced in Matthew and in Josephus (*BJ* 2.142). Goodman sums up his position as follows:

> What I suggest, therefore, is that *proselytos* in the first century had both a technical and a non-technical sense, and that in that latter sense it could quite easily be applied to Jews.[14]

It seems that such a non-technical understanding of the term would relieve Matthew's text of a certain incongruity. Let us have a closer look at the context in which it is inserted. It is one of the seven woe oracles, in which Jesus charges the Scribes and the Pharisees with a contradiction between their inner attitudes and their outward behaviour. There are serious reasons to believe that the words of Jesus are more or less authentic.[15] In the first two woes[16] the Jewish leaders are accused of locking people out of the Kingdom of heaven and imposing on them their own, i.e. false, understanding of the Law. Jesus opposed 'the Kingdom of heaven', which he preached (v.13), and 'Gehenna', to which Pharisees recruited newly converted members (v.15). Instead of listening to Jesus who preached to all the Jews, Pharisees included, they, with the force of their authority, do not allow other Jews to join him. They present in place of his message their own false teaching and make their followers even more damnable, and even more deserving of the punishment of hell than themselves, because such people had a choice between Jesus' teaching and that of the Pharisees. Both woes are connected and develop the same idea with rhetorical intensification. Apparent reference to Gentile proselytes in this Jewish context would weaken the strength of accusation and the connection between the two parts. Besides, it is difficult to explain why Gentiles who converted to Judaism would be worse than their Pharisaic teachers.[17] The expression 'the sea and the land' has a strong idiomatic colouring and it seems that we need not view it as an itinerary of missionary journeys.[18]

---

[14]Goodman, 'Jewish Proselytizing', 62f. = *Mission and Conversion*, 73.

[15]Jeremias, *Jesus' Promise to the Nations*, 17-18, n. 4.

[16]The woe in Matt. 23:14 is treated by the majority of text critics as an interpolation derived from the parallel text in Mark 12:40 or Luke 20:45. It is absent from the best witnesses of the Alexandrian and western types of texts, and manuscripts which include it have it in different places. See B.M. Metzger, *A Textual Commentary on the Greek New Testament. A Companion Volume to the United Bible Societies' Greek New Testament*, (Stuttgart: United Bible Society, 1994⁴), 60.

[17]The usual explanation is that newly adopted members as a rule tend to be far more zealous than the old adherents of the doctrine.

[18]McKnight, *A Light among Gentiles*, 154, n. 30.

II. Later Christian Evidence

It seems that Goodman's interpretation of the word προσήλυτος can be supported by some additional arguments. Though it is used as a technical term in a number of inscriptions and some literary texts, προσήλυτος retains the basic literal meaning of the cognate verb. This consideration, implicit already in Philo's etymology, served to facilitate expansion of the term's sphere of usage. Προσήλυτος had the same potential as Christian νεόφυτος, which meant at first 'a new convert to Christianity', and then expanded its meaning to a more general one and was used to designate anyone who was newly initiated into anything. That this potential was to a certain extent realised can be seen from the following examples.

In Justin's *Dialogus cum Tryphone* 28.2, it is said that the Jews have but a short time left in which to accept Christianity: Βραχὺς οὗτος ὑμῖν περιλείπεται προσηλύσεως χρόνος. It looks as if the word προσήλυσις (a *hapax*, according to *TLG*) was coined by Justin himself instead of προσέλευσις and was definitely used by him here with προσήλυτος in mind. In the mainstream of his argument envisaging Christians as a new Israel he interprets Isaiah 49:6 (Dial. cum Tryph. 122) as referring to Christians as proselytes of Christ:

> Ἐπεὶ δὲ καινὴν διαθήκην καὶ νόμον αἰώνιον καὶ πρόσταγμα ὁ θεὸς προεκήρυσσε πέμψειν, οὐχὶ τὸν παλαιὸν νόμον ἀκουσόμεθα καὶ τοὺς προσηλύτους αὐτοῦ, ἀλλὰ τὸν Χριστὸν καὶ προσηλύτους αὐτοῦ, ἡμᾶς τὰ ἔθνη, οὓς ἐφώτισεν.

> But since God announced beforehand that he would send a new covenant, and an everlasting law and commandment, we will not understand this of the old law and its proselytes, but of Christ and his proselytes, namely us Gentiles, whom he has illuminated.

> (trans. Dods and Reith, *ANF*)

A similar line of interpretation (and, accordingly, the new meaning of the word) was very much in evidence, not to say inevitable, in Christian commentaries on Isaiah 54:15 (LXX). Here are two examples from the fourth and fifth centuries. They differ in the details—one author considers proselytes to be Gentile Christians, the other to be Gentile as well as Jewish— but both apply the term to Christians.

Theodoret of Cyrus (*PG* 81, 445)

> Ἰδοὺ προσήλυτοι προσελεύσονται. Προσηλύτους καλεῖ τοὺς καθ' ἑκάστην, ὡς ἔπος εἰπεῖν, ἡμέραν ἐκ τῶν ἐθνῶν ἀγρευομένους, καὶ τοὺς θείῳ προσιόντας βαπτίσματι. Καὶ ταύτης τοίνυν τῆς προφητείας ὁρῶμεν τὸ τέλος.

Behold, proselytes will come. He calls 'proselytes' those who were hunted out from among the Gentiles practically each day and who came to divine baptism. And so we see the fulfilment of this prophecy.

Procopius of Gaza (*PG* 87, 2544D)

> Καὶ ἰδοὺ προσήλυτοι προσελεύσονται, φησί δι' ἐμοῦ, τοὺς ἐν ἑκάστῳ καιρῷ προσιόντας τῇ πίστει δηλῶν ἐξ ἐθνῶν, ἢ καὶ ἐξ αὐτῶν Ἰουδαίων. Κατόπιν γὰρ τεθείνται τῶν ἐθνῶν, καίτοι πρώτην ἔχοντες τάξιν, καὶ γεγόνασι προσήλυτοι τοῖς ἐξ ἐθνῶν, οἱ πάλαι τούτους προσηλύτος δεχόμενοι. Πλὴν καὶ τοῦτο δι' ἐμοῦ, φησί. Διὰ γὰρ Χριστοῦ ἡ πάντων ἐπιστροφή, καὶ πρὸς τὸν Πατέρα καὶ Θεὸν ὁδός.

And behold, proselytes will come, he says, through me, meaning those who come at each opportunity to the faith from among the Gentiles or even from the Jews themselves. For they have been placed below the Gentiles, although they [originally] were ranked first, and they became proselytes to the Gentiles, they who previously received these as proselytes. But he adds that this is through me. For every conversion is through Christ, and the way is to the Father and God.

Didymus the Blind, in his Commentary on Psalm 21: 31 (καὶ ἀναγγελήσεται τῷ κυρίῳ γενεὰ ἡ ἐρχομένη), toys with the complete reversal of the situation: now, after the Incarnation, a Jew, if he believes in the Christian good news, will become a proselyte of the Gentiles:

> ὥσπερ γὰρ πρότερον πρὸ τῆς ἐπιδημίας οἱ προστιθέμενοι τῷ νόμῳ τοῦ θεοῦ προσήλυτοι ἐγίνοντο τῶν Ἰουδαίων, οὕτω νῦν Ἰουδαῖος ἐάν πιστεύσῃ τῷ εὐαγγελίῳ καὶ τῷ θεῷ, τοῦ εὐαγγελίου προσήλυτος γίνεται του{ς} τῶν {Ἰουδαίων} ἐθνῶν.[19]

---

[19]The papyrus with Didymus' text was published in vol. 7 of *Papyrologische Texte und Abhandlungen: Didymos der Blinde, Psalmenkommentar (Tura-Papyrus) Teil I: Kommentar zur Psalm 20-21*, eds. L. Doutreleau, A. Gesche and M. Gronewald (Bonn: Rudolf Habelt Verlag, 1969).

For just as earlier, before the coming [of Christ] those who became adherents of the law of God became proselytes of the Jews, so now if a Jew believes in the gospel and in God, he becomes a proselyte of the gospel of the Gentiles.

But in the case of a certain Mary of Cassobela (Μαρία ἐκ Κασσοβήλων) the situation is quite different. The author of a letter to Ignatius (which is regarded as spurious by modern scholars), she designates herself in the *praescriptio* as Μαρία προσήλυτος Ἰησοῦ Χριστοῦ. This shows that the word could sometimes be used with a new meaning outside an exegetical or theological context, as a self-definition.

What other shades of meaning this term could acquire can be seen from examples in the writings by Asterius, Bishop of Amasea in Pontus in the fourth century AD.[20] They all belong to one and the same Homily VIII, an *encomium* on Peter and Paul. Four times Asterius used the word to designate Christian neophytes. Speaking about Peter as the one to whom the Lord entrusted care of his flock, Asterius says:

καὶ σχεδὸν ἀνθ' ἑαυτοῦ τὸν πιστότατον μαθητὴν ἔδωκεν ὁ Κύριος τοῖς προσηλύτοις πατέρα καὶ νομέα καὶ παιδευτήν (ΊΙΙ 15,2).

And the Lord gave to the proselytes, instead of himself as it were, the most faithful disciple to be their father, and shepherd, and teacher.

In another place, after having depicted how Paul confused and astonished Jews and the whole city by his teaching in the synagogues of Damascus immediately after his conversion, he called Paul a noble proselyte:

εἰς ταύτην τὴν ἀμηχανίαν ἐνέβαλε πόλιν μεγάλην, δῆμον πολυάνθρωπον, τὸ πρῶτον τοῦ γενναίου προσηλύτου κήρυγμα καὶ πλέον τότε Δαμασκὸς ἐταράττετο ἢ πρώην ἐν Ἱεροσολύμοις χριστιανοί, ἡνίκα Στέφανον Παῦλος ἐλίθαζεν (VIII 25,4).

The first proclamation of the noble proselyte threw a great city, a densely populated community into such turmoil, and then Damascus was even more stirred up than the Christians in Jerusalem had previously been, at the time when Paul stoned Stephen.

Re-telling Acts 18:1-8 (the conversion of the ruler of the synagogue), Asterius calls him a proselyte:

[20]Asterius of Amasea, *Homilies I-XIV. Text, Introduction and Notes* by C. Datema (Leiden: Brill, 1970).

καὶ λαλήσας ἐν ταῖς συναγωγαῖς τὸ σωτήριον δίδαγμα ᾤχετο ἄγων προσήλυτον, οὐχ ἕνα τῶν πολλῶν οὐδὲ τῶν ἐπιτυχόντων, ἀλλὰ αὐτὸν τὸν ἀρχισυνάγωγον (VIII 29,1).

And, having recounted the teaching of salvation in the synagogues, he left taking a proselyte [with him], not one from the crowd nor someone who just happened to be there, but the ruler of the synagogue himself.

Asterius contrasts Christians and proselytes, comparing the latter with newly-planted trees:

χριστιανοὺς βεβαιῶν, προσηλύτους οἰκοδομῶν καὶ τρέφων τοῖς προσφόροις παιδεύμασιν ὡς φυτουργοὶ τὰ νεαρὰ τῶν φυτῶν τῇ συμμέτρῳ καὶ πεφεισμένῃ τῶν ὑδάτων ἐπιρροῇ (VIII 27, 6).

Strengthening Christians, building up and nourishing proselytes with the appropriate teaching as gardeners nourish young plants, with the right and carefully measured dose of water.

In the last example προσήλυτος comes very close to the meaning of νεόφυτος and Asterius actually makes the next step, creating a neologism νεοπροσήλυτος, as a description of the young Christian community in Jerusalem. He recalls the story of Ananias and Sapphira (Acts 5:1-5) and explains Peter's action toward them through his anxiety to impose a new Christian way of life on the community:

Ἐπειδὴ γὰρ νεοπροσήλυτος ἦν καὶ νεοπαγὴς ὁ λαός, ἑλληνικῆς καὶ ἰουδαικῆς ἀδιαφορίας ὑπάγουν τοὺς εὐαγγελικοὺς δεξάμενος νόμους, εἰκότως ἐνόμισεν οὐ τῆς ἐκ λόγων νουθεσίας μόνον χρῄζειν τοὺς μαθητάς, ἀλλὰ καὶ φόβου τινὸς ἐμπράκτου (VIII 7, 1).

For since the people were neoproselytes and newly built up, and were in the process of abandoning Greek and Jewish indifference, having accepted the laws of the gospel, he reasonably considered that his pupils needed not only instruction by words but also a certain practical fear.

It looks as if the use of προσήλυτος to mean 'a potential convert' (in contrast with someone who had belonged to the faith for some time) can be found in a passage from Clement of Alexandria:

καὶ τοὺς ἀδελφούς, οὐ τοὺς κατὰ πίστιν μόνον, ἀλλὰ καὶ τοὺς προσηλύτους λέγων. εἰ γὰρ ὁ νῦν διεχθρεύων ὕστερον πιστεύσει (Stromata 7,14).

'and these your brethren,'—not meaning those in the faith only, but also the proselytes. For whether he who now is hostile shall afterwards believe, we know not as yet.

(trans. Wilson, *ANF*).

If we compare the texts of Asterius, the *praescriptio* of Maria of Cassobela and the passage from Clement, we can see how wide was the range of meanings of the word. Nevertheless one particular tendency can be traced. Alongside the traditional meaning there began to develop another one, namely 'a convert to Christianity'. To a certain degree this development was prompted by theological exegesis. But this was not the only reason. The word, as was mentioned before, had strong links with the verb προσέρχομαι—hence its appearance in a persistently repeated *figura etymologica*, προσήλυτος προσέρχεται, not only in quotations from the Septuagint. The meaning emphasised in the word is not the idea of being a newcomer to Judea or the Jewish religion, but the idea of approaching anything new.

We must also bear in mind that Christian technical language was only beginning to develop in the first centuries. There existed a certain degree of flexibility. Even later some terms which seem to have an established meaning were used with surprising freedom. Thus the term Χριστιανός, according to the seventh canon of the First Council of Constantinople in 381, was applied in a restricted sense only to those who were admitted to the first grade of the catechumenate,[21] though usually the word was applied to those who were actually baptized.

Possible evidence for the Christianizing of the term προσήλυτος can be found in the intriguing inscriptions on ossuaries from the Dominus Flevit necropolis in Jerusalem, dating from the end of the 1st century to the beginning of the 2nd century AD. The suggestion that these could have belonged to Christian proselytes has been put forward by P.B. Bagatti, and this is not impossible, as it is sometimes assumed.[22] The first inscription is incised on the cover of the ossuary and consists of a name of a certain Diogenes son of Zenon, a proselyte (Διογένης προσήλυτος Ι Ζηνᾶ). The same name is cut also on the edge of the chest. Below and to the left of the inscription there is an incised cross mark in the sideways position. The inscription on the edge of the ossuary is

---

[21]The seventh canon does not belong to the Second Ecumenical Council and probably was composed in the middle of the fifth century. It was afterwards adopted by the Quinisext Synod under the number 95: C.J. Hefele, *A History of the Councils of the Church. Vol. 2 AD 326 to AD 429* (Edinburgh: T. & T. Clark: 1876), 368.

also followed by a cross mark.[23] On the second ossuary there are two names, both drawn in charcoal. The first name traced on the centre of the cover is female and in Hebrew letters. The second graffito is in Greek and the deceased marked as a proselyte.[24] On this ossuary is drawn (also in charcoal) a *chi-rho* monogram, which served as Bagatti's main reason for identifying the Chamber 79 at '*Dominus Flevit*' as Jewish-Christian. To the left of the *chi-rho* sign there is a drawing of an eight-pointed star, which was interpreted either as a combination of *iota* and *chi* for Jesus Christ plus additionly a horizontal stroke for a cross, or as a combination of two cross marks.

In arguing his case, Bagatti went too far in proposing that the Judaeo-Christians had an institution similar to a catechumenate, which after the same pattern he called 'proselytate'. The example which he gave from Justin to support his hypothesis of this technical usage of the word was also rather unfortunate and, at the very least, ambiguous.[25] But on the whole, if we put aside all fantasies about a 'proselytate', the

---

[22]P.B. Bagatti–J.T. Milik, *Gli Scavi del 'Dominus Flevit'*, No. 21, 13a. Bagatti argues for his hypothesis in details in: P.B. Bagatti, *The Church from Circumcision. History and Archaeology of Judaeo-Christians*, The Studium Biblicum Franciscanum, Smaller series, 2, ET by E. Hoacle (Jerusalem: Franciscan Printing Press, 1971), 237-239 (first published in French in 1965 also as Studium Biblicum Franciscanum, Collectio Minor, 2). For another interpretation see: P. Figueras, *Decorated Jewish Ossuaries* (Leiden: Brill, 1983), 17-23. For the most radical criticism of Bagatti see: J. Taylor, *Christians and Holy Places. The Myth of Jewish-Christian Origins* (Oxford: Clarendon Press, 1993), 11-12. See also J.T. Sanders, *Schismatics, Sectarians, Dissidents, Deviants. The First One Hundred Years of Jewish-Christian Relations* (London: SCM,1993), 35-37, who, though sceptical about Bagatti's interpretation, is in general agreement with the careful conclusion of J. Finegan, that it 'comes within the realm of possibility' that at least some ossuaries belonged to 'Jewish families some of whose members had become Christians', J. Finegan,*The Archaeology of the New Testament. The life of Jesus and the Beginning of the Early Church* (Princeton: Princeton University Press, 1969), 249.

[23]Bagatti—Milik, *Gli Scavi del 'Dominus Flevit'*, 21. According to *NewDocs* 4, 268, M. Guarducci *EG* 4, 441-44 discerned beneath the name of Diogenes to the left a *chi-rho* sign, which she dated to the end of the 2nd century, i.e. nearly a century later than the inscription itself. This sensational information in what is generally a reliable and carefully prepared edition is a regrettable misunderstanding.

[24]The reading in Bagatti-Milik 13a was ᾽Ιούδα ν(εωτέρου) προσηλύτο[υ] τυρᾶ (cheesmaker). But later Bagatti changed the reading of the last word to Τύρου, (SBF 3, 1952-53), 163; he was followed by B. Lifshitz, 'Beiträge zur palästinischen Epigraphic', *Zeitschr. des Deutschen Palästina-Vereins* 78 (1962) 79, who also suggested, that ν should belong to the name: ᾽Ιούδαν. M. Guarducci made a careful guess that the last word could be patronymic: *EG* IV, 443, n. 4.

[25]Justin, *Dial. cum Tryph.*, 23.3.

hypothesis that both Judah and Diogenes were Christian proselytes cannot be ruled out.

It seems that a Latin epitaph from Rome, carved on a marble plaque, can also contribute to this discussion. It starts with the name of the deceased: Cresces Sinicerius | Iudeus proselitus. There are different interpretations of this combination of *Iudeus* and *proselytos*.[26] The most evident and reasonable, as I see it, is that Iudeus modifies proselytos, giving it the meaning 'Crescens Sinicerius, a Jewish proselyte', and that the use of the modifying adjective can be explained by the fact that 'proselyte' without additional definition, could be understood as a Christian proselyte.[27]

To sum up, some tendencies in the usage of the word προσήλυτος in the Christian era seem to confirm the assumption that in Matthew 23:15 this term could mean 'a Jew converted to Pharisaism', in which case the text of Matthew loses its significance as the main Christian proof text for Jewish proselytizing activity in the first century.

III. The Proselytes in Acts

Now let us turn to the book of Acts. Proselytes are mentioned for the first time in the list of nations who were present in Jerusalem on the day of Pentecost, when the miracle of glossolalia took place (Acts 2:11). Though there exist some differences in opinion as to the understanding of the grammatical structure of the sentence—specifically over whether we are to take προσήλυτοι to refer to proselytes from all the peoples mentioned,[28] or just proselytes from Rome,[29] the meaning of the term we are discussing is clear. The term is used technically and denotes Gentile converts.

The second time Luke uses the term προσήλυτος, it is with reference to Antiochone of the Seven appointed for disbursing the resources among the needy (Acts 6:5). In this case also the word is also used

---

[26]See Kraemer, 'On the meaning', 326.

[27]Cf. also another possible interpretation discussed by Kraemer, 'On the meaning', 327, n. 44: 'One might argue that Crescens is a Christian proselyte born to a mother who initially sympathized with Judaism and thus named her son Iudeus. The terminology of the inscription would not contradict such a reading, nor does the photograph in Frey indicate any Jewish symbols'.

[28]So Haenchen, *The Acts of the Apostles*, 413, n. 5; 'The phrase 'Jews and proselytes' does not refer to any specific national group with its own language. . . but covers all the preceding groups with respect to religious affiliation'.

[29]So the majority of commentaries and translations.

technically. But the third and the last mention of the term in Acts is puzzling.

In Pisidian Antioch, after Paul finished preaching in the synagogue, he and Barnabas were followed by many of the Jews and by 'worshipping proselytes', and Paul and Barnabas persuaded them to continue in the grace of God:

λυθείσης δὴ τῆς συναγωγῆς, ἠκολούθησαν πολλοὶ τῶν Ἰουδαίων καὶ τῶν σεβομένων προσηλύτων τῷ Παύλῳ καὶ τῷ Βαρναβᾷ, οἵτινες προσλαλοῦντες αὐτοῖς, ἔπειθον αὐτοὺς ἐπιμένειν τῇ χάριτι τοῦ θεοῦ.

(Acts 13:43)

The combination of the two terms προσήλυτοι and σεβόμενοι looks very strange. It is the first time that Luke has used the term σεβόμενοι instead of the φοβούμενοι, characteristic of the previous narrative. If by this word he designates, as I believe,[30] a definite category of Gentiles, what can this combination of words mean?   Two possible explanations are suggested. The first one is to assume that προσήλυτοι is the wrong word. It could be either an ancient gloss[31], or a result of inaccuracy—'a careless expression', as H. Conzelmann puts it.[32] The second repudiates the technical character of σεβόμενοι.[33]

I would like to discuss another possibility, namely that προσήλυτοι is used here in the same manner as in Matthew in a basic 'verbal' sense of coming to any-thing new. This meaning fits the context. From the outset in the Pisidian synagogue, Paul addressed two groups: Jews (ἄνδρες Ἰσραηλῖται) and God-fearers (οἱ φοβούμενοι τὸν θεόν), as is made clear by the article before φοβούμενοι. In the middle of his speech he repeated his address (13:26): Ἄνδρες ἀδελφοί, υἱοὶ

---

[30]The problem of σεβόμενοι/φοβούμενοι will be discussed in full in the next chapter. Cf. C.K. Barrett, A Critical and Exegetical Commentary on The Acts of the Apostles, vol. 1, (Edinburgh: T & T Clark, International Critical Commentary, 1994), 654, who does not see any problem at all: 'there is only one group before us, consisting of proselytes, devout proselytes, perhaps worshipping proselytes, that is, proselytes who had duly attended the Sabbath service in the synagogue. There is no problem, and there is no evidence here that should lead us to think of synagogue adherents, even if σεβόμενος τὸν θέον, θεοσεβής, or θεοσέβιος, were current as technical terms describing such adherents'.
[31]Kuhn, TDNT 6, 743; Haenchen, The Acts of the Apostles, 413, n. 5; Conzelmann, Acts of the Apostles, 106.
[32]Conzelmann, Acts of the Apostles, 106.
[33]BC V, 88; Bruce, The Acts of the Apostles, 313; M. Wilcox, 'The "God-Fearers" in Acts–A Reconsideration', JSNT 13 (1981), 108f.

γένους Ἀβραὰμ καὶ οἱ ἐν ὑμῖν φοβούμενοι τὸν θεόν. If 'God-fearers' means here the more devout Jews, as Wilcox observed, it sounds 'mildly sarcastic', to use this phrase, rather than flattering.[34] Such an attitude of Paul, in Wilcox's view would be explicable in terms of his intention to turn from Jews to Gentiles—'after all it is in this very section that we find Paul's first threat to abandon a Jewish mission and go to the Gentiles'. Such an explanation does not sound justified.

If we assume that φοβούμενοι has no technical meaning here and if we bear in mind the presence of an article, then it follows that Paul addressed some Jews whom he called ἄνδρες Ἰσραηλῖται and another group of Jews whom he called οἱ φοβούμενοι τὸν θεόν. For Judaism φόβος θεοῦ is *conditio sine qua non*.[35] It acquired the meaning of Latin *pietas, religio*.[36] Every Jew is φοβούμενος τὸν θεόν while he follows the Jewish law and stops being so if he breaks with it. So if Paul was sarcastic it was not a mild kind of sarcasm—basically the implication is that ἄνδρες Ἰσραηλῖται are not φοβούμενοι τὸν θεόν, i.e. not Jews at all—the worst insult one can think of. Of course, a critical attitude towards one's audience is quite possible—the Jewish prophets supplied us with an abundant number of examples—but it seems that such an attitude is inappropriate for someone who is seeking to convert. And it would have been very cunning and insidious if Paul had started insulting Jews with an aim to cause their strong reaction and use this as an excuse to abandon preaching Christ to them.

It seems more in keeping with the context to assume that the presence of two groups in the synagogue was known to Paul and he addressed them separately. After the synagogue was dismissed, Paul was followed by representatives of both of the groups he addressed. Luke stressed that Paul's speech was successful and that he converted many in both groups. Luke gives the same pattern for other synagogues visited by Paul: Jews and God-fearers, i.e. Gentiles.

As Luke saw it, and in reality, proselytes were indistinguishable from native Jews in outlook where matters of religion were concerned, and the psychology of these people, who had formally become new members of the Jewish community, was not such as to make them easy converts to a new faith. It is quite easy to imagine that people who were attracted by Judaism, but who did not take the last step and bind

---

[34]Wilcox, 'The "God-Fearers" in Acts', 108.
[35]L.H. Feldman, 'Jewish "Sympathizers" in Classical Literature and Inscriptions', *TAPA 81* (1950), 203. See also G. Wanke, *TDNT* 9, 201f.
[36]K. Romaniuk, 'Die "Gottesfürchtigen" im Neuen Testament: Beitrag zur neutestamentlichen Theologie der Gottesfürcht', *Aegyptus* 44:1-2 (1964), 71.

themselves to the community, could easily turn to a new teaching. But it is almost impossible to imagine how people who had taken this last step (and for males it was a difficult decision) and who might have sought to be accepted in the new community, could be among the first to start a new life and reject some of basic things they had just learned to follow. It was possible for individuals, like Nicolas of Antioch, whose proselyte-status Luke referred to probably because it was not an ordinary thing, but it is difficult to imagine for masses of proselytes. Taking all this into consideration, it seems worthwhile at least to consider the possibility of a new interpretation of the meaning of the word προσήλυτοι in Acts 13:43.

To summarise, the sources from the first century do not support the view that there was large scale Jewish missionary activity. Luke's sporadic mention of proselytes without any special attention to the phenomenon of proselytizing and without any reference to a Jewish mission corresponds to the historical setting. It was to another group of Jewish sympathizers that he paid special attention. This group was central both for his historical and theological conception. To this group I shall now turn in the next section of this book.

CHAPTER 4

GOD-FEARERS:
EPIGRAPHIC EVIDENCE

The prominent place which is assigned to God-fearers in Acts is one of the main reasons why some scholars give little credence on the whole to the work as an authentic source of information. Until recently the very existence of such a category of Gentiles was questioned. This chapter surveys the possible epigraphic traces of Jewish sympathizers. While all the findings before the Aphrodisias inscription became known were inconclusive and open to different interpretations, the latter tipped the balance and proved both the existence of a category of friendly Gentiles and the application to this category of the term theosebes *which was known from other inscriptions.*

I. Introduction

For those studying the Acts of the Apostles a question often posed is whether Luke was writing a work of history or whether we are dealing with 'theology in narrative form'.[1] In other words, should we dismiss Luke as a historian and trust him only as a theologian? Was all he did as an historian to solve 'as best as he could the theological problem posed by the mission to the Gentiles without the law'?[2] Besides contradictions between some of the details in Luke and Paul's letters—and the latter were always treated as a far superior and trustworthy source of information compared to Acts[3]—one of the main reasons for suspecting Luke's historical reliability, was the prominent place he assigned to the God-fearers, i.e. Gentiles who became adherents of the Jewish God without becoming proselytes.

During the last century scholars have wavered in their choice of an appropriate term to designate this particular class. At first they were called 'semi-proselytes'. However, G.F. Moore drew attention to the fact that this term is not quite appropriate from the point of view of Jewish legislation, since 'Jewish law knows no semi-proselytes'. Furthermore the term gave rise to much confusion, especially in attempts 'to find a category for them in the rabbinical deliverances concerning proselytes'. Therefore it gradually ceased to exist, though not everybody agreed that this was a necessary development.[4] C.K. Barrett thinks that as the definition 'semi-proselyte' means a person 'who was half-way to being a proselyte, one who had taken several steps but not the final decisive step towards becoming a proselyte; and this is a description that makes sense'.[5]

Following a discussion by Feldman the use of the term 'sympathizers' became widespread, along with the translation of Luke's φοβούμενοι τὸν θεόν—God-fearers.[6] Siegert attempted to introduce a

---

[1]A.T. Kraabel, 'The Disappearance of the "God-Fearers"', *Numen* 28,2 (1981) 118.
[2]Haenchen, *The Acts,* 102.
[3]Cf., for instance, E.R. Goodenough with A.T. Kraabel, 'Paul and the Hellenization of Christianity', *Religion in Antiquity: Essays in Honour of Erwin Ramsdell Goodenough,* ed. J. Neusner, (Leiden: Brill, 1968, Supplements to Numen, 14), 233: '. . . it is sheer perversity to go from Acts to Paul's letters, from a second-hand account to a man's own exposition of his thought'. For a response to this view see T. Hillard, A. Nobbs and B. W. Winter, 'Acts and the Pauline Corpus I: Ancient Literary Parallels', *The Book of Acts in Its First Century Setting,* vol. 1, *The Book of Acts in its Ancient Literary Setting,* eds. B.W. Winter and A.D. Clarke (Grand Rapids, Carlisle: Eerdmans, Paternoster, 1993), 183-213.
[4]Moore, *Judaism in the First Centuries,* 326.
[5]Barrett, *A Commentary on the Acts,* Vol. 1, 500.

differentiation between those who became real adherents of the Jewish God, 'God-fearers', and those who expressed some curiosity about the Jewish religion (first of all about festivals) or patronized Jews politically, 'Sympathizers'. The problem is that given the fragmentary character of our information and lack of sensitivity to this difference on the part of our informants, it is in fact impossible to follow this differentiation.[7] At the present time the terms 'God-fearers' and 'sympathizers' are used interchangeably, but not by everybody, for instance, Trebilco prefers the translation of the epigraphic term θεοσεβεῖς—'God-worshippers'.[8]

In the theological scheme the role of proselytes is that of mediators in the passage to Christianity from the Jewish world to the Gentile one. Luke has drawn a vivid picture of the God-fearers, giving his readers the feeling that they constituted a significant class of Gentiles. This has begun a search for traces of God-fearers in the inscriptions in the light of archaeological discoveries which, since the Second World War, have enormously increased our knowledge of Diaspora Judaism in the Roman Empire.

There are two ways of conducting this research. The first is to examine the inscriptions for the terms which Luke used. The second is to search for inscriptions which do not look perfectly at home in a purely Jewish context but nevertheless bear, or seem to bear, some traces of Jewish influence, or what seems to be Jewish influence. Both ways present problems. First of all, Luke himself used different names for these adherents of the Jewish God: φοβούμενοι τὸν θεόν Acts 10:1-2; 10:22; 13:16; 13:26), σεβόμενοι τὸν θεόν (13:50; 16:14; 18:6-7), σεβόμενοι (17:4), σεβόμενοι προσήλυτοι (13:43), σεβόμενοι "Ελληνες (17:17). The abrupt change in terminology in Acts is puzzling. From 13:26 φοβούμενοι disappears completely giving way to σεβόμενοι. K. Lake did not rule out the possibility that it was somehow connected with the sources underlying Luke's narrative.[9] Wilcox considers that the change 'corresponds to the shift in emphasis in Acts from the basically Torahcentred piety of the earlier part to the Gentile mission of the later section'.[10] P.L. Couchoud and R. Stahl made an unsuccessful attempt to explain it within their theory of two different authors, one of whom

---

[6]L.H. Feldman, 'Jewish "Sympathizers" in Classical Literature and Inscriptions', *TAPA* 81 (1950), 200-208.
[7]F. Siegert, 'Gottesfürchtige und Sympathizanten', *JSJ* II, 2 (1973), 110.
[8]P. Trebilco, *Jewish Communities in Asia Minor* (Cambridge: CUP, 1991), 246, n. 1.
[9]K. Lake, 'Proselytes and God-fearers', *BC V*, 86.
[10]Wilcox, 'The "God-Fearers" in Acts', 118.

called the Holy city Ἰερουσαλήμ and used the term φοβούμενοι, the other preferred Ἱεροσολύμων and σεβόμενοι.[11]

Secondly, no such terms as the ones Luke used exist in the Greek inscriptions—the only possible exception known at present is provided by the evidence for cult associations worshipping the Most High God in the imperial period at Tanais (one of the cities in the estuary of the Don, that belonged to the Bosporan Kingdom).[12] These usually employ the term θεοσεβής, which has been equated with Luke's usage, though such an equation was considered by many as wrong and unproven.[13] They stressed, and not without reason, that it could not be deduced from the inscriptions themselves whether θεοσεβής had a special technical meaning designating a group of Judaizers, or was a commonplace one, namely 'pious' or 'devout'. The main difficulty with the latter conclusion is that here, more than usual, historical research depends upon one's presuppositions, underlying theory and imagination.

In a recent article, Goodman outlines in an intentionally provocative way, the limits of our capacity to interpret archaeological and epigraphic material.[14] To show how flimsy the foundation on which we build is, and to illustrate the fragility of the scholarly assumptions which lie behind attempts to describe Diaspora Judaism in the Mediterranean region, he suggests the new, absolutely implausible, but at the same time absolutely logical identification of the famous synagogue at Sardis as a cult building of the Gentile polytheist God-worshippers. It is impossible not to agree with his basic premise that we need more caution than was first realized when drawing conclusions and building theories about first century evidence, no matter whether Jewish, Christian or Greco-Roman.

But is all as hopeless as it is sometimes assumed? Are we forever doomed not to generalize and to assume that each piece of evidence is valid only within the particular context with which it is associated? I

---

[11]'Les deux auteurs des Actes des Apôtres', *RHR* 97 (1928), 6-52; cf. critical remarks in J. Dupont, *The Sources of Acts*, ET (London: Darton, Longman & Todd, 1964), 21. Cf. also Haenchen, *The Acts*, 81, who insists that no sources can be discerned in Acts with the help of stylistic criteria and explains the more Semitic character of the first part of Acts by 'a more intensive use of "biblical" language'.
[12] This will be discussed in the chapter 6.
[13]See, for instance, L. Robert, *Nouvelle inscriptions de Sardes* (Paris: Librairie d'Amérique et d'Orient, 1964), 39-45, (hereafter referred to as *NIS*).
[14]M. Goodman, 'Jews and Judaism in the Mediterranean Diaspora in the Late-Roman Period: the Limitations of Evidence', *Journal of Mediterranean Studies*, 4, 2 (1994), 208-224.

think not. The greatest sceptics cannot escape the temptation to construct a new theory, even after concluding that the old theories no longer fit the current levels of knowledge, and that the new information, which shows a much more complicated, diverse and uncertain picture does not entitle us to make any generalisations. The new challenge unfortunately does not make us wiser. We are still trying, despite all the reservations and complaints, to understand what happened in this mysterious first century when the foundation of modern European civilization was laid.

But let us return to Acts and the problem of the God-fearers. It is not at all surprising that given the terminological discrepancy between Acts and the epigraphic evidence on the one hand, and the different terms within Acts itself on the other, the first stage of the discussion was centred on the issue of terminology. The main question was whether all these similar, though slightly different words in Acts, in Greek and Roman literature, in inscriptions (including Latin with *metuens*) and in the rabbinic sources from about AD 300 (*yirei shamayim*) can be treated as variants (and translations) of a single technical term, or whether our evidence is insufficient to draw such a conclusion.[15]

The most radical view was expressed by Wilcox who denied that either Lucan expression in Acts had any kind of technical meaning and considered both merely refer to any pious members of the Jewish community, whether Jews, Gentiles, proselytes or adherents'.[16] Such scepticism did not become widespread and little by little a consensus has emerged according to which 'God-fearers' is treated as a semi-technical term, which Luke used to describe a category of Gentiles who reverenced God and existed on the fringes of first-century synagogues. Throughout the debate no one doubted the existence of such a group no matter how vague and indeterminate its boundaries were. This point is especially important. For a long time the discussion about the God-fearers had been less fruitful than it could have been, because those who contributed to it treated the words as technical terms found in a modern dictionary. Hence, the sceptical and negative reaction of some (how was it possible for a word to be a technical term if it could

---

[15]The most important works for this stage of the discussion are: Lake, *'Proselytes and God-Fearers'*, 74-96; Feldman, *'Jewish "Sympathizers"'*, 200-208; Romaniuk, 'Die "Gottesfürchtigen"', 66-91; Robert, *NIS* 39-45; Siegert, 'Gottesfürchtige und Sympathizanten', 109-164; Wilcox, 'The "God-fearers" in Acts: a Reconsideration', *JSNT* 13 (1981), 102-122.

[16]Wilcox, 'The "God-fearers" in Acts', 118.

be used otherwise?), and attempts by others to show that all the words involved were synonyms and related to a firmly established category. Now since it is assumed (especially after the publication of the Aphrodisias inscription, about which *infra*) that the words in question were used semi-technically, it is discussion of how to define the category of God-fearers and to what extent that is possible, if at all, which dominates the field.[17] Discussion was concentrated on the epigraphical evidence, mainly whether the word θεοσεβής could designate a Gentile sympathizer with Judaism or just meant 'pious' or 'devout' Jew. The balance was tipped in favour of the latter, not insignificantly without the authority of L. Robert, the most prominent epigraphist of the twentieth century.[18]

It was at this stage of the discussion that A.T. Kraabel intervened and 'put the cat among pigeons', as J. Murphy-O'Connor describes his action.[19] Kraabel does not reject the technical character of the expressions in Acts. It was the very idea of the existence of a category of marginal converts that he questioned and attacked. He insists that God-fearers served Luke's kerygmatic purpose and were just

> a symbol to help Luke argue that Christianity had become a Gentile religion *legitimately*, without losing its Old Testament roots. The movement of the Jewish sect of the Christians into Gentile society was God's will. . . . But there is also justification in Jewish history itself, says Luke: witness the God-fearers.[20]

Kraabel's main arguments were based on archaeological evidence. He believes that the quantity of information now available about the Jew-

---

[17]See, for instance, Cohen, 'Crossing the Boundary', 32f.

[18]See, first of all *NIS*, 39-45.

[19]'Lots of God-Fearers? *Theosebeis* in the Aphrodisias Inscription', *RB*, 99, 2 (1992), 418.

[20]A.T. Kraabel, 'The God-fearers Meet the Beloved Disciple', *The Future of Early Christianity: Essays in Honour of Helmut Koester*, ed. B.A. Pearson, A.T. Kraabel, G.W.E. Nickelsbourg and N.R. Peterson (Minneapolis: Fortress Press, 1991), 280, cf. also other articles by Kraabel and especially the first one: 'The Disappearance of the "God-Fearers"', *Numen* 28, 2 (1981), 113-126; '*Synagoga Caeca*: Systematic Distortion in Gentile Interpretations of Evidence for Judaism in the Early Christian Period', '*To See Ourselves as Others See Us': Christians, Jews, 'Others' in Late Antiquity*, eds. J. Neusner & E.S. Frerichs (Chico: Scholars Press, 1985), 219-246; (with R.S. MacLennan) 'The God-Fearers—A Literary and Theological Invention', *Biblical Archaeology Review* (Sept.-Oct. 1986), 47-53; 'Immigrants, Exiles, Expatriates, and Missionaries', *Religious Propaganda and Missionary Competition in the New Testament World: Essays Honoring Dieter Georgi*, eds. L. Bormann, Kelly Del Tredici, A. Stadhartinger (Leiden, New York, Koln: E.J. Brill, 1994), 71-88.

ish Diaspora 'allows scholars to reconstruct Jewish life entirely on the basis of archaeological finds',[21] and as 'archaeology shows no traces of God-fearers, their historicity is questionable in the extreme'.[22]

This position seems to me untenable for a number of reasons.[23] First of all, our epigraphic and archaeological information about first century Diaspora Judaism is very limited. Among six excavated synagogues (Dura Europos in Syria, Priene and Sardis in Asia Minor, Delos in the Aegean Sea, Ostia in Italy and Stobi in Macedonia)[24] only the one on Delos dates from the first century AD and the identification of the building as a synagogue was questioned by some scholars[25] though this seems unjustified. There is also a first-century structure beneath the fourth-century building of another synagogue in Ostia which was identified by the excavator as a synagogue.[26] What would be our perception of the importance, the number, or the role of synagogues in the Diaspora in the first century from archaeological evidence alone with only a limited number of synagogue sites excavated?

For pre-Constantinian Christianity there is an extraordinary contrast between the abundance of epigraphic sources in Phrygia for which the literary tradition is rather modest, on the one hand, and the literary evidence for the western coastal area, where epigraphic information is practically non existent, on the other.[27] The picture built from archaeological findings or literary testimonia alone is insufficient.

Thirdly, Kraabel's view that extant archaeological evidence can deliver the goods is, on the whole, far too optimistic. Without under-

---

[21]Kraabel, 'The Disappearance', 115.

[22]Kraabel, 'The Disappearance', 120.

[23]Contrary to S.J.D. Cohen, 'Respect for Judaism by Gentiles according to Josephus', *HTR* 80:4 (1987), 419, n. 30 who thinks that this position 'requires no rebuttal', I consider that it is necessary to discuss it, taking into consideration the theoretical issue underlying Kraabel's scepticism and dissemination of his ideas. See also critical evaluation of Kraabel's position in Th.M. Finn, 'The God-fearers Reconsidered', *CBQ* 47 (1985), 75-84.

[24]There is probably also a synagogue of the fourth century in Elche in Spain. The building was excavated in 1905, and uncovered again in 1948, Noy, *JIWE*, 241ff.. The remains of a synagogue of the fourth-fifth century were found also in Bova Marina in Southern Italy, Noy, *JIWE*, No. 140.

[25]See, for instance, B.D. Mazur, *Studies in Jewry in Greece* I (Athens: Hestia, 1935), I, 15-24.

[26]On Diaspora synagogues see a most helpful account by A.T. Kraabel in *ANRW* II 19,1 (1979), 477-510. See also *Ancient Synagogues: The State of Research*, ed. J. Gutmann (Ann Arbor: Scholars Press, 1981, *JS* 22).

[27]S. Mitchell, *Anatolia: Land, Men and Gods in Asia Minor*, vol. 2 (Oxford: Clarendon Press, 1993), 38.

estimating the importance of information that can be harvested from archaeological evidence, it is also important to remember that archaeology by its very nature is not able to produce a complete picture of cultural and religious life. To cite once more the article by Goodman which was discussed earlier in this chapter:

> It is worth asking what, if historians totally lacked the benefit of evidence from literary texts, they would deduce about Judaism from archaeology and inscriptions. I doubt if they would ever discover that Judaism was distinguished from most other religions by being a system, or number of systems, with a complex mythology based on the covenant and revelation on Mount Sinai. . . . None of the archaeological and epigraphic evidence gives any hint of the really distinctive traits of Judaism as it appears in late-antique Jewish and Christian sources: the centrality of a written scripture, and its proclamation and explanation in public assemblies. To deduce that, we would need more inscriptions affirming the status of liturgical readers, which are curiously rare. Nothing in the iconography would give a clue to the main Jewish identity markers as we know them from elsewhere: shabbat, kashrut (dietary laws), and circumcision. [28]

Only the combination of the information received from the different sources, and the careful cross-checking of them, can produce reliable results.[29]

So much for the theoretical issue. I believe, in any case, that Kraabel is incorrect in denying any traces of God-fearers in the extant epigraphic material. Let us have a closer look at the evidence in question and, first of all, at the inscriptions containing the word θεοσεβής, a word which is usually treated as an inscriptional equivalent of Luke's terms.

---

[28]Goodman, 'Jews and Judaism', 219.

[29]The same over-estimation of the archaeological potential can be found in R.S. MacLennan, *Early Christian Texts on Jews and Judaism* (Atlanta: Scholars Press, 1990, Brown Judaic Studies). His approach, sober in the extreme where the limitations of literary texts are concerned, while over-enthusiastic about archaeology, creates a biased picture.

II Evidence for God-fearers

CIJ I² 500, uncertain provenance

 Ἀγρίππας Φού-
σκου Φαινή-
σιος θεοσεβής

Agrippas, the son of Fuscus, from Phaena, God-fearer (or pious).

The inscription is cut on a marble slab with two lulabs and a crown under the text. Its original provenance is uncertain. Phaena, the native city of Agrippas was a centre of Trachinitis in Syria. Schürer considered Agrippas to be the member of the sect of *Theosebeis* which, according to Cyril of Alexandria,[30] existed in Phoenicia and Palestine.[31] This is purely a guess, since nothing is known about the existence of this sect in Phaena. On the whole the inscription can be interpreted either way.

CIJ I² 202, Noy, *JIWE* 2 392, Rome

 [....'.Io]υδέα προσή-
 [λυτος.... θ]εοσεβ⌈ή⌉
 [ς?......] νον
 [....] ν

Jew proselyte ...God-fearer (pious) (?)[32]

The inscription is cut on a marble piece of sarcophagus, found in the catacomb of Vigna Randanini in Rome. Near the inscription a menorah is engraved.[33] Feldman notes that, if Frey's restoration is correct, this inscription may refer either to two individuals, one a proselyte and one a God-fearer', or to one individual who is described

---

[30]*De adoratione et cultu in spiritu et veritate*, 3,92 (*PG* 68, 281 BC).

[31]E. Schürer, *Geschichte des jüdischen Volkes im Zeitalter Jesu Christi*, vol. 3 (Leipzig, 1909⁴), 174, n. 70. About this sect and similar groups see pp. 98-101.

[32]Leon doubted the supplement θεοσεβίς (ι=η) and offered a restoration, eliminating the word θεοσεβής· ...[εος ἐβίωσε βίον κοι?]νόν: *The Jews of Ancient Rome*, 292, No. 202. Noy, *JIWE* 2 392 follows Leon's interpretation, although doubts his restoration βίον κοινόν and proposes that N at the end of l.4 'is likely to have been either ὑμῶν or αὐτῶν at the end of an "in peace. . . sleep" formula, or ἐποίησεν'.

[33]As Siegert, 'Gottesfürchtige', 156, n. 8, supposes the menorah on the stone dates this inscription to the third century AD.

as a God-fearing' (i.e. pious proselyte)'.[34] This immediately reminds us of Acts 13:43, but the scanty character of this inscription and the serious doubts about the correctness of Frey's restoration do not allow us to jump to any conclusion.

CIJ II 754, Deliler, Lydia

[Τ]ῇ ἁγιοτ[άτῃ]
[σ]υναγωγῃ
τῶν Ἑβραίων
Εὐστάτιος
ὁ θεοσεβὴς
ὑπὲρ μνίας
τοῦ ἀδελφοῦ
Ἑρμοφίλου
τὸν μασκαύ-
λην ἀνέθη-
κα ἅμα τῇ νύμ-
φ⌈η⌉ μου᾽ Ἀθανασία.

To the most holy synagogue of the Hebrews, Eustatios God-fearer (or pious), in remembrance of brother Hermophilos, I have dedicated the wash-basin[35] together with my bride (or sister-in-law)[36]Athanasia.

The inscription cut on a rectangular column dates to the third century AD. Deissmann was sure that Eustathios was a proselyte.[37] On the other hand, Bickerman, Bellen and Wilcox considered him to be a God-fearer.[38]

Robert, who held the opinion that all inscriptions containing the word θεοσεβής referred to Jews or in the last resort to proselytes, noted the presence of the definite article before θεοσεβής ('la presence de l'ar-

---

[34]Feldman, 'Jewish "Sympathizers"', 204, n. 24.

[35]Traditionally μασκαύλης was treated as a transcription of the Hebrew משכל; see, for instance, *CIJ* II 754; Lifshitz, 28. C. Hemer, 'Reflections on the Nature of New Testament Greek Vocabulary', *TynB* 38 (1987) 73, n. 27 however insisted that the correct Hebrew form must be משיכלא.

[36]Frey translated νύμφη as *fiancée*. Lifshitz, *DF*, 25f. accepted Robert's understanding of the term as 'sister in-law'.

[37]*Light from the Near East*, ET (London: Hodder & Stoughton, 1927), 427, n. 2.

[38]Bickerman, 'The Altars of the Gentiles', 158, n. 58; H. Bellen, 'Συναγωγὴ τῶν Ἰουδαίων καὶ Θεοσεβῶν. Die Aussage einer bosporanischen Freilassunginschrift (CIRB 71) zum Problem der "Gottfürchtigen"', *JAC* 8/9 (1965-1966) 175; Wilcox, 'The "God-Fearers" in Acts', 102, 118, n. 1.

ticle est intéressante') and concluded that 'Eustathios peut être un prosélyte, surement pas un sympathisant'. In general he considered this term to be too honorable to be applied to non-Jews.[39]

Influenced by the famous inscription from Aphrodisias, where the θεοσεβεῖς were listed under a separate heading after the members of the Jewish community, the editors of the revised English edition of Schürer's work paid attention to the possible contrast between the dedicator with his Greek name and the *Hebraioi* which made it 'slightly more probable' that Eustathios is to be seen as a gentile God-fearer.[40]

Trebilco, however, argued that, if Eustathios was a Gentile God-fearer, his brother Hermophilos similarly was of non-Jewish birth and in this case would be likely to be described in such an inscription as a proselyte or a God-fearer. 'It is, after all, unlikely', writes Trebilco, 'that Eustathios if he were a God-worshipper, would make a dedication *in the synagogue* in memory of his brother if Hermophilos himself had no connection at all with the synagogue'. It seems more probable to Trebilco that all three people mentioned in the inscription were Jews and that θεοσεβής means 'pious' and 'records the noteworthy piety of Eustathios'.[41] This argument is not convincing. There is no reason why a God-fearer could not make a donation in memory of someone who had no connections with the syngogue. Gentiles sent their donations to the Temple, brought votive offerings and offered sacrifices—all this was accepted without any objection and without proof of the identity of those who paid for the rites or sent expensive gifts.[42] The Roman emperors and the monarchs of Ptolemaic Egypt, for the safety of whom, or alternatively, on behalf of whom, donations to the synagogues were made, definitely had no connection with the synagogues. If all three persons mentioned in the inscription are Jews and θεοσεβής means 'pious' it seems very unusual that the honorary term is applied not to the deceased but to the donor. The normal practice, which still exists, is to pay tribute to the one who is no more with us. This makes

---

[39]Robert, *NIS*, 43-45. He considers, for instance, that Capitolina, who was not an ethnic Jew, was a proselyte. See pp. 65–6.

[40]Schürer, Vermes, Millar, Goodman, *The History of the Jewish People*, 3, 1, 167. Though it is very difficult to define in which cases the word Ἐβραῖοι has a different meaning from Ἰουδαῖοι, it was sometimes used as a term for Hebrew- and Aramaic-speaking Jews (who would usually have Jewish names) as opposed to Ἑλληνισταί, i.e. Greek-speaking Jews. See *TDNT* III 367ff.; N. de Lange, *Origen and the Jews* (Cambridge, London, New York, Melbourne: CUP, 1978, University of Cambridge Oriental publications, 25), 29f.; see also p. 163.

[41]Trebilco, *Jewish Communities*, 162.

[42]Schürer, Vermes, Millar, Black, *The History of the Jewish People*, 2, 309-313.

it more probable that θεοσεβής here is used as a technical term. But on the whole, it is impossible to say for sure that Eustathios was a God-fearer.

CIJ I² Lifshitz, Prolegomenon 731e, Rhodes

> Εὐφρο⌐σ⌐ύνα θεοσεβής
> χρηστὰ χαῖρε.

> Euphrosyna the God-fearer (or pious), the worthy, farewell.

This inscription is found on a rectangular altar made of black marble. L. Robert considered it to be Jewish or judaizing.[43]Either option is equally tenable.

W.R. Paton, E.L. Hicks, *The Inscriptions of Cos* (Oxford, 1891) No. 278.

> Εἰρήνη θεο-
> σεβὴς χρηστ-
> ὴ χαῖρε

> Eirene, the God-fearer (or pious), the worthy, farewell.

The inscription is on a small stele. In view of the form of *sigma* used, F. Siegert dates it to the Roman period.[44] L. Robert noted that the name Eirene is well attested in the Jewish milieu as a rendering of the name Salome.[45] There are no clear indications in the inscription as to whether Eirene was a God-fearer or not.

Six *theosebes* inscriptions were found in the great synagogue of Sardis. Two of them were in the central parts of the mosaics in the forecourt of the synagogue.[46]

Robert, *NIS* No. 3; Lifshitz, *DF* 17

> Αὐρ(ήλιος) Εὐλό-

---

[43]L. Robert, *Etudes anatoliennes: recherches sur les inscriptions grecques de l'Asie Mineure* (Paris: 1937), 441, n. 5.
[44]Siegert, 'Gottesfürchtige', 156, n. 4.
[45]Robert, 44.
[46]Four more inscriptions, which will be published in J.H. Kroll's forthcoming, Nos. 22, 57, 59, 66, until then can be seen in Trebilco, *Jewish Communities*, 252, n. 60. In the final publication of the Sardis synagogue, Kroll is responsible for the Greek inscriptions.

γιος θεο-
σεβὴς εὐ-
χὴν ἐτέ-
λεσα.

Aurelios Eulogios, God-fearer (or pious), I have fulfilled my vow.

Robert, *NIS* No. 5, Lifshitz *DF* 18.

Αὐρ(ηλιος)
Πολύιππος
θεοσεβὴς εὐ-
ξάμενος ἐ-
πλήρωσα.

Aurelios Polippos, God-fearer (or pious), I, having made a vow, fulfilled it.

Robert thought that both donors were Jews since the inscriptions were found in the synagogue. His opinion was approved by Lifshitz. However, Trebilco pays attention to the fact that Robert did not support his contention which is far from being self-evident. Trebilco thinks that the word could have a technical meaning. His grounds are: first, the involvement of the members of the Jewish community in Sardis in the city's life, which could have attracted the curiosity of the local population and made them interested in the Jewish way of life. That in turn could have made them adopt some of the practices of Judaism and become God-fearers; second, the decoration, mosaics and what may possibly have been a public fountain in the synagogue forecourt also could have attracted visitors who would have then been impressed by the 'grandeur and splendour of the Jewish faith and the Jewish community'.[47] Trebilco himself sees all this as a strong possibility. The technical meaning of the term, however, cannot be proved even with the help of these inscriptions.

CIJ II 748, Miletus

τόπος Ειουδέων τῶν καὶ θεοσεβίον.

Place of the Jews who are also called God-fearers (or pious).[48]

---

[47]Trebilco, *Jewish Communities*, 158f.

This inscription dates to the Roman period in the second or third century AD. It was found *in situ* beside many others on the seats in the fifth row from the front in the theatre at Miletus. This small inscription, has given rise to a very long and extensive discussion.[49] Some argue that τῶν καὶ θεοσεβῶν was erroneously inscribed instead of καὶ τῶν θεοσεβῶν and emended the text.[50] Others think that the text must be preserved as it stands and that the honorary epithet θεοσεβεῖς marks the piety of Jews.[51] B. Lifshitz paid attention to the fact that the theatre was not the best place for Jews to advertise their piety. If the inscription was issued, as he believes, by the theatre administrators, then the word 'pious' would sound very strange, because the Greeks would hardly regard themselves as less pious than the Jews and give to them alone this honorary epithet. Thus the inscription refers to two groups—the Jews and Jewish sympathizers, and the God-fearers.[52]

Another interpretation was suggested by H. Hommel. He analysed the formula ὁ καί and came to the conclusion that this inscription belongs to the category of 'synthetic relative clauses' and that its true meaning is 'place of (only) those Jews who are called God-fearers'. The meaning would be that the section in the theatre was reserved only for the group of God-fearers who, being closely associated with Jews, were called 'Jews' by the citizens of Miletus who knew about their connection with the Jewish community and were not concerned to understand the difference between the two groups.[53] But irrespective of

---

[48]Whereas the first editor of the inscription, A. Deissmann, *Light from the Near East*, 451f., also E. Schürer, *Geschichte*, 174, n. 70, G. Bertram,*TDNT* III, 125, L. Robert, *NIS*, *169*, and Trebilco *Jewish Communities*, 159f. all understand θεοσεβίον as a genitive plural of θεοσέβιοι (as an analogue to group names like Λεοντίοι etc.), J.-B. Frey, *CIJ* II 748 and H. Hommel, 'Juden und Christen im kaiserzeitlichen Milet', *IM* 25 (1975), 183, see it as the genitive plural of θεοσεβεῖς (θεοσεβίων for θεοσεβείων = θεοσεβέων as a result of an itacism).

[49]As T. Rajak, 'Jews and Christians as Groups in a Pagan World', *'To See Ourselves as Others See Us': Christians, Jews, 'Others' in Late Antiquity*, eds. J. Neusner and E.S. Frerichs (Chico: Scholars Press, 1985), 258 remarks: 'These few Milesian words offer, in a way, almost as much food for thought as the longer inscription'.

[50]e.g. Schürer, *Geschichte*, 174, n. 70, and recently Rajak, 'Jews and Christians', 258 who thinks that the incorrect formula can be explained by the poor quality of Greek language in Miletus: 'it is not unusual to find ungrammatical constructions, improper idioms and simple errors of word transpositions in this kind of provincial notice', also to some extent Trebilco, *The Jewish Communities*, 161. In this case the phrase should be translated 'Place of the Jews and the God-Fearers'.

[51]J.–B. Frey *ad. loc.*; G. Bertram, *TDNT* III, 125, 'The Jews prefer to call themselves "God-fearers" in an exclusive sense'; L. Robert *NIS*, 39.

[52]Lifshitz, *DF* 25f.

what line of interpretation seems more probable, it is impossible, on the basis of this inscription, to establish with certainty that such a group as Gentile God-fearers really existed in Miletus. 'Other interpretations are possible, none is conclusive.'[54]

CIG 2924, Lifshitz, DF 30, Tralles (Caria)

Καπετωλῖνα
ἡ ἀξιόλογ(ος) καὶ
ꞁθꞁεοσεβὴ(ς) <π>οήσα-
σα τὸ πᾶμ βάτρο[ν]
ἐσκούτλωσα τ[ὸν]
[ἀ]ναβασμὸν ὑπ[ὲρ]
εὐχῆς ἐ<α>υτῆς [καὶ?]
πεδίων τε καὶ ἐγ-
γόνων. Εὐλογία.

I, Capitolina, worthy of mention and God-fearer (or pious)[55] having made all the platform, having decorated the stairs with mosaics in fulfilment of a vow for myself and my children and my grandchildren. Blessing.

The inscription dates to the third century AD. It was regarded as Christian[56] and for that reason was not included in CIJ. Robert was the first to recognise this inscription as relating to the synagogue at Tralles.[57] It seems that the dedicator, Capitolina, belonged to a well-known family among whose members were a proconsul of Asia, a sen-

---

[53]Hommel, *Juden und Christen*, 184f. See the serious critical analysis of Hommel's interpretation by Trebilco, *Jewish Communities*, 161, though not all of the critical remarks of Trebilco in fact disprove this hypothesis. If the inscription was written by theatre management, the evidence of Dio Cassius, 37.17.1 that the title Ἰουδαῖοι 'applies also to all the rest of mankind, although of alien race, who affect their customs' (trans. E. Cary, *LCL*), can be legitimately used as an analogue to the inscription at Miletus.

[54]Reynolds and Tannenbaum, *Jews and God-Fearers*, 54.

[55]ΘΕΟΣΕΒΗΟΗΣΑ on the stone. Lifshitz reads ἀξιολογ(ωτάτη) καὶ θεοσεβ(εστάτη). Robert, *NIS* 44 considers ἡ ἀξιολογ(ωτάτη) καὶ θεοσεβ(ής) also to be a possible reading; Schürer, Vermes, Millar, Goodman, *The History of the Jewish People*, 3, 1, 167 prefer ἀξιόλογ(ος) καὶ θεοσεβ(ής). In Christian inscriptions θεοσεβής is mostly used in the superlative degree. Can the possible explanation be that the positive degree was known to have a special meaning? Later when the difference became of no importance the superlative form was traditionally used by Christians.

[56]Groag, 'Notizen zur Geschichte kleinasiatischen Familien', *JÖAI* 10, (1907), 283.

[57]Robert, *Etudes Anatoliennes*, 411.

ator and priest for life of Zeus Larasios in Tralles.[58] She was definitely not Jewish.

Can we be sure that θεοσεβής, at least in this inscription, is being used technically? Robert insisted that Capitolina was a proselyte.[59] Trebilco, rejecting this possibility, notes: 'If this was the case the Jewish community in a synagogue inscription would surely have proudly proclaimed the fact when such an important person was involved.'[60] But no matter how proud the Jewish community was, Capitolina, if she became a proselyte, could have preferred not to publicize the fact of her full membership in the community. Besides, it was not safe. Trebilco, arguing that Capitolina was a God-fearer, also noted that

> as a Gentile she would not be regarded as θεοσεβής by the Jews unless she was considerably involved in the synagogue. . . . Capitolina must have been a regular attender at the synagogue; thus we conclude that θεοσεβής here means 'God-worshipper.[61]

However, I cannot see why Jews could not apply an honorary title to a person of high rank who acts as a patron towards the community by making substantial donations. We have the same situation with Poppaea, Nero's consort, who interceded with the emperor on behalf of the Jews and whose pro-Jewish activity Josephus explained by saying that she was θεοσεβής.[62] Neither the remark of Josephus nor Capitolina's inscription can testify with certainty to the existence of a definite category of Judaizers.

---

[58]Groag, 'Notizen zur Geschichte', 283 considered that Capitolina of this inscription being Christian could not be identified with Claudia Capitolina known from another inscription who was the wife of a senator and priest for life of Zeus Larasios. But he admitted that she had belonged to the same family: 'Es gehet wohl nicht an, diese Claudia Capitolina mit der gleichnamigen Gattin des Stasikles Metrophanes zu identificieren... In jedem Falle gehören jedoch die beiden Damen denselben Hause an'. Robert, *Etudes anatoliennes*, did not doubt the identification. Trebilco, *Jewish Communitites*, 157 wrote about Capitolina as though her identity with Claudia Capitolina is beyond doubt. I think that more caution is needed in such matters.

[59]Robert, *Etudes Anatoliennes*, 411.

[60]Trebilco, *Jewish Communities*, 252, n. 56.

[61]Trebilco, *Jewish Communities*, 157.

[62]Josephus, *AJ* 20, 195. For a discussion of Poppaea see: E.M. Smallwood, 'The Alleged Jewish Tendencies of Poppaea Sabina', *JThSt* 10 (1959) 325-335; M.H. Williams '"Θεοσεβής γὰρ ἦν" –The Jewish Tendencies of Poppaea Sabina', *JTS*, n.s. 39 (1988), 97-111.

Noy, *JIWE* 1 12, Lorium

> ἐνθάδε ἐν εἰρήνῃ κεῖτε ˙ Ρουφεῖνος ἀμύμων
> θεοσεβὴς ἁγίων τε νόμων σοφίης τε συνίστωρ·
> ἐτῶν κα΄ ἡμ(ερῶν) η΄ ὥρ(ᾳ) νυ(κτὸς) ι΄.

Here in peace lies Rufinus, blameless, God-fearer (or pious), learned in holy laws and wisdom. He lived 21 years, 8 days, (died) at the 10th hour of night.

This metrical epitaph is difficult to date. Noy suggests a broad period from the second to the fourth century AD.

It is impossible to decide with confidence whether Rufinus was a Jew, a God-fearer or a pagan. Reference to the holy laws more likely indicate that he was a Jew, but he could have been a student of Roman *lex sacra* as well[63] or even (with less probability) a Christian.[64]

E. Pfuhl–H. Mobius, *Die ostgriechischen Grabreliefs* (Mainz am Rhein: Verlag Philipp von Zabern, 1979) No. 1697, plate 248, unknown provenance

> ˙ Ἐπιθέρσῃ τῷ θεοσε-
> βῆ κ<α>ὶ Θεοκτίστῃ
> τὰ τέκνα Μα<ρ>κιανὸς
> καὶ ˙ Ἐπιθέρσης μετὰ
> τῶν ἀδελφῶν ἐκ τῶν
> εἰδείων μνήμης χάριν.

To Epitherses the God-fearer (or pious) and Theoktiste their children Marcianos and Epitherses with the brothers [put this stele] in memory on their own expense.

This epitaph dates to the third century AD and is cut in a tabula ansata-like panel on a white marble stele under a relief representing a man lying on a couch, a seated woman, and a boy pouring a libation on an altar. Both the inscription and relief would look perfectly at home in a pagan context. Nevertheless the possibility that Epitherses was a Jewish sympathizer in a pagan family, and that this was marked in the epitaph by his children, cannot be completely ruled out.

---

[63]Reynolds and Tannenbaum, *Jews and God-Fearers*, 31.
[64]See discussion and references in Noy, *JIWE* 1.

In two Latin inscriptions we have a transcription of the Greek θεοσεβής into Latin letters.

CIJ I² 228, Noy, *JIWE* 2 207, Rome

> Hic posita Epar-
> chia theose-
> bes qu(a)e [v]i-
> xit annos LV
> d(ies) VI dorm[i]-
> tio tua in b[onis?][65]

Here is laid Eparchia the God-fearer (or pious), who lived 55 years, 6
days. Your sleep among the good.

This epitaph probably dates back to between the third and fourth century AD. Frey took *theosebes* as Eparchia's surname.[66] Some scholars
consider the transcription of the Greek word to be proof that it has a
special technical meaning here.[67] But Siegert has reasonably argued
that, given the transliteration of certain Greek words or phrases in
some Roman Jewish inscriptions, it is difficult to ascribe a special
meaning to the word.[68] Once again, here we have two conflicting in-

---

[65]This reading was accepted by J. Leon, *Jews in Rome*, 297, No. 228, who referred to
CIJ I² 250 for the same formula. Both Frey and Noy here follow J.B. de Rossi, who
claimed to have seen *bono* on a separate fragment. Others restorations are: *in p[ace]*
and *in d[omino]*. See references in *CIJ*, and *JIWE*, 1; cf. also van der Horst, *Ancient
Jewish Epitaphs*, 117.
[66]*CIJ* I², Index. *Noms propres latins*, 625. Cf. the remark of Feldman, *Jewish
"Sympathizers"*, 204, n. 24: 'Frey, who is very eager to find "sympathizers" in his
inscriptions, is wrong in not recognizing a possible one here'.
[67]See, for instance, Hommel, 'Juden und Christen', 174, n. 38; L. Feldman,
'Proselytes and "Sympathizers" in the Light of the New Inscription from
Aphrodisias', *REJ* 148,3-4 (1989) 41; L. Kant, 'Jewish Inscriptions in Greek and
Latin', *ANRW* II 20,2, 688.
[68]Siegert, 'Gottesfürchtige', 157. He cited as a parallel two Latin inscriptions: *CIJ* I
482 = *JIWE* 2 No. 564 (*dicea, osia, filentolia*) and *CIJ* I² 210 = *JIWE* 2 No. 343 (*dormitio
tua in dicaeis*). Cf. also *CIJ* I 224 = *JIWE* 2 No. 379 (*en irene ae cymesis su*) and many
others (see list in *JIWE* 2, p. 514, to which it is necessary to add *JIWE*,2 343). On
linguistic confusion in Venosa, where sometimes Greek words in the epitaphs
have Latin case-endings and Latin words are transliterated into the Greek
alphabet and or vice versa see D. Noy, 'The Jewish Communities of Leontopolis
and Venosa', *Studies in Early Jewish Epigraphy*, ed. by J.W. van Henten and P.W. van
der Horst, *Arbeiten zur Geschichte des antiken Judentums und des Urchristentums*, XXI,
(Leiden, New York, Köln: Brill, 1994), 175.

terpretations, both of which are possible. The same is also true of the next Latin inscription.

CIJ I² Lifshitz, *Prolegomenon* 619a, Noy, *JIWE* 1 113, Venosa

> Marcus
> teuseues
> qui vixit
> annu qui-
> ndecim hic
> receptus est
> in pac<e>.

Marcus the God-fearer (or pious), who lived fifteen years, is received here in peace.

This inscription was ingraved on a tomb in the NW gallery of the burial-vault in Venusia (now Venosa) and dates to between the fourth and fifth century AD. It is the first known case of a θεοσεβής buried in a Jewish cemetery, although in a different part of the hypogeum than those with Jewish titles.

Apart from the inscriptions with θεοσεβής, there are a number of Latin epitaphs with the word *metuens*,[69] that have been suspected of referring to the category of God-fearers, mainly because of the Lukan φοβούμενοι τὸν θεόν. Sometimes the inscriptions have the full formula *deum metuens*.[70] Though *deum* could be both accusative singular and genitive plural,[71] in which case all these inscriptions would belong to Gentiles, the participle *metuens* normally governs the genitive case. The Christian inscriptions, which borrowed some features of Jewish ones, regularly use the accusative.[72] By contrast, in undoubtedly pagan inscriptions the genitive is used.[73]

In one of the Latin epitaphs dated somewhere between the third and the fifth century, there is an unusual formula with *metuens* which is unparallelled in other inscriptions:

---

[69]*CIJ* I² 5, 285, 524, 529, 642.

[70]M. Stern considered that *metuens* could be only an abridgment of the fuller formula and hence was definitely used technically: 'It is hard to conceive that either *metuens* or σεβόμενος is used in the general sense of religious' (*GLAJJ* II, 105).

[71]Siegert, 'Gottesfürchtige', 152.

[72]E. Diehl, *ILCV* 3359a, 3416a, 4779, 6. The Christian inscriptions also employ the participle *timens*: *LCV*, 1172, 1339, 1340, 1341.

[73]*CIL* VI, 1 390a (Rome).

CIJ I² 642, Noy, *JIWE* 1 9, Pula (Pola)

> Aur(elius) Soter et Aur(elius)
> Stephanus Aur(eliae)
> Soteriae matri pien-
> tissimae religioni
> Iudaicae metuenti
> f(ilii) p(osuerunt)[74]

Aurelius Soter and Aurelius Stephanus to Aurelia Soteria, the most devout mother, a fearer of the Jewish religion, her sons set up (this monument).

The name Aurelia Soteria is known from another inscription in which she commemorated her *alumna*. The second inscription starts with the *Dis Manibus* formula, which slightly increases the probability that Aurelia Soteria was a God-fearer, though it is not impossible to find this formula in Jewish inscriptions.[75] However, given that the name Aurelia Soteria is quite a common one, it is doubtful whether both inscriptions refer to the same woman.[76]

Thus the fragmentary evidence for God-fearers in the inscriptions reviewed to this point is far from clear, and until recently interpretation of the inscriptions depended on the underlying theoretical presuppositions of particular modern scholars. The discovery of the Aphrodisias inscription changed the picture completely, and has now become the central point of the discussion.

The Aphrodisias inscription, published by Reynolds and Tannenbaum,[77] is engraved on two faces of a block of marble. Concerning the original use of the stone, the editors suggested that this stele stood 'to the left of an entry' of the synagogue, so that

---

[74]The sequence of words *matri pientissimae religioni Iudaicae metuenti* has been variously interpreted. Frey separated *religioni Iudaicae* from *metuenti*: ('a Aurelia Soteria, leur très bonne mère, de religion juive, craignant [Dieu]'). Lake *BC* 5 89 connected *pientissimae* and *metuenti* — 'very devout fearer of the Jewish religion'. The version given by Noy ('their very devout mother, a fearer of the Jewish religion') seems preferable.

[75]Siegert, 'Gottesfürchtige' 153, n. 4. Siegert draws attention to the fact that this formula is quite often used in Christian inscriptions. There are more than 100 from the fourth and fifth centuries AD. His conclusion runs as follows: '"D.M", nahezu bedeutungslos, diente nur mehr als Kennzeichen einer Grabinschrift'.

[76]See discussion with statistics for the name in Noy, *JIWE* 1, 17, 285f.

face *a* would greet the visitor with an explanation of the feature that he was approaching and the names of the donors who initiated the construction, while he would see face *b* as he passed into the entry and could learn the names of others associated with it.[78]

G.W. Bowersock, in an unpublished article (reported by Feldman), conjectured that it could be the door-frame of the synagogue. The two main texts were inscribed by different hands with some additions by another hand or hands. Face *a* starts as follows:

Θεὸς βοηθός, πατέλλᾳ ? δο[- ὲ.2 -]
Οἱ ὑποτεταγμέ-
νοι τῆς δεκαν(ίας)
τῶν φιλομαθῶ[ν]
τῶν κὲ παντευλογ(--ων)
εἰς ἀπενθησίαν
τῷ πλήθι ἔκτισα[ν]
'εξ ἰδίων μνῆμα

God our help. Givers to the soup kitchen (?).[79] The below-listed (members) of the decany[80] of the learned persons, also known as those who continually praise God,[81] for the relief of suffering in the community erected at their personal expense (this) memorial (building).

---

[77]Reynolds and Tannenbaum, *Jews and God-Fearers*. I cannot but express my surprise at some remarks in a short article by J. Murphy-O'Connor, 'Lots of God-fearers? *Theosebeis* in the Aphrodisias Inscription', *RB* 99:2 (1992), 418-424, who calls the form of this publication obscure (sic!) and suggests that this fact is responsible for the lack of any serious debate subsequent to the publication. He complains that scholars are forced to rely on pre-publications, in which some details of the inscription were confused. After such remarks, he devotes half of his article to an unnecessary summary of the contents of the book by Reynolds and Tannenbaum. All this is a regrettable misrepresentation. Not only does the volume follow what is accepted scholarly convention when epigraphists and historians discuss an inscription, but since its publication, which I would call exemplary with the exception of the poor quality of the photographic reproduction, the inscription has been the centre of lively debate. This will be seen from the account, later in this chapter, of an interchange of scholarly views, which, for unknown reasons appears to have escaped the attention of J. Murphy-O'Connor. There is no danger that 'this inscription may enter the NT domain in the form of observations made before the complete text became available'. Cf. for instance the account of the recent stage of the continuing debate in *SEG* 41 (1994), 302-303, No. 918.
[78]Reynolds and Tannenbaum, *Jews and God-Fearers*, 19.

After this, the text provides a list of sixteen male names[82]—thirteen of which belong to persons who were born Jews, three to proselytes and two to θεοσεβεῖς. The editors date the inscription on face *a* to the third century AD, though the case seems to them far from certain.[83] They consider face *a* to be the introduction to face *b*.

Face *b* is dated in the third century, and on onomastic grounds the editors suggested an even more precise date, i.e. before the *Constitutio Antoniana* of AD 212.[84] It contains a list of male names, a number of which are followed by trade designations. The text is arranged in

---

[79]Bowersock, who had a chance of seeing better photographs than the ones included in the monograph, expresses serious doubts about the reading πάτελλα (see Feldman, 'Proselytes and "Sympathizers"', 287), but these seem unwarranted: the photograph No. 3 (pl. 16) despite the surprisingly bad quality of all photographs for such an edition, is quite clear where this reading is concerned. The interpretation of πάτελλα as a soup-kitchen was firmly rejected by M. Williams, 'The Jews and Godfearers Inscription from Aphrodisias—a Case of Patriarchal Interference in Early 3rd Century Caria?', *Historia* 51,3 (1992), 297-310. Though many of her critical remarks are justified (for instance, Williams quite rightly notes that *tamhui*, which, as the editors consider, was rendered by πάτελλα, is unparalleled with the meaning of a special building) the new interpretation that she suggested (the decania as a funeral association, μνῆμα as a synagogal triclinium, πατελλαδό[ς] as imperative and the line interpreted as an appeal to God 'put <food> upon our plate') is less convincing and has many weak points. Cf. G. Mussies, 'Jewish Personal Names in Some Non-Literary Sources', *Studies in Early Jewish Epigraphy*, ed. J.W. van Henten and P.W. van der Horst (Leiden, New York, Koln: Brill, 1994), 256f., who pointed out that an alleged verb πατελλαδίδωμι contradicted the norms of the Greek word-formation (the first compound-member should become πατελλο-, δίδωμι cannot occur as second compound-member after a substantive). Mussies at first proposed the reading πατελλάδος which in the context of the inscription should mean 'charity dish-man' (*Mnemosyne* 44(1991), 293-295) (cf. the discussion of this interpretation by C. Brixhe and A. Panayotou, *BE* (1992) No. 434), but later changed his opinion and suggested that πάτελλα was the neuter plural of a substantive πάτελλον/βάτελλον and that δο[.] should be restored as δο[ῖ] or δό[η]; the first line can then be translated as 'May God the Helper provide meals' ('Jewish Personal Names', 257). Van Minnen, 'Drei Bemerkungen zur Geschichte des Judentums in der griechisch-romischen Welt', *ZPE* 100 (1994), 255-257 suggests the restoration πατελλάδο[ς] or πατελλάδω[ν] and translates the line as follows: 'Gott ist der Helfer der πατελλάδες'. He gives a parallel for πατελλᾶς ('eine Art Imbissinhaber'), which was considered by the first editors to be non-attested, from a Byzantine inscription of unknown provenance.
[80]Bowersock suggested another reading in place of τῆς δεκαν(ίας): τῆσδε κανονίδος (a door-frame). Feldman, 'Proselytes and "Sympathizers"', 280, n. 58 did not mention how Bowersock coordinated this reading with the rest of the text; cf. also Feldman, *Jew and Gentile*, 575, n. 116.
[81]παντευλογ[οῦντες]—a plausible restoration by Reynolds and Tannenbaum, 35. *Contra* G. Mussies, 'Jewish Personal Names', 257f.

two parts with a sizeable vacant area between. The upper list names fifty-five persons. Taking into consideration that nearly all of them have patronymics, there are names of seventy-four persons in all. Twenty-one of these names, used with reference to forty-one persons, have obvious Jewish connections. There are transliterated biblical names, Greek and Latin equivalents of biblical names, etc. The lower list is introduced by the heading καὶ ὅσοι θεοσεβῖς (=θεοσεβεῖς)—as many as [are] *theosebeis'*. This line is followed by the names of fifty-two persons (the list includes sixty-three names in all). Among these names only two are connected with the Jewish tradition (Εὐσαββάθιος and Ὁρτάσιος), one may be Semitic (Ιουνβαλος), two could be regarded by Jews as equivalents of biblical names ('Αλέξανδρος, Ζωτικός), but the rest are Greco-Roman. The first nine people listed among the *theosebeis* are described as town-concillors (βουλευτής).

---

[82]With one possible exception of ΄Ιαηλ in l. 9 of face *a*. The assumption that Iael was a woman (discussed and rejected by the editors) was strongly advocated by B. Brooten: 'The Gender of Ίαηλ in the Jewish Inscription from Aphrodisias', *Of Scribes and Scrolls. Studies on the Hebrew Bible, Intertestamentary Judaism, and Christian Origins presented to John Strugnell on the occasion of his sixtieth birthday*, eds. H.W. Attridge, J.J. Collins, Th.H. Tobin, Lanham: University Press of America, 1990, Resources in Religion, 5, 163-173; 'Iael προστάτης in the Jewish Donative Inscription from Aphrodisias', *The Future of Early Christianity. Essays in Honor of Helmut Koester* , ed. B.A. Pearson, (Minneapolis: Fortress Press, 1991), 149-162. See, however, G. Mussies, 'Jewish Personal Names', who argued that Iael could be both a male name in accordance with its grammatical gender, and a female name contrary to its grammatical gender but given to women because of the fame of the biblical Iael. He concludes that the name itself cannot allow us to come to any decision but that the title προστάτης given to Ίαηλ can and does point to a man rather than a woman.

[83]Reynolds and Tannenbaum, *Jews and God-fearers*, 21. Bowersock thinks that the inscription *a* came from a much later hand and 'may not be much earlier than the fifth century' (Feldman, 'Proselytes and "Sympathizers"', 287). The possibility of later dating was examined by the editors, but on the whole they incline for the earlier one and their arguments seem convincing.

[84]Reynolds and Tannenbaum propose this date for the face *b* with more confidence than for face *a*. Their onomastic arguments sound very persuasive. Reynolds and Tannenbaum pay attention to the absence in the inscription of the *nomen* Aurelius, or its derivatives popular after the Antonine Constitution, and of the Roman citizen nomenclature adopted after 212. The latter was likely to be absent only before 212 or in the late fourth and fifth centuries when this nomenclature was abandoned. These observations were not understood by Williams, 'The Jews and God-fearers', 311, n. 4, who insists that, as there are no *gentilicia* in the inscription the absence of the *gentilicium* Aurelius cannot be regarded as meaningful, and prefers 'a broad mid-third century date'.

The contrast between the two lists on face *b* is quite obvious and provides the strongest argument in favour of the interpretation that the people mentioned in the second list are Gentile sympathizers with Judaism, i.e. God-fearers, distinguished from both the Jews and proselytes. After establishing that, at least in one inscription, in one particular city of Asia Minor at the beginning of the third century, θεοσεβής was used technically, we have to decide the implications of this fact. Can we extend the same interpretation to other inscriptions? What can be deduced about God-fearers and their relations with the Jewish community from this inscription?

I shall commence with the second question. The fact that two God-fearers were members of the decany of the students of the law made the editors, and many after them, believe that they were members of the community, though somehow inferior to the proper Jews. They were 'not quite kosher'.[85] If this is true, then it is an extremely important observation. The assumption that Gentiles could have been members of the Jewish community is usually supported by the references to the inscription from Panticapaeum. Let us have a closer look at this particular inscription, which was published in *CIRB* as No.71.[86]

[-$^{c.10}$-]+A++[-$^{c.6}$-]KA[-?]
κου ἀφίημι ἐπὶ τῆς προσευχῆς ᾽Ελπία<ν>[ἐμ]α[υ]τῆς θρεπτ[ὸν]
ὅπως ἐστὶν ἀπαρενόχλητος
5   καὶ ἀνεπίληπτος ἀπὸ παντὸς
κληρονόμου χωρὶς τοῦ προσ-
καρτερεῖν τῇ προσευχῇ ἐπι-
τροπευούσης τῆς συναγω-
γῆς τῶν ᾽Ιουδαίων καὶ θεὸν
10   σέβων.

I free in the prayer-house Elpias, my household slave, so that he will be undisturbed and unassailable by any of my heirs, on condition that he works for the prayer-house under the guardianship of the Jewish community, and honours God.

---

[85]Reynolds and Tannenbaum, 'Proselytes and "Sympathizers"', 55; Trebilco, *Jewish Communities*, 153; Kant, 'Jewish Inscriptions', 689f.
[86]Various restorations of the text are discussed in the Appendix 3, II, 2.

This inscription, first published in 1935,[87] is datable in the first century AD.[88] It belongs to a series of Panticapaean manumissions, stating that the freedman is liberated in the synagogue and remains from this time under the protection of the Jewish community.[89] H. Bellen and B. Lifshitz, puzzled by the grammatical awkwardness of the addition καὶ θεὸν σέβων at the end of the inscription, independently made the same emendation to this inscription—θεο{ν}σεβῶν,[90] which has been approved by the majority of scholars working in this field.[91] Thus we get συναγωγὴ τῶν Ἰουδαίων καὶ θεοσεβῶν, which can be understood either as *the synagogue of the Jews and God-fearers* or as *the synagogue of the Jews who are also pious*.[92] The advantage that is obtained by adopting this emendation (if we accept the first interpretation, which on balance seems more probable[93] and is generally accepted) is quite obvious—we acquire epigraphic evidence for the existence of God-fearers as a distinct group considered part of the Jewish community by this very community.[94]

The emendation suggested by Bellen and Lifshitz is not necessary, however and can be challenged. Briefly, objections to this emendation are as follows:

1. An awkwardness of phrasing is not exceptional in the Bosporan inscriptions and is explicable against the background of Bosporan Greek grammar.[95]

2. Usually in this type of manumission there are two requirements for the freedman: firstly, that he should respect the cult, and secondly, that he should work for the prayer-house.[96] Accepting Bellen and Lifshitz's emendation we lose the first condition.

---

[87]J J Marti, 'Novye epigraficheskiye pamyatniki Bospora', *Izvestiya GAIMK* 104 (1935) 66, No. 5. See the description of the stone and commentary in App.III,II,2.
[88]B. Lifshitz, *CIJ*² *Prolegomenon*, No. 683a, wrongly reports that the editors of *CIRB* date this inscription to the second century.
[89]*CIRB* 70, 72, 73; App. 3, II, 1, 3, 4.
[90]H. Bellen, 'Συναγωγή', 171-176; Lifshitz 'Notes d'épigraphie grecque', *RB* 76 (1969), 95f., see also Lifshitz, *CIJ* I² *Prolegomenon*, No. 683a).
[91]See, for instance, Siegert, '*Gottesfürchtige und Sympathizanten*', 158f., Hommel, 'Juden und Christen', 175, n. 38, Simon, 'Sur les débuts', 518f.; Schürer, Vermes, Millar, Goodman, *The History of the Jewish People*, 3, 1, 166, 168; Reynolds and Tannenbaum, 'Jews and God-Fearers', 54; Rajak, 'Jews and Christians', 259; Trebilco, *Jewish Communites*, 155f.; Cohen, 'Crossing the Boundary', 32.
[92]Nadel, 'Actes', 278.
[93]See, for instance, Trebilco, *Jewish Communites*, 156.
[94]Reynolds and Tannenbaum, 'Jews and God-Fearers', 54; Trebilco, 156.
[95]See the literature devoted to deviations from Greek grammar in the Bosporan inscriptions in: Nadel, 'Actes' 278, n. 33.

3. The word θεοσεβής has never been found in Bosporan inscriptions. In all other manumissions mentioning συναγωγὴ τῶν ᾿Ιουδαίων these words stand at the end of the inscription. The fact that the inscriptions are in good condition allows us to assert that no additions were made after the last words. The emendation would mean that in this letter of manumission another Jewish community was being mentioned which had Gentiles among its members, and which has left no epigraphic trace other than this inscription. Though this possibility cannot be absolutely ruled out it seems rather unlikely.

B. Nadel, in a critical discussion of the emendation, noted that we are dealing here with a general question 'sur la nécessité ou non des émendations philologiques dans les cas où une interprétation suffisante est possible sans appliquer la chirurgie philologique'.[97] Using 'philological surgery' in the case of a literary text, we risk editing an ancient author and even improving him—the latter can be very tempting. In the case of an inscription, we sometimes risk creating a fact which never existed, and ultimately a past reality which never was.[98]

To sum up it seems more prudent to leave the inscription as it stands and not to use it too hastily as a parallel for the inscription from Aphrodisias.[99]

Is it possible to conclude that in Aphrodisias God-fearers were members of the Jewish community? Those who incline towards this view[100] have in mind the presence of God-fearers among the members of δεκανία, though the nature of this institution is far from clear.[101] It could be a guild, it could be a charitable society, it could be a general-purpose benevolent society, it could be the *batlanim* who guarantee a quorum at synagogue services. Without further evidence, we cannot know which.[102] Not all such institutions require participants to be members of a Jewish community. The inscription testifies that the re-

---

[96]See Appendix 3, II, 1, app. crit. l.13-15. For προσκαρτερέω with dat. cf. Acts 10:7 (στρατιώτην εὐσεβῆ τὸν προσκαρτερούντων αὐτῷ) about Cornelius' orderlies.
[97]B. Nadel, 'Actes', 278.
[98]Some scholars using this inscription even forget to mention that the reading that they refer to is the emendation. See, for instance, Cohen, 'Crossing the Boundary', 32.
[99]For more detail see I.A. Levinskaya, 'The Inscription from Aphrodisias and the Problem of God-fearers', *TynB* 41.2 (1990), 312-318.
[100]Cf. Kant, 'Jewish Inscriptions', 690: 'God-fearers were often members of Jewish synagogues'.
[101]See a detailed discussion in Reynolds and Tannenbaum, *Jews and God-Fearers*, 28-38.
[102]Reynolds and Tannenbaum, *Jews and God-Fearers*, 37.

lationship of the God-fearers to the Jewish community was close but
there we have to stop. To establish the possibility of the membership
of the Gentiles in the Jewish community is to go beyond the evidence.

Let us return to the first question. What can be said about other
inscriptions in the light of the one from Aphrodisias? The buzz-word
among modern Jewish scholars is 'diversity'. The traditional, twofold,
straightforward division of Judaism into Hellenistic and Palestinian
(which in its time was a great step forward) has now been completely
abandoned.[103] Some scholars even prefer to speak not about Judaism,
but about *Judaisms*.[104] Variety in Judaism is seen now both in Palestine
and in the Diaspora.[105] The fact that, in the past, later sources were
happily used as evidence for an earlier period, and vice versa, has led
to an unnecessarily sceptical attitude in modern scholarship towards
the possibility of making generalisations from any information which
was obtained from a source which has a specific reference. Between
the extreme sayings, 'All human beings are similar' and 'Each human
being is a universe of his own' there is a vast distance and thus plenty
of room for scholarly negotiation.

One extreme position is epitomized by Murphy-O'Connor who
refuses to use the information from one part of the Aphrodisias inscription to analyse the other part of the same inscription. He distinguishes between θεοσεβεῖς who were members of *decania* and thus
were firmly attached to the synagogue and other Aphrodisian θεοσεβεῖς on the grounds that this group included city councillors who
could not avoid participating in public pagan sacrifices. He agrees that
the former were 'what NT scholarship has traditionally considered
God-fearers to be', but insists that the latter were Gentiles 'with a sense
of civic duty' to subscribe to the institution, this being beneficial to the
city. As to the the council members, their main interest might have

---

[103]For the view that the separate study of Judaism in the Diaspora and of that in
the land of Israel is desirable, see Goodman, 'Jews and Judaism', 208. For the
opposite position see J.A. Overman, 'The Diaspora in the Modern Study of Ancient
Judaism', *Diaspora Jews and Judaism: Essays in Honor of, and in Dialogue with, A.
Thomas Kraabel*, eds. J.A. Overman, R.S. MacLennan (University of South Florida,
1992), 64-78.

[104]Overman, 'The Diaspora', 64; cf. the title *Judaisms and their Messiahs at the Turn
of Christian Era*, eds. J. Neusner, W.S. Green, E. Frerichs (Cambridge: CUP, 1987).
For a critical evaluation of this approach see Rutgers, *Jews in Rome*, 206ff., who
applies E.P. Sanders' term 'normal' or 'common Judaism' to Diaspora Judaism in
late antiquity.

[105]Cf. the title of the recently published book: *Diasporas in Antiquity*, eds. S.J.D.
Cohen, E.S. Frerichs (Atlanta: Scholars Press, 1993).

been in winning the Jewish vote or in preventing the 'Jewish proletariat' from becoming troublesome.[106] Murphy-O'Connor appears not to be concerned by the notion that in one inscription one word is used with different meanings.[107] On the contrary, from his assumption that this is the case he jumps to the general conclusion that 'the meaning of the term must be determined in each instance from the context'.[108]

The Aphrodisias inscription provides, in fact, information very different from that adduced from it by Murphy-O'Connor, and it offers an explanation for what was formerly seen as contradictory. It shows how wide and how loose in reality the category of God-fearers was.[109] Aphrodisian city councillors, and similarly Nero's consort, Poppaea Sabina, participated in public sacrifices; for instance Poppaea offered a sacrifice after the birth of her child. At the same time, the former subscribed to a charitable Jewish institution and the latter patronized Jews, and toyed with Judaism, quite probably because it was fashionable among the pagan women of high standing.[110] Nevertheless they as much as members of the Jewish *decania*, whatever that may mean, who studied the law and continually praised God, were perceived as belonging to the same category of 'God-fearers' and were called by the same name. What was important about them was that they were Gentiles and did not join the chosen people.

Some of the God-fearers were only one step from becoming converts, while others just added the Jewish God to their pantheon. So long as they showed some kind of sympathy with the Jewish religion they were considered God-fearers. Cohen divided those who show affection for Judaism into seven categories: those who did it by '(1) admiring some aspect of Judaism; (2) acknowledging the power of the

---

[106]'Lots of God-fearers', 422.

[107]It is undoubtedly the case that one and the same word, even one that is usually used technically, can be used with different meanings (cf. the discussion of προσήλυτος in the previous chapter), but it is unusual for this to happen in the same inscription and, when it occurs, it is usually somehow marked in the context.

[108]It is not surprising that this article was immediately welcomed by Kraabel, 'Immigrants, Exiles', 80f. He somehow did not pay attention to the fact that at least some of the θεοσεβεῖς were, in Murphy-O'Connor's view, God-fearers in the Lukan sense.

[109]The definition given by Reynolds and Tannenbaum, *Jews and God-fearers*, 65, seems very balanced and well formulated. I again can only express my surprise at the remark by Murphy-O'Connor, 'Lots of God-fearers', 421, that, in accordance with this definition 'a polytheistic psychopath could be classified as a God-fearer simply because he had once looked in the synagogue and expressed some interest in Judaism'.

[110]Williams, 'The Jewish Tendencies', 111.

God of the Jews by incorporating him into a pagan pantheon; (3) benefiting the Jews or being conspicuously friendly to Jews; (4) practising some or many of the rituals of the Jews; (5) venerating the god of the Jews and denying or ignoring the pagan gods; (6) joining the Jewish community; (7) converting to Judaism and "becoming a Jew"'. Those whose behaviour fitted the categories 2-5 could be called God-fearers. For instance, Cornelius, a model God-fearer, described by Luke in Acts 10 can be described as belonging to categories 2-4, but not the fifth, since, as a Roman centurion, he participated in a pagan cult.[111]

Cohen rightly stresses that there is absolutely no reason to assume that all venerators of God throughout the Roman empire over the course of several centuries followed a single fixed pattern of practice and belief.[112] A fixed pattern just had not existed; but that a loose one had, is seen from the Aphrodisias inscription. Goodman argues that there was no formal recognition by Jews of Gentile God-fearers before the second century AD (or at least we have insufficient evidence to say that such recognition existed) and that the change in Jewish attitudes took place about the time when the Aphrodisias inscription was written.[113] He approves of a modified version of Kraabel's position, i.e. the rejection of 'a formal category of Gentile God-fears recognized as such by Jews in the first century'[114], while Kraabel actually rejects the existence of such a class of Gentiles. He admits, however, that the Greeks who were attracted by Judaism, 'filled a rôle equivalent to that filled in later centuries by "Godfearers" attached to synagogues with a status formally recognized by the Jews among whom they lived'. What can be called 'formal' in this context? Definitely in the first century (and up to the first half of the third century as well) there was no formal recognition in the later rabbinical sense because there was no central authority to produce a clear definition. It is only in the late fourth century that we can assert with confidence that rabbinic influence reached the Mediterranean Diaspora.

However, this does not mean that, in practice, such definitions did not exist. If there is some evidence, as Goodman admits, 'of a Jewish mission to win gentile *sympathizers* in the first century', how was

---

[111]Cohen, 'Crossing the Boundary', 14f. See below p. 121.
[112]Cohen, 'Crossing the Boundary', 32.
[113]Goodman, *Mission and Conversion*, 47. Kraabel rejects not the existence of 'a formal category of gentile Godfearers recognised as such by Jews in the 1st century', but the existence of such a class of Gentiles. He approves of the position of Kraabel, 'Disappearance', 47, n. 14, which he presents in a modified way.
[114]Goodman, *Mission and Conversion*, 87.

such a mission possible without some kind of recognition of these sympathizers by the Jewish community? Why is the separate list of θε-οσεβεῖς in the Aphrodisias inscription a proof of the formal status of the God-fearers and of a change in Jewish attitudes towards them, while the description of the φοβούμενος τὸν θεόν Roman centurion Cornelius in Acts 10:22 as someone who was approved by the Jewish community is not? How can we explain that the same set of expressions is constantly applied to those who showed sympathy with Judaism and that in the talmudic period the rabbis used one of these expressions to designate those Gentiles who ought to be recognised by Jews? It seems that the category of God-fearers which existed on the fringes of Jewish synagogues in the first century, and probably earlier, acquired formal status when the general formalisation of Jewish life came on the agenda.[115]

The importance of this inscription for the historical controversy about Gentile sympathizers with Judaism lies in the fact that, once and for all, it has tipped the balance and shifted the onus of proof from those who believe in the existence of Luke's God-fearers to those who have either denied or had doubts about it.[116] All the θεοσεβής-inscriptions discussed above could have been interpreted either way. However, since the publication of the Aphrodisian text, each one must now be scrutinized in the light of it.

Now that it has been established that θεοσεβής could be used as a term designating a particular category of Gentiles, it seems that the best procedure, when we find this term in an inscription, is to assume that the reference is to a Gentile 'God-fearer', unless, as may quite possibly happen, it is able to be demonstrated that this cannot be its meaning. The close relationships with the synagogue of the Aphrodisian God-fearers is another matter. It shows only one type of relationship that existed. There existed others. The impulse picked up by the Gentiles from Jews could give way to the development of independent structures.

---

[115]Kraabel, 'Disappearance', 47, n. 14.
[116]Kraabel, 'Immigrants, Exiles', 80ff. adamantly rejects the existence of Gentiles with a religious interest in Judaism. He is ready to accept that God-fearers were friends of local Jews for economic and political reasons, but never for religious ones.

III. Indirect Epigraphic Evidence for God-Fearers

Now let us examine indirect epigraphic traces of God-fearers.

P.W. van der Horst has drawn attention to a most interesting inscription from Belkis, a town in Pamphylia, recently published by French epigraphists.[117] It is engraved on a small altar and dates to the first or second century AD. The text of the inscription is as follows:

θεῷ ἀψευδ[εῖ καὶ]
ἀχειροποιήτῳ
εὐχήν

For the truthful and not-handmade god (in fulfilment of) a vow.

Van der Horst argued that this inscription 'derives from a pagan deeply influenced by Judaism, especially by its view of idolatry, and who belongs to the category met in the New Testament under the names φοβούμενοι or σεβόμενοι, and who are θεοσεβεῖς or *metuentes* in the epigraphic sources'.[118] His main arguments are that: (1) the word ἀχειροποίητος is used in a sense which originated in Jewish polemics against idolatry—χειροποίητος, a neutral Greek word used since Herodotus, became in the Septuagint a technical term for an idol and its negation, ἀχειροποίητος, came to designate the only true God; (2) being an altar-inscription, it cannot be Christian or Jewish; (3) the combination of the two terms, ἀψευδής and ἀχειροποίητος points in a Jewish direction. As a parallel, van der Horst cites another private altar-inscription from Pergamon which dates to the second century AD. At the top of the altar it is inscribed: θεὸς κύριος | ὁ ὢν εἰς ἀεί (God the Lord, He who is forever), and at the bottom: Ζώπυρος τῷ κυρίῳ τὸν βωμὸν | καὶ τὴν φω{ι}τοφόρον μετὰ τοῦ | φλογούχου (Zopyros [dedicated] to the Lord this altar and the lantern with its stand). The combination of θεὸς κύριος and ὁ ὢν εἰς ἀεί cannot belong to the Gentile religious vocabulary[119] and an altar makes it very doubtful that this inscription could be produced by a Jew.[120]

---

[117]P.W. van der Horst, 'A New Altar of a Godfearer?', *JJS* 43 (1992), 32-37.
[118]van der Horst, 'A New Altar', 36.
[119]The only possible exception, which was carefully assessed by van der Horst, relates to the cult of the Egyptian God, Sarapis. Evidence for the use of similar terminology in his cult is very limited: ἀψευδής in only one inscription, and ἀχειροποίητος once in a work of Clement of Alexandria (*Protrepticus*, IV 48,1). Van der Horst's interpretation of this material is judicious.

Such altars are not the only possible traces of the God-fearers. All over the Mediterannean world there exist numerous dedications to the Most High God, which some view as such and which will be discussed in the following chapter.

---

[120]See the references to the different interpretations of this inscription in Trebilco, *Jewish Communities*, 254, n. 84. He suggests that βωμός could be translated as 'a base' for the lantern stand and that in this case Zopyros was a Jew. In the absence, so far as I am aware, of parallels, I cannot see how either interpretation could be possible.

CHAPTER 5

GOD-FEARERS AND THE CULT OF THE MOST HIGH GOD

This chapter contests the commonly held belief that the epithet ὕψιστος was widely used by Gentiles and was applied to 'a whole range of exalted deities'. In the overwhelming majority of cases this assumption is not based on direct evidence, but is the result of scholarly interpretations rooted ultimately in the theory of syncretism. On the other hand, the Jewish background of this title is beyond any doubt. The very limited amount of pagan evidence for the independent usage of this epithet makes it highly unlikely that the cult of the Most High God combined elements of Jewish and pagan beliefs. This chapter also questions the interpretation according to which Paul exorcised the demon from the slave-girl in Philippi (Acts 16:16-18) because of the pagan content of her proclamation. The adherents of the Most High God were Judaizing Gentiles (God-fearers), some of whom remained close to the synagogue while others developed structures of their own, the existence of which is attested by Patristic literature.

It was first suggested long ago that the cult of 'the Most High God', θεὸς ὕψιστος, was developed by pagans under Jewish influence. The theory was that the Most High God was a syncretistic[1] deity in whom elements of pagan and Jewish beliefs were merged.[2] This theory was first of all based on a belief that the epithet ὕψιστος was widely used by Gentiles, irrespective of whether they were influenced by Jews or not, and that it became a point of convergence for Jewish monotheism and the Gentile search for the only true god at the beginning of the first century—in a 'trend towards monotheism', as M.P. Nilsson called it.[3] Other scholars have denied Jewish influence and argued that the Most High God was a purely pagan venture.[4] Now, P. Trebilco in his recent book on the Jewish Diaspora in Asia Minor has re-examined the bulk of evidence for θεὸς ὕψιστος and concluded that in a limited number of cases Judaism did stand behind the use of the title 'Hypsistos'. He argues, however, that in the majority of inscriptions this title was used independently: 'There were many "Highest gods" and a pagan hearer or reader would understand the referent of the term to be the deity he or she considered to be supreme, if in fact he or she considered any deity in this position'.[5] The belief that the title ὕψιστος was widely applied to pagan deities is commonplace in the study of the religion of the Hellenistic and Roman periods. Let us test this hypothesis.

I. Pagan Background

The existence of the cult of Zeus the Most High (Ζεὺς Ὕψιστος) is well documented, though its rôle in Greek religion was of little importance.[6] The title was used sporadically by Greek poets, such as Pindar, Aeschylus, Sophocles and Theocritus.[7] The cult was officially recognized in Corinth (Pausanias II.2,8), in Olympia where there were two altars to *Zeus Hypsistos* (*ibid*. V.15,5), and in Thebes where there was also a temple (*ibid*. IX.8,5). There was possibly a sanctuary in Argos.[8]

---

[1]See Appendix 1.
[2]F. Cumont, *Les mystères de Sabazius*, 63-79; id. 'A propos de Sabazius et de judaïsme', *Musée Belge* 14 (1910) 55-60; id. '"Ὕψιστος', *RE* 9, 444-450.
[3]M.P. Nilsson, *Geschichte der griechischen Religion*, vol. 2 (Munich, 1961²), 569-578. Trebilco, 'Paul and Silas - "Servants of the Most High God" (Acts 16.16-18)', *JSNT* 36 (1989), 65, n. 1 remarks that more correctly that this trend should be called a trend towards henotheism, that is worship of one god who becomes the supreme among the gods and supplants them. Actually both trends existed.
[4]A.T. Kraabel, '"Ὕψιστος and the Synagogue at Sardis', *GRBS* 10 (1969), 87ff.
[5]Trebilco, *Jewish Communities*, 143.
[6]Cumont, '"Ὕψιστος', 444.

We know about a cult association at Philadelphia.[9] Four altars were found in Sparta and there probably was a temple there in the agora.[10] The epigraphic evidence for this cult is spread over a large territory, including Macedonia, Thrace, Dacia, the southern part of Asia Minor and Egypt.[11] The earliest inscription comes from Macedonia and dates from the second century BC.[12] In some places dedications to *Zeus Hypsistos* have been found together with dedications to *Theos Hypsistos* or simply to *Hypsistos*. This has prompted the conclusion that quite often it was Zeus who was called by the name of *Theos Hypsistos*. Some dedications to *Theos Hypsistos* were found in regions where a prominent place was occupied by another particular deity. The conclusion has been drawn that this deity was called by this name.

How well founded are such conclusions? If dedications to Zeus and Hermes are found in close proximity, are we to conclude that they must be treated as the same deity?[13] The assumption that *Zeus Hypsis-*

---

[7]C.F.H. Bruchman, *Epitheta deorum quae apud poetas graecos leguntur* (Leipzig, 1893), 142; E. Schürer, 'Die Juden im bosporanischen Reiche und die Genossenschaften der σεβόμενοι θεὸν ὕψιστον ebendaselbst', *SPAW* XII-III (1897), 209. This epithet has no literary attestations from Asia Minor, *NewDocs* 1 (1981), 28 with reference to M. Santoro.

[8]*IG Pelop.* I.620, 4.

[9]C. Roberts, T.C. Skeat and A.D. Nock, 'The Guild of Zeus Hypsistos', *HTR* 29 (1936), 39ff..

[10]A.M. Woodward, 'Excavations at Sparta 1924-1925', *BSA* 26 (1924-1925), 222-224, No. 16-18, *BSA* 29 (1927-1928) 49-50, No. 71, 73).

[11]The evidence for both cults is collected in: Schürer, 'Die Juden im Bosporanischen Reiche', 209-213; Cumont, '"Ὕψιστος', 445-450; A.B. Cook, *Zeus: A Study in Ancient Religion*, 2.II (Cambridge: CUP, 1925), 876-890, Addenda, 1162-1164; C. Roberts, T.C. Skeat and A.D. Nock, 'The Guild of Zeus Hypsistos', 56-59; M. Tacheva-Hitova, *Eastern Cults in Moesia Inferior and Thracia* (Leiden: Brill, 1983. EPRO, 95), 190-215; *eadem*, 'Dem Hypsistos geweihte Denkmaler in Thrakien. Untersuchungen zur Geschichte der antiken Religionen, III', *Thracia* 4 (1977) 274-90; J. Keil, 'Die Kulte Lydiens', *Anatolian Studies Presented to Sir William Mitchell Ramsey*, edd. W.H. Buckler & W.M. Calder (Manchester, 1923), 255; P. Aupert, O. Masson, 'Inscriptions d'Amathonte, I', *BCH* 103 (1979), 380, n. 53; F.T. van Straten, 'Gifts for the Gods. Appendix. Votive Offerings Representing Parts of the Human Body (in the Greek World)', *Faith, Hope and Worship. Aspects of Religious Mentality in Ancient World*, ed. H.S. Versnel (Leiden: Brill, 1981), 116-119.

[12]S. Pelecides, 'Ἀνασκαφὴ Ἐδέσσης', *Ἀρχαιολογικὸν δελτίον* 8, 1923 (1925), 268.

[13]This is exactly the logic exploited by some scholars. Cf., for instance, Kraabel, '"Ὕψιστος and the Synagogue at Sardis' 88: 'Two inscriptions from Aezani in Phrygia honor θεὸς ὕψιστος, one because of 'merciful delivery from many sufferings'; a large temple of Zeus has been discovered nearby, along with a number of inscriptions in his honour—it appears that the dedicators of the two θεὸς ὕψιστος-inscriptions had this Zeus in mind.'

tos and *Theos Hypsistos* were easily interchangeable is not supported by
the evidence. If we look at the territorial distribution of the dedications
to *Zeus Hypsistos* and *Theos Hypsistos*, we can see that they originate in
different regions.[14] In continental Greece, with the exception of Athens, there are no dedications to the Most High God. In the central part
of Asia Minor there are no dedications to *Zeus Hypsistos*. They were
found only in the southern part in a rather small area which does not
cover the whole of Caria. The localities where the dedications to both
were found together are rather exceptional. They are situated along
the coast of the Aegean sea, in Thrace and in Dacia.

    Dedications to *Theos Hypsistos* are noticeably different from the
ones to *Zeus Hypsistos*, the former being marked by a complete absence
of anthropoid images of the deity. Trebilco mentioned a bas-relief
from Delos in which Cybele was shown along with *Theos Hypsistos*[15]
and supported this observation with a reference to Cumont.[16] This bas-
relief however has a dedication not to *Theos Hypsistos* but to *Zeus Hypsistos*—Διὶ τῷ πάντων κρατοῦντι καὶ Μητρὶ μεγάληι τῆι πάντων κρατού-
'σηι. The identification with *Theos Hypsistos* is a product of modern interpretation. Cumont compared ὁ πάντων κρατῶν of this inscription
with παντοκράτωρ of the Septuagint and concluded that the dedication
was made to the God of Israel.[17] Such a conclusion was characteristic
of his theory of religious Jewish-pagan syncretism. Trebilco, though he
quite rightly rejects this theory, nevertheless uses the material which is
interpreted in accordance with the same pattern of thought which un-
derlies Cumont's theory. As to the reliefs with eagles carrying on their
wings small busts which were found together with the dedications to
the Most High God in Serdica (Thrace),[18] they do not represent the image of the god. Cumont connected such images with the apotheosis of
emperors.[19] The traces of a footprint on a dedication to *Theos Hypsistos*
from Pisidian Termessus is a sign of the epiphany of the god in answer

---

[14]The map of the distribution of the dedications to *Zeus Hypsistos* and *Theos
Hypsistos* and the full catalogue of inscriptions see in my forthcoming book in
Russian, *The Cult of the Most High God in the Bosporan Kingdom.*
[15]Trebilco, *Jewish Communities*, 131.
[16]*The Oriental Religions in Roman Paganism*, ET (Chicago: The Open Court
Publishing Co, 1911) 227, n. 30).
[17]On the pagan usage of παντοκράτωρ and similar see p. 109.
[18]M. Tacheva-Hitova, 'Dem Hypsistos geweihte Denkmaler in Thrakien', *Thracia* 4
(1977), 278f., fig.3; M. Tacheva-Hitova, *Eastern Cults in Moesia Inferior and Dacia*
(Leiden: Brill, 1983, EPRO 95), 192.
[19]F. Cumont, 'L'aigle funéraire des Syriens et l'apothéose des empereurs', *RHR* 62
(1910), 119-164.

to a worshipper's prayer.[20] Sometimes the dedications to the Most High God are accompanied by representations of an eagle (or a pair of eagles),[21] with or without wreaths (for instance in Thyateira[22], Mytilene,[23] Crete,[24] Nicomedia,[25] Tanais[26] etc.). Dedications to *Zeus Hypsistos* were sometimes decorated with representations of an eagle but in accordance with pagan tradition, could also have anthropoid images.[27] This important iconographical difference, as well as the geographical distribution of the evidence, shows that we are dealing with rather different cults with significantly different backgrounds.

It has been argued that many pagan gods were called ὕψιστος. Let us examine the data that are usually cited in support of this assertion. The standard reference works are those of A.B. Cook,[28] A.D. Nock,[29] H. Gressman,[30] A.S. Hall[31] and M. Tacheva-Hitova.[32] The deities who are considered to receive the epithet include Men, Attis, Poseidon, Sabazios, Eshmun, Eshmun-Melkart, Helios.[33] However, the works of the scholars mentioned above provide no list of inscriptions giving the names of different gods with the title *Hypsistos*. The reason

---

[20]The first editor read θεῷ ἐπηκόῳ˙ Ὑφιστοτυχος κτλ. The presently accepted reading θεῷ ἐπηκόῳ ὑ[ψ]ίστ(ῳ) Τυχ<ι>ος κτλ. was suggested by F. Cumont, 'Hypsistos', *Supplement à la Revue de l'instruction publique en Belgique* (Bruxelles, 1897), 14, No. 16. The stone carried not a brown statue of a left foot, as Mitchell, *Anatolia*, II, 50, n. 294 proposed, but, as is evident from the word ἴχνος, a thin sheet of metal shaped in the form of a footprint (*TAM* 3, 1, 32). For footprints on Greco-Roman monuments see K.M.D. Dunbabin, '*Ipsa deae vestigia*... Footprints divine and human on Greco-Roman Monuments', *JRA* 3 (1990), 85-109.
[21]The eagle is a universal symbol. For the Greeks it was connected with Zeus; in the east it represented so many gods that, as E. Goodenough, *Jewish Symbols in the Greco-Roman Period*, 8, 129, remarks, the eagle 'had come to represent God, or the power of God, and could have been so regarded by Jews'. See also *RLAC* s.v. Adler (Th. Schneider).
[22]F. Cumont, 'Un *ex-voto* au *Theos Hypsistos*', *BullAcadBelg* (1912), 251-253.
[23]*IG* XII 2, 115.
[24]*IKret* I, VII, 7 (Chersonesos).
[25]J. Robert and L. Robert, *BE* (1974), No. 579.
[26]*CIRB* 1260, 1261, 1277, 1281, 1285.
[27]See for instance, dedications from the region of Cyzicus (A.B. Cook, *Zeus*, 834, fig. 793, 881, pl. XXXIX) and from Byblos, R. Dussaud, 'Voyage en Syrie. Notes archéologiques' *Revue archéologique*, ser. 3, 28 (1896) 299f., fig. 1.
[28]A.B. Cook, Zeus 2, II, 889.
[29]Roberts, Skeat and Nock, 'The Guild of *Zeus Hypsistos*', 422-423.
[30]H. Gressman, 'Die Aufgaben der Wissenschaft des nachbiblischen Judentums', *ZAW* 43 (1925), 18-19.
[31]A.S. Hall, 'The Klarian Oracle at Oenoanda', *ZPE* 32 (1978), 264-267.
[32]*Eastern Cults*, (Leiden: Brill, 1983. EPRO 95), 212-215.
[33]Trebilco, *Jewish Communities*, 131.

for this is that in the overwhelming majority of cases the assumption that a certain deity bears this title is simply an interpretation.

For instance, Trebilco writes that 'in Syria "Theos Hypsistos" (and also "Zeus Hypsistos") was used to refer to the local Baal of the region'.[34] He obtained this information from A.B. Cook, who wrote that the Syrian Zeus was *probably* Ba'al-samin, and three pages later, that in Syria it *definitely* means Ba'al-samin.[35] The only reason for this identification is that the dedications to *Theos Hypsistos* were found in the same region where Ba'al-samin was predominant. Eshmun appears in the list of the Most High Gods as a result of a remark by Nock.[36]

In another characteristic example, Trebilco very strongly criticizes Cumont's theory of 'syncretism between the Sabazios cult and Judaism'.[37] One of the main arguments in favour of this connection had been derived from an inscription from Pirot, in the territory of Serdica (Sophia), in which it was presumed that an association of Sabazios-worshippers was making a dedication to the Most High God. Those who have considered *Theos Hypsistos* to be Yahweh have seen this inscription as an important link between the cult of Sabazios and Judaism. Trebilco rejects this link, but accepts the traditional assumption that the title 'Hypsistos' was widespread and finds another explanation: 'a number of pagan deities were given the epithet "Hypsistos", so it is highly likely that in this instance Sabazios is being called "the Highest God" by some of his own worshippers'.[38] He failed to mention that an association of Sabazios Hypsistos had been postulated only as a result of the *restoration* of a lacuna in the inscription which was made by A. von Domaszewski when he first published it.[39] Let us have a closer look at this inscription and see whether, on the basis of the actual wording of the last lines of the inscription, it is possible to arrive at an interpretation different from those of Cumont and Trebilco.

---

[34]Trebilco, *Jewish Communities*, 128.

[35]Cook, *Zeus*, 886, 889.

[36]Roberts, Skeat and Nock, 'The Guild of Zeus Hypsistos', 64: 'at Athens *Theos Hypsistos* is a god of healing, perhaps some form of Esmun'.

[37]See also the critical analysis of Cumont's theory in Johnson, 'The Present State', 1583-1613, whose verdict runs as follows: 'this impressive edifice has, to a degree, crumbled, and should perhaps be demolished', 1602.

[38]Trebilco, *Jewish Communities*, 141.

[39]A. von Domaszewski, 'Griechische Inschriften aus Moesien und Thrakien', *AEM* 10 (1886), 238f.

The text which is inscribed on an altar of limestone is dated to the second—early third century AD and on the basis of onomastic analysis before the Antonine Constitution.[40]

    Ἀγαθῇ [τύ]χ[η]
    Θεῷ ἐπηκόῳ ὑψίστῳ
    εὐχὴν ἀνέστησαν
    τὸ κοινὸν ἐκ τῶν ἰ-
5   δίων διὰ ἱερέως
    Ἑρμογένους καὶ προ-
    στάτου Αὐγουστιανοῦ
    (list of the names)
    καὶ Ἀλέξανδρος Ἀσκ-
    ληπιάδου ΘΙΑ---ΣΕΒΑΖΙ
15 ΑΝΟΣΘΗ---ΤΟΥΤΑΣ[41]

With good fortune. To the Most High God, who listens, the association through the priest Hermogenos and the president Augustianos . . . and Alexander the son of Asklepiades . . . set up at their own expense in fulfilment of a vow [this altar].

Domaszewski suggested the restoration θίασος for ΘΙΑ in line 14 and connected it with Σεβαζιανός and thus the association of adherents of Sabazios the Most High was born. His proposition was approved by the majority of scholars.[42] Another interpretation of this inscription was given by D. Detschev, who suggested that Σεβαζιανός was a personal theophoric name which was well-represented in the region where the inscription was found.[43] His idea received very limited scholarly support,[44] partly because he did not give arguments in its favour. Let us consider his interpretation more closely.

There is nothing impossible in the supposition that a religious association in one and the same inscription was described as both τὸ κοινόν and ὁ θίασος. The former was a general term for any kind of association and can be found in inscriptions in association with such

[40]B. Gerov, *Godishnik na Sofijskiya universitet* (Sofia 1969), 224. *(in Bulgarian)*
[41]Domaszewski wrote that the last three lines are given in accordance with the squeeze 'da ein heftiges Gewitter mich hinderte die Copie von dem Steine zu Ende bringen'; 'Griechische Inschriften', 239.
[42]Cf., for instance, Johnson, 'The Present State', 1606.
[43]D. Detschev, *Godishnik na norodniya muzei v Sofia*, 5 (1926-1931) 158f. *(in Bulgarian)*
[44]It was approved by Gerov, *Godishnik,* 224f. and M. Tatscheva-Hitova, *Eastern Cults*, 197.

words as θιασῖται (θιασῶται), ὀργεῶνες and ἐρανισταί.[45] But the word θίασος was usually linked with a noun in the genitive, which could be either the name of the head (or founder) of the association: ὁ θίασος ὁ Φαιν[ε]μάχου (B 146),[46] ὁ θίασος ὁ ᾿Αναξιπόλιδος (B 338a), ὁ θίασος ὁ [Σ]ιμαλ[ίων]ος (340), or the name of the deity: θίασοι Βάκχοιο (B 320a), or the names of the members of the association, derived from the name of the deity with the suffixes -ισταί, -ασται in the genitive plural: θιάσος ᾿Αφροδιαστᾶν (B 231 α,β), θίασος ῾Ερμαστ[ᾶν] (B 232), or some special names connected with a certain cult, mostly the cult of Dionysos, also in the genitive plural: θίασος τῶν Πλατανιστηνῶν (320a). According to Domaszewski's restoration, θίασος is combined with an adjective derived from the name Σεβάζιος.[47] Generally speaking, θίασος can be coupled with adjectives, though such a combination is rather uncommon: τοῦ Βακχικοῦ θιάσου (SEG 27, 384). An adjective could also be used with other designations of associations: σύνοδος Εἰσιακή (B 470), though in this case also, combinations with the genitive or with prepositions are much more common: ἔρανος ὁ Βακχίου (B 46A), ἡ σύνοδος ἡ περί κτλ. (CIRB 1260, 1263, 1264 etc.). The members of Sabazios' association were called Σεβαζιασταί (CCIS II 28, 46, 51) cf. ᾿Ασκλαπιασται, ᾿Απολλωνιασταί, Σεραπιασταί, Διονυσιασταί.[48] Thus the designation of the *thiasos* of the adherents of Sabazios, formed in accordance with the traditional pattern, must have been ὁ θίασος (τὸ κοινὸν, ἡ σύνοδος) τῶν Σεβαζιαστῶν.

In accepting Domaszewski's suggested restoration of the inscription from Pirot, Cumont noted that σεβαζιανός is a regular derivative from Σεβάζιος.[49] He is right in a general sense, insofar as adjectives with the suffix -ανος do exist in the Greek language. But as far as we know, the adjective σεβαζιανός is not recorded. Besides, the meaning 'devoted or belong to some deity' is not characteristic for adjectives with such a suffix.[50] It was used in the Latin language to designate supporters of a political or military leader (*Caesariani, Pompeiani*) and with this meaning, penetrated into Greek (cf. ῾Ηρωδιαν-

---

[45]F. Poland, *Geschichte des griechischen Vereinwesens* (Leipzig, 1909), 1f., 550f.
[46]The references to the inscriptions follow Polland's classification.
[47]A parallel form of the more common Σαβάζιος.
[48]Poland, *Geschichte*, 57-62.
[49]F. Cumont, 'Les mystères de Sabazius et le judaïsme', *CRAIBL* (1906), 67.
[50]R.Vulpe, 'Le sanctuaire des Zeus Casios de Serêmet et le problème d'un *vicus cassianus*', *Epigraphica* (Bucarest, 1977), 113f. argued that the word was the name of the members of the association of the adherents of *Zeus Casios*. His arguments were rightly contested by J. and L. Robert, *BE* (1991), 447, No. 337.

οἱ Mt. 22:16; Mk. 12:13; 3:6). The Latin form of the name 'Christian' does not mean that it was coined by the Romans.[51] Neither does it mean that Christians understood themselves as those who belong to Christ as God. It rather implies that they labelled themselves to be followers of the Messiah, their leader: 'they were agents, representatives of the Messiah'.[52] They tried to do what the rich youth could not: to take up the cross and follow (ἀκολουθέιν) Christ (Mk. 10:21; Mt. 19:21; Lk. 18:22). In Christian circles this model became a norm in designating members of the heretical sects as followers of their leader: Σαβελλιανοί, Σαββατιανοί, Μακεδονιανοί etc.[53] It became so common that it was used even if the name of the sect was not connected with the name of the heresiarch as in the case of the Μασσαλιανοί, whose name was a rendering the Syriac word for 'praying'.

The suffix -ανος/-ηνος can be found in a limited number of ancient adjectives and in the onomastic adjectives from toponyms in the north-western corner of Asia Minor and adjacent regions.[54] The Greek

---

[51]The name 'Christians' was traditionally considered to have been invented by the Gentile population of Antioch. Some scholars have held that the authorship belonged to the Roman authorities. It was viewed as a term of derision, or as a name with an unfavourable political connotation, or even as a synonym for sedition; cf. for instance, E. Peterson, 'Christianus', *Miscellanea Giovanni Mercati*, vol. I (Biblioteca Apostolica Vaticana, 1946, 355-372; H.B. Mattingly, 'The Origin of the Name *Christiani*, *JTS* n.s. 9 (1958), 26-37; J. Taylor, 'Why were the Disciples First called "Christians" at Antioch? (Acts 11:26)', *RB* 101:1 (1994), 75-94; E.A. Judge, 'Judaism and the Rise of Christianity: a Roman Perspective', *TynB* 45.2 (1994), 363. Another interpretation was suggested by E. Bickerman, 'The Name of Christians', *HTR* 42 (1949), 109-124 (reprinted in *Studies in Jewish and Christian History*, 3 (1986). He argued that the name 'Christians' was a self designation. The starting point for this hypothesis was an analysis of the verb χρηματίζω. In Bickerman's view the correct translation of this verb in the active voice should be not 'to be called', as it was assumed, but 'to call oneself', 'to take on the style of'. The attempt of Taylor, 'Why were the Disciples', 83, to refute Bickerman's grammatical and lexicographical considerations is not convincing. Bickerman's interpretation of the name 'Christians' as introduced by the Christians themselves is supported by J.Moreau, 'Le nom des chrétiens', *La nouvelle Clio* 1/2 (1949-1950), 190-192 and C. Spicq, 'Ce que signifie le titre de chrétien', *Stud. Theol.* 15 (1961), 68-78; cf. also B. Lifshitz, 'L'origine du nom des chrétiens', *VC* 16 (1962), 65-70.
[52]Bickerman, 'The Name of Christians', 123.
[53]Ναυατιανοί· αἱρεσῖται τὰ Ναυάτου φρονοῦντες (Suid. *s.v.* Ναυατιανοί); cf. also Μακεδονιανοί and οἱ τὰ Μακεδονίου φρονοῦντες in Theophanes' *Chronographia* (ed. De Boor, I, 68; 77; 156).
[54]E.A. Schwyzer, *Griechische Grammatik* I (Munich, 1953), 490; P. Chantraine, *La formation des noms en grec ancien* (Paris: Librarie ancienne Honoré Champion, éditeur Edouard Champion, 1933), 206; M.Leumann, *Lateinische Laut- und Formenlehre* (Munich: C.H. Beck'sche Verlagsbuchhanglungs, 1977), 323.

language also transliterated, borrowed and imitated some Latin expressions referring to Roman names: *Antonianus fundus* (the former property of Antonia)—οὐσία ᾽Αντωνιανή (instead of πρότερον ᾽Αντωνι-᾽ας).[55] There are also some astrological terms with the meaning, 'under the influence of—(a zodiac sign)', e.g. Σκορπιανοί, and a few derivatives from personal names, such as μαγιανόν (bracelet, from the name of the manufacturer).[56] In the Roman period, under the influence of the Roman onomastics, personal names ending in -(ι)ανος (including theophoric names) gradually gained popularity (cf. the name of *Augustianos*, the president of this association). It is in the realm of personal names that this suffix flourished from the second century AD onwards.

Theophoric personal names ending in -ιανος quite often form a pair with adjectives ending in -ιακος: ᾽Απολλωνιανός—᾽Απολλωνιακός, ᾽Αμμωνιανός—᾽Αμμωνιακός, Δημητριανός—Δημητριακός. The latter were employed as adjectives (cf. the above example, σύνοδος Εἰσιακή) while the former, in view of the popularity of the model in onomastic contexts, came to be perceived for the most part as personal names.

Thus, taking into consideration the rarity of the using of adjectives with θίασος, the absence in our sources of the adjective Σεβαζιανός as well as the absence of adjectives with the suffix -ιανος with the meaning 'the adherents of a deity', the popularity of the model ending in -ιανος for personal names and the presence of the parallel adjectives ending in -ιακος, it seems to me that the only plausible interpretation of Σεβαζιανός in the inscription from Pirot is that it is a personal name.[57] This interpretation undermines the Sabazios Hypsistos association completely.

It is actually quite surprising how rarely the title ὕψιστος was used with the names of the pagan gods. Several times we find Helios called *Theos Hypsistos*,[58] once Apollo;[59] the epithet ὕψιστος was used with the name of Attis[60] and in the dedication πατρὶ θεῷ Σαμοθρᾶκι ἀθανάτωι ὑψίσ[τωι].[61] We know of one dedication to Isis the Most

---

[55]Bickerman, 'The Name of Christians', 117.

[56]Bickerman, 'The Name of Christians', 117.

[57]The fact that καί in this case appears not to stand before the last name in the list cannot be used as an argument against this interpretation, since such an order of words is not exceptional, cf. *IGBulg* I, 287. On this interpretation ΘΙΑ, ΘΗ, ΤΟΥΤΑΣ are parts of the names such as, for instance, Θῆρις, Θήρων, Τουτας: F. Bechtel, *Die historischen Personennamen des griechischen bis zur Kaiserzeit* (Halle: Niemeyer, 1917), 210; L. Zgusta, *Kleinasiatische Personennamen*, (Prague: Tschechoslovakischen Academie Wissenschaften, 1964), 1596-I.

High[62] and one to *Thea Hypsiste* in Lydia.[63] These scanty testimonies do not allow us to conclude that the epithet Hypsistos, or the name *Theos Hypsistos*, was used for pagan deities throughout the Roman Empire'.[64] The idea that it was very easy for the Gentiles to abandon the name of the god and replace it by the anonymous and colourless *Theos Hypsistos* seems to me to simplify a much more complicated reality. An understanding that the one divine essence is hidden under the names of different gods, and indifference towards what name to use, was characteristic of the intellectual stratum of society,[65] especially of those who were imbued with Stoic teaching. The so-called Zeus of the Stoics was a very exalted philosophical conception, but philosophical speculations affect the popular views only to a limited extent. In some parts of Asia Minor anonymous divinities with vague titles, ὅσιος, δίκαιος became widespread,[66] which shows that an innovative movement in popular religion towards a less anthropomorphic and more abstract conception of the deity was in progress. This does not mean, however, that the pagan believer could simply, without being offensive to the god, rename him. What he could easily do was to add the new divinity to the pantheon, and gradually make this divinity its centre. Given the lack of evidence for the pagan tradition behind *Theos Hypsistos*, and the ample evidence for the Jewish usage of the term (to

---

[58]Ἡλίῳ θεῷ ὑψίστῳ (Cook, *Zeus*, 882); Θεῶι ὑψίστωι ἐπηκό[ω]ι˙ Η λ[ίωι], E. Kalinka, 'Aus Bithynien und Umgegend', *JÖAI* 28,1 (1933) 65. Taking into consideration that Helios as a sun-god was high in the sky in the literal sense of the word, the paucity of the inscriptions with this title shows that it was not well incorporated into the language of Greek religion.

[59][Ἀπόλ]λωνι Λαιρβήνῳ θεῷ ὑ[ψίστῳ] (W.M. Ramsay, *JHS* 10 (1889) 223).

[60][Ἀττει ὑψίστῳ καὶ συνέχοντι τὸ πᾶν (*CIL* VI. 509), see also Nock, Roberts, and Skeat, 'The Guild of Zeus Hypsistos', 68, n.77.

[61]L. Robert, 'Documents d'Asie Mineure', *BCH* 107 (1983) 584.

[62]G. Ronchi, *Lexicon theonymon rerumque sacrarum et divinarum ad Aegyptum pertinentium quae in papyris, titulis, Graecis Latinisque in Aegypto repertis laudantur* (Milan, 1977, Testi e Documenti per lo studio dell'Antichità XLV), 1120.

[63]Roberts, Skeat, and Nock, 'The Guild of Zeus Hypsistos', 62f.

[64]Trebilco, *Jewish Communities*, 128.

[65]Cf., for instance how Augustine described Varro's attitude (*De consensu evangelistarum* I.22:30): *deum Judaeorum Jovem putavit nihil interesse censens, quo nomine nuncupetur, dum eadem res intellegatur.* '[Varro] thought the God of the Jews to be the same as Jupiter, thinking that it makes no difference by which name he is called, so long as the same thing is understood' (trans. Stern, *GLAJJ* I, 210 No. 72b).

[66]L. Robert, 'Reliefs votifs et cultes d'Anatolie', *Anatolia*, 3 (1958), 112-122 = *Opera minora selecta* I (Amsterdam: Adolf M. Hakkert, 1969), 411-421. Robert demonstrates a tendency in some inscriptions from Lydia to use more abstract θεῖον instead of θεός and to substitute θεὸς ὅσιος καὶ δίκαιος by ῞Οσιον καὶ Δίκαιον.

be discussed later), would it not be reasonable to see Jewish influence in the choice of a title which could also incorporate some Jewish ideas of the divinity? This could account for the absence of images of the god in the majority of pagan dedications to *Theos Hypsistos*.[67] Even in cases when there are dedications in one place to both *Zeus Hypsistos* and *Theos Hypsistos*, it is not self-evident (though quite probable) that the same deity was meant. It could be argued, for instance, that while the Gentiles honoured Zeus the Most High, some Jews, or some Gentiles under the Jewish influence, for some reason found it necessary to honour in the same place the God of Israel. This supposition cannot be proved and I would not hold to it, but such a possibility at least is not without a parallel. In the temple of Pan east of Apollinopolis Magna (Edfu) in Upper Egypt there were found on a rock two votive inscriptions for which Jews were responsible.[68] The first expresses gratitude to God (θεοῦ εὐλογία) on the part of Theodotos the son of Dorion, a Jew, for, as Guarducci suggested, being saved from some kind of disaster at sea, e.g. a shipwreck, or as Dittenberger supposed, for returning safely from a journey (σωθεὶς ἐκ πελ<αγ>ους).

The second inscription commences with εὐλογεῖ τὸν θεόν[69] and then has the name of the dedicator along with the indication of his Jewish origin. Though the occasion of the second inscription is not mentioned, it is clear that, being found among ninety other inscriptions, the majority of which were addressed to *Pan Euodos* (Pan of the Successful Journey), it is also connected with travelling.[70]

How can the Jewish inscriptions in the pagan sanctuary be explained? J.–B. Frey proposed two explanations—the first one is that it

---

[67]The necessary reservation must be made for the regions with Semitic pagan populations, where *Theos Hypsistos* fitted quite naturally the religious perception and vocabulary. Cf. F. Cumont, "Ὕψιστος', 445, 'Eliun עליון bedeutet nicht 'der höchste' dem Range nach, sondern nur 'der Hohe', d.h. der Gott der in der Höhe des bestirnten Himmels wohnt und durch Donner und Blitz seinen Zirn offenbart'. See, for instance, Philo, *Bibl.* ap. Euseb. *Praep.ev.* 1.10,14: ᾿Ελιοῦν καλούμενος ὕψιστος. On the whole Ba'al-samin in Syria may possibly be found in the inscriptions under the name of *Theos Hypsistos* (see *supra* p. 86), but an assertion that this is so must be proved by more than just a reference to the general probability.

[68]Horbury and Noy, *JIGRE* No. 121, No. 122; cf. also *CIJ* II, *1537, 1538*, W. Dittenberger, *OGIS* 73, 74; A. Bernard, *Le Paneion d'El Kanais: les inscriptions grecques* (Leiden: Brill, 1972), 34, 42. M. Guarducci, *Epigraphia Graeca*, vol. 3 (Rome, 1974), 205-206. The site was usually referred to as Redesiyeh, but A. Bernard proved that the correct place-name to use is El-Kanais.

[69]G. Dittenberger and M. Guarducci understand εὐλογεῖ as a present indicative, A. Bernard as an imperative; he accentuates εὐλόγει. Horbury and Noy follow Bernard. See discussion in *NewDocs* 4 (1987), 113.

was possible, though assuredly not very orthodox, to thank Yahweh even in the temple of Pan, and the second one that in Egypt Pan could have been viewed as a universal deity (Πᾶν = τὸ πᾶν).[71] Whichever explanation is accepted, and the first one seems more plausible since there is no evidence for the perception of Pan as a universal deity, it is obvious that both Jews were expressing their gratitude to God, but not to the same deity, Pan Euodos, as others did.[72] What otherwise was the point of indicating their Jewishness, which implied not only their ethnicity but also their religious affiliation?[73]

To sum up, the pagan background of *Theos Hypsistos* has been given exaggerated prominence by modern scholars. We in fact know only a few examples where the title ὕψιστος was definitely used with the name of a pagan deity.

II. Jewish Background

Let us now examine the Jewish background of the title. That Jews addressed God as *Theos Hypsistos* is beyond any doubt. In the Septuagint ὕψιστος occurs over one hundred and ten times, usually as a translation of אֵל עֶלְיוֹן or עֶלְיוֹן.[74] It is found in some Jewish writings[75] and quite probably was in official use by Roman authorities as a designation of the God of the Jews.[76] The term was also used in some undoubtedly Jewish inscriptions. For instance, three inscriptions from Egypt com-

---

[70]For two more possibly Jewish inscriptions in the same temple see Horbury, Noy, *JIGRE*, No. 123 (temple graffiti on the rock-face to the east of the temple with the name Lazarus), No. 124 (on a column inside the temple, the restoration of the name Lazarus is speculative); in both cases the dedicators recorded that they had come to the *Paneion* τρίτον (for the third time, or 'with two others'), cf. G. Mussies, review of *JIGRE*, *BiO* 1 (1995), 777, who thinks that all four dedications were made to Pan 'or rather Min'.

[71]*CIJ* II 445. Cf. M. Hengel, *Judaism and Hellenism: Studies in their Encounter in Palestine during the Early Hellenistic Period*, ET (London: SCM Press, 1991), 264, for whom it was just another example of *theocrasia*: "Pan" as the universal God was for them presumably identical with the God of the Jews'.

[72]A. Bernard pays attention to the fact that both inscriptions are inside a frame isolating them from the dedications to Pan, *Le Paneion* , 34, 42. In general, he minimizes the relation between the pagan temple and the Jewish dedications. Cf. critical remarks concerning this approach in L. Robert, *BE* (1973), 530 and in Kant, 'Jewish Inscriptions', 685, n. 85.

[73]The geographical interpretation of the terms *Ioudaia, Ioudaios, Iudaeus* and *Ioudaea* proposed by A.T. Kraabel, 'The Roman Diaspora', 455 and supported by Kraemer, 'On the Meaning', does not sound convincing to me.

[74]*TDNT* VIII, 617; Trebilco, *Jewish Communities*, 129.

[75]See the list in Trebilco, *Jewish Communities*, 129, 239, n. 11.

memorate the dedication of the prayer-house (προσευχή) to the Most High God.[77] The other generally accepted Jewish ὕψιστος-inscriptions are as follows:[78]

1. Two inscriptions from the island of Rheneia, which was the burial place of the inhabitants of Delos. Both inscriptions date back to the end of the second century, or the beginning of the first century BC. They have a nearly identical text marked by allusions to the Septuagint, and they appeal to the Most High God for vengeance against the murderer of two girls.[79]

2. Five inscriptions from a building in Delos which is believed to be a synagogue of the first century AD.[80] In one of them προσευχή is mentioned, which, no matter whether it means a 'prayer'[81] or a 'prayer house',[82] is an exclusively Jewish term.[83]

3. An inscription from Acmonia in Phrygia probably from the third century AD with an allusion to Zech 5:1-5 (Septuagint version): καὶ τὸ ἀρὰς δρέπανον εἰς τὸν οἶκον αὐτοῦ εἰσέλθοιτο ('and let the sickle of the curse enter his house').[84]

4. An inscription from Sibidunda in Pisidia with the dedication θεῷ ὑψίστῳ καὶ ἀγείᾳ καταφυγῇ.[85] The reference to the Holy Refuge

---

[76]Schürer, 'Die Juden', 216. Philo twice uses the term when he refers to official documents of Julius Caesar and Augustus (*Leg.* 157, 317), but there is no certainty that he is citing the documents *verbatim* (Roberts, Skeat and Nock, 'The Guild of Zeus Hypsistos', 67, n. 74). The fact, though, that Josephus used the same term quoting Augustus' decree (*AJ* 16.163), and Joannes Lydus (*De mens.* 4.53) when quoting Julian's, makes such a conclusion rather probable.

[77]Horbury and Noy, *JIGRE* No. 9 (2nd century BC ?, Alexandria), No. 27 (2nd or 1st century BC, Athribis (Bencha): the synagogue is dedicated to the Most High God on behalf of king Ptolemy and queen Cleopatra by the chief of police and the Jewish community; No. 105, mid-2nd century BC - early 2nd century AD, Leontopolis (Tell el-Yehoudieh): fragmentary text, the restoration of *proseuche* is uncertain.

[78]Trebilco, *Jewish Communities*, 133-137.

[79]Deissmann, *Light from the Ancient East*, 413-424, fig. 75, 76, 77; *CIJ* I² 725 a, b.

[80]*CIJ* II 726, 727, 728, 729, 730.

[81]So Mazur, *Studies in Jewry*, 21.

[82]So, for instance, Lifshitz, *DF* 15.

[83]A very helpful analysis of the term is given in M. Hengel, 'Proseuche und Synagoge: Judische Gemeinde, Gotteshaus und Gottesdienst in der Diaspora und in Palästina', *Tradition und Glaube: Festgabe für K.G. Kuhn* (Göttingen, 1971) 157-183 = *The Synagogue, Studies in Origins, Archaeology and Architecture*, ed. J. Gutmann (New York: Ktav, 1975) 110-148. See, in detail, Appendix 2.

[84]*CIJ* II 769.

[85]C. Bean, 'Notes and Inscriptions from Pisidia', *Anatolian Studies* 10 (1960), No. 122.

seems to have been inspired by the Septuagint, the only ancient religious text in which the God is understood as the Refuge.[86]

5. (Less certain.) An inscription from Thessalonica in which the letters ΙΟΥΕΣ have been interpreted as the transliteration of Yahweh.[87]

6. A dedication from Kaleciuk, north-east of Ankara, of the late second or third century AD, to the Great and the Most High and Heavenly God and to his holy angels and to his revered prayer house—τῷ μεγάλῳ θεῷ ὑψίστῳ καὶ ἐπουρανίῳ καὶ τοῖς ἁγίοις αὐτοῦ ἀγγέλοις καὶ προσκυνητῇ αὐτοῦ προσευχῇ.[88] The wording of the inscription has a strong Jewish colouring and the word προσευχή which was used only in a Jewish context excludes a pagan interpretation.

In general terms, the Jewish religious affiliation of these inscriptions is evident. But can we insist that all of them belonged to Jews? It seems that some of them could with equally well have been produced by Jewish sympathizers—God-fearers. The Aphrodisias inscription shows how close the relations of this Gentile group with the synagogue could be. We cannot exclude that the dedications from the synagogue in Delos were made by the involved Gentiles. We cannot be sure that the inscription from North Galatia, probably from the first century AD, with the words δύναμις ὑψίστου—a characteristic Jewish allusion to the power of God,[89] is to be included among Jewish inscriptions, but it is definitely to be included among the inscriptions in which Jewish influence is detected. Likewise the dedication to the Most High God from Acmonia[90] which, despite the fact that it starts with a pagan formula 'With good fortune' (Ἀγαθῇ τύχῃ), could be Jewish,[91] or could belong (and in this case the formula does not need any kind of excuse) to God-fearers. It is very unlikely to be pagan.

---

[86]J. and L. Robert, BE 1965, No. 412;

[87]CIJ I², B. Lifshitz, Prolegomenon No. 693 d.

[88]Mitchell, RECAM II: The Ankara District: The Inscriptions of North Galatia (British Institute of Archaeology at Ankara Monograph No. 4, B.A.R. International Series 135, Oxford: British Archaeological Reports, 1982), No. 209B.

[89]Mitchell, RECAM II, No. 141. Cf. Trebilco, Jewish Communities, 137, 243, n. 51.

[90]T. Drew-Bear, 'Local Cults in Graeco-Roman Phrygia', GRBS 17 (1976), 249.

[91]This phrase was a common formula, like Dis Manibus in epitaphs, and lost its specific reference to Tyche, a goddess of Fortune (E.R. Goodenough, 'The Bosporus Inscriptions to the Most High God', JQR 47 (1956-1957), 225f. Cf. references to Hades, Lethe, Moira, and the like in Jewish inscriptions (Kant, 'Jewish Inscriptions', 678, 685; Horbury and Noy, JIGRE, Index: Non-Jewish Divine and Mythological References, 275). On the Dis Manibus formula in Jewish inscriptions see Rutgers, Jews in Rome, 269-272.

III. The Most High God in Acts: Pagan or Jewish?

Trebilco has proposed a new interpretation of Acts 16:16-18, according to which Paul exorcised the demon from the slave-girl in Philippi because of the pagan content of her proclamation.[92] Trebilco argues that

> this content must have been misleading to pagans. Only to a Jew or Judaizer would the title Theos Hypsistos have suggested that Yahweh was meant. To others, the referent would be one of a number of other gods. . . . She was proclaiming that the way of salvation was found in whichever god the hearer considered to be 'the highest god'. Paul's annoyance and consequent action was caused by the fact that the girl was confusing those to whom he was preaching. His anger was aroused by the fact that she was exposing his own proclamation to a syncretistic misunderstanding. He acted to remove the danger.[93]

Trebilco also supposes that Luke distinguished between the pagan and Jewish backgrounds of the term *Hypsistos* and used it differently in Jewish and Gentile settings.[94] These suppositions could be valid only if the title *Hypsistos* had an actually strong pagan background. However, as I have shown above, the extent of pagan usage of the title has been strongly exaggerated and most of the pagan highest gods are merely the result of scholarly reconstruction.

But one possibility for real confusion did actually exist at the linguistic level. The Greek ὕψιστος could be understood both as an absolute and as a relative superlative.[95] The translators of the Septuagint definitely had the first option in mind. But for the pagans the second interpretation probably was more natural.

Philo was well aware of the problem when in his commentary on Gen. 14:18 ('he [Melchizedeck] is the priest of the Most High God')[96] he had to make a provision against this interpretation:

---

[92]Trebilco, 'Paul and Silas', 51-73. The list of those whom Trebilco sees as his predecessors in developing this interpretation see in his article, p. 71, n. 65.
[93]Trebilco, 'Paul and Silas', 62.
[94]Trebilco, 'Paul and Silas', 59.
[95]M. Simon, '*Theos Hypsistos*', *Ex orbe religionum* (Leiden, 1972), 375 = id., *Le Christianisme antique et son contexte religieux. Scripta Varia*, vol. 2 (Tübingen: J.C.B. Mohr [Paul Siebeck], 1981), 498.
[96]In his quotation from Genesis Philo omits the noun θεός, which is present in the LXX. Simon considers this fact to be instructive ('*Theos Hypsistos*', 377 = *Le Christianisme*, II, 500), cf. *infra* n. 102.

οὐχ ὅτι ἐστί τις ἄλλος οὐχ ὕψιστος - ὁ γὰρ θεὸς εἷς ὤν, ἐν τῷ οὐρανῷ ἄνω
ἐστὶ καὶ ἐπὶ τῆς γῆς κάτω, καὶ οὐχ ἔστιν ἔτι πλὴν αὐτοῦ [Deut. 4:39]'
(*Leg. all.* 3, 82).

Not that there is any other not Most High—for God being One is in
heaven above and on earth beneath and there is none besides Him

(trans. G.H. Whitaker, *LCL*).[97]

If we assume that *Theos Hypsistos* was not a designation of 'a whole
range of exalted deities',[98] how then could this name have been
perceived by the pagan audience? There are several possibilities. Some
Gentiles could consider it to be just the name of the Jewish God.[99] Some
could identify *Theos Hypsistos* with the highest god of the pagan
pantheon in accordance with the tradition of *interpretatio graeca*[100]—
and this perception was to some extent promoted by Jews
themselves.[101] The opposite trend was the identification by some
people in Jewish circles of Zeus with the God of Israel and their
recognition that Greek philosophers and poets, while speaking about
Zeus, actually had in mind the true God.[102] Thinking along somewhat
similar lines, Plutarch, having compared Greek and Jewish rituals,
identified the Jewish God with Dionysus.[103] Some might even think of
there being a highest god in a Jewish pantheon, though this would be

---

[97]It was proposed by Hengel, *Judaism and Hellenism*, v. 2, 201, n. 265 that Jews, in
order to avoid the possible ambiguity in the interpretation of the title 'Hypsistos',
gradually abandoned it in synagogue usage. The evidence from the Bosporan
Kingdom, where the term was definitely in synagogue usage till at least the beginning of the fourth century AD, does not support this assumption (see App. 3, I, 1).
Trebilco, 'Paul and Silas', 56, asserts that, after the first century AD, the term was
abandoned by Jews except in areas 'which had a large Jewish population, or in
groups where its use had become traditional'. The last reservation invalidates the
main thesis.

[98]Trebilco, 'Paul and Silas', 52.

[99]Cf., for instance, Celsus's view in Origen, *Contra Celsum* I,24.

[100]Cf. Augustine's commentary on Varro's assertion that Jews worshipped Jupiter.
Though the starting point of Varro's reflection differs from the popular views the
choice of the name is explained in terms of traditional *interpretatio graeca*: *Nam quia
nihil superius solent colere Romani quam Jovem, quod Capitolium eorum satis aperteque
testatur, eumque regem omnium deorum arbitrantur, cum animadverterent Iudaeos
summum deum colere, nihil aliud potuit auspicari quam Jovem* (August., *De cons. evang.*
I.22:30 = Stern, *GLAJJ*, I, 72b). 'Since the Romans habitually worship nothing superior to Jupiter, a fact attested well and openly by their Capitol, and they consider
him the King of all the gods, and as he perceived that the Jews worship the highest
God, he could not but identify him with Jupiter', (trans. Stern, *GLAJJ*, I, 210). Cf.
also *Letter of Aristeas*, 15-16.

rather exceptional—on the whole the Greeks knew about Jewish 'atheism' (ἀθεότης).[104]

The Gentile passers-by in Philippi, hearing the slave-girl's proclamation, could have various different ideas about Jewish religion and the Jewish *Theos Hypsistos*. But they would not, I believe, have been thinking primarily in terms of their own pantheon and the pre-eminence of any one God within its hierarchy: these were not the associations that would have been conjured up by the name *Theos Hypsistos*. The demon was exorcised by Paul, not because of the content of his proclamation, but because the Christian mission did not need allies such as these.

----

[101]For the Jewish identification of Zeus with the God of Israel and the identification of Greek philosophers and poets of Zeus with the true God, see Aristobulus cited by Eusebium *Pr.Ev.* 13,12,4-8. Aristobulus quoted the verses of Aratus replacing the name of Zeus (in the genitive case, Διός) by Theos and explained that this was what the author had actually in mind. The same poem of Aratus Phae was cited by Paul in Athens (Acts 17:28) with the same idea that Greek poets had grasped the understanding of the true God: ἐν αὐτῷ γὰρ ζῶμεν καὶ κινούμεθα καὶ ἐσμέν, ὡς καί τινες τῶν καθ᾽ ὑμᾶς ποιητῶν εἰρήκασιν· τοῦ γὰρ καὶ γένος ἐσμέν. - 'for in him we live, and move, and have our being; as certain also of your own poets have said, For we are also his offspring'. See discussion in Hengel, *Judaism and Hellenism*, 261-267.

[102]Simon, *Theos Hypsistos*, 376 (= 499) detects a tendency towards differentiation between the usage of the title by Jews and Gentiles, the former preferring *Hypsistos* alone, the latter *Theos Hypsistos*. Though inscriptions do not support this observation, on the whole in literary texts such a tendency can be detected. It seems that Jews deliberately introduced the full form to the Gentiles to stress— since they had no hope and no intention of making monotheists out of them—at least the prominent place of their God as compared to pagan gods. The same differentiation can also be traced in the Book of Acts, Trebilco, 'Paul and Silas', 59). Luke did distinguish between Jewish and Gentile *settings*, but this does not mean that he distinguished between Jewish and Gentile *provenances* or *backgrounds* of the term.

[103]Plutarch, *Quaest. conv.* IV,6,1-2 = Stern, *GLAJJ*,I, No 258. Judging by the fact that Tacitus took the trouble to refute this interpretation (*Hist.*V.5.5) it seems to have been rather widespread. Cf. also A. Alfoldi, 'Redeunt Saturnia regna', II: An iconographical pattern', *Chiron* 3 (1973), 138, who explains the attempt of Seleucid kings 'to force the Jews to conform to the Hellenistic Dionysos cult in order to control their loyalty' by the affinity, from the Gentile point of view, of the Jewish rites to that of Dionysus' cult.

[104]A standard accusation of Jews, since they had no images of God and had not recognized other gods; see in detail Schürer, Vermes, Millar, Goodman, *The History of the Jewish People*, 3, 1, 612f. cf. also *supra*, 5ff.

Patristic Evidence

Patristic literature preserves for us information about the religious development of the adherents of the Most High God. As distinguished
from those who remained close to the synagogue, these God-fearers
formed structures of their own. Several groups of this type are known.
One of them existed in the fourth century in Cappadocia and is recorded by both Gregory of Nazianzus[105] and Gregory of Nyssa.[106] According to Gregory of Nazianzus, they were called Ὑψιστάριοι, according
to Gregory of Nyssa Ὑψιστιανοί. This group rejected all images and
sacrifices and, while observing the Jewish sabbath and some of the
food laws, they rejected circumcision. Gregory of Nazianzus reports
that they revered fire and light and combined in their beliefs both Hel-
lenic and Jewish elements which actually were sharply opposed (ἐκ
δυοῖν ἐναντιωτάτοιν Ἑλληνικῆς τε πλάνης καὶ νομικῆς τερατείας). His
father (and his oration was delivered at his father's funeral) belonged
to this group and was converted to Christianity by the bishops who
passed through Cappadocia on their way to the Council of Nicaea in
325 (καὶ δὴ συμβὰν τηνικαῦτα πλείους ἀρχιερεῖς ἐπὶ τὴν Νικαίαν σπεύ-
δειν). Gregory of Nyssa mentioned them together with Jews among
those who feigned another god beside God the Father—εἰ δὲ ἄλλον
τινα παρὰ τὸν πατέρα θεόν, ἀναπλάσσει, Ἰουδαίοις διαλεγέσθω ἢ τοῖς
λεγομένοις Ὑψιστιανοῖς. They acknowledged the only one God, whom
they called the Most High or Almighty. The major difference with
Christians was in their denial of his role as God the Father—ὧν αὐτὴ
ἐστιν πρὸς τοὺς Χριστιανοὺς διαφορὰ τὸ θεὸν μὲν αὐτοὺς ὁμολογεῖν αὐτὸν
εἶναι τινα, ὃν ὀνομάζουσιν ὕψιστον ἢ παντοκράτορα· πατέρα δὲ αὐτὸν
εἶναι μὴ παραδέχεσθαι. The next phrase can be understood either as a
general statement or as a recognition of the fact that Hypsistarii considered themselves to be Christians—ὁ δὲ Χριστιανός, εἰ μὴ τῷ πατρὶ
πιστεύοι, Χριστιανὸς οὐκ ἔστιν. That there was only a fine line distinguishing Christians from groups like Hypsistarians is seen from the
Phrygian epitaph to a certain Gourdos who was the priest of the Most
High God. Were it not for the term ἱερεὺς θεοῦ ὑψίστου this epitaph
could not be distinguished from Christian ones. According to one of
the reports of the inscription, it may have been flanked by crosses.[107]

Another group of a similar type is known from Epiphanius.[108]
The members of the group were called Μασσαλιανοί (a Greek tran-

---

[105]Gr.Naz. Or.18.5 (PG 35. 989 D ff.)
[106]Gr.Nys. Eun. 2 (PG 45. 481 D 484 A).

scription of the Syriac for 'praying') or Εὐφημῖται. According to Epiphanius, earlier (πρὸ χρόνου τινός, ὡς ἀπὸ τῶν καιρῶν Κωνσταντίου καὶ δεῦρο) there existed a pagan sect and later a Christian sect (ἀπὸ ὀνόματος Χρίστου ὁρμωμένων) with the same name (both were known by a number of additional different names),[109] which at first emerged in Mesopotamia and then appeared in Antioch. This Christian sect was condemned by synods at Side and Constantinople.[110] In Epiphanius' eyes, apart other faults, it was discredited by the very fact of its inheritance from the pagan Messalians. From his description, however, it is evident that this group was strongly influenced by Judaism.[111]

A third sect is known from Cyril of Alexandria.[112] Its members worshipped ὕψιστος θεός (καθάπερ ἀμέλει καὶ Μελχισεδέκ, commented Cyril) but they also revered the objects of creation—τὰ ἐξαίρετα τῶν κτισμάτων—such as the moon, the sun, the heaven. This sect survived till the time of Cyril (καὶ πλημμέλημα μὲν ἀρχαῖον ἡ ἐπὶ τῷδε καταφθορὰ καὶ πλάνησις, διήκει δὲ καὶ εἰς δεῦρο καὶ παρατείνεται) and existed then in Phoenicia and Palestine. Its followers called themselves θεοσεβεῖς and, in Cyril's view, their beliefs were somewhere between those of the Gentiles and those of the Jews—οἴμοι δέ τινα θρησκείας διαστείχουσι μέσην, οὔτε τοῖς Ἰουδαίων ἔθεσι καθαρῶς οὔτε τοῖς Ἑλλήνων προσκείμενοι, εἰς ἄμφω δὲ ὥσπερ διαπιπτούμενοι καὶ μεμερισμένοι.

At the beginning of the fifth century the attention of Roman legislators was attracted by a group called *Caelicolae*. Two laws prohibit-

[107]Mitchell, *Anatolia*, 50. His other example of a possible Hypsistarian on the epitaph from Yapidak in the Phrygian Highlands does not seem to be apposite. I rather agree with R.L. Fox, *Pagans and Christians* (Viking, 1986), 404, that this epitaph is Christian, though λαοῦ ὑψιστοίο I am inclined to understand not as 'the highest people' as both Fox and Mitchel, but as 'people of the highest (God)' as in the Christian funerary epigram of the fourth century from Hadrianoi in Mysia (*SEG* XXVIII, 946: ἐν [ὅλ]ῳ τε λαῷ Θεοῦ ὑ[ψίστ]ου).
[108]Epiph. Pan. 80.1-3 (*GCS*, Epiphanius, ed. K. Holl, vol.3, 485-488). Some consider Messalians and Hypsistarians, given the similarity in their beliefs, to be the same group, cf., for instance, *GCS*, 485; Mitchell, *Anatolia*, 50.
[109]Such as *Martyriani, Enthusiastae* etc. The collection of ancient testimonia and detailed discussion of Messalians see in *Patrologia Syriaca*, part I, vol. 3: *Liber Graduum*, ed. M. Kmosco (Paris: Firmin-Didot, 1926), CXV-CXLIX (discussion), CLXX-CCXCII (testimonia). Ephraem Syrus was the first to mention Christian Messalians, but it was Epiphanius who gave the description of their Gentile predecessors.
[110]References in G.W.H. Lampe, *A Patristic Greek Lexicon*, (Oxford: Clarendon Press, 1961), 833.
[111]See in detail App. 2, pp. 218-20.
[112]*De adoratione in spiritu et veritate* 3, 92 (*PG* 68, 281 BC).

ing them were issued—one in 407 AD in the names of Honorius, Arcadius and Theodosius II and the second one in 409 AD in the names of Honorius and Theodosius II.[113] In the law of 407, the heaven-worshippers were condemned along with the heretics (the Donatists, the Manichaeans, and the Priscillianists) and pagans. The law of 409 was directed against *Caelicolae*, conversion to Judaism and profaning of Sunday. The legislation concerning *Caelicolae* was preserved in both *Codex Theodosianus* (16:5:43; 16:8:19) and *Codex Justinianus* (1:9:12). In both laws it was emphasized that the sect was a recent development (*novum crimen superstitionis*) and it was suggested that the members should return to Christian worship (the law of 409 gave them a year to rejoin the Church under the threat of being prosecuted under anti-heresy legislation afterwards). Their buildings were to be confiscated by the churches for the reason that everything that differed from the Christian teaching contradicted the Christian law: *Aedificia autem eorum, quae nescio cuius dogmatis novi conventus habent, ecclesiis vindicentur. Certum est enim, quidquid a fide Christianorum discrepat, legi Christianae esse contrarium.*

It is important to note that in the second law the measures against the Caelicolae were followed by a reiteration of the prohibitions of proselytism. This suggests that the legislator considered these two phenomena to be linked together.[114]

The existence of the group with the same name in Africa is known from the letter of Augustine dated to 396, or the beginning of 397, or even to 398[115]:

> I had already sent a messenger to the chief man[116] of the Coelicolae, of whom I had heard that he had introduced a new baptism among them, and had by this impiety led many astray, intending, so far as my limited time permitted, to confer with him.
>
> (trans. J.G. Cunningham, *NPNF*).

It is evident from this letter that Augustine means a Christian sect.

---

[113]A. Linder, *The Jews in Roman Imperial Legislation, edited with Introductions, Translations and Commentary*, ET (Detroit: Wayne State University Press, 1987), 226-236, 256-262.

[114]Linder, *The Jews*, 256.

[115]Letter 44, 6, 13.

[116]Lat. *maior*. Linder notes that this title was used in Roman law to refer to the leaders of the Jewish communities.

CHAPTER 6

GOD FEARERS: THE BOSPORAN KINGDOM: A CASE STUDY

Jewish presence in this remote part of the Mediterranean world is well attested by a unique set of inscriptions from the first century AD (see Appendix 3). This was a period when the traditional ethno-cultural situation of this state was destabilized. Such conditions are usually favourable to religious innovations. Jewish religious beliefs, which were so much in line with the general tendency of this period towards monotheism, created interest among the local population and attracted sympathizers. The cult of the Most High God became the most popular with the Bosporan inhabitants. Some God-fearers manumitted their slaves in the Jewish synagogues on condition that as freedmen they would be attached to them. The freedmen joined, and widened the circles of God-fearers connected with Jewish communities. In some parts of the Bosporan Kingdom, Jewish influence gave rise to a proliferation of religious associations worshipping the Most High God. The possibility cannot be excluded that some Christians, whose presence in the Bosporan Kingdom is registered from the beginning of the fourth century AD, were former members of the thiasoi of the Most High God. This development would be in harmony with one of the types of reaction described by Luke of the God-fearers to the Christian message.

A most extraordinary development took place in the Bosporan Kingdom which is situated in the Crimea and on the Taman peninsula.[1] Beginning in the first century AD there was a remarkable increase of
private dedications to the Most High God, so that by the fourth century
this cult undoubtedly became, in some parts of the state, the central
one. And what is more important for the present study is that it can be
argued that this cult was formed under Jewish influence. Let us have
a closer look at the religious developments in this remote part of the
Graeco-Roman world.

When Greek colonists arrived in the sixth century BC in the territory of the future Bosporan Kingdom, they brought with them their
own religious system. Being a pagan system, it was an open one and
was able to adopt the local deities, albeit in accordance with certain traditions. The normal practice was *interpretatio graeca*, i.e. the identification of a foreign god with a Greek one, whereby a proper place for this
god was established in the pantheon. The contacts of the Greeks with
local barbarians and the infiltration of the latter in the newly founded
Greek *poleis* had its impact on Bosporan religious life. Local influence
changed the cult composition, so that some divinities who were identified with the local protectors gained a more prominent place in the
hierarchy. But on the whole the extant data indicates that the Greek-
speaking population worshipped the Greek gods, or gods long ago
adopted by the Greeks such as, for instance, Cybele.

In the sixth to fourth century BC the Bosporan Kingdom was in
the process of territorial expansion and nationhood. The new period
in the political history of the state started at the end of the fourth to the
beginning of the third century BC. This coincided chronologically with
the beginning of the new Hellenistic period, which was marked by the
development on an unprecedented scale of innovations in Greek reli-

---

[1]The literature devoted to the history of the Bosporan Kingdom is extensive, but
mostly in the Russian language which is not widely read (I hope not for ever)
within the scholarly community. Occasionally I shall refer to some Russian works,
giving a translation of the titles and a transliteration of publication details. E.H.
Minns, *Scythians and Greeks* (Cambridge, 1913) is still the main reference work in
English. The views of M. Rostovtzeff as always must be thoroughly considered,
though the conception of religious development which is defended in this book
differs from what he wrote (in my view he exaggerated the Iranian impact). For a
different approach see my commentary on the newly discovered and published
article by Rostovtzeff, 'The Iranian Rider-God and the South of Russia', in *Vestnik
drevnej istorii*, 2 (1990), No. 5, 198-199 (*in Russian*) and the German translation in M.
Rostowzew, *Skytien und der Bosporus. Bd.II: Wiederendeckte Kapitel und Verwandtes*,
ed. and trans. by H. Heinen (Stuttgart: Franz Steiner Verlag, 1993), 164-167.

gious life. Intensive contact between the Greeks and the local population in the vast Hellenistic monarchies stimulated the possibility of
such innovations. But this alone is not sufficient to explain why the innovations commenced. Two 'organized' religions could happily exist
side by side for centuries with no exchange between them.[2] In fact, the
official policy of the Hellenistic states encouraged the mingling of religions. The best example is the cult of Serapis introduced by Ptolemy I.
Yet even more important was the crisis of the traditional Greek *polis*
which created new problems and new demands. A new religious development was an answer to a new challenge.

If we look for circumstances conducive to religious innovation in
the Bosporan Kingdom during this period, it is immediately obvious
that nothing happened comparable to these developments. Thanks to
its outlying location, no matter how dramatic and troubled its history
was in this period, the Bosporan Kingdom was at least not involved in
the major international military conflicts of the time. The symbiosis of
the Greeks and the local barbarians had been established long before.
According to prosopographical analysis, there were no large, sudden
migrations to the Bosporan Kingdom from different parts of the Mediterranean world. Instead, there were continuous small scale migrations and continuous infiltration of the local population. On the whole
the ethno-cultural situation was fairly stable. The Bosporan Kingdom
had not suffered from the crisis of the *polis* system. During the fifth
century BC the cities were gradually consolidated into a territorial tyr-
anny which developed into a monarchy of the Hellenistic type.[3] This
transition was smooth when compared with that of the Hellenistic
states.

Real changes in the religious life of the Bosporan Kingdom began only in the first century AD with the end of a relatively stable period. As a result of Mithridates' activity, the Bosporan Kingdom
became involved in a worldwide political struggle which resulted in
its subjection to Rome. Migrations to the Bosporan Kingdom from
Asia Minor and Thrace increased dramatically, as did the infiltration
of the local Iranian tribe of Sarmatians into the cities. The traditional
ethno-cultural situation in the state was destabilized. Such conditions
are usually favourable to religious innovations. Whether they start, or
what direction they take, is another matter.

---

[2]H. Ringgren, 'The Problems of Syncretism', *Syncretism*, ed. S.S. Hartman (Stockholm, 1969, Scripta Instituti Donneriani Aboensis, 3), 7.
[3]Yuri G. Vinogradov, 'Polis at the North Black Sea Shore', *Antichnaya Grecia*, I
(Moscow, 1983), 420 (*in Russian*).

In the Bosporan Kingdom the changes in religious life began and developed along two lines. First of all, for obvious political reasons, the cult of the Roman emperors was officially introduced. The phrase 'the chief priest for life of the emperors'— ἀρχιερεὺς τῶν Σεβαστῶν διὰ βίου was added to the title of the Bosporan kings.[4]

Secondly, the cult of θεὸς ὕψιστος came into being and became extraordinarily popular with the local people. In Tanais, a remote Bosporan city on the Taman peninsula, nearly all free male inhabitants[5] in the third century AD were members of thiasoi, worshipping the Most High God. All private dedications by the locals in this city were made to θεος ὕψιστος.[6] What is especially important for our study is that, according to the inscriptions, the worship of the Most High God was connected with the Jewish synagogues from the very beginning.

It cannot be determined precisely when Jews arrived in the Bosporan Kingdom. M. Rostovtzeff suggested that it would have happened in connection with the initiative of Mithridates.[7] B. Nadel believed that it had occurred much earlier, but could not propose any appropriate date.[8] Epigraphically their presence is recorded from the first century AD. One of the earliest dated inscriptions which registered a Jewish presence in the Bosporan kingdom shows that the Most High God was a title used by the Jewish community.[9] The inscription

---

[4]CIRB 41, 42, 44, 53, 982, 983, 1045, 1047, 1118, 1122.

[5]We know the names of about three hundred members of thiasoi of the Most High God between the year 225 and the year 330. According to D.V. Shelov (Tanais and the Lower Don in the First Centuries of the Common Era (Moscow: Nauka, 1972), 277f, (in Russian), the number of the adult free males at this time was between 250 and 300 (with the whole population being 1500 to 2000).

[6]The nature of this phenomenon has intrigued several generations of scholars. The main hypotheses have included: a Jewish genesis, an Iranian background, influence from the Thraco-Macedonian Zeus-Sabazius and even Christian roots. See, for instance, A. Salac, 'At the Estuary of the Quiet Don', Pražská universita Moskovské universite. Sbornik k výroči 1755-1955 (Prague, 1955), 213-230 (in Russian); V. Blawatsky, and G. Kochelenko, Le culte de Mithra sur la côte septentrional de la mer Noire (Leiden, 1966). For a recent work reviving the old theory of Theos Hypsistos as a syncretistic deity in which Thracian Sabazios was fused with the Iranian solar god see Ju. Ustinova, 'The Thiasoi of Theos Hypsistos in Tanais', History of Religions 31 (1991), 152-180, who ignores modern discussions. All the main hypotheses are discussed in full in I. Levinskaya, The Cult of the Most High God, forthcoming (in Russian).

[7]M. Rostovtzeff, Iranians and Greeks in South Russia (Oxford, 1922), 150.

[8]B. Nadel, The Bosporan Manumissions, PhD Thesis, Leningrad, 1947, 146f. (in Russian).

[9]CIRB 1123 (App. 3, II, 7). The earliest inscription dates back to AD 16 (see App. 3, II, 5).

dates from 41 AD and belongs to the acts of enfranchisement. It was produced in Gorgippia (modern Anapa) and, like two more manumissions of the same provenance,[10] it commences with the formula θεῷ ὑψίστῳ παντοκράτορι εὐλογετῷ. The notion of godhead implicit in the use of the epithet παντοκράτωρ[11]—ὁ πάντων κράτος ἔχων—is not completely alien to the pagan world.[12] The title itself was used sporadically with the names of Isis,[13] Mandulis Apollon (who was an Egyptian sun god), Hermes, Cybele and Attis.[14] As O. Montevecchi supposed, the word was first coined in the Hellenistic circles of Alexandria. Though it is impossible to say that it owes its origin to the Septuagint, the word was spread through its occurrence in the Septuagint. Whereas the title παντοκράτωρ was at least used by the pagans on rare occasions, the other epithet of the manumissions, εὐλογητός, was never registered outside Jewish and later Christian vocabulary.[15] Since Christian provenance is out of the question in first century Gorgippia, this epithet is definitely Jewish. Even more instructive is that in this manumission the freedwoman is devoted to the *proseuche*, i.e. to the Jewish synagogue.[16] And that the Jewish prayer-house was called *proseuche* in the Bosporan Kingdom as it was everywhere else, is evident from the manumission from Phanagoria and three manumissions from Panticapaeum, the earliest of which dated from AD 51[17] and the latest from the first half of the second century.[18] All these manumissions in-

---

[10]*CIRB* 1125, 1126.

[11]See *TDNT* III 914 (Michaelis); O. Montevecchi, 'Pantokrator', *Studi in onore di Aristide Calderini e Roberto Paribeni* (Milan, 1957), 401-432; (H. Hommel, 'Pantokrator', Schöpfer und Erhalter 1956), 81-137, and Nachtrage, 146f.

[12]First of all this idea is connected with Zeus, for instance, Soph. *Trach.* 127: ὁ πάντα κραίνων βασιλεύς, but also with Hera, Moira, Apollo and Athene. In classical literature the usual epithet was παγκρατής.

[13]Isis was once called παντοκράτειρα, in the first century BC in Egypt (Arsinoites), and once παντοκράτωρ in an Arcadian inscription: Ronchi, *Lexicon thèonymon.*, 880.

[14]Hommel, 'Pantokrator', 96. He remarks that in all these cases Jewish or even Christian influence cannot be excluded.

[15]Roberts, Skeat, Nock, 'The Guild of *Zeus Hypsistos*', 64: it 'has no chance of being Greek'. The verb εὐλογέω and the noun εὐλογία rarely occur in pagan usage, cf. *CIG* 4705c and confessional inscriptions from the north-eastern part of Lydia and adjacent regions of Mysia and Phrygia (G.Petzl, 'Die Beichtinschriften Westkleinasiens', *Epigraphica Anatolica* 23 (1994), VII-XVIII (for the reference to the latter, I am indebted to A.Bij de Vaate and J.W. van Henten).

[16]One of the other manumissions lacks the end of the text (*CIRB* 1125) and the other has a big lacuna in the middle (1126). It cannot be excluded that the Jewish prayer house was mentioned in these inscriptions also.

[17]App. 3, II, 6.

[18]*CIRB* 73 = App. 3, II, 4.

form us that the slaves are set free in the prayer house (προσευχή), that the Jewish community appears as a guardian of the legal act, and that the freedmen are connected by certain obligations to the synagogue.[19]

The latest of the Hypsistos-inscriptions is also connected with the synagogue. It informs us that in AD 306 (that is, two years later than the earliest Christian epitaph from Panticapaeum)[20] the imperial governor of Theodosia, Aurelius Valerius Sogus, built a προσευχή to the Most High God in Panticapaeum, the capital of the Bosporan King-dom.[21] Between the first and the beginning of the fourth century the main centre of the worship of θεὸς ὕψιστος became Tanais, where the Most High God had possibly been known as early as the first century.[22]

---

[19]It is difficult to decide whether these manumissions (or at least part of them) were produced by Jews. B. Nadel in his article about the Bosporus manumissions ('The Bosporan Manumissions and Greek Law', Listy filologické 91, 3 (1968), 271f., in Russian) suggested that the acts of enfranchisement from the Bosporus should be divided into three groups: 1) Greek sacred manumissions in a form of a dedication to the god (CIRB 74, 1021); 2) proselyte's manumissions with a dedication to the Jewish prayer house and/or an address to the Most High God; 3) Jewish manumissions with obligations towards the prayer house and the Jewish community (CIRB 70, 71, 72, 73 = App. 3, II, 1; 2; 3; 4). The main criterion for singling out the Jewish manumissions is the mention of the guardianship of the Jewish synagogue. This criterion seems to me insufficient without additional data such as the Jewish names of the manumittors or reference to their ethnicity. (For instance, in CIRB 1124 = App. 3, II, 8 the patronymic of the manumittor is Γαδειος, and for the name Γαδεις Hebrew or Aramaic etymology can be proposed, see App. 3, II, 8. What is more interesting is that in this manumission, if the restoration is correct, the Jewish ethnicity of the freedmen is mentioned. It cannot be excluded that here we have a Jewish family that manumitted Jewish slaves.) It can be argued that the manumissions with obligations towards the Jewish community as a paramone could have been produced by Jewish sympathizers, God-fearers, as a benefaction to the Jewish community. On the whole, it seems prudent, for the sake of caution, not to divide these documents into Jewish and proselytes' manumissions. Recently the acts of enfranchisement from the Bosporan kingdom have been discussed by J.A. Harrill, The Manumission of Slaves in Early Christianity (Tübingen: J.C.B.Mohr [Paul Siebeck], 1995), 174-177. He argues that 'paramone obligations do seem to be part of the financial and/or legal arrangement by which Jews redeemed fellow Jews', 177, and rejects the possibility that 'paramone services were given in return for nothing', 177, n. 84). But if the manumittors were God-fearers it does not seem so unlikely. In this case the paramone services were given for 'something': friendly relations with the people who taught them to worship the true God.
[20]CIRB, Addenda 3.
[21]CIRB 64, App. 3, I, 1.
[22]CIRB 1316. The inscription was found in Rostov-on-the-Don and, as Latyshev supposed, had been brought here from the near-by Tanais Izvestiya Archeolog-icheskoj Komissii 14 (1905), 134, No. 55. If Latyshev's guess is correct, this is the earliest inscription from Tanais.

As mentioned before, the scale of involvement of the inhabitants of the city in the worship of the Most High God was unprecedented. Let us have a closer look at the evidence.

At present there are sixteen known inscriptions from the *thiasoi* of the adherents of the Most High God.[23] Fifteen of them are from Tanais. They date from AD 155 to the first half of the third century. Five of them are decorated with representations of eagles. Some of them commence with the formula Ἀγαθῇ τύχῃ. The inscriptions are mainly lists of the names of various officials (including the head of the *thiasos* with the title ἱερεύς, the father of the synodos, πατὴρ συνόδου, a promoter of goodness—(lit. 'lover of goodness'), φιλάγαθος, the director of the gymnasium, γυμνασιάρχης etc.) and ordinary members of the associations. A few lists have different headings. They belonged to εἰσποιητοὶ ἀδελφοὶ σεβόμενοι θεὸν ὕψιστον.[24] This formula was the closest epigraphic parallel to the σεβόμενοι τὸν θεόν in the book of Acts and was quite naturally attracted a great deal of attention to the inscriptions from Tanais. The most important article was written by E. Schürer nearly a hundred years ago but it still retains its significance.[25] His aphoristic conclusion about the nature of the cult in Tanais ('weder Judentum, noch Heidentum, sondern eine Neutralisirung beider')[26] became a kind of maxim, referred to in all subsequent publications.

What brought Schürer, who was the first to fully recognise the Jewish features of the worship of the Most High God,[27] to such a conclusion? First of all, the term ἱερεύς applied to the head of the *thiasoi* and the images of the eagles on the stones. He also considered the usage of the formula ὑπὸ Δία, Γῆν, Ἥλιον in the acts of enfranchisement from Gorgippia to be impossible in a purely Jewish context. E. Goodenough was not impressed by these considerations. In line with his general conception of Hellenistic Judaism he argued that all these fea-

---

[23]*CIRB* 1260, 1260a, 1261, 1277, 1278, 1279, 1280, 1281, 1282, 1283, 1284, 1285, 1286, 1287, 1289, 1231 (probably from Gorgippia). The number of these inscriptions would be greater if it were not for the bad preservation of some of the stones. Many of them lack the upper part with the heading where θεὸς ὕψιστος was usually named. There is also a considerable amount of material from recent excavations not yet published.

[24] *CIRB* 1281, 1283, 1285, 1286, Appendix 2, III, 3; 4.

[25]'Die Juden', 225.

[26]'Die Juden', 225.

[27]The Jewish colouring of the inscriptions was noted to by the first publishers. See, for instance, L. Stephani, 'Parerga archaeologica', *Mélanges greco-romains*, II (St.Petersburg, 1866), 203, but Schürer was the first to collect and to discuss in full all the relevant material.

tures fitted the Hellenistic Jewish pattern: there is nothing in these inscriptions alien to what we know of the practices of loyal Jews of the
period.[28] He referred to the eagles which decorated a number of the
synagogues of Palestine (Capernaum, Umm el-Kanatir, Khirbet Dubil,
Yafa) and were used as funerary monuments for Jews there.[29] He
showed that the word ἱερεύς was used in a Jewish milieu.[30] He gave
parallels for the use of the formula ὑπὸ Δία, Γῆν, Ἥλιον in manumissions of slaves, which showed that it had nothing to do with one's beliefs.[31] Nevertheless he quite reasonably hesitated to conclude that
members of the *thiasoi* were native Jews.[32] His verdict was that the *thiasoi* consisted of Jewish converts who 'may or may not have been circumcised' and 'who became fully Jewish in their point of view'. It is
impossible to say whether *thiasotai* thought themselves to be 'fully
Jewish' or how closely they related to the Jewish community, if they related at all.[33] The structure of the *thiasoi* was traditional for the Bosporan Kingdom and the titles of the officials were the same as in other
purely pagan associations.[34]

From the onomastic point of view, it does not seem that many
Jews were members of the associations.[35] Two names Ἀζαρίων and
Σαμβατίων, were identified as Jewish by Schürer.[36] The last one, derived from 'Sabbath' is especially interesting. V. Tcherikover demonstrated that this Jewish name gained popularity among Gentile Jewish
sympathizers in connection with their veneration of *festi sabbata*.[37] On

---

[28]Goodenough, 'The Bosporus Inscriptions', 223.
[29]Goodenough, 'The Bosporus Inscriptions', 230ff.
[30]Goodenough, 'The Bosporus Inscriptions', 226 ff.
[31]Goodenough, 'The Bosporus Inscriptions', 222f. Cf. also examples in Juster,
Juifs, 125 and S. Luria, *Antisemitism in the Ancient World* (Petrograd, 1922),
Addenda (Petrograd, 1923) 1, n. 21 *(in Russian).*
[32]The very fact that E. Goodenough considers such a possibility shows that he did
not realise what a proportion of the population was involved.
[33]So far the excavations have produced no material proving the existence of a
Jewish community and a synagogue building in Tanais. The presence of some
Jews in Tanais is supported by the onomastic data. The most convincing example
is a dipinto Ἰούδα on the amphora (first half of the third century). Among dipinti
on amphoras of the third century from Tanais there are also a few abbreviations of
the names that could possibly be Jewish. The Jewish names from the Bosporan
Kingdom are discussed in detail in I. Levinskaya, S. Tokhtas'ev, 'The Jewish
Names in the Bosporan Kingdom', *Acta Associationis internationalis. Terra Antiqua
Balcanica* (Serdica, 1991), 118-128 *(in Russian),* but the number of misprints in
linguistic arguments makes this publication invalid. For the list of the names see
SEG XLII (1992), No. 687.
[34]See list of the titles and inscriptions in *CIRB,* Index II.

the whole, nine bearers of this name are recorded in the Bosporan Kingdom and seven among them are members of the *thiasoi* of the Most High God.[38]

In my view, on the basis of the epigraphic data, the development of the veneration of the Most High God in the Bosporan Kingdom can be reconstructed as follows. The name θεὸς ὕψιστος was used by Jewish communities in their synagogue worship when they arrived in the Bosporan Kingdom. Their arrival roughly coincided with the destabilization of the ethno-cultural situation in the state, which made the population more amenable to religious change. From the very beginning, Jewish religious beliefs which were so much in line with the general tendency of the time, caused interest among the local population and attracted sympathizers. Some of these God-fearers showed their sympathy by following the Jewish example and manumitting their slaves in Jewish synagogues on condition that the freedmen would be attached to the synagogues. Evidently this move was encouraged by the Jewish community, which became a guarantor of these legal transactions. The freedmen joined and widened the circles of God-fearers connected with the synagogues. The social status of at least some of the God-fearers was quite high. This can be seen from the fact that in fourth century Panticapaeum, the Jewish prayer house was built by a highly-placed official.[39] In some parts of the Bosporan Kingdom the Jewish message gave rise to the development of religious associations

---

[35]It is inappropriate to make a judgment about someone's ethnicity on onomastic grounds. Jews in the Roman period preferred Greek and Latin names. 85 % of Jews buried in Rome and 73% in Teucheira (Cyrenaica) had Greek or Latin names (L.H. Kant, 'Jewish Inscriptions', 673, n. 7). Nevertheless even 85% is not 100%, and taking into consideration the number of names in inscriptions, it is reasonable, if Jews were members of these associations, to expect at least some to have Jewish names.

[36]As an alternative to Schürer's interpretation, an Iranian etymology has been suggested for the first name. See, for instance, M. Vasmer, Untersuchungen über die altesten Wohnsitze der Slaven, vol. 1 (Leipzig, 1923), 30; L. Zgusta, Die Personennamen griechischer Städte der nordlichen Schwarzmeerkuste (Praha, 1955), # 44. But the Jewish etymology looks much more convincing (see discussion in Levinskaya and Tohktas'ev, 'Jewish Names').

[37]V. Tcherikover, The Sambathions; CPJ III, 43-56. Later this name became popular also with Christians (J. Kajanto, Onomastic Studies in the Early Christian Inscriptions of Rome and Carthago (Helsinki, 1963) 106f.) partly due to tradition and partly because of the veneration of the Sabbath among some Christian groups. See, however, G. Mussies, 'Jewish Personal Names', 270-272, who insists that the popularity of the name among Egyptians can be understood only by assuming that in addition to its Hebrew meaning it acquired also a popular Egyptian etymology.

[38]CIRB 1231, 1278 (three different persons), 1279, 1280, 1282.

worshipping the Most High God within a structure traditional for the Gentile associations in the Bosporan Kingdom.[40] Though the form of veneration was Gentile, there is nothing in these inscriptions that contradicts Jewish monotheism or, as E. Goodenough puts it— 'practices of loyal Jews of the period'.[41]

In the book of Acts, the God-fearers were very receptive to the Christian message. It is interesting to look from this point of view at the Bosporan Kingdom. The documentary evidence for Christianity there dates back to the beginning of the fourth century.[42]

How should we interpret this fact? From a letter of Pliny we know that on the opposite side of the Black Sea, in Pontus, Christianity had established itself by the early second century.[43] It was reported by Hippolytus that the father of Marcion, who moved to Rome about 140, was bishop in Sinope.[44] The route into the Bosporan Kingdom from there was quite short. Scarcity of information may be of little significance when we consider how surprisingly little epigraphic evidence of Christianity before Constantine exists in Pontus. There are just 'a handful of Christian inscriptions'.[45] Did the early Christian communities in the Bosporus, if they existed, leave no epigraphic traces? Or was the situation quite different, with strong Jewish communities impeding the development of Christianity?[46] The latter assumption is not particularly probable in view of later developments. In the fourth century, for which there exists epigraphic evidence, we run into an inter-

---

[39]In the neighbouring city of Olbia the Jewish prayer house was repaired by the city's chief magistrates—ἄρχοντες (IPE I² 176)—a fact that seemed so unbelievable for many scholars in the past that they preferred to dismiss the meaning of proseuche as a Jewish prayer house (a preference which was epitomized in LSJ) rather than to accept that the city authorities supported Jews. Now after the Aphrodisias inscription, with its members of the city council involved with the synagogue, it does not sound so astonishing; see in detail Appendix 2.

[40]The association from Cilicia worshipping the god Sabbistes, i.e. as it was suggested, the god of Sabbath, could be a possible parallel for the religious associations of the God-fearers in Tanais (V. Tcherikover, 'The Sambathions', 84; Schürer, Vermes, Millar, Goodman, The History of the Jewish People, 3, 1, 161; L.H. Feldman, 'Proselytes and "Sympathizers"', 278).

[41]'The Bosporus Inscriptions', 233.

[42]Recently, during the excavations in Cytae, in a complex with an upper date of the third century AD, there was found a silver finger-ring with a cornelian with an engraved T-form cross and two fishes: V.A. Krshanovsky, 'The Excavations of the Necropolis of Kitei', Archaeological Researches in the Crimea (Simferopol: Tavria, 1994), 265, fig. on p. 264 (in Russian).

[43]Ep. 10.96.9.

[44]Epiphanius, Haer. 42,1.

[45]Mitchell, Anatolia, 37.

esting phenomenon. In one of the inscriptions from Hermonassa, which includes a list of names which is very badly preserved, we can nevertheless discern a word συνθειασεῖτ[αι] (members of the *thiasos*) in the fifth line, μετὰ τῶν ἁγίων in the second and a cross in the middle of the sixth.[47] It looks as if the early Bosporan Christians were following a pattern which had existed previously and forming *thiasoi* like the God-fearers worshipping the Most High God earlier.[48] In view of this, we cannot exclude the possibility that some of the members of the Christian communities in the Bosporan Kingdom were former members of the thiasoi of Theos Hypsistos. This would explain why they preserved the customary form of worship. S. Pines revealed the fact that in three Iranian languages (Pahlavi, New Persian and Sogdian) one of the names for Christians, *tarsakan*, was derived from the Iranian root with the meaning fear'.[49] He explains this by historical and semantic continuity between God-fearers and Christians:

> It is a vestige that testifies to the fact that, in countries in which Aramaic or an Iranian language were spoken, on the borders of the Parthian and Persian Empire or within it, the Christians, during a certain historical period, were identified with the God-fearers' in the technical sense of the term. This may have been due to the fact that many of them had formerly been, or were the sons of, God-fearers', or may else be explained by a certain similarity in customs. The designation of the Christians by the name *tarsakan* is, consequently, further proof of the strong connections which existed in the Iranian regions and in the eastern border-lands of the Roman Empire between primitive Christianity and the circles of the σεβόμενοι.[50]

Comparisons with *Hypsistarioi, Coelicolae, Theosebeis* and Massalians point in the same direction. All these groups were formed

---

[46]P.W. van der Horst, 'Jews and Christians in Aphrodisias', *Nederlands Theologisch Tijdschrift* 43:2 (1989), 113, argues that the strong Jewish presence sometimes thwarted the success of Christian propaganda. For further discussion see 123f.

[47]*CIRB* 1099.

[48]Nothing is known about the veneration of the Most High God or the existence of the Jewish community in this particular place. In one of the epitaphs of the first half of the first century AD, the patronymic Ὤνια (nom. Ὤνιας) was correctly defined as Jewish, V.V. Schkorpil, *Isvestiya Archeologicheskoj Komissii* 27 (1908) 68f., No. 6, (*in Russian*). The name of the deceased Βοθυλις could theoretically be a rendering of the biblical name Batu'el (LXX, Gen. 22:22: Βαθουηλ, Βαθουλ), but no occurrence of this name among Jews is known.

[49]"The Iranian Name for Christians and the 'God-Fearers'", *Proceedings of the Israel Academy of Sciences and Humanities*, 2 (1968), 143-152.

[50]Pines, 'The Iranian Name', 152.

by Gentiles and were under Jewish influence. In fact, the Messalians even called their places of worship by a Jewish term. And, as we know, at least some of these groups were at one stage or another connected with Christianity. The Coelicolae were condemned as Christian apostates and obliged by law to rejoin the Church.[51] The Messalians were the forerunners of the Christian sect with the same name. The father of Gregory of Nazianzus, a member of Hypsistarii, was readily converted by bishops on their way to the Council of Nicaea in 325, at which the bishop of Bosporus was also present. It is very exciting to imagine that he could be among this group of bishops. The previous religious experience of Gregory's father among the Hypsistarioi, who worshipped the Most High God, was good preparation for conversion to Christianity.

Finally, if we compare the spread of Christianity among the population of the Bosporan Kingdom with that of the nearby Chersonese, a striking dissimilarity comes to light, which can be explained by the presence of numerous God-fearers who prepared the way for Christianity in the former. In the Bosporus we know nothing about any clashes accompanying the conversion to the new religion, while in Chersonese, which retained the political and religious traditions of the ancient *polis* this transition was accompanied by serious public disturbances.[52] So much for the epigraphic traces of the God-fearers. Let us now have a brief look at the literary evidence.[53]

---

[51]On the influence of Judaism on Christians and on the blurring of the distinctions between Christian and Jewish groups in some parts of Asia Minor see van der Horst, *Jews and Christians*, 115f..

[52]The spread of Christianity along the nothern shore of the Black Sea is discussed in a number of works by P.D. Diatroptov: 'The Spread of Christianity in Chersonesus in the Fourth-Fifth Century', *Antichnaya Grazhdanskaya Obshchina* (Moscow, 1986), 127-150 (*in Russian*); 'The Spread of Christianity along the Northern Shore of the Black Sea', Synopsis of dissertation (Moscow, 1988), (*in Russian*).

[53]I shall refer only to a few, the most instructive of them. The full list and discussion can be found in Feldman, *Jew and Gentile*, 345ff., though not all of his interpretations seem to me to be acceptable; for instance, I think that there is no reference to the God-fearers in Petronius' fragment.

CHAPTER 7

GOD-FEARERS:
THE LITERARY EVIDENCE

This chapter is a review of some of the most instructive evidence for the God-fearers from Gentile literature, as well as a discussion of Luke's picture. Luke shows God-fearers to be the first among the Gentiles to accept Christianity. The responsiveness of the God-fearers to the Christian message posed a serious problem for Jews. Their status quo and a certain social stability which was secured by their links with the God-fearers, many of whom belonged to the upper class of the society, were put at risk. As a response to the Christian mission Jews intensified relations with their sympathizers. With very perceptive insight, Luke registered this turning point in Jewish relations with their well-disposed Gentile neighbours in his description of the events in Pisidian Antioch (Acts 13:50). It is not surprising that God-fearers play such an important rôle in Acts. As Luke showed, they were either the backbone of the Christian communities, or a serious impediment to the spread of the Christian mission. Both of these models of behaviour were repeated in the Christian history of the next centuries.

I. Non-Christian Literary Evidence

Following our examination of the epigraphic evidence for God-fearers, it is now time to consider briefly some relevant literary sources. The most famous example from the Gentile literature is beyond doubt a passage from Juvenal XIV. 96ff:

> *quidam sortiti metuentem sabbata patrem*
> *nil praeter nubes et coeli numen adorant,*
> *nec distare putant humana carne suillam*
> *qua pater abstinuit; mox et praeputia ponunt.*
> *Romanas autem soliti contemnere leges*
> *Iudaicum ediscunt et servant ac metuunt ius*
> *tradidit arcano quodcumque volumine Moyses.*
> *non monstrare vias eadem nisi sacra colenti,*
> *quaesitum ad fontem solos deducere verpos.*
> *Sed pater in causa, cui septima quaeque fuit lux*
> *ignava et partem vitae non attigit ullam.*

Some who have had a father who revere the Sabbath, worship nothing but the clouds, and the divinity of the heavens, and see no difference between eating swine's flesh, from which their father abstained, and that of man; and in time they take to circumcision. Having been wont to flout the laws of Rome, they learn and practice and revere the Jewish law, and all that Moses handed down in his secret tome, forbidding to point out the way to any not worshipping the same rites, and conducting none but the circumcised to the desired fountain. For all which the father was to blame, who gave up every seventh day to idleness, keeping it apart from all concerns of life.

(trans. G.G. Ramsay, *LCL*)

Discussion of this passage with reference to the God-fearers started with an article by J. Bernays[1] which developed the suggestion of J. Selden that *metuentes* here had the special meaning of 'Judaizers'. The discussion went along the traditional line, i.e. whether the word is used technically and can be compared with φοβούμενος in Acts and in later rabbinic usage.[2] But no matter what position one adopts in this debate[3]—and I think that Juvenal selected his words rather carefully

---

[1]'Die Gottesfürchtigen bei Juvenal', *Gesammelte Abhandlungen* 2, ed. H. Usener (1885), 71-80. Reprint Hildesheim: Georg Olms, 1971.
[2]See *supra* p. 54-55.
[3]See survey in Stern, *GLAJJ* II, 103f.

using a term which was sometimes used technically though it also had a general meaning—the sense of these verses is very straightforward: the sons of fathers who observe some Jewish practices and thus set their children a bad example, become proselytes. As satire is meant to be appealing (or at least understandable) to the general public, the figure of the God-fearer must have been recognizable.

Another classical example is found in Epictetus:

τί ὑποκρίνῃ Ἰουδαῖον ὢν ῞Ελλην; οὐχ ὁρᾷς, πῶς ἕκαστος λέγεται Ἰου-δαῖος, πῶς Σύρος, πῶς Αἰγύπτιος; καὶ ὅταν τινὰ ἐπαμφοτερίζοντα ἴδωμεν, εἰώθαμεν λέγειν· οὐκ ἔστιν Ἰουδαῖος, ἀλλ᾽ ὑποκρίνεται. ὅταν δ ἀναλάβῃ τὸ πάθος τὸ τοῦ βεβαμμένου καὶ ᾑρημένου, τότε καὶ ἔστι τῷ ὄντι καὶ κα-λεῖται Ἰουδαῖος.[4]

Why do you act the part of a Jew, when you are a Greek? Do you not see in what sense men are severally called Jew, Syrian, or Egyptian? For example, whenever we see a man halting between two faiths, we are in the habit of saying, 'He is not a Jew, he is only acting the part'. But when he adopts the attitude of mind of the man who has been baptized[5] and has made his choice, then he both is a Jew in fact and also is called one.

(trans. W.A. Oldfather, *LCL*).

Here a similar contrast is implied between God-fearers, who were not Jews but only imitated some features of the Jewish way of life, and proselytes, who actually became Jews. The expression εἰώθαμεν λέ-γειν shows that such behaviour was quite common.

As for Jewish literature, we have a number of remarks by Philo and Josephus[6] testifying that the Gentile world was attracted by Judaism and that many Gentiles developed sympathy towards it. Especially important is the passage from Josephus where he describes the wealth of the Temple, and notes that contributions to it were made by Jews throughout the world, and by the God-fearers from Asia and

[4]Epictetus cited by Arrianus, *Dissertationes* 2.9.19-20 = Stern, *GLAJJ*, I No. 254.
[5]This statement made some scholars believe that Epictetus confused Christians with Jews. See summary of the discussion in Stern, *GLAJJ* I, 543f. It also gave rise to a discussion on what was the ritual of initiation of the proselytes and whether circumcision was obligatory or whether baptism was the ultimate step. See, for instance, N.J. McEleney, 'Conversion'; J. Nolland, 'Uncircumcised Proselytes?' *JSJ* 12:2 (1981), 173-194.
[6]S.J.D. Cohen, 'Respect for Judaism by Gentiles According to Josephus', *HTR* 80:4 (1987), 416-419, counted as many as five instances in the *AJ* (3.217; 3.318-319; 20.34; 20.41; 20.195) and four in *BJ* (2.454; 2.463; 2.560; 7.45).

from Europe (σεβομένων τὸν θεόν, ἔτι δὲ καὶ τῶν ἀπὸ τῆς ᾽Ασίας καὶ τῆς Εὐρώπης) (*AJ* 14.110).[7]

In the talmudic period the rabbis started to determine the status of the God-fearers. The term they used is יראי שמים—'Heaven-fearers' where Heaven is a traditional substitute for God. The term however appears only in later writings and is not found in the Mishnah.[8] It seems to me that the use of the same term by rabbis and in the book of Acts cannot be explained as mere coincidence. The choice was made among a number of similar words expressing the same idea and loosely attached to a certain category within vague borders.

Following on from the review of this evidence for the God-fearers it is time to address the evidence in the book of Acts.

II. God-fearers in the Book of Acts

Luke devoted a substantial part of the book of Acts to the God-fearers. The whole of chapter 10 gives a paradigmatic description of a Gentile sympathizer with Judaism and, if we agree that σεβόμενοι, used attributively, is an abbreviation of, or an allusion to, the full formula σεβόμενοι (φοβούμενοι) τὸν θεόν, God-fearers are mentioned eight times in the book of Acts (13:16; 13:26; 13:43; 13:50; 16:14; 17:4; 17:17; 18:6-7).[9] The references to God-fearers cover a wide geographical area including Caesarea, Pisidian Antioch, Philippi, Thessalonica, Athens, and Corinth. In all these places the God-fearers are portrayed as having close relations with Jews and frequenting their synagogues. Thus, naturally, they were the first group among the Gentiles to hear the Christian message. On the whole, they showed themselves to be very receptive to it—but not always. Let us have a closer look at the episodes relating to the God-fearers in Acts.

---

[7]Lake suggested that σεβόμενοι in this sentence referred to Jews, because otherwise the definite article would have been used (*BC* V, 85). He was followed by L. Feldman, 'Jewish "Sympathizers"', 206f. But now the latter is convinced by one of R. Marcus's arguments and agreed that the passage could hardly have any logic without accepting the distinction between the Jews and the God-fearers (*Jew and Gentile*, 350). In his article Marcus ('Σεβόμενοι in Josephus', *JSS* 14 [1952], 247-250) also gave a parallel from Xenoph. *Anab.* I.7.2 for anarthrous mentioning of different groups.

[8]All relevant passages are collected and discussed in the articles by I. Levi ('Le proselytisme juif', *REJ* 50 (1905), 1-9; 51 (1906), 29-31) and F. Siegert ('Gottesfürchtige,' 110-127). See also Feldman, *Jew and Gentile*, 353-356.

[9]See the discussion of the change in Luke's terminology on pp. 52–3.

In the first one, Luke gives his most detailed description of a model God-fearer. Cornelius is pious, his piety being, in a very Jewish way, expressed as almsgiving and constant praying (10:2 ποιῶν ἐλεη-μοσύνας πολλὰς τῷ λαῷ καὶ δεόμενος τοῦ Θεοῦ διὰ παντός) and he enjoys a good reputation among Jews (10:22— μαρτυρούμενός τε ὑπὸ ὅλου τοῦ ἔθνους τῶν' Ἰουδαίων). Nevertheless, he is not a member of the Jewish community, and the Jewish Christians who came with Peter to Cornelius' house are astonished that Cornelius was qualified to receive the Holy Spirit (10:45). Though Cornelius is not the first Christian Gentile in Acts—earlier, in 8:27-39, Luke has given a detailed account of the conversion of the Ethiopian eunuch by Philip—it is from Cornelius' conversion thanks to Paul that the mission to the Gentiles began and that the news of Gentiles receiving the word of God reached the other apostles and Christians in Judea (11:1). It is the turning point of the book: from there Acts is the history of this mission. The importance of the event is marked by the repetition of the whole story in the next chapter, which is not a usual literary device for Luke, as it is only Paul's conversion that he retells several times. It is of no less importance that Cornelius[10] holds an official position: he is a centurion in the *Cohors Italica*[11] which means that he, like the magistrates from Aphrodisias, participated in the official cult. Thus, at the very beginning Luke takes as an example the most complicated case of a God-fearer who, because of his official duties and despite his belief in one God, has to demonstrate publicly his polytheism. On the one hand, Cornelius is accepted by God since he fears him and works righteousness (10:35); on the other, Cornelius is a Gentile in the true sense of the word: he is an idolater, participating in offerings to the pagan gods. This second facet of Cornelius' identity has important implications for the further development of the mission from the God-fearers to the Gentiles.

---

[10]This name became widely spread after P. Cornelius Sulla's liberation of 10,000 slaves in 82 BC. The use of the simple *nomen*, as C.J. Hemer, *The Book of Acts in the Setting of Hellenistic History*, ed. K. Gempf (Tübingen: Mohr-Siebeck, 1989, *Wissenschaftliche Untersuchungen zum Neuen Testament*, 49), 177, pointed out, is connected with 'an older Roman practice which persisted into the Julio-Claudian period among older and more conservatively minded men in the army'.

[11]The presence in Syria of the auxiliary *Cohors II Miliaria Italica Civium Romanorum Voluntariorum* in AD 69 is witnessed by inscriptions (Dessau *ILS* 9168, *CIL* 6.3528, 11.6117). It is doubtful, however, whether Roman troops could have been stationed in Caesarea in 41-44 AD, when Agrippa I was reigning over Judea. This means that either the conversion of Cornelius took place outside this time interval, or Luke is chronologically incorrect (see commentary *ad. loc.* by Bruce, Conzelmann, BC V, 427-445, Haenchen, Barrett).

The next time Luke mentions the God-fearers, it is to identify them in Paul's audience in the synagogue in Pisidian Antioch.[12] The success of Paul's preaching in Pisidian Antioch was tremendous: almost the whole city (σχεδὸν πᾶσα ἡ πόλις) came to the synagogue to hear the word of the Lord. It is here that for the first time the mission to the Gentiles is proclaimed as a recognized aim (13:46). Before Paul and Barnabas visited Pisidian Antioch, the evangelization of the Gentiles was accepted (not without serious hesitations, cf. ἄρα in 11:18, which gives the whole paragraph a hesitant, if not an interrogative sense)[13] as a part of God's plan of salvation, but not as a primary aim. It is also in Pisidian Antioch that Luke registered an event which was very important for the future development of the Christian mission: some of the God-fearers rejected the Christian message. Let us have a look at the episode in question.

> οἱ δὲ ᾿Ιουδαῖοι παρώτρυναν τὰς σεβομένας γυναῖκας τὰς εὐσχήμονας καὶ τοὺς πρώτους τῆς πόλεως, καὶ ἐπήγειραν διωγμὸν ἐπὶ τὸν Παῦλον καὶ Βαρνάβαν, καὶ ἐξέβαλον αὐτοὺς ἀπὸ τῶν ὁρίων αὐτῶν,

Acts 13:50.

> But the Jews incited the worshipping women of high standing and the leading men of the city and raised a persecution against Paul and Barnabas and drove them out of their borders.

The crucial word for understanding what had actually happened in Antioch is σεβόμεναι. Can we assume that the word here is used technically to designate God-fearers as σεβόμενοι (φοβούμενοι) τὸν θεόν is used in other contexts?[14] Or is it possible that these women were Jewish?

From epigraphic evidence it is known that the upper class of Antioch, a Roman colony founded by Augustus, were Roman citizens of Italian descent. Though that does not exclude them from being Jewish, on the whole it is unlikely that they were.[15] The supposition is also absurd from the logical point of view, because if these high-standing women were Jewish, this means that Jews incited the female part of the community, which somehow possessed a higher status than the male

---

[12]See Acts 13:16, 26.
[13]Barrett, *The Acts of the Apostles*, vol. 1, 543.
[14]Cf. Siegert, 'Gottesfürchtige', 137: 'σεβομένων ist nicht Abkürzung, aber Anspielung auf die Formel σεβ.τ.θ., die Lukas ja nicht jedesmal gebrauchen mußte'.
[15]Mitchell, *Anatolia*, v. 2, 8.

part, to initiate a persecution of Christian preachers.[16] It is clear that their piety was attached to Judaism, since it is impossible to imagine that Luke would call a pagan idolater by the term σεβόμενος, –η. So they could be either proselytes[17] or God-fearers. If they were proselytes, this means that at least some women who belonged to the upper class in Pisidian Antioch were full members of the Jewish community, and thus had cut themselves off from the traditional social life, which implied participation in public ceremonies and, inevitably, in pagan religious rituals. This seems very unlikely and would have been very exceptional, for in the whole first century we know of just a few, and not very reliable, examples of high-standing women who were probably proselytes. One such an example is reported by Josephus as a pretext for the expulsion of Jews from Rome.[18] According to Dio[19], Flavius Clemens, Domitian's first cousin and the *consul ordinarius* for AD 95, with his wife Flavia Domitilla, were accused of 'atheism and Jewish ways'.[20] It was impossible for them (especially for Clemens) to be proselytes,[21] since Clemens, being the supreme magistrate, could not avoid performing pagan rituals. What is quite probable is that both of them were God-fearers, like Julia Severa, who built a synagogue in Acmonia and at the same time was High Priestess of the imperial cult,[22] or Capitolina from Tralles, or Nero's consort Poppaea Sabina.[23] A loose link with fashionable Judaism was much more common, since such a link would cause no social complications (cf., for instance, Cornelius who, while he continued to be a Roman centurion could not become a proselyte). Historically it would be more sensible

---

[16]Cf. Wilcox, 'The God-Fearers', 110, who considers that these women are *probably* to be distinguished from 'the Jews', but then adds: 'There is nothing in the text to compel us to conclude that the women in question . . . were or were not Jews or proselytes'.

[17]So Haenchen, *The Acts of the Apostles*, 414. *Contra* Siegert, 'Gottesfürchtige', 139f., who considers that Acts 13:43 does not allow us to draw the conclusion that σεβόμενοι could be used as a designation for proselytes.

[18]*AJ* 18. 8. See above pp. 30-31.

[19]Dio Cassius 67.14.2

[20]See in detail p. 5ff.

[21]The tradition that Clemens and Domitilla were Christian martyrs, advocated by quite a number of scholars, is rather late (fourth century for Domitilla and eighth for Clemens) and must be rejected. See Leon, *Jews in Rome*, 34f., Smallwood, *The Jews under Roman Rule*, 381f.

[22]*MAMA* VI. 262 = *CIJ* 766. Julia Severa was related to the Galatian dynasty and connected with the influential Italian family of Turronii. One of the members of this family is mentioned in the same inscription as *archisynagogus*, the other was a priest of the imperial cult (Mitchell, *Anatolia*, vol. 2, 9).

to suppose that these high standing women from Pisidian Antioch were God-fearers. This is also more in accordance with Luke's usage of the word in other places.

The other places where σεβόμενοι is used attributively are 17:4 and 17:17. The first case describes the visit of Paul and Silas to the synagogue in Thessalonica. Paul preached for three sabbath days and, as a result, some Jews and many of the worshipping Gentiles and women of high standing, became Christians: καί τινες ἐξ αὐτῶν ἐπείσθησαν καὶ προσεκληρώθησαν τῷ Παύλῳ καὶ τῷ Σίλα, τῶν τε σεβομένων Ἑλλήνων πλῆθος πολύ, γυναικῶν τε τῶν πρώτων οὐκ ὀλίγαι.[24] Ἕλληνες here, as quite often in Jewish usage, means 'Gentiles'[25] which makes the meaning 'proselytes' to be very unlikely. Actually the word Ἕλληνες here is superfluous which is seen from Acts 17:17 where, in the synagogue in Athens, plain οἱ σεβόμενοι are opposed to Jews: διελέγετο (Paul) μὲν οὖν ἐν τῇ συναγωγῇ τοῖς Ἰουδαίοις καὶ τοῖς σεβομένοις. To sum up, it seems more in accordance with the historical setting of the first century and with Luke's usage if σεβόμενοι has the same meaning as the full formula.

If the word is used as a designation for Jewish sympathizers, the events in Pisidian Antioch acquire an important historical significance. Luke records, with the insight of a good historian, a turning point in Jewish relations with their well-disposed Gentile neighbours. The beginning of a Christian mission to the Gentiles posed a serious problem for Jews. Before then, in the course of centuries of living among the Gentiles, they had achieved (at least in Asia Minor)[26] a certain *status*

---

[23]See above, p. 64ff. Josephus reports that nearly all Damascene women were subject to Judaism (ὑπογμένας τῇ Ἰουδαικῇ θρησκείᾳ, BJ 2.560). It is evident that these women were not proselytes but God-fearers since they were married to the Gentiles and were separated from Jewish community; Cohen, 'Respect for Judaism', 417.

[24]Some manuscripts (P[74], A, D, lat, bo) read καί before Ἑλλήνων: 'a great crowd of the worshipping and of the Greeks'. This can be explained by the unusual collocation of σεβομένων Ἑλλήνων, which prompted several copyists to insert καί, Metzger, *A Textual Commentary*, 401. Wilcox 'The God-Fearers', 112 overestimates the quality of external attestation of this variant; it is inferior to the one without καί and easier to explain. For variants in the Western text see Metzger, *A Textual Commentary*, 401.

[25]Siegert, 'Gottesfürchtige', 138.

[26]It looks as if in Syria and in Egypt, especially in Alexandria, the situation was more complicated than in Asia Minor. Though we have some information about Jewish attempts to win sympathizers there (cf., for instance, Josephus' evidence for Antioch in BJ 7,45) the rivalry between Jews and the local population impeded the formation of a stratum of Jewish sympathizers around synagogues.

quo which was now suddenly being challenged. Christian preachers were aiming at, and gaining, success among people whose social links with the Jewish community secured Jewish life in the Gentile milieu. The Jewish community was forced to take measures to fight for influence over the God-fearers. As a response to the Christian mission, the Jews intensified relations with their sympathizers. M. Goodman found 'evidence of a Jewish mission to win gentile sympathizers in the first century'. He also noted that 'the intensity of this mission varied from place to place and period to period'.[27] In describing the events in Pisidian Antioch, Luke marked the starting point of this intensification—Christian mission to the God-fearers.

It is not at all surprising that the Jews had greater success among the God-fearers with whom they had enjoyed good relations for some time, than did the Christian newcomers unless the latter were supported by direct intervention from God, as in the case of Cornelius. A.T. Kraabel has rather sarcastically remarked that 'the God-fearers are on the stage as needed, off the stage after they have served their purpose in the plot' and explained this 'disappearance of the God-fearers' from the pages of Acts in terms of Luke's theological scheme.[28]

The God-fearers definitely played an important rôle in Luke's theology. But their 'disappearance' is justified not by the theological, but by the historical setting. If the Jewish community in a particular place decided to put a stop to the Christian mission, it was by far the easiest way to do so by using their influence on the God-fearers, among whom there were socially high-ranking and influential people. Consequently God-fearers, in places where these happened, ceased to be responsive to the Christian message and the missionaries found that those Gentiles who were not connected with the synagogues were easier to approach. The more widespread Christian teaching became, the more actively Jews looked for the support of Jewish sympathizers. In his picture of the events in Pisidian Antioch, Luke revealed a tendency which was to play an important rôle in spreading Christianity in the next few centuries.

Let us examine the impact on the spread of Christianity in the first centuries AD, and of the Jewish 'mission' to win the God-fearers, the beginning of which was registered by Luke in the episode in Pisidian Antioch. In an article devoted to the Jews and Christians in Aphrodisias, P.W. van der Horst paid attention to an instructive

---

[27]*Mission and Conversion*, 87.
[28]Kraabel, 'The Disappearance of the 'God-fearers'', 120.

phenomenon. While in all districts of western Asia Minor Christian presence is attested either by literary or epigraphic testimonia[29] no later than the third century AD, and sometimes as early as the first, in the district of Caria of which Aphrodisias was the capital, the earliest testimonies are from 325 or even later.[30] He explains this as follows:

> Although it must remain somewhat speculative, there can hardly be serious doubts that the late appearance and success of Christianity in the province of Caria and its capital Aphrodisias is due to the very strong position Judaism had built up there in cooperation with the gentiles.[31]

The Aphrodisias inscription shows how close were relations between members of the city council and the local community. These close relations seem to have been a response of the Jews to Christian missionary activity. Goodman argued that the change of Jewish attitude towards God-fearers took place about the time the inscription was written,[32] but Luke's account of the events in Pisidian Antioch shows that this change had happened much earlier. Jews had no chance to wait till the third century; the threat of Christianity to the social stability of their communities demanded an immediate answer.

Thus it is no surprise that God-fearers were such an important issue for Luke, the historian. They could be (and actually were) either the backbone of the Gentile Christian communities or the greatest impediment to the spread of the Christian mission. Which way they chose to adopt depended upon the reaction of Jewish communities to Christian propaganda. Luke presents examples of both models of their behaviour and, as the future history of Christianity revealed, both models were realized.

---

[29]For an amazing contrast of epigraphic and literary evidence about the spread of early Christianity in parts of west and south-west Asia Minor and in inland regions of northern Isauria, Lycaonia, and Phrygia see *supra* p. 57.
[30]'Jews and Christians', 113.
[31]*Mission and Conversion*, 119f.
[32]*Mission and Conversion*, 47. Cf. p. 78, n. 107.

CHAPTER 8

ANTIOCH

The importance of the city of Antioch and of the Jewish community there during the first century AD is very clear from the book of Acts. Other evidence for Antiochian Jews in this period is limited. This chapter discusses all the known evidence from all periods of the Graeco-Roman world in the belief that it gives a context in which to understand better the references to it in Acts: in particular, the description of Malalas of disturbances in Antioch under Gaius is assessed for its historical value, and the considerable debate over the size of the community is also presented.

According to Josephus, the largest concentration of Jewish people lived in Syria because of its proximity to Judaea, and most were congregated in Antioch.[1] He claims that the Jewish community in Antioch went back to the foundation of the city by Seleucus I Nicator.[2]

As to the political status of the Antiochene Jews, Josephus supplies us with at least two versions in three passages. In one of the relevant passages he reports that Jews received honours from the Asian kings when they served with them in war. As an example of such honours Josephus refers to Seleucus I who granted Jews citizenship (πολιτεία) in the cities which he founded both in Syria and in Asia Minor; they still enjoyed this status in his time.[3] The other runs as follows: 'Our Jewish residents in Antioch are called Antiochenes, having been granted rights of citizenship by its founder, Seleucus'.[4] In the third he claims that citizen rights on a par with those of the Greeks were granted to Jews by the successors of Antiochus Epiphanes.[5] Some scholars who have tackled this issue have attempted to resolve the contradiction[6] by proposing that only certain Jews, such as for instance ex-soldiers, were enrolled in the citizen lists from the foundation of the city,[7] while from the middle of the second century BC Jews were organized as a separate community (πολίτευμα) within each their *polis*.[8] Others

---

[1]*BJ* 7.43. On the official administrative position of Antioch, see R. Tracey, 'Syria', *The Book of Acts in Its Graeco-Roman Setting*, eds. B.W. Winter & A.D. Clarke (Grand Rapids, Carlisle: Eerdmans, Paternoster, 1994), 237ff.

[2]*AJ* 12. 119.

[3]*AJ* 12. 119.

[4]*Contra Ap.* 2.39 (trans. H.St.J. Thackeray, *LCL*).

[5]*BJ* 7. 44.

[6]But cf. A. Kasher, *The Jews in Hellenistic and Roman Egypt*, (Tübingen: Mohr-Siebeck, 1985), 298f., who thinks that there is no contradiction between Josephus' passages at all.

[7]This interpretation seems to be supported by the first of the Josephus' passages mentioned above (*AJ* 12.119), which quite possibly does not imply more than that Jewish mercenaries got citizenship rights upon discharge.

[8]C.H. Kraeling, 'The Jewish Community at Antioch', *JBL* 51 (1932), 137f.; G. Downey, *A History of Antioch in Syria from Seleucus to the Arab Conquest* (Princeton: Princeton University Press, 1961), 80; cf. the more sceptical view of R. Marcus (Josephus, vol. VII, *LCL*, Appendix C), who thinks that the attribution by Josephus of pro-Jewish enactments to the founders of the Ptolemaic and Seleucid dynasties is an apologetic motif, and that it is very improbable that the Jewish communities were granted either citizenship rights or any kind of privileges before the time of Antiochus III; the same sceptical attitude towards Josephus' assertion is shared by J.M.C. Barclay, *Jews in the Mediterranean Diaspora from Alexander to Trajan (323 BCE - 117 CE)*, (Edinburgh: T & T Clark, 1996), 245, n. 29.

saw in Josephus' statement a hint that citizen rights were curtailed by Antiochus Epiphanes IV and restored by his successors.[9]

But despite disagreement over the dating of the citizen rights of Jews in Antioch, until recently no one questioned the common assumption that Jews in Antioch and in other Diaspora cities were organized as a πολίτευμα within the larger community.[10] Then in 1994, Lüderitz issued a warning that

> one has to reckon with the possibility that the Jewish *politeuma* in the two inscriptions from Berenice is a local peculiarity of the Jewish Diaspora in Cyrenaica. This might explain why the term is not really attested outside Cyrenaica, and why it is not mentioned in Josephus or other ancient authors in connection with the Jewish Diaspora in contrast with the considerable career the term *'politeuma'* has had in the modern historiography of the Diaspora.[11]

However, no matter what the legal status of the community was, it is clear that, at some date during Seleucid rule, Jews in Antioch were given the official privilege of living in accordance with their laws and of following their mode of worship. Josephus reports on one such privilege, which he attributes to Seleucus Nicator: 'those Jews who were unwilling to use foreign oil should receive a fixed sum of money from the gymnasiarchs to pay for their own kind of oil'.[12] In AD 70, the pagan

---

[9]Schürer, Vermes, Millar, Goodman, *The History of Jewish People*, 3, 1, 127; W.A. Meeks, R.L. Wilken, *Jews and Christians in Antioch in the First Four Centuries of the Common Era*, (Missoula: Scholars Press, 1978, SBLSBS, 13), 3.

[10]See, *e.g.* Kraeling, 'The Jewish Community', 138; Downey, 'A History of Antioch', 107; Meeks, Wilken, *Jews and Christians*, 2; 'The Jewish Diaspora', *CRINT, section 1. The Jewish People in the First Century*, I (Assen, 1974),138.

[11]G. Lüderitz, 'What is Politeuma?', *Studies in Early Jewish Epigraphy*, eds. J.W. van Henten, P.W. van der Horst, (Leiden, New York, Köln: Brill, 1994, Arbeiten zur Geschichte des antiken Judentums, 21), 222; cf. now also the remark by Barclay, *Jews*, 245, n. 30, that 'there is, in any case, no evidence that the Jews in Antioch were constituted as a *politeuma'*.

[12]*AJ* 12.120 (trans. R. Marcus, *LCL*). On kosher olive oil in general see M. Goodman, 'Kosher Olive Oil in Antiquity', *A Tribute to Geza Vermes*, eds. P.R. Davies, R.T. White (Sheffield: JSOT Press, 1990), 227-245. Goodman thinks that Josephus ascribes this privilege to an earlier period than it was actually granted and follows Marcus in assuming that it was Antiochus III who was responsible for Jewish privileges in Syria, 228f. Barclay, *Jews*, 256f., n. 63, also views the date given by Josephus as implausible, and considers Josephus to obscure the issue by generalizing it, since this privilege concerned only those Jews who were training in gymnasia. His main argument is that the gymnasiarchs were unlikely to have had a monopoly over the complete oil supply in such a large city as Antioch. But note the different view taken by Kasher, *The Jews*, 303f.

population of Antioch presented a petition to Titus with a request to remove Jewish privileges which were inscribed on bronze tablets. They failed to secure his approval.[13]

It seems that, on the whole, under Hellenistic kings the Jewish community grew considerably and became quite prosperous. Tensions between Jews and other inhabitants of Syria started in the time of Antiochus Epiphanes and continued in the following period of warfare in Palestine. The expansion of Jewish power and such actions as the destruction of pagan temples[14] or the deportation of the whole population of cities,[15] gave rise to ill-feelings towards Jews among the Gentile population.[16] It is reasonable to suppose that the transportation to Antioch of Jewish prisoners would not contribute to the popularity to local Jews.[17] But, apart from general considerations, we know nothing about the particularities of Jewish—Gentile tensions in Antioch. The successors of Antiochus Epiphanes, as Josephus testifies, were favourable to Jews:

> For, although Antiochus surnamed Epiphanes sacked Jerusalem and plundered the temple, his successors on the throne restored to the Jews of Antioch all such votive offerings as were made of brass, to be laid up in their synagogue, and, moreover, granted them citizen rights on an equality with the Greeks.[18]

On the other hand, the action of Demetrius II could hardly have added a peaceful note to Jewish-Gentile relations. Demetrius, after he ordered discharged native troops to be disarmed by his Cretan mercenaries, which began a kind of civil war in Antioch, appealed for help to his ally, the Jewish leader, Jonathan. Jewish soldiers numbering about three thousand put down an insurrection of the Antiochenes, killed one hundred thousand Antiochenes (according to I Maccabees) and burned much of the city.[19]

When Syria became a Roman province, the status of the Jews was not changed and their privileges were secured.[20] But the third year of

---

[13]*BJ* 7.110.
[14]1 Macc. 5:68; 10:82-85; 13:47-48; *AJ* 13. 356-364.
[15]1 Macc. 13:11.
[16]See the examples of growing tension and of 'ideological warfare' between Jews and Greeks in Syria in Barclay, *Jews*, 248.
[17] Kraeling, 'The Jewish Community', 146.
[18]*BJ* 7.44-45 (trans. H.St.J. Thackeray, *LCL*).
[19]*AJ* 13.135-142.
[20]Kraeling, 'The Jewish Community', 139.

Caligula's reign (AD 40) was marked by an outburst of anti-Jewish violence. The only literary source for information concerning the events in Antioch, the sixth century *Chronicle* of Malalas is, sadly, not reliable for this period.[21] Malalas reports a Jewish pogrom in Antioch, which had started with the clash of the two circus factions, the Green and the Blue.[22] In the theatre, in the presence of the consular governor, the Blue faction chanted insults against the Greens. Then Malalas' story runs as follows:

> There followed a great faction riot and disaster fell on the city. For the Hellenes of Antioch fought with the Jews there in a faction brawl, killed many Jews and burnt their synagogues. When the priest of the Jews in Palestine, named Phineas, heard of this, he collected a large number of Jews and Galileans who were citizens. With about 30,000 of these[23] he came suddenly to the city of Antiochos from the city of Tiberias and killed many there, for he made a single unexpected attack with armed men. Then Phineas broke off the attack and returned to Tiberias. When the emperor Gaius learnt of these events he was angry with Pontous and Varius, the senators in the city of Antioch; he requisitioned the houses in Antioch that belonged to them. These houses were called 'the Imperial Houses' in Antioch in Syria from that time. The senators themselves were led away in chains, since they neither put an end to the riot in the city, nor did they resist the priest Phineas when he was ravaging the city. Gaius sent to the city of Tiberias in Palestine, captured Phineas the priest of the Jews and be-

---

[21]For the discussion of Malalas' sources and the evaluation of his usage of them see E. Jeffreys, 'Malalas' sources', *Studies in Malalas* (Sydney: Australian Association for Byzantine Studies, 1990, Byzantina Australiensia, 6), 167-216.

[22]Downey, *A History of Antioch*, 194, refers to the similar disorders in Alexandria in connection with athletic games and festivals, in which Jews took part. Malalas also described clashes between the Greens and the Blues in the reign of Zeno, in which Jews were involved. The Greens murdered Jews ('sparing no one', as Malalas notes) who supported the Blues (the faction which was traditionally viewed as representing the interests of the government, for a different view see A. Cameron, *Circus Factions: Blues and Greens at Rome and Byzantium* (Oxford: Clarendon Press, 1976), 97) and plundered and burned the synagogue called Asabiani (Malalas, *Chronographia*, 15.15 (389-390 Dindorf); a longer account of the events is preserved in the *Excerpta de insidiis*, 35 (166-167 de Boor) and the fullest in the Slavonic version); cf. Downey, *A History of Antioch*, 498f. and n. 120, for the explanation for the name of the synagogue. The connection of Jews with the Blues has been questioned by Cameron, *Circus Factions*, 149f., but graffiti from Aphrodisias and evidence at Tyre seem to confirm this connection, Reynolds and Tannenbaum, *Jews and God-Fearers*, 132.

[23]In the Slavonic version the figure is 230,000.

headed him as a rebel; he also put many Jews and Galileans to death. He put the head of the priest Phineas on a pole outside the city of Antioch, on the other side of the river Orontes. He sent money and reconstructed the areas of the city that had been burnt.[24]

Although fantastic details of Malalas' narrative, such as the retaliatory expedition led by the high priest Phineas, make his story unlikely in the extreme, the fact of a disturbance at that time is plausible. It coincides with the time when Caligula decreed that his statue be erected in the Jerusalem Temple. It is quite probable that a protest against this project began at Antioch, which was the residence of the governor of Syria who was responsible for carrying out the decree. When Claudius in AD 41 ordered the cessation of pogroms in Egypt, a copy of his proclamation was sent to Antioch, and this can be interpreted as proof of the existence in Antioch of a situation similar to that in Egypt.[25]

The period of tranquillity after the events of AD 40 was very short. The next crisis in Syria began with the outbreak of the great revolt of AD 66-70. Throughout the whole of Syria, with the exception of Antioch, Sidon and Apamea, Jews were killed and imprisoned.[26] However, this fortunate exception did not last long for the Antiochene Jews. Soon after the arrival of Vespasian in Syria in AD 67 they were accused by a certain apostate named Antiochus. He was the son of the ἄρχων of the Jewish community and was for this reason highly respected. He alleged they had plotted to burn Antioch to the ground in one night. After his disclosure, a pogrom and religious persecution of Jews commenced. Several foreign Jews who were named by Antiochus as participants in the conspiracy were burned to death on the spot. On the advice of the same Antiochus, Jews were required to bring sacrifices to pagan gods. Failure to do so would implicate them in the conspiracy. All recalcitrants were to be executed.[27] When in AD 70 a great fire

---

[24]Malalas, *Chronographia* 10.20 (244-246 Dindorf); trans. E. Jeffreys, M. Jeffreys and R. Scott, *Byzantina Australiensia* 4 (1986), 130.

[25]Kraeling, 'The Jewish Community', 148; Downey, *A History of Antioch*, 192ff.; Meeks, Wilken, *Jews and Christians*, 4. Downey suggests that the disturbances at Alexandria and Antioch would have been provoked by the Christian missionaries. His point was developed for Antioch by Taylor, 'Why were the Disciples', 88-94, who argues that the name Christians, which was synonymous with sedition and crime, was given to the disciples by the Roman authorities at Antioch towards the end of Gaius' reign when they by their Messianic preaching provoked the revolutionary and nationalistic commotion among Jewish population. On the name 'Christian', see p. 88 n. 50.

[26]*BJ* 2. 462-463, 479.

[27]*BJ* 7. 46-52.

occurred in Antioch and destroyed some public buildings, including magistrates' quarters, the Law-courts and the record-office, the same Antiochus again accused Jews of the deed. The following pogrom was even more violent than the previous one had been.[28] The Jews were only saved by the intervention of the legate, Gnaeus Pompeius Collega, who had been left in charge until the arrival of the new governor, Gaius Caesennius Paetus. The legate cleared the Jews after an investigation. But it was only after the arrival of Titus who refused to sanction both the expulsion of the Jews and the revocation of their citizenship privileges, that the imminent danger to the Jewish community's very existence in Antioch was removed.[29] However, according to Malalas, this was not a total Jewish triumph, as Josephus tries to make us believe. At the same time the emperor fixed several bronze figures of Cherubim, which were possibly taken from the Jerusalem Temple, outside the city gate as a reminder of the fall of Jerusalem. On the site of the Jewish synagogue in Daphne, a famous suburb of Antioch, a theatre was built with the inscription 'from the spoils of Judaea' (*Ex praeda Iudaea*).[30]

There is little else known about the life of the Jewish community until the time of Constantine. It seems that during this obscure period the legal status of Antiochian Jews remained the same, although their civic standing was substantially lowered.[31] Gradually recovering from the disasters they suffered in the first century, in the better documented post-Constantine period Jews seem to have played an important role in the life of Antioch.[32]

Not much is known about the inner structure of the Antiochian Jewish community. From Josephus' account of the events of AD 67 we know that the title of a chief official was ἄρχων. All other references are much later. A fourth century letter by Libanius mentions 'the chief of their officials' (τὸν τῶν ἀρχόντων τῶν παρ᾽ αὐτοῖς ἄρχοντα).[33] Chrysostom refers to ἄρχοντες, προστάται and πατριάρχαι and calls the organi-

---

[28]Kraeling, 'The Jewish Community', 150f. considers that actually there was only one outbreak of violence at Antioch, and that Josephus gives 'two different accounts of one and the same series of events'. See arguments against his theory in Downey, *A History of Antioch*, 586f. Downey's defence of Josephus' version of events is accepted by Meeks, Wilken, 4f., 38, n. 13.
[29]*BJ* 7.54-60; 100-111.
[30]Malalas, *Chronographia*, 10.45 (260-1, Dindorf).
[31]Kraeling, 'The Jewish Community', 152ff.
[32]Kraeling, 'The Jewish Community', 13f.; Meeks, Wilken, *Jews and Christians*, 6.
[33]*Ep.* 1251. For the discussion of the meaning of this title see Meeks, Wilken, *Jews and Christians*, 7f.

zation of the community a πολιτεία.[34] He also speaks of a Jewish court of law[35] and perhaps of a Jewish hospital.[36] From two dedicatory inscriptions on the mosaic floor of the synagogue in Apamea, which was built in AD 391 and shortly afterwards destroyed, we know that the mosaic entry-way was donated by the ἀρχισυνάγωγος of the Antiochian Jewish community who was related through marriage to the Apamean community.[37] He was a descendant of the Antiochian γερουσιάρχης (the head of the Council of Elders in Antioch), whose burial chamber was uncovered in Beth She'arim in Galilee.[38]

As is the usual case, estimates of the size of the community are very unreliable.[39] Kraeling's figures of forty-five thousand in the time of Augustus and sixty-five thousand for the fourth century[40] seem to be too high. Meeks' and Wilken's estimate of twenty-two thousand looks more truthworthy though it is far from being precise.[41]

The number of synagogues in Antioch is unknown. Archaeological evidence is non-existent.[42] From Josephus we know of at least one that stood in Seleucid times.[43] There is no doubt that in the Roman period there existed more than one.[44] There was also a synagogue in Daphne[45] which, according to Malalas, was the one destroyed in the reign of Vespasian and replaced by a theatre.[46] But in the fourth centu-

---

[34]Chrysostom, Adv. Iud. 5.3; 6.5; 1.3. See Kraeling, 'The Jewish Community', 137.
[35]Adv. Iud. 1. 3; cf. P.T. Sanhedrin, III, 21a.
[36]Adv. Iud. 8. 6.
[37]CIJ I, 803, 804 = Lifshitz, DF 38, 39 = Meeks, Wilken, 53f., No. 1, 2.
[38]M. Schwabe, B. Lifshitz, Beth She'arim. Vol. 2: The Greek Inscriptions (New Brunswick: Rutgers University Press, 1974), 141f., No. 141.
[39]See p. 23, n.19.
[40]The Greek Inscriptions, 136.
[41]The Greek Inscriptions, 8. Being well aware of this fact, they comment on their own calculations as follows: 'Obviously the margin of error in such guesswork is enormous'.
[42]Meeks, Wilken, Jews and Christians, 8 and 39, n. 32.
[43]BJ 7.44.
[44]Meeks, Wilken, Jews and Christians, 8f.
[45]The Jewish settlement near Daphne existed at least in 170 BC, since the former Jewish high Priest Onias III took refuge in the sacred precincts of the pagan sanctuary of Daphne (perhaps the temple of Apollo), which suggests that he lived in or near Daphne, 2 Macc 4:33-34; Kraeling, 'The Jewish Community', 24, 140f.; Downey, A History of Antioch, 109f.
[46]Chronographia, 10.45 (261 Dindorf), see in more detail above. Downey (A History of Antioch, , 206f., n. 28) noted that Kraeling 'by a slip of the pen' wrote that the synagogue was destroyed 'in the days of Tiberius'. An even more unfortunate slip occurred in Meeks and Wilken, Jews and Christians, 9: 'At least since Tiberius there was a synagogue in Daphne', with a reference to the same passage in Malalas.

ry, besides synagogues in Antioch herself, Chrysostom also mentioned synagogues outside the city, the one in Daphne that presumably replaced the destroyed building, being among them.[47]

Josephus, in one of his accounts of the Antiochian Jewish community, specially noted that local Jews

> were constantly attracting to their religious ceremonies multitudes of Greeks (πολὺ πλῆθος Ἑλλήνων), and these they had in some measure incorporated with themselves (κἀκείνους τρόπῳ τινὶ μοῖραν αὐτῶν πεποίητο).[48]

It is instructive that the only one proselyte who is mentioned by name in the book of Acts is Nicolas described as a native of Antioch (Acts 6:5). But on the whole the wording of Josephus points more in the direction of God-fearers than proselytes. The intensive Jewish religious influence on the Antiochene Gentiles seemed to create a substantial stratum of these sympathetic Gentiles.[49] Josephus' remark fits well, on the one hand, with Luke's description of Antioch as the starting point of preaching the gospel among Gentiles and, on the other, it shows that the fourth century's 'fatal attraction' of Judaism for Christians in Antioch had a long tradition and was deeply rooted in the pre-Christian period.[50]

---

[47]*Adv. Iud.* I.6; 5.ult. (PG XLVIII, 96).

[48]*BJ* 7.45 (trans. H.St.J. Thackeray, *LCL*).

[49]Cf. Barclay, *Jews,* 254, who stresses the importance in the analysis of Jewish-Gentile relations of positing distinctions between social levels; for the attractiveness of Judaism for Gentiles who belonged to the higher echelon of the society see pp. 65–6.

[50]See pp. 101–2.

CHAPTER 9

ASIA MINOR

Asia Minor as a region, and specific cities therein, provide the main stage on which the events of the Book of Acts are played out. For each city, respectively Ephesus, Miletus, Pisidian Antioch, and Iconium, all known evidence about Jewish communities has been discussed in order to illuminate what is said about it in Acts. For the region as a whole, discussion focusses on the documents of the Roman period concerned with the privileges conferred on the Diaspora community by the Romans and their attitudes towards the Jews.

137

I. Introduction

In the Hellenistic and Roman periods Asia Minor had a substantial Jewish population. Philo said that Jews inhabited every city of Asia in large numbers.[1] When Jews first settled there is not clear. Clearchus, Aristoteles' disciple, reports that his teacher met an educated Hellenized Jew from Coele-Syria[2] who was travelling from the interior of Asia Minor to the coast,[3] but this does not necessarily imply the presence of Jewish settlers in this part of the world. Perhaps there was a Jewish community in Sardis in the Persian period.[4]

The massive influx of a Jewish population into Asia Minor took place at the end of the third century BC, when Antiochus III settled two thousand Jewish families from Mesopotamia and Babylonia in Lydia and Phrygia,[5] in order to maintain the security of his hold over this region. This information is preserved by Josephus, who quoted to this end the letter of Antiochus III to his governor Zeuxis.[6] In the same letter the Jewish settlers were granted the right to follow their own laws (νόμοις αὐτοὺς χρήσεσθαι τοῖς ἰδίοις), to get land for homes and farming, to receive exemptions from tax for their harvest for a period of ten years and to secure as much grain as was needed to feed their servants

---

[1]*Legatio* 245. The meaning of the term 'Asia' in Philo is not absolutely clear, cf. *Legatio* 282, where Philo's usage of 'Pamphilia' and 'Cilicia' would suggest that he could be using 'Asia' as a designation of the Roman province, while the next part of the sentence τὰ πολλὰ τῆς᾽ Ἀσίας ἄχρι Βιθυνίας καὶ τῶν τοῦ Πόντου μυχῶν would rather suggest that at least most of Pontus was being covered by the term 'Asia' (contrast Trebilco, 'Asia', *The Book of Acts in Its Graeco-Roman Setting*, 301, n. 38, who assumes that this is clear evidence of Philo's usage of the word in the sense of the Roman province).

[2]A very vague geographical term, used mostly of the southern area surrounding Mount Lebanon and Anti-Lebanon, but also of the region south of Damascus and east of Jordan, and of Palestine and Transjordania together (R. Marcus, note on *AJ* 11.25, *LCL*). Septimius Severus 'with remarkable perversity', as F. Millar comments, *The Roman Near East* (Cambridge, Mass., London: Harvard University Press, 1994), 423, chose it as the official name for the *northern* part of Syria when it was divided into two provinces.

[3]Clearchus quoted by Josephus, *C. Ap.* 1.22 (176-182) = *GLAJJ* I No. 15.

[4]M. Stern, 'The Jewish Diaspora', *CRINT*, I, 143; Kraabel, ' "Ὕψιστος and the Synagogue at Sardis', 81.

[5]Romans divided the territory of Phrygia between two provinces: in Asia (the main part) and Galatia changes of the borders were made several times during the Roman period.

[6]Josephus, *AJ* 12.149-150. See literature on the discussion of the authenticity of the letter of Antiochus III in Schürer, Vermes, Millar, Goodman, *The History of the Jewish People*, 3, 1, 17, n. 33; add Trebilco, *Jewish Communities*, 5f. to the list.

until they could get their own harvest. But on the whole it must be admitted that very little is known about actual status of the Jews, and the existence of any Jewish 'charter' is somewhat doubtful.[7]

The coming of Roman control to the region, and the creation of the Roman province of Asia between 129 and 126 BC,[8] seem not to have affected the status of Jewish communities. We do know that it was the Romans' standard policy to retain the *status quo* in the newly acquired territories. There is nothing to suggest that they deviated from it in this new province.

Direct documentary evidence for Jewish rights and privileges in Asia exists only from c. 50 BC. Most of it is preserved in Josephus.[9] The documents in question have been the subject of more than two centuries of discussion,[10] in the course of which their authenticity has been both questioned and confirmed several times.[11] What has emerged from these discussions is confirmation of the fact that the formal features of the documents are correct for their genre and the period,[12] but does this fact make it 'very difficult to conceive of them as forgeries', as Rajak thinks?[13] Do we not have to agree with Moehring that 'any forger would be careful to imitate the proper form as exactly as possi-

---

[7]Rajak, 'Was there a Roman Charter?', 108.

[8]On the history of the province of Asia and the range of meanings of the term in Acts, see Trebilco, 'Asia', 292-302.

[9] *AJ* 14.185-267; 16.160-178. See the discussion on the authenticity of the documents and literature in Trebilco, *The Jewish Communities*, 7f.

[10]See E.J. Bickerman, 'Les privilèges juives', *Mélanges Isidore Levi*, 1953 (Bruxelles: Secretariat des Editions de l'Institut, 1955, Annuaire de l'Institute de Philologie et d'Histoire Orientales et Slaves XIII), 11-34, who provides a exhaustive survey of the early period of the discussion. He showed that the motivations which stood behind the decisions concerning the authenticity of the documents were mainly theological. Cf. also the helpful summary of his article in H.R. Moehring, 'The *Acta Pro Judaeis* in the *Antiquities* of Flavius Josephus. A Study in Hellenistic and Modern Apologetic Historiography', *Christianity, Judaism and Other Graeco-Roman Cults: Studies for Morton Smith at Sixty*, ed. J. Neusner, Part 3 (Leiden: Brill, 1975, SJLA, 12), 126-128.

[11]The latest sceptical treatment of these documents belongs to Moehring, 'The *Acta Pro Iudaeis*', 124-158.

[12]Smallwood, *The Jews under Roman Rule*, App. B, 588. Cf. Moehring, 'The *Acta Pro Iudaeis*', 149, who concludes that the style and language of some documents vary significantly from the standard which emerged from epigraphic evidence and that on this ground their authenticity must be seriously doubted. His own table of correspondence between Josephus' *senatus consulta* and epigraphic evidence (p. 143f.) seems to testify otherwise.

[13]Rajak, 'Was there a Roman Charter?', 109.

ble'?[14] On the other hand, I would not dismiss as mere bluff the invitation of Josephus to inspect the documents at the Capitol:

> ... against the decrees of the Romans nothing can be said — for they are kept in public places of the cities and are still to be found engraved on bronze tablets in the Capitol.

> (trans. R. Marcus, *LCL*).[15]

If his aim was to gain respect for Jews among the educated élite of Graeco-Roman society, a statement which could so easily be checked and proved false would be of no advantage to him. Are we right to assume that Josephus' Gentile audience had a perception of truth and falsehood quite different from the one we have, and that the reputation of the truthworthiness of an historian was of no importance in antiquity?[16] The fact that Josephus failed to mention that the authentic documents were destroyed by fire in AD 69 does not invalidate his claim, since Vespasian had replaced three thousand destroyed documents.[17] As to the Moehring's doubts that 'Vespasian would restore documents conferring privileges upon members of a people against whom he was still waging a costly war'[18] it can be argued that it was precisely what Vespasian would have done in order to give conclusive proof of the wickedness of the Jewish people who had commenced a war against their benefactors. As a general principle, it seems necessary to agree that each document must be treated individually, and that even if some of them (or some parts of them) are not genuine, they correspond in essentials to the nature of Roman-Jewish relations in the period when they are claimed to have been produced and reveal what were the burning issues for the Jewish communities of Asia.[19]

The documents collected by Josephus and presented by him in a rather chaotic way, are meant to demonstrate that Roman authorities granted certain rights and privileges to the Jewish communities in different places of Asia, and that local authorities obediently carried out Rome's decision.[20] Thus, for example, the Pergamene decree dated from the time of Antiochus VII Sidetes or Antiochus IX Cyzicenus, as-

---

[14]Moehring, 'The *Acta Pro Iudaeis*', 154.
[15]*AJ* 14:188; cf. *AJ* 14:265-267.
[16]Cf. Moehring, 'The *Acta Pro Iudaeis*', 16: 'If he did include forged documents, he would only indicate how well he had learnt the tricks of his Gentile audience'.
[17]Suetonius, *Vespasianus*, 8, 4.
[18]Moehring, 'The *Acta Pro Iudaeis*', 151.
[19]Cf. Barclay, *Jews in the Mediterranean Diaspora*, 263f.

sured Jews that the Pergamenes 'would do everything possible on behalf of the Jews in accordance with the decree of the (Roman) Senate'.[21]
In Sardis, Jews were permitted to have autonomous jurisdiction, to
build a synagogue, to form associations, and to supply the Jewish community with suitable food through the agency of the market-officials
who were charged with this duty.[22] The decree of Halicarnassus, 'following the example of the people of Rome', allowed Jews to perform
their rites in accordance with their Law and to build synagogues near
the sea; it also threatened to fine anyone who might seek to prevent
them.[23]

Until recently it was generally assumed that these documents,
and in particular those associated with Julius Caesar,[24] could be described as a 'Jewish Magna Carta'[25] which guaranteed privileges to the
whole Jewish population all over the Roman Empire.[26] Recent research
has raised doubts about the universal application of these privileges,
and has shown that they fall short of being 'an overall definition of
Jewish religious liberty'.[27]

In 12 BC Augustus issued an important edict concerning the
Jews of Asia.[28] He ruled that the Jews

> may follow their own customs in accordance with the law of their
> fathers . . . and that their sacred monies shall be inviolable and may be
> sent up to Jerusalem and delivered to the treasurers in Jerusalem, and
> they need not give bond (to appear in court) on the Sabbath or on the
> day of preparation for it (Sabbath Eve) after the ninth hour. And if

---

[20]See the discussion of the documents in Juster, *Les Juifs*, vol. 1, 132-158 and also in
A.M. Rabello, 'The Legal Condition of the Jews in the Roman Empire', *ANRW* II,
13 (1980), 682-685, who follows Juster's classification of the documents and whose
aim is 'to bring Juster's work up to date'. A helpful classification of the documents
and the critical evaluation of the traditional legalistic approach to them can be
found in Rajak, 'Was there a Roman Charter?', 109-123.

[21]*AJ* 14.247-255. The text of the Pergamene decree incorporates part of a Roman
senatus consultum, which was probably inserted into it by mistake Schürer,
Vermes, Millar, Goodman, *The History of the Jewish People*, 3, 18; T. Rajak, 'Roman
Intervention in a Seleucid Siege of Jerusalem?' *GRBS* 22 (1981), 65-81.

[22]*AJ* 14. 235; 261.

[23]*AJ* 14. 256-258.

[24]*AJ* 14. 185-267.

[25]This popular expression originally belongs to B. Niese, *Hermes* 2 (1876), 488.

[26]See, for instance, Juster, *Les Juifs*, 217; Rabello, *The Legal Condition*, 692; Smallwood, *The Jews under Roman Rule*, 124 ff.

[27]Rajak, 'Was there a Roman Charter?', 109f., followed by Trebilco, *Jewish Communities*, 10.

[28]*AJ* 16. 162-165.

anyone is caught stealing their sacred books or their sacred monies from a synagogue or an ark (of the Law) (ἐκ τε σαββατείου ἐκ τε ἀ[α]ρῶνος (ἀνδρῶνος codd.), he shall be regarded as sacrilegious, and his property shall be confiscated to the public treasury of the Romans.[29]

(trans. R. Marcus, *LCL*)

The decree was set up in the temple which was dedicated to Augustus by the Commonwealth of Asia (κοινὸν τῆς ᾿Ασίας).[30] Despite the fact that Augustus' ruling applied to the whole of Asia, the same privileges were repeatedly guaranteed by Roman officials in different documents issued for different cities. This leaves an impression that they were not properly carried out or, that in the face of tensions in Graeco-Jewish relations in individual cities, they needed to be reiterated. Each time, the renewal of the privileges was the result of intervention by individuals of standing in Roman eyes— 'every batch of documents is part of an exchange of *beneficia*'. This conforms well with the general Roman practice of distributing privileges 'as tokens of esteem for meritorious individuals'.[31]

It was the emperor Claudius who, for the first time in AD 41/42, at the request 'of my dearest friends' Agrippa I and Herod of Chalcis', promulgated a general enactment,[32] which allowed Jews throughout the whole Roman Empire (ἐν πάσῃ τῇ ὑπὸ ᾿Ρωμαίοις ἡγεμονίᾳ) to observe their customs unimpeded.[33] Nevertheless, the policy towards Jews was not spelt out in detail and, as Rajak notes,

> it is fair to say that Claudius is not doing much more than expressing his goodwill towards the practice of the Jewish cult and establishing a lead for Greek cities to follow.[34]

---

[29] *AJ* 16.162-165.
[30] *AJ* 16.162-165.
[31] Rajak, 'Was there a Roman Charter?', 116.
[32] The letter written by Tiberius after the death of Sejanus (Philo, *Legatio* 161) in which he confirmed Jewish rights, though it was addressed to the governors of all the provinces, was not a general edict, but an official briefing.
[33] *AJ* 19.288. On the Claudian edict and its limitations see Rajak, 'Was there a Roman Charter?', 115f. and Trebilco, *The Jewish Communities*, 10, who fully accepted her interpretation.
[34] Rajak, 'Was there a Roman Charter?', 115; for Claudius's policy towards Jews see in more detail pp. 172–81.

On the whole, the documents leave an impression that in a number of cities in Asia Minor, Jews often met with local opposition to their rights and privileges and had to appeal to Roman authorities who always ruled in their favour.[35] To present a more balanced picture we must not forget that Josephus' aim was apologetic[36] and that it is reasonable to suppose that he selected only those documents which were suitable for this aim, while omitting those which witnessed against his point.[37] It is also beyond doubt that by collecting documents which were intended to illustrate Rome's general support, Josephus inevitably highlighted the tensions between the Jews and the Gentiles, since the documents were issued at the times when Jews actually needed Roman backing. Periods of normal peaceful relations naturally left no documentary evidence of the type Josephus was looking for.[38]

In Acts, Luke usually depicts Paul beginning his preaching among Jews in the Jewish synagogues, even after he had proclaimed the mission to Gentiles as his goal.[39] This suggests that in all the places in which Paul stopped there were Jewish communities. Let us examine the evidence for Jews in the cities of Asia Minor (the Roman provinces of Asia and Galatia) mentioned in Acts.

II. Ephesus

According to Josephus, Jews were granted Ephesian citizenship (πολιτεία) by Antiochus II Theos.[40] Among the Roman documents grant-

---

[35]Stern, 'The Jewish People', 145.

[36]Moehring, 'The *Acta Pro Iudaeis*', 156f., especially stresses this point, insisting that the documents presented by Josephus 'must first and foremost be read as part of his apo-logetic scheme'.

[37]Rabello, 'The Legal Conditions', 682. Cf. also Rajak, 'Was there a Roman Charter?', 120ff., who scrutinized this collection of documents as a part of Josephus' political struggle in the aftermath of the fall of the Jerusalem Temple: 'The decrees were weapons in a polemic which was often intense and fierce. It is not surprising that in his presentation he overestimates respect for the Jews, exaggerates the scope of grants in their favour and tells us nothing of the times when Roman support was denied', 122.

[38]Trebilco, *Jewish Communities*, 11. Thus Josephus presents the favourable edict of Claudius, but says nothing about Claudius' measures against Jews in Rome; see 168-174.

[39]Cf. Acts 13:46 and Acts 14:1; 17:1; 17:10; 17:17 or 18:6 and 18:19.

[40]*AJ* 12. 125; c. App. 2. For understanding of πολιτεία as citizenship in *AJ* 12.125 see Schürer, Vermes, Millar, Goodman, *The History of the Jewish People*, 3, 1, 129f., n. 15 (with reference to more detailed and recent studies).

ing or confirming Jewish privileges there are a number concerning Ephesus. They are mostly connected with military service, which always caused serious problems for Jews because of their dietary laws and their inability to fulfil any duty on the Sabbath.[41] After Marius' reforms, voluntary enlistment was substituted for conscription into the Roman army, and Jews with Roman citizenship had no reason to worry. But in periods of crisis the Romans practised conscription and Jews, like other citizens, became liable for military service. Thus in 49 BC Lucius Lentulus Crus, one of the consuls for that year, was commissioned by the Roman Senate to recruit two legions in the province of Asia. He issued an edict which granted an exemption to Jews with Roman citizenship.[42] His resolution is also referred to in a letter 'to the magistrates, council and people of Ephesus' by Titus Ampius Balbus, *legatus pro praetore*, who claimed that the exemption of Jews in Asia was guaranteed as a result of his petition to the consul and that the same request was granted later by the propraetor Gaius Fannius and the proquaestor Lucius Antonius.[43]

This privilege was renewed in 43 BC at the request of Hyrcanus by the governor of Syria, P. Cornelius Dolabella, who for a short time became governor of Asia.[44] Apart from exemption from military service, the same decree granted Jews the right

> to follow their native customs (χρῆσθαι τοῖς πατρίοις ἐθισμοῖς) and to come together for sacred and holy rites in accordance with their law, and to make offerings for their sacrifices

(trans. R. Marcus, *LCL*).

Similar privileges were granted to Ephesian Jews in 42 BC by Marcus Junius Brutus:[45]

---

[41]Jews who became mercenaries under the Seleucids may have served in separate units (Smallwood, *The Jews*, 127, n. 23).

[42]*AJ* 14.228-229; 234; 237-240.

[43]*AJ* 14.230. It looks as though the exemption covers the whole of Asia, cf. a decree of Delos AJ 14.231-232, which, probably at this period, was attached to the province of Asia; see Smallwood, *The Jews*, 127, n. 24.

[44]*AJ* 14.223-227.

[45]*AJ* 14.262-264. The name in # 263 is corrupt, but it is generally held that the privileges were granted by the famous Marcus Brutus; see Juster, *Les Juifs*, 148f., n. 12; Schürer, Vermes, Millar, Goodman, *The History of the Jewish People*, 3, 1, 22; Stern, 'The Jewish Diaspora', 144.

3, I, 1, *CIRB* 64, Panticapaeum, AD 306

3, II, 1, *CIRB* 70, Panticapaeum, AD 81

3, II, 2, *CIRB* 71, Panticapaeum, First Century AD

3, II, 3, *CIRB* 72, Panticapaeum,
End of the first–beginning of second century AD

3, II, 5, *CIRB* 985, Phanagoria, AD 16

3, II, 6, Phanagoria, between AD 45 and 52

3, II, 6, Phanagoria, between AD 45 and 52

3, II, 7, *CIRB* 1123, Gorgippia, AD 41

3, II, 8, *CIRB* 1124, Gorgippia, AD 59

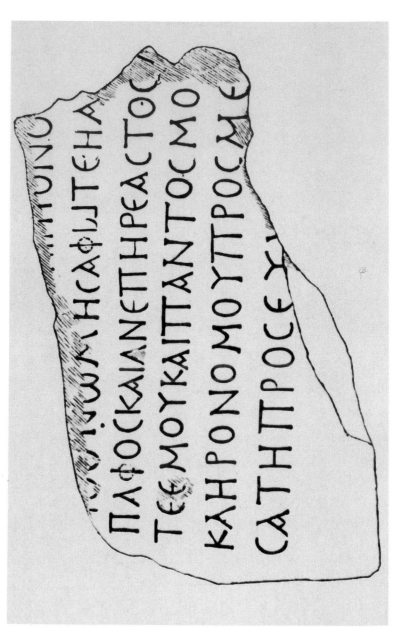

3, II, 9, *CIRB* 1127, Gorgippia,
First half of the second century AD

3, III, 1, *CIRB* 1260, Tanais, AD 155

3, III, 2, *CIRB* 1280, Tanais, AD 225

3, III, 3, *CIRB* 1281, Tanais,
First quarter of the third century AD

3, III, 3, *CIRB* 1281, Tanais,
First quarter of the third century AD

3, III, 3, *CIRB* 1281, Tanais,
First quarter of the third century AD

3, III, 4, *CIRB* 1283, Tanais, AD 228

> No one shall be prevented from keeping the Sabbath days nor be
> fined for so doing, but they shall be permitted to do all those things
> which are in accordance with their own laws.
>
> (trans. R. Marcus *LCL*).

Another legal issue connected with Ephesus, as it emerges from the
literary sources, is the payment of the Temple tax. The main concern
of the Jews was to ensure that the money would reach Jerusalem. To
achieve this aim they needed practical collaboration on the part of the
authorities, i.e. for the protection of the transport. A special
'concession' (*privilegium*) was necessary, since the export of gold and
silver from the provinces could on some occasions be banned by the
Roman Senate or by a governor of a province. In the period of civil
disturbances and economic troubles in the first century BC caused by
the wars against Sertorius, Mithridates and the pirates, the Roman
Senate issued a series of *senatus consulta*, the latest in 63 BC, forbidding
the export of silver and gold from Italy. Cicero (*Pro Flacco* 28.67) refers
to these rulings in his defence of Flaccus who, in 62 BC while he was
governor of Asia, issued an edict banning the export of gold from his
province. In accordance with his ruling, he confiscated the Jewish
Temple tax which the Asian Jews were attempting to send to
Jerusalem, and deposited it in the *aerarium*.[46] It is probable that we
have quite a number of documents from Ephesus concerning the
Jewish tax simply because, since the time of Augustus, it had become
the capital of the province, and for that reason was viewed as the
centre from which decisions were to be forwarded to other Asian
cities. But we cannot exclude the possibility that it was in Ephesus that
especially serious conflicts with the local Gentile population took place
over the issue. It is probable that the latter attempted to appropriate

---

[46]See in detail A.J. Marshall, 'Flaccus and the Jews of Asia (Cicero *Pro Flacco* 28.67-
69)', *Phoenix*, 29:2 (1975), 139-154, who argues that Flaccus in his action was motivated not by his anti-Jewish feelings but rather by economic considerations. He
also proposes that, since there is no evidence that Jewish organisations were
exempted from a *senatus consultum* of 64 BC, which had dissolved the *collegia*
(though it is not clear whether the ban was in force outside Rome), 'Jews may theoretically have lost their right to hold a common fund and with it their right to send
communal payments to Jerusalem.' 149f. The argument of Smallwood, *The Jews
under Roman Rule*, 134, that an exception seemed to have been made in favour of
the synagogues, since Cicero's speech implied the legal status of Jewish organisations in Rome, does not impress me. Their legal status in Rome quite possibly was
not specified at this time and this could allow the Roman authorities to use the ban
when it was convenient.

the Temple tax, which was perhaps accumulated in the provincial capital before being sent to Jerusalem. Philo in *Legatio* 315 quotes a letter by Gaius Norbanus Flaccus, proconsul of Asia, to the magistrates of Ephesus, in which he referred to a letter of Augustus:

> Caesar has written to me saying that it is a native traditional custom of the Jews, wherever they live, to meet regularly and contribute money, which they send to Jerusalem. He does not wish them to be prevented from doing this. I am therefore writing to you so that you may know that these are his instructions.[47]

(trans. E.M. Smallwood)

Josephus supplies us with two letters to the Ephesians. One, from Marcus Agrippa, not only expresses his will that the care and custody of the Temple-tribute should be given to Jews, but equates those who steal the sacred monies of the Jews with temple-robbers.[48] Another is from the proconsul Julius Antonius, arising from a request of the Asian Jews who approached him while he was administering justice in Ephesus. Among other privileges granted by Augustus and Agrippa, he confirms the right to forward the Temple tax to Jerusalem under escort and without any kind of impediment.[49]

Extant epigraphic evidence for the Jewish community in Ephesus is sparse given that there exist more than five thousand Ephesian inscriptions. This is understandable in terms of the fact that the part of the city where Jews could have had their quarters has not been excavated. The officials of the synagogue (ἀρχισυνάγωγοι,[50] πρεσβύτεροι[51]) are mentioned in a fragmentary inscription of uncertain date.[52]

We have also an interesting epitaph from the second or third century of a chief doctor (ἀρχιατρός) whose tomb was built by the Ephe-

---

[47]See the commentaries to the letter in *Philonis Alexandrini Legatio ad Gaium*, ed. with an introduction, translation and commentary by E.M. Smallwood (Leiden: Brill, 1961), 309f.

[48]*AJ* 16.167-168.

[49]*AJ* 16.172-173.

[50]See in detail pp. 186–87.

[51]It seems that the word could be used both as a title and as a designation of age. For the use of *presbyteros* as a title among the Jews in the Diaspora see Schürer, Vermes, Millar, Goodman, *The History of the Jewish People*, 3, 1, 102 and n. 55; *presbyteros* was also among the officials of the *thiasoi* of the adherents of the Most High God in Tanais, see p. 111ff. For the New Testament usage see Schürer, Vermes, Millar, Black, 2, 212, n. 43.

[52]H. Engelmann, D. Knibbe, 'Aus ephesischen Skizzenbüchern', *JÖAI* 52 (1978-80), 50, No. 94 = *IEphes* IV 1251.

sian Jews.[53] Only two Jewish chief doctors are known from inscriptions, the second one being commemorated in an epitaph from Venosa.[54] The title ἀρχιατρός (*archiater*) is well-known both from epigraphic and legal sources.[55] It is first attested in the Hellenistic period when an *archiatros* was a personal physician to a ruler. In the Roman period the title referred to someone working in the imperial palace or as a public physician. Until the early 140s, cities had the right to employ unrestricted numbers of doctors who were granted the privileges connected with this title. After the edict of Antoninus Pius to the *koinon* of Asia, the number of doctors which a city could employ with an exemption from liturgies was restricted to three in the small towns, seven in *conventus* centres and ten in *metropoleis*. After this edict a new two-class system of doctors, some with immunity and some without, gradually came into being and the term ἀρχιατρός may thus imply that its bearer was a civically-approved, tax-exempted doctor.[56]

Another Jewish epitaph dates to the end of the second century. The first publishers of the inscription read: τὸ μνημεῖόν ἐστι Μαρμουσσίου Ἰαίρεος. Ζῆ. Κήδονται οἱ Ἰουδαῖοι. ('This is tomb of mar-Moses [= rabbi Moses] son of Jair. He has finished his life. The Jews took charge of it').[57] L. Robert suggested another more plausible interpretation of the name of the deceased as Μ(ᾶρκος) Α<ὐ>ρήλιος Μούσσιος·

---

[53]*IBM* III,2 67=*CIJ* I 745=*IEph* 1677, the form in inscription is ἀρχιατροῦ (*IEph* after Heberdey) ἀρχειάτρου (*IBM, CIJ*). Confusion about the accent of this word goes so far that sometimes in one and the same article it is given different accents. The issue was discussed by Herodian the grammarian as early as the second century AD and resolved in favour of the last syllable (V. Nutton, 'Archiatri and the Medical Profession', *PBSR* 45 (1977), 191, n. 4).

[54]*CIJ* I 600=Noy, *JIWE* 1 76. The third example (*CIJ* I 5*=Noy, *JIWE* 2 341) was regarded by Frey as dubious because he thought the standard of lettering was too high to belong to a Jewish sarcophagus. See, however, the commentary of Noy, who is inclined to consider it Jewish, though with some reservations.

[55]See a detailed study of the term by Nutton, 'Archiatri', 191-226, and his list of relevant inscriptions, papyri and coins pp. 218-226; cf. also *NewDocs* 2 (1982), 10-25 and Noy, *JIWE* 1 76.

[56]Nutton, 'Archiatri', 201f, 215. However, the distinction between doctors who were liable to an exemption from liturgies (*archiatroi*) and doctors who were not (*iatroi*) seems not to be absolute, and the system did not develop simultaneously everywhere, for we know at least two cases when immune doctors are called *iatroi* (Nutton, 'Archiatri', 201f.). Cf. also an important discussion of the term by G.H.R. Horsley, who drew attention to a tendency to compound words with ἀρχι- in Koine in order to make the titles sound more impressive; *NewDocs* 2, 18f. For Christian usage of the term which was metaphorically applied to Christ see Nutton, 'Archiatri', 197, n. 40, Horsley, *NewDocs* 2, 17f.

[57]*BM* III.2, 676 = *CIJ* II 746.

(Marcus Aurelius Mussius [the last part is *nomen*] and proposed that ΙΑΙΡΕΟΣ stands for ἱερέως–priest).[58]

III. Miletus

Josephus quotes only one document concerning Milesian Jews. It probably dates from the time of Julius Caesar and was written by a proconsul whose name is given in a corrupted form as Publius Servilius Galba, son of Publius. The correct name will almost certainly have been P. Servilius Isauricus, who was proconsul from 46 to 44 BC.[59] The letter was written in response to a complaint by Milesian Jews which was brought to a court held by the Roman proconsul in Tralles. It stated that, contrary to the expressed wish of the Romans, Gentile Milesians 'are attacking the Jews and forbid them to observe their Sabbaths, perform their native rites or manage their produce (τοὺς καρποὺς μεταχειρίζεσθαι)[60] in accordance with their custom'. After hearing the case, the proconsul decided in favour of the Jews and the letter informing them of this decision was sent to the Milesian authorities.[61]

The only inscription from Miletus which is definitely Jewish should be dated in the late Roman period. It was found in the theatre, among others which reserved fifth-row seats for named persons.[62]

On the outer wall of the north-west corner of the same theatre there is an inscription from the early Byzantine period with an invocation to the archangels to preserve the city and its inhabitants.[63] In another part of the theatre there was found a fragment of the same text. Apart from the prayer addressing the archangels collectively, the inscription originally contained seven symbols of the archangels and seven ovals with their magic names (only five of both have survived) consisting of a series of seven vowels and an adjuration, which was ad-

---

[58]L. Robert, *Hellenica* XI-XII (1960), 381-384. His reading was adopted by *IEph* 1676.
[59]Schürer, Vermes, Millar, Goodman, *The History of the Jewish People*, 3,1, 117, n. 2, 3.
[60]The meaning of καρποί is not clear; the word could refer to food supply, but also to funds, including temple dues. S. Safray, 'Relations between the Diaspora and the Land of Israel', *CRINT* 1, 201f. and J.D.G. Dunn, 'The Incident at Antioch', *JSNT* 18 (1983), 15, consider that the word means tithes; E.P. Sanders, *Jewish Law from Jesus to the Mishnah* (London: SCM Press, 1990), 296f., decides in favour of food supply.
[61]*AJ* 14. 244-246.
[62] See p. 64ff. for the detailed discussion of this inscription.
[63]A. Deissmann, *Light from the Ancient East*, ET (London: 1927), Appendix IX, 453-460.

dressed to each of the archangels individually, to preserve the city and all who dwell therein. The inscription was considered by Deissman to be most certainly Christian. He thought that it belonged to a period when the theatre was converted into a citadel, and proposed that the inscription was the work of guardsmen for whom the prayer in the form of a protective charm seemed to be particularly efficacious. De-issman admitted, however, that 'in itself it might be Jewish'. He also noted that the prayer to the archangels had been influenced by the Sep-tuagint. His decision in favour of the Christian origin of the inscription was determined by two considerations: first, by the prominent posi-tion of the inscription[64] and its repetition in another place, and second, by the size of Jewish community in the city, which he assumed to have been very small.

This second argument must be rejected at once since we know nothing about the size of Jewish minority in Miletus at this time. The first one is more serious. From general considerations, it seems to be unlikely that the Jewish community was influential in Christian Miletus in the early Byzantine period. On the other hand, though the worship of the archangels was popular in Christian Asia Minor, the unorthodox magical colouring of the inscription in such a prominent place is in many ways surprising. On the whole, even if the inscription was produced by Christians, it bears the traces of a stronger Jewish influence than one normally finds in Christian inscriptions, even against the background of the widespread Christian adoption of things Jewish.

Among the Jewish epitaphs from Athens, one belongs to a certain Martha, daughter of Nicias from Miletus. The epitaph has been dated to the first century AD.[65] At the beginning of this century German archaeologists excavated what they thought had been a Jewish synagogue at Miletus.[66] The building had two or three construction periods, the earliest dating to the third or early fourth century. The complex was not fully excavated and the initial identification is highly doubtful. As Kraabel pointed out, 'in actuality much of the restoration was conjectural, and no Jewish evidence was found in or near the complex'.[67]

---

[64]I am most grateful to D. Feissel, who had a chance to inspect this inscription personally and, in discussion with me, confirmed that it had been placed centrally.
[65]CIJ I², *Prolegomenon*, 715g.
[66]A. von Gerkan, *Synagoge in Milet*, (1921). The identification was accepted by a number of scholars, see references in A.T. Kraabel, 'The Diaspora Synagogue: Archaeological and Epigraphic Evidence since Sukenik', *ANRW* II 19.1, 489.

IV. Pisidian Antioch

There is only one Jewish inscription which has been thought to refer to
Pisidian Antioch, namely one referring to an Antiochian woman called
Deborah. It is a verse epitaph from Apollonia in Phrygia which is datable in the second or the third century AD. It starts with the words
[κλεινῆς ᾽Α]ντιόχισσα πάτρης, γονέων πολυτείμων, οὔνομα Δεββῶρα[68]
('Antiochian by famous fatherland, from ancestors who held many
honours').[69] It was regarded as obvious by Ramsay and many others
that the 'Antioch' is the neighbouring Pisidian one (*Colonia Caesareia
Antiocheia*). But this identification is only one of four possibilities. This
type of epitaph (metrical, with the details of birth and place of burial)
usually indicates a contrast and requires a more distant place of birth.[70]
Carian Antioch on the Maeander[71] or Syrian Antioch[72] would perhaps
be more likely.

V. Iconium

In Stephanus Byzantius *s.v.* Ἰκόνιον we read that the legendary king of
Phrygia Annakos (in all other sources named Nannakos), who lived to
be over three hundred years old, received an oracle that after his death
all people would die. The Phrygians lamented so much that it gave
rise to a proverb— 'To weep as in the time of Annakos' (τὸ ἐπὶ ᾽Αννα-
κους κλαύσειν). The oracle was fulfilled in the time of Deucalion
(Stephanus did not mention how much time passed between Annakos
and Deukalion). After the flood, the earth was peopled anew with the
help of Prometheus and Athena who at Zeus' command made images
(εἰκόνες) of mud. From these the name of the city Ἰκόνιον was derived.[73]

---

[67]Kraabel, 'The Diaspora Synagogue', 489.

[68]*MAMA* IV 202; In *BCH* 17 (1893), 257 No. 37 and *CIJ* II 772 the text is not correct.

[69]The translation follows Robert's understanding of syntactical connections (*Noms
indigenes* (1963), 401, n. 3); Ramsay *The cities of St.Paul* (1907), 256f. interprets differently. Also Frey (*CIJ* II 772) and Schürer, Vermes, Millar, Goodman, 3,1, 32.

[70]*MAMA* VII, (1956), X, n.1.

[71]*MAMA* VII, (1956), X, n. 1, followed by B.M. Levick, *Roman Colonies in Southern
Asia Minor* (Oxford: Clarendon, 1967), 128; Schürer, Vermes, Millar, Goodman, *The
History of the Jewish People*, 3, 1, 32.

[72]Mitchell, *Anatolia*, vol. 2, 8f., n. 60. He thinks that the Semitic name of the
deceased is more congruous with Syria and refers to the fact that 'several persons
with Semitic names from Syrian Antioch occur at Athens'.

Zenobius (second century AD) knows two meanings of the proverb relating to Nannakos, which he gives in a compressed form as τὰ Ναννάκου: it can refer to things (people) amazing for their great antiquity (ἐπὶ θαυμαζομένων ἐπὶ παλαιότητι) or to those who lamented a great deal. Actually he is speaking about two different proverbs which though based on the same legend highlighted different aspects of it. Citing Hermogenes, he retells the story of Nannakos, who is described as the one who lived before Deucalion's time (this explains the first proverb) and his prediction of the Deluge and the subsequent lamentations (the second proverb). Then he quotes the second proverb with a reference to Herodas (Mimes 3.10) 'Even if you weep as in the story of Nannakos' (κἢν τὰ Ναννάκου κλαύσῃ).[74]

In the *Suda* it is also mentioned that Nannakos lived before Deucalion and the story of the prediction is also retold, but the proverb is quoted as ἀπὸ Ναννάκου with the explanation ἐπὶ τῶν πάνυ ἀρχαίων ('which refers to those who lived very long ago').[75]

It has been proposed that the original form of the name of the king was Annakos and that here we have a Phrygian reflection of the Biblical flood story with Annakos rendering the name of Enoch. But the mention of this proverb by Herodas in the third century BC in a form which implies knowledge of the flood legend, and is accompanied by other relevant details, testifies that the flood legend existed before Jews were settled in the region.[76] It seems that the Phrygian story was at quite an early stage combined with a Greek myth about Deucalion's flood, and a sequence of events (first Nannakos and prediction, then Deucalion and fulfilment of the prediction) was established. It cannot be ruled out, however, that the original proverb[77] underwent a

---

[73]Steph. Byz. *s.v.* Ἰκόνιον (=*FGrHist* III, C 800, Fr. 3).
[74]Herodas gives the proverb with a verb in a first person and in an active voice.
[75]Suda, *s.v.* Νάννακος (ed. A.Adler, III, 435). The remark of Stern (*GLAJJ* I, 452) that the same proverb as in the fragment of Hermogenes preserved by Zenobius, occurs in the Suda is misleading: though the Suda knows the story about the prediction of the flood and the following lamentations, the proverb which it refers to, unlike the one in Herodas's *Mimes*, has nothing to do with the details of the story.
[76]Trebilco, 'Jewish Communities', 88f.
[77]Stern, *GLAJJ*, I, No. LXXIV (Hermogenes); cf. also Trebilco, *Jewish Communities*, 86-99 on Phrygian flood legends and Noah coins from Apamea; for a different interpretation ('there is no doubt concerning the Jewish origin of the legends') see cf. Schürer, Vermes, Millar, Goodman, *The History of the Jewish People*, 3, 1, 30 with a critical remark on Schürer's view by the English editors; for the list of those who support the Jewish interpretation, see Trebilco, 'Jewish Communities', 223, n. 22.

transformation under Jewish influence and became connected with Enoch, but this proposition seems rather questionable.

CHAPTER 10

MACEDONIA AND ACHAIA

Literary and epigraphic sources are discussed here to shed light on the Jewish community in Thessalonica: there is also evidence for a Samaritan community. For Beroea, two epitaphs constitute the evidences for Jewish presnece. In Athens, as in Beroea, epitaphs are the principle records, one of which refers to a 'proscholos'—a very rare word which is examined in detail. Finally, the evidence from Corinth reveals an inscription from A synagogue which some have associated with the time of Paul himself: two other inscriptions survive in fragments.

The existence of Jewish communities in Macedonia and Greece is first registered in literary sources by the letter from Agrippa to Caligula, quoted by Philo.[1] Among regions with a Jewish population, it mentions Thessaly, Boeotia, Macedonia, Aetolia, Attica, Argos, Corinth and the largest and best parts of the Peloponnese.

The earliest epigraphic evidence for Jews in this part of the world dates back to the first half of the third century BC (Oropus, shrine of Amphiaraos).[2] There are also three manumissions of Jewish slaves from Delphi from the second century BC.[3] Among the most important discoveries has been a late-second or, more probably, third century inscription from Stobi (in the north of the province of Macedonia), consisting of thirty-three lines, in which the donor described construction work on the synagogue.[4] The excavations revealed that in the second to third century there was a synagogue in Stobi which was replaced by a later one destroyed by the end of the fourth century and replaced in turn by the Christian basilica.[5]

Luke mentions Jewish synagogues in Philippi, Thessalonica, Beroea, Athens and Corinth (Acts 16:12-13; 17:1,10,17; 18:4,7). Let us examine the extant evidence for Jews in these cities.

I. Thessalonica

From Thessalonica we have a late second century AD epitaph of a certain Abrameos and his wife, Theodote.[6] There are no special Jewish

---

[1]Philo, *Legatio*, 281.

[2]*CIJ* I², *Prolegomenon*, 711b; cf. D.M. Lewis, 'The First Greek Jew', *JSS* 2 (1957), 264-266.

[3]*CIJ* I² 709, 710, 711. In 710 the slave who is manumitted through a fictitious sale to Apollo is described as σῶμα ἀνδρεῖον ᾧ ὄνομα Ἰουδαῖος, τὸ γένος Ἰουδαῖον (a male person by the name Ioudaios, Jewish by race). It does not seem necessary to treat Ioudaios as Ioudas, as Schürer, Vermes, Millar, Goodman, *The History of the Jewish People*, 3, 1, 65 suggest; cf. 711, in which a man with the name Ioudaios manumitted a slave named Amyntas. As there is no clear cut evidence for the usage of Ioudaios as a personal name among Gentiles the remark in Schürer, Vermes, Millar, Goodman that the name does not necessarily imply that a man was Jewish seems to be superfluously cautious; for Ioudaios as a personal name cf. Kraemer, 'On the Meaning', 324, cf. also pp. 162–63.

[4]*CIJ* I², 694 and Lifshitz, *Prolegomenon*, p. 76f.; Lifshitz, *DF*, 10; see also a very important article by M. Hengel, 'Die Synagogeninschrift von Stobi', *ZNW* 57 (1966), 145-183 (reprinted in *The Synagogue*, ed. J. Gutmann).

[5]Kraabel, 'The Diaspora Synagogue', 494-497.

[6]*CIJ* I² 693.

symbols on the tomb and thus Christian provenance cannot be excluded. Two other epitaphs, however, do have these symbols. They are inscribed along with the symbol of the menorah, on two sarcophagi in the Palaeochristian necropolis to the east of Thessalonica. One of them has a formula not known in Jewish inscriptions but quite common in Christian ones: Κύριος μεθ' ἡμῶν ('The Lord is with us'). It is a paraphrase of Ps. 45:8,12.[7] The other is on the marble door of the sarcophagus and has the name of the deceased Benjamin (Βενιαμής), who was also called Domitios.[8] Taking into consideration the place where the inscriptions were found and the rather Christian formula in one of them, one should consider the possibility of their Jewish-Christian origin.

There is also possibly a Jewish dedication to the Most High God, in which the letters of the last word ΙΟΥΕΣ have been interpreted by the majority of scholars as a transliteration of the name Yahweh.[9]

The most interesting Jewish inscription in Thessalonica was found in 1965 and published quite recently, in 1994.[10] It is inscribed on a sarcophagus in a *tabula ansata* and dates to the late second or third century AD (the latter is more probable). The sarcophagus belonged to a certain Marcus Aurelius Iakob who was also called Eutychios and his wife Anna who was also called Asyncrition. The inscription states that, if anyone places another body in the sarcophagus, he will have to pay the fine of 75,000 denarii[11] to the synagogues (ταῖς συναγωγαῖς).[12]

---

[7]*CIJ* I², *Prolegomenon*, 693b; D.Feissel, *Recueil des inscriptions chrétiennes de la Macédoine du IIe au VIe siècle* (Paris, 1983), 292.

[8]*CIJ* I², *Prolegomenon*, 693c; Feissel, *Recueil*, 293.

[9]*CIJ* I², *Prolegomenon*, 693d; Schürer, Vermes, Millar, Goodman, *The History of the Jewish People*, 3, 1, 67; for the Jewish background of the cult of the Most High God see pp. 95-97; cf. also D. Feissel, M. Sève, 'Inscriptions de Macédoine', *BCH* 112 (1988), 455, with a short survey of interpretations, among which, alongside the Jewish one, that proposed by Ch. Habicht, *Gnomon* (1974), 491 (to understand the letters as the abbreviation of a personal name of which the cognomen was incompletely cut 'Ἰού(λιος)'Εσ-) should be considered seriously; cf. p. 96.

[10]P.M. Nigdelis, 'Synagoge(n) und Gemeinde der Juden in Thessaloniki: Fragen auf grund einer neuen jüdischen Grabinschrift der Kaiserzeit', *ZPE* 102 (1994), 297-306. I am grateful to G. Green who drew my attention to this inscription.

[11]The editor of the inscription considers the size of the fine to be an additional argument for the third century dating. In Rome in the second century the fine for violation a tomb was between 2,500 and 5,000 denarii, but in the third century, with inflation, the sum varied in the range between 12,500 and 25,000. In Thessaloniki the second century fine was 5,000, but in the third century it ranged between 50,000 and 100,000 denarii (Nigdelis, 'Synagoge[n] und Gemeinde', 299, with references to the literature); cf. also Noy, *JIWE* 2, 306.

The plural form of the word συναγωγή implies that in the third century there were several Jewish communities in Thessaloniki. The editor thinks that a fine was to be paid to that synagogue which would set in motion the prosecution for tomb violation.[13] This does not sounds convincing. It seems more plausible that the Jewish cemetery did not belong to any particular synagogue but was shared by all communities and that there existed some kind of an overall, communal body to manage the cemetery and receive the payment of fines.[14] But we cannot go further than this supposition. It is impossible to say whether the Jewish congregations in Thessalonica had a unified organisation or were completely independent of each other.[15]

From the epigraphic evidence we know also of the existence of a Samaritan community in Thessalonica.[16] This is attested by the bilingual (Greek and Samaritan) inscription, which is datable in the fourth to sixth century AD,[17] and consists mostly of a quotation from Num. 6:22-27. S. Pelekidis considered that the inscription commemorated the building of a synagogue by a benefactor (whom he identified with the sophist Siricius from Neapolis), but this is not clear from the text.[18] The

---

[12]As inscriptions show, the fines might be payable to a city as a village or a temple or indeed to a trade organisation, and increasingly in the Roman imperial period to the Roman *aerarium* or the fiscus; the trade organisation provides a useful parallel to the synagogue(s) as recipient. In Jewish inscriptions the body to receive fines could be κατοικία τῶν' Ιουδαίων or λαὸς τῶν' Ιουδαίων or συναγωγή; sometimes the fines had to be paid to a number of bodies, such as the *fiscus* and *gerousia* or the *fiscus* and the Jewish community simultaneously, Nigdelis, 'Synagoge[n] und Gemeinde', 304.

[13]Nigdelis, 'Synagoge(n) und Gemeinde', 306.

[14]Cf. for Rome G.La Piana, 'Foreign Groups in Rome during the First Centuries of the Empire', *HTR* 20 (1927), 363f.; S.W. Baron, *A Social and Religious History*, vol. 2, 199; A. Konikoff, *Sarcophagi from the Jewish Catacombs in Rome* (Stuttgart, 1986), 34. For a different view see Leon, *Jews in Rome*, 169, n. 4. who thinks that, 'at most one can say that a group of congregations probably administered one cemetery on some sort of co-operative basis'. Cf. M. Williams, 'The Organisation of Jewish Burials in Ancient Rome', *ZPE* 101 (1994), 165-182, who puts forward a hypothesis of the existence in Rome of a plurality of burial consortia, since the size of the Roman community was too great to be controlled by a single organisation.

[15]Cf. p. 186.

[16]*CIJ* I², *Prolegomenon*, 693a; Feissel, *Recueil*, 291; for the most detailed discussion of the inscription see in B. Lifshitz, J. Schiby, 'Une synagogue samaritaine à Thessalonique', *RB* 75 (1968), 368-378; cf. also J. Robert, L. Robert, *BE* 1969, 369. *NewDocs*, 1 (1981), 108-110.

[17]The first editor (S. Pelekidis) suggested an earlier date in the 4th century, which was corrected in view of the Samaritan script, J.D. Purvis, 'The Palaeography of the Samaritan Inscriptions from Thessalonica', *BASOR* 221 (1976), 121-123.

inscription has provoked a discussion concerning problems arising from the translation of the Hebrew text into Greek.[19] The inscription includes the 'God is one' formula, which, while fairly common in Christian epigraphy, can also be found in Jewish texts.[20]

II. Beroea

Jewish presence in Beroea is attested by two late epitaphs. The first one, perhaps from the fifth century AD, has the menorah and probably the lulab at the right and an open scroll or the Holy Ark at the left.[21] The second line of the inscription, with the name of the deceased, was read differently by A. Orlandos (the first editor) and subsequently by L.Robert and B.Lifshitz[22] as ([Ἰ]ωάννο[υ] κὲ ʼΑνδρέου), but differently by D. Feissel[23] who considersthat there was only one deceased person, Joses from Alexandria: Ἰωσῆς ʼΑλεξανδρεού(ς). While his reading of the name Ἰωσῆς is beyond doubt, the interpretation of the next word is not so certain.

The second epitaph is perhaps from the fourth to fifth century.[24] It registers the existence of a Jewish synagogue in the city at the time when it was inscribed on the tomb of a certain Maria, daughter of Tertia and Leontius, by her son-in-law. At the end of the inscription there is a warning that if anyone opens the tomb he will have to pay to the most holy synagogue (τῇ ἁγιωτά[τῃ] συναγω[γῇ]) one pound of silver.[25]

---

[18]A more sceptical view, that the inscription does not prove the existence of a building, nor of any Samaritan communal organisation, can be found in Schürer, Vermes, Millar, Goodman, *The History of the Jewish People*, 3, 1, 67. Cf., however, Lifshitz (*Prolegomenon*, 71), who argued that the fact that one of the four towers of Thessalonica was later called the Samaritan Tower showed that a memory of the Samaritan community had been preserved for a long time.

[19]For the details of the discussion, see *NewDocs*, 1, 109.

[20]*NewDocs*, 1, 110.

[21]*CIJ* I², *Prolegomenon*, 694a; Feissel, *Recueil*, 294.

[22]A.K. Orlandos, ʼΑρχαιολογικὸν Δελτίον, 2 (1916), 163, N 32, fig. 15 (photograph); L. Robert, *Hellenica*, III, 104; *CIJ* I², *Prolegomenon*, 694a. The quality of the photograph in Orlandos' publication is very poor, but even this photograph shows that the suggested reading is incorrect.

[23]*Recueil*, 294, pl. LXV.

[24]*CIJ* I², *Prolegomenon*, 694b; Feissel, *Recueil*, 295.

[25]The sum is modest, as Feissel pointed out. See also the discussion of the inscription, including the sums of fines calculated in pounds in Robert, *Hellenica*, III, 106f.

III. Athens

There are a number of Jewish epitaphs which have been found in Athens dating from the second century BC to the second to third century AD, with a rather high proportion of inscriptions from the first century AD.[26] Some of the Jews buried in Athens are recorded on their gravestones as having originated from other places: from Jerusalem,[27] Antioch[28], Aradus,[29] Miletus.[30] This is not surprising. Aliens from all parts of the world lived in Athens, and the proportion of people from Asia Minor and the Levant was very high.[31] We know that Phoenicians and Egyptians had their own corporations in Athens with the right to build temples in Piraeus. The merchants from Kition (in Cyprus) formed their own association. It seems that Salaminioi also had the same right.[32]

Epigraphic evidence does not supply us with much information about Jewish life in Athens: the epitaphs give just the names of the deceased without any details except, sometimes, for the place of origin. In one epitaph, dated in the second to third century AD and decorated with a seven-branched menorah, the deceased is called πρόσχολος: Βενιαμὴς(?) πρόσχολος Λαχάρους.[33] The word πρόσχολος is a very rare one indeed. *LSJ* provides us with two examples. One is in Ausonius, *Commemoratio professorum Burdigalensium*, 22. The second is in Augustine's *Sermon* 178, c.7, 8. L. Robert refers to Πρόσχολος as the name of

---

[26]*CIJ* I² 712, 713, 714 (?), 715, *Prolegomenon*, 715a,b, c, d, e, f, g, h, i; cf. also L.B. Urdahl, 'Jews in Attica', *Symbolae Osloenses* 43 (1968), 39-46, who suggested that there were some other inscriptions from Athens which could be Jewish; but his conjectures cannot be proved. His article contains numerous errors, which were discussed by J. Robert and L. Robert in *BE* (1980), 230.
[27]*CIJ* I², *Prolegomenon*, 715a.
[28]*CIJ* I², *Prolegomenon*, 715d, 715e.
[29]*CIJ* I², *Prolegomenon*, 715f.
[30]*CIJ* I², *Prolegomenon*, 715g.
[31]Schürer, Vermes, Millar, Goodman, *The History of the Jewish People*, 3, 1, 109 give a figure of 2,649 epitaphs of aliens dating from the period from fourth century BC to the Roman empire.
[32]Schürer, Vermes, Millar, Goodman, *The History of the Jewish People*, 3, 1, 109f.
[33]*IG2*, II, 10949; *CIJ* I², *Prolegomenon*, 715b; L. Robert, *Hellenica*, III, 101; M. Schwabe, *Tarbitz* 21 (1950), 112-123 (*in Hebrew*); B. Lifshitz, 'Notes d'épigraphie grecque', *RB* 70 (1963), 257f. The name of the deceased has been read either as Βενιδάης (G. Klaffenbach, L. Robert) or as Βενιαμής (M. Schwabe, M.T. Mitsos, B. Lifshitz). The words of the inscription has also construed in two different ways: (1) 'Beniamin *proscholos* of Lachares' (*IG*, Robert, Schwabe); (2) 'Benjamin son of Lachares, *proscholos*' (Lifshitz). See in detail commentary by Lifshitz to 715b.

an *ephebus* in Athens.[34] With reference to the title of one of Ausonius' poems, *proscholos* is usually explained as a synonym for a Latin *subdoctor* ('assistant teacher'). The equation seems to me to deserve some thought and the history of the English word *usher* (originally a doorkeeper, later in some contexts, a depreciatory description of an underteacher, is worth remembering.

The usage of the word by Augustine and Ausonius creates a curiously different impression from that of Ausonius of the professional duties of someone who held this post. According to Augustine, the position of a *proscholos* was very humble:

> *dicam quod fecerit pauperrimus homo, nobis apud Mediolanum constitutis; tam pauper, ut proscholus esset grammatici: sed plane christianus, quamvis ille esset paganus grammaticus; melior ad velum, quam in cathedra.*

> I shall tell you what an extremely poor man did at the time when I was living in Milan. He was so poor that he was *proscholos* of a teacher of grammar. But he certainly was a Christian, while the other was a pagan teacher of grammar. A better person was at the curtains than the one in the teacher's chair.

The remark about curtains is clear from another passage by Augustine *Confessiones* I,13.22:

> *at enim vela pendebant liminibus grammaticarum scholarum, sed non illa magis honorem secreti quam tegimentum erroris significant.*

> True it is, that there are curtains at the entrance of Grammar schools; but they signify not so much the cloth of state to privacy, as serve for a blind to the follies committed behind them.

> (trans. W. Watts, *LCL*)

It seems evident from Augustine's sermon that the *proscholos* (from προσχόλιον— ante-room of the school, according to a gloss) was not in principle an assistant teacher, but rather was in charge of introducing students to the auditorium or even simply a doorkeeper.[35]

Ausonius' text gives another picture. He starts his epitaph *Victorio subdoctori sive proscholo* with the words:

---

[34]*Hellenica* III, 101: *IG*, II^2, 2130, l.141.

[35]*proscholos* was translated as 'usher' by H.G.E. White in his edition of Ausonius in *LCL* and as 'doorkeeper' by E. Hill in his translation of Augustine's sermons *Sermons III/5 on the New Testament: The Works of Saint Augustine. A Translation for the 21st Century* (New Rochelle, New York: New City Press, 1992).

Victori studiose, memor, celer, ignoratis
adsidue in libris nec nisi operta legens...

Scholarly Victorius, gifted with memory and a quick brain, how pa-
tiently you used to pore over books which no one read.

(trans. H.G.E. White, *LCL*)

Ausonius mentions that Victorius' status was lower than that of a
grammaticus, but there is no doubt that Victorius was a scholar as well
as an assistant teacher:

exili nostrae fucatus honore cathedrae,
libato tenuis nomine grammatici...

Your post here in our city had brought you only a faint tincture of re-
nown, and given you but a slight foretaste of the title grammarian.

(trans. H.G.E. White, *LCL*)

The description of Ausonius does not correspond well with Augustine's sermon, but it corresponds well with a passage in the *Confes-
sions*. In *Confessiones* 8.6 Augustine mentions that his friend Nebidius
at his own request lectured under Verecundus, a grammarian of Milan
who was very friendly with Augustine's circle:

*Nebridius autem amicitiae nostrae cesserat, ut omnium nostrum familiaris-
simo Verecundo, Mediolanensi et civi et grammatico, subdoceret.*

It seems evident that here *grammatico subdoceret = subdoctor grammatici
esset*[36] Augustine also stresses that his friend was not motivated to accept this position by any desire of profit, and might have done better
as writer. This means that though the position (and payment) was
rather modest, it was not humiliating for a man with good connections
to accept it. The comparison with Augustine's description of the position of a *proscholos* in his sermon shows that they were different and
that Augustine distinguished between them.

The corresponding word to *subdoctor* in the Greek language is
ὑποδιδάσκαλος. It was used of an under-teacher of a chorus,[37] but we
also have an example from Cicero of its usage in a general sense of un-

---

[36]W. Heraeus, 'Die Sprache des Petronius und die Glossen', *Kleine Schriften*, ed. J.B.
Hofmann (Heidelberg: Carl Winter's Universitäts-Buchhandlung, 1937), 94.
[37]Plato, *Ion* 536a.

der-master: Cicero offered the seat of the *hypodidascalus* in an imaginary school of rhetoric about which he was fantasizing to his friend Papirius Paetus.[38]

The only basis for equating *proscholos* and *subdoctor* is the title of Ausonius' epitaph to Victorius, where both words are connected by the conjunction *sive*. One can suppose that in Bordeaux for some reason these terms were used as synonyms. For instance, we may conjecture that the office of an assistant teacher was located in a *proscholion* and for this reason he was nicknamed 'a doorkeeper'. Gradually the nickname became a synonym of an official title and both were used in Bordeaux interchangeably. We cannot assume that *proscholos* was used with the same meaning everywhere; by putting the two terms together Ausonius could have been recording a peculiar local usage. But this is not the only possible explanation. The Latin conjunction *sive* does not necessarily imply the equation of the words connected by it. It may introduce an alternative in case the preceding should not be thought appropriate, or might introduce a more precise expression.[39] It seems that to view the *subdoctor* and the *proscholos* as designations of two *different* occupations would be the best way to understand the title. Perhaps, Victorius had two jobs. Or perhaps according to his official status he was *proscholos*, but actually was fulfilling the duties of *subdoctor*, and Ausonius marked this pecularity of his position by putting the more honourable title in the first place and after that designating his actual status. In any case there is no firm basis for equating both terms automatically.[40]

With this in mind, let us return to our inscription. It has been referred to as possible evidence for the existence of a Jewish school in Athens. M. Schwabe proposed that it could have been a Greek school for Jewish children.[41] The deceased has even been styled the head of a Jewish school.[42] This last supposition must be ruled out. Even if *proscholos* had regularly had the same meaning as *subdoctor*, it would have been very surprising indeed for the title of 'assistant teacher' to have been used to designate the head of a school. It seems that the inscription has to be interpreted with more caution. It does not prove the ex-

---

[38]*ad Fam*. IX.18.4.

[39]See examples in *Oxford Latin Dictionary*, s.v., 9a,b.

[40]For the opposite conclusion see Heraeus, 'Die Sprache' 92-94, who adds to the pair *proscholos/subdoctor* also *antescolanus* in a passage of Petronius 81.1 which adds no helpful information.

[41]Schwabe, *Tarbitz* , 116.

[42]J. and L. Robert, *BE* 1964, No. 146; van der Horst, *Jewish Epitaphs*, 97.

istence of a Jewish school in Athens. The deceased may quite possibly have been a humble doorkeeper for a pagan grammarian in a Greek school, like that poor honest Christian to whom Augustine referred.

IV. Corinth

The finding of an inscription from the Corinthian synagogue caused a sensation among New Testament scholars especially since the date proposed by some epigraphists suggested that it could be from the very synagogue in which Paul had preached.[43] The inscription is preserved on a large block of white marble with irregular letters and poor quality of cutting. It consists of one line: [Συνα]γωγὴ τωςν ʹΕβρ[αίων] ('The synagogue of the Hebrews'). Originally the block may have been a cornice, but later it was trimmed, chiselled and reused, probably as the lintel over a doorway of the synagogue. The first editor of the inscription, B. Powell,[44] having in mind the place where the stone was found, located the Jewish synagogue east of the Lechaeum road and a short distance north of the fountain of Pirene, not more than a hundred metres from the Propylaea at the entrance to the market. The basis of this location was the large size of the stone (93 cm x 42 cm x 29 cm) which, as Powell thought, made it very improbable for the block to have been removed from its original site. But as W.A. Meeks rightly observed 'the violence with which stones were smashed and scattered in the Herulian and Gothic attacks on Corinth somewhat undercuts Powell's confident claim that the stone was too large to have been moved far from its site'.[45]

The date of the inscription is far from certain. Deissmann and Frey dated it to any time from 100 BC to AD 200.[46] N.A. Bees believed that it is from the time of Paul.[47] He argues that though the synagogue may have been restored at a later date, it never changed its location. B.D. Meritt, however, assumed that 'it is considerably later than the time of Paul', though he suggested that the synagogue in which Paul

---

[43]Cf. Deissmann, *Light from the Ancient East*, 16, n. 7: 'It is therefore a possibility seriously to be reckoned with that we have here the inscription to the door of the Corinthian synagogue mentioned in Acts XVIII.4, in which St. Paul first preached!'
[44]'Greek Inscriptions from Corinth', *AJA* Second Series 7 (1903), 60f., N0. 40.
[45]W.A. Meeks, *The First Urban Christians* (New Haven, London: Yale University Press, 1983), 49.
[46]Deissmann, *Light from the Ancient East*, 13; *CIJ* I 718.
[47]*IKorinthChr*, 6.

preached should be located in the same area.[48] V.J.M. de Waele proposed a second or even third century date.[49] V.P. Furnish considers that 'the inscription could be as late as the fourth century CE'.[50]

One of the most important problems raised by the inscription is the meaning of the word Ἑβραῖοι[51] which was used instead of a much more common Ἰουδαῖοι. The difference between the two terms is rather hard to define precisely, but the basic distinctions can be formulated as follows:[52]

(1) The term Ἑβραῖοι was used as an archaic name for Jews in the earliest times while the contemporary Jews were called Ἰουδαῖοι.[53] This is characteristic of Josephus, who used Ἑβραῖοι also to describe what was peculiar to the Jewish nation and then was lost in the dispersion, i.e. language, coins, etc.[54] It could also stress the purity of an ethnic descent.[55]

(2) Sometimes Ἰουδαῖοι could take on derogatory overtones and in this case Ἑβραῖοι became the polite term,[56] though this difference must not be exaggerated.

(3) Ἑβραῖοι could be used as a term for Hebrew- or Aramaic-speaking Jews as opposed to Ἑλληνισταί, i.e. Greek-speaking Jews (Acts 6:1).[57]

The last usage makes it necessary to consider the possibility that the language of the Corinthian synagogue was Hebrew or Aramaic. There are four inscriptions from Rome[58] and one from Deliler (near Philadelphia)[59] in which there is a reference to 'the synagogue of the Hebrews' (or simply 'the Hebrews'). Among the Roman inscriptions one is bilingual (Aramaic and Greek), the three others are in Greek, the one from Deliler is in Greek (with a transcription of a Hebrew word)

---

[48]*IKorinthMeritt*, 111.
[49]*Studia Catholica* 4 (1928) 165, 170.
[50]*II Corinthians* (Garden City, New York: Doubleday and Company, 1984, The Anchor Bible), 21.
[51]A soft breathing is also used for this word, cf. Bl.-Debr. 39, 3; WH Intr.[2] § 408, MM).
[52]*TDNT* III, 367ff. (K.G.Kuhn); de Lange, *Origen*, 29f.
[53]Cf. *AJ* I.146 and Tertullian, *Apol.* 18.6.
[54]*AJ* 1.36, 146; 5.323; 9.20; 10.8; *BJ* 6.96 etc.
[55]*Phil.* 3:5; II Cor. 11:22.
[56]See *e.g.* 4 Macc.
[57]Cf. Chrysostom, *Hom. 14 on Acts 6:1*; Philo, *De conf. ling.* 129; see Str.-Bill. II, 448.
[58]*CIJ* I 291, 317, 510, 535 = Noy, *JIWE* 2, 33, 2, 578, 579.
[59]*CIJ* II 754 = *DF* 28, see p. 60.

and is a dedication by a θεοσεβής.[60] Taking into consideration that the
Roman inscriptions are epitaphs on the tombs of officers of the community and members of their families, it seems reasonable to expect
that if the language of the community was Aramaic the epitaphs
would be also in Aramaic.[61] But do epitaphs reflect the vernacular language of the community? Could Greek have been used as the conventional language of the inscriptions without any connection with the
actual language of the congregation, as Momigliano believed?[62]
Against this view, one must consider the high proportion of Latin epitaphs, and the linguistic confusion in some of them (Latin in Greek
characters and *vice versa*; both Greek and Latin in the same inscription).[63] Analysing the linguistic material from the Jewish catacomb in
Venosa, Noy noted that the Latin inscriptions are on the whole later
than the Greek ones and that eventually Latin replaced Greek as the
language of commemoration.[64] The four epitaphs which belonged to
the successive generations of a family show that, while the first gener-
ation used Greek and Hebrew, the third and fourth switched to Latin
and Hebrew. Some of the Greek epitaphs in Venosa were written by
people who were thinking in Latin.[65] This demonstrates that although
the language of the epitaphs has a tendency to reflect the language
spoken by the individuals concerned, there also existed a tradition of
using a particular language in epitaphs and there was a certain gap between the time when the new language became vernacular and the
time when it supplanted the old one in lapidary style.

---

[60]See p. 60ff.

[61]Cf. Leon, *The Jews of Ancient Rome*, 156 and de Lange, *Origen*, 30.

[62]I nomi delle prime 'synagoghe' romane e la condizione giuridica delle commu-
nita in Roma sotto Augusto', *Rassegna Mensile di Israel* 6 (1931-1932), 291; cf. also
Smallwood, *The Jews*, 133.

[63]See distribution of languages in the Roman Jewish inscriptions in Noy, *JIWE* 2,
Index, 513f.

[64]Cf. also the very detailed and helpful study of the linguistic features of Jewish
funerary inscriptions from Rome in L.V. Rutgers, *Jews in Rome*, 176-201. He proves
that the Jewish community in Rome was in the process of linguistic change and
marks the main stages of this process as follows (p. 181): 'The earliest inscriptions
that were set up by the Jewish community of ancient Rome were all in Greek. The
high percentage of Latin names used in these inscriptions suggests that at a relatively early stage a tendency towards Latinization started to manifest itself (late
second and third century C.E.) . . . . In the course of the fourth century, the influence of Latin became even more palpable. In this period the first inscriptions in
Latin started to be carved'.

[65]Noy, 'The Jewish Communities of Leontopolis and Venosa', 175.

G. La Piana put forward the following explanation of the name of the Roman synagogue of the Hebrews,[66] which was supported by H.J. Leon.[67] The Jewish colony in Rome had come into being before Pompey's conquest. At the beginning it must have been rather small and when its members organized a synagogue, there will have been no need for more than one. The congregation sought to differentiate itself from other religious or ethnic groups. Other Jews coming to Rome later formed congregations of their own and gave them appropriate names, but the first congregation retained its original name. La Piana, referring to a Greek-Aramaic epitaph of a daughter of the archon of the synagogue, considered it to be possible that this particular Roman synagogue had conservative traditions in language. However, we must not press this point against the background of other inscriptions from the same community.

M. Hengel suggested that the Corinthian congregation might have been an 'offshoot' of the Roman one.[68] This cannot be completely ruled out. All things considered, however, a more plausible explanation would be that it was quite natural for the first congregation to be called by its ethnic name; and that as in Rome, the synagogue of the Hebrews derived its name from the fact that it was the first one (or the only one) in Corinth.[69] It cannot be excluded that the term 'Hebrew' did imply at first that the language of the community was Hebrew (or Aramaic), but, even if that was true, it would have been most likely replaced by Greek at a later time.

Apart from this inscription, seven more have been found in Corinth. Five of them are in such small fragments that no one word survived completely. The date cannot be determined, and the conclusion of the editor of the corpus, that they are in Hebrew, is accepted.[70] Near the Theatre was found a tablet bearing the seven-branched menorah upon a base flanked by a seven-branched menorah, a lulab, and an ethrog. Two fragments of Jewish inscriptions were also found in the eastern area of the Theatre.[71] They yield some information. The first one is bilingual (Greek and Hebrew) with a Hebrew word *miscab*

---

[66]Foreign Groups, 356, n. 26.

[67]Leon, *The Jews of Ancient Rome*, 149.

[68]'Proseuche und Synagogue', 183.

[69]Cf. Meeks, *The First Urban Christians* , 213, n. 276.

[70]They are listed in *IKorinthKent*, p.214.

[71]D.I. Pallas, S.P. Dantes, Ἀρχαιολογικόν Ἐφήμερις (1977), 80f. No. 29, 30; cf. J. Robert, L. Robert, BE. (1980), 230; SEG XXIX, 300; *IKorinthKent* 8.3 (1966) 304 = *CIJ* I², 718a.

(tomb).[72] The second contains two titles διδάσ[καλος] and ἀρχ[ισυνάγ-ωγ]ος. After the last title the editors restored τῆ[ς συναγωγῆς Κορίν-θου?]. The restoration is very insecure and the last word ought to be ruled out, since 'given the size of Corinth in the Roman period, it is certain to have had more than the one synagogue which Κορίνθου might imply'.[73] Moreover it would be very difficult to find a parallel for the use of a city's name within that city in a text of this category.[74]

---

[72]Pallas, Dantes,Ἀρχαιολογικόν Ἐφήμερις (1977), 80f. No. 29.
[73]Cf. NewDocs 4, 113, 213.
[74]For a discussion of the preliminary hearing before Gallio in Acts 18:12–17 see B.W. Winter, 'Acts and Roman Religion B' The Book of Acts in its Graeco–Roman Setting edd. D.W.J. Gill and C. Gempf (Grand Rapids and Carlisle: Eerdmans and Paternoster, 1994) 98–103.

CHAPTER 11

ROME

For Rome there is a great deal more evidence on the resident Jews. From the late Republic, Cicero's alleged anti-Jewish comments are discussed, as is Suetonius' account of Julius Caesar's benevolence to the Jews. Under the Empire, the development of imperial attitudes to the Jewish people are explored, with special reference to Suetonius' mention of Chrestus— and the evidence for whether that name is an alternative for Christ is weighed. Finally, the eleven synagogues for which evidence survives are described, as well as their organization, and the roles of synagogue officials.

I. Literary Evidence

For the Jewish community in Rome we clearly have much more literary and epigraphic evidence than for any other Diaspora site.[1] The Jews appeared in Rome relatively late. Evidence for their presence in Rome as early as 139 BC has been questioned and even rejected as apocryphal by some scholars, because of a rather puzzling and much discussed passage in *Facta et dicta memorabilia*, 1.3.2 by Valerius Maximus.[2] It has, however, been accepted by others and Valerius' report of the expulsion of Jews from Rome has been treated as proof that they engaged in proselytizing activity as soon as they arrived in Rome.[3]

Evidence from the late Republic and the Early Empire

The first contemporary and absolutely reliable literary evidence for the Jewish community in Rome is in Cicero's oration *Pro Flacco*.[4] The speech is coloured by contempt for Jews. Cicero makes a few scornful remarks about the Jewish religion, which he stigmatizes as a *barbara superstitio* incompatible with the dignity of the Roman name and the customs of the Roman people's forefathers. These remarks have provided grounds for some scholars to accuse Cicero of anti-semitism. His anti-Jewish feelings, however, should not be exaggerated on the basis of his racist comment. His invective against the Jews was to a certain degree conditioned by a standard rhetorical technique: incrimination of the national character of opposing witnesses with the aim of discrediting them as individuals. Cicero himself admitted that there existed a difference between his own views and those he expressed in a court-room.[5] Thus 'the most one can safely conclude is that Cicero counted on arousing anti-Jewish prejudice in the juror's minds to colour their consideration of charges against Flaccus'.[6] But even if we make allowances for the rhetorical devices and exaggera-

---

[1]Not surprisingly, there exists a vast amount of literature on Jews in Rome; see list in Schürer, Vermes, Millar, Goodman, 3, 1, 73f., n. 75; add to the list Smallwood, *The Jews*, 201-219; Noy, *JIWE* 2, especially bibliography on pp. 550-562; Barclay, *Jews in the Mediterranean Diaspora*, 282-319.
[2]S. Alessandri, 'La presunta cacciata dei Giudei da Roma nel 139 a. Cr.', *Studi Class. e Orient.* 17 (1968), 187-198; cf. also Marshall, 'Flaccus', 140f.
[3]See in detail p. 29.
[4]*Pro Flacco*, 28.66-69 = Stern, *GLAJJ* I, No. 68.
[5]*Pro Cluentio*, 139.

tions,[7] the information which the speech provides is very important indeed. In Augustus' reign the majority of Jews were said by Philo to have been freedmen who were brought to Rome as prisoners of war by Pompey and subsequently manumitted by their owners.[8] Cicero's speech, however, bears witness to the fact that a Jewish community had existed there some time before the arrival of Pompey's captives, and that in 59 BC there was a noticeable Jewish population in Rome.[9] Otherwise we cannot explain Cicero's complaints of Jewish social cohesion, for this could not have developed so rapidly.

> *Hoc nimirum est illud quod non longe a gradibus Aureliis haec causa dicitur. Ob hoc crimen hic locus abs te, Laeli, atque illa turba quaesita est; scis quanta sit manus, quanta concordia, quantum valeat in contionibus.*

Pro Flacco 28, 66.

This, no doubt, is the reason why this case is being tried nat far from the Aurelian Steps. You procured this place and that crowd, Laelius, for this trial. You knnow what a big crowd it is, how they stick together, how influential they are in informal assemblies.

(trans. L.E. Lord, *LCL*)

But the influx of Jewish slaves significantly enlarged the Jewish population of Rome. More importantly, it gradually changed the civil status of a certain part of the Jewish community, since all the Jews who were formally manumitted were granted full Roman citizenship,[10] and there is no doubt that at least some of the Jews in Rome acquired this right.[11]

---

[6]Marshall, 'Flaccus', 141f. See discussion of this issue in Stern, *GLAJJ* I, XXXIV, . 194, n. 4 (references to literature); Leon, *The Jews in Ancient Rome*, 7f.; Marshall, 'Flaccus'; Barclay, *Jews in the Mediterranean Diaspora*, 287f.

[7]Thus Cicero, *Pro Flacco*, 28.66, informs the judges that he has to lower his voice so that only the jurors may hear, since he is afraid of Jews who have come to offer support for their compatriots.

[8]Philo, *Legatio* 155.

[9]The possibility of Jewish political influence in Rome in this period, which Leon *The Jews of Ancient Rome*, 8, advocates, seems, however, to be rather doubtful.

[10]Informal manumission gave to freedmen *peregrine* status, but after the *Lex Junia* was passed in 25 BC, 17 BC, or AD 19, they secured a Junian Latin status (rights similar to those which were granted to Latin colonies); see Smallwood, *The Jews under Roman Rule*, 131f.

[11]Philo, *Legatio*, 157-158.

The most important factor forwarding the interest of the Jews in Rome was the favourable attitude shown towards them by Julius Caesar, who issued a number of decrees which granted them important privileges in certain cities of Asia. The first was freedom of worship.[12] In one of these decrees, addressed to the people of Parium, there is a reference to the exemption which was made for Jews in Rome from the ban on *collegia*:[13] Jews were permitted to assemble in the city, to collect contributions of money and to hold common meals in accordance with their customs.[14]   That Jews saw in Caesar their protector and treasured his benevolence is evident from the way they mourned after his assassination. According to Suetonius, (*Julius* 84.5)

> at the height of the public grief a throng of foreigners went about lamenting each after the fashion of his country, above all the Jews, who even flocked to the place for several successive nights.

(trans. J.C. Rolfe, *LCL*).

Augustus continued the same benevolent policy. When he reenacted the ban on *collegia*, Jews again were exempted and their rights of association were confirmed.[15] He even granted an additional privilege to Jews in Rome who held Roman citizenship and were thus entitled to the monthly dole. If the distribution happened to fall on a Sabbath, the Jews were allowed to collect their share on the following day.[16] Augustus' patronage of Jews was commemorated in the name of one of the Roman synagogues: συναγωγὴ Αὐγουστησίων (the synagogue of the Augustans).[17] Noy rightly observed that, in principle, 'the eponym *could* be anyone with the title Augustus, but few if any 1st or 2nd century emperors had such good relations with the Jews'.[18]

---

[12]Josephus, *AJ* 14.185-216. Caesar's favourable policy was to a certain extent caused by the support of Judaean rulers which he enjoyed during the civil war between him and Pompey; Hyrcanus II played an important role in the issuing of these documents; see Leon, *The Jews of Ancient Rome*, 9f.; Smallwood, *The Jews under Roman Rule*, 135; Rajak, 'Was there a Roman Charter for the Jews?', 110.

[13]Cf. Suetonius, *Julius* 42.3: *cuncta collegia praeter antiquitus constituta distraxit* ('He disbanded all *collegia*, except those of ancient foundation'). The first ban on *collegia*, which was imposed in 64 BC and rescinded in 58 BC, did not explicitly exempt Jewish communities; unlike the previous one, which could possibly have been in operation only in Rome, this ban on *collegia* was empire-wide; see Smallwood, *The Jews under Roman Rule*, 134; cf. p. 145 n. 46.

[14]Josephus, *AJ* 14. 215-216.

[15]Philo, *Legatio* 157; Suetonius, *Augustus* 32.1; cf. Josephus, *AJ* 16.162-165 (Asia).

[16]Philo, *Legatio* 158.

[17]*CIJ* I² 284, 301, 338, 368, 416, 496 = Noy, *JIWE* 2 547, 96, 169, 189, 194, 542.

Under Tiberius the life of the Jewish community was not as peaceful as before. In 19 AD, Jews were expelled from Rome.[19] Despite the expulsion, it seems that a considerable part of the community managed to remain in Rome and many of the deported returned after some time, for, by the 40s, the Jewish community had again become substantial. Philo testifies that after the death of Sejanus (October, AD 31) who 'wanted to destroy that race completely'[20] the rights of the Jews were restored.[21]

During the short reign of Gaius the actual status of Jews in Rome as far as it is known, was not changed. However, the eccentric behaviour of the emperor, his wicked jokes at the expense of some Jewish envoys, who came to Rome to complain of the abuses which were inflicted upon Jews in Alexandria, his hostility towards them[22] and lastly his intention to set up his statue in the Jerusalem Temple,[23] could not but threaten and horrify the Jewish community. But it was the next reign that brought serious troubles for them.

Evidence from the Principates of Claudius and Nero

Two important events concerning Jews are reported by our sources to have happened during Claudius' principate. The first one is a general edict issued at the very beginning of his reign which authorized Jews throughout the whole empire to observe their customs without let or hindrance.[24] The second one is the expulsion of Jews from Rome, dated by Dio Cassius (who, however, did not speak about expulsion, but about a ban on meetings) to Claudius' first year in power (AD 41). These actions of Claudius are sometimes viewed as contradictory. In an attempt to resolve this contradiction, some scholars date the expulsion later in Claudius' reign and develop a theory of two periods in Claudius' attitude towards Jews: at first benevolent (under the

---

[18]*CIJ* I² 284, 301, 338, 368, 416, 496 = Noy, *JIWE* 2, 79.
[19]See in detail p. 30.
[20]For Sejanus' anti-Jewish policy we have only Philo's testimony (Eusebius cannot be viewed as an independent source, since he only summarises *Legatio* 160 in *HE* II,5.7); see Smallwood, *The Jews under Roman Rule*, 201f.
[21]*Legatio* 160-161.
[22]Philo, *Legatio* 349-367: 'As soon as we came into Gaius' presence, we realized from his appearance and gestures that we were standing not before a judge but before an accuser more hostile to us than our actual opponents'.
[23]Philo, *Legatio* 203.
[24]Josephus, *AJ* 19. 286-291; cf. p. 141ff.

influence of his friend Agrippa I), he is supposed then to have made a complete reversal, resulting in hostile measures against the Jews (and there was no longer an Agrippa to take in their side, for he died in AD 44).[25] The testimony of the Christian historian Paulus Orosius (of the beginning of the fifth century) is usually cited as a justification for accepting this solution. Orosius, with a reference to Josephus, dated Claudius' expulsion to the 9th year of his reign, i.e. AD 49.[26] There is no such record, however, in the works of Josephus and it is not known where Orosius, who is a very unreliable source, got his date. Tacitus, whose account of the events of AD 49 has survived (although admittedly not in full form), while those for the year 41 are missing completely, reports nothing about the expulsion in the first-mentioned year. Neither does Dio, though, for the sake of accuracy, we must bear in mind that from AD 47 to 54 his history exists only in excerpts. But, before discussing the real contradictions in the extant evidence, it is necessary to eliminate an alleged one, i.e. between the edict and the expulsion. This cannot be used as the ground for dating the expulsion later in Claudius' reign.

In AD 41, Claudius produced a number of documents concerning Jews. There were two edicts—one dealing with the rights of Alexandrian Jews and another granting Jewish rights throughout the whole empire, both of which were reported by Josephus.[27] Fortunately, we also possess the letter of Claudius to the Alexandrians, preserved on papyri and first published in 1924.[28] Not surprisingly, the letter is sharper in tone than the edicts. But all three documents have a common feature: a warning to Jews to behave reasonably. In the letter the warning is expressed in very strong words indeed:

---

[25]See e.g. Schürer, Vermes, Millar, Goodman, The History of the Jewish People, 3, 1, 77, n. 91: 'An edict unfavourable to the Jews is not likely to belong to the earliest years of his reign for it was just then that he published an edict of tolerance in their regard'; see the list of scholars who hold this view in D. Slingerland, 'Suetonius Claudius 25.4 and the Account in Cassius Dio', JQR 79:4 (1989), 308. However, S. Benko, 'The Edict of Claudius of A.D. 49 and the Instigator Chrestus', TZ 25 (1969), 408, who strongly supports the idea of incompatibility of the edict and the expulsion, exaggerates when he writes that AD 49 (the date is taken from Orosius, see below) 'is now the generally accepted date of the edict'.
[26]Historiae adversum paganos 7.6.15-16. The work was composed at Augustine's request in the year 417-418. B. Altaner, Patrology, ET (Freiburg, Edinburgh/London: Herder/Nelson, 1960), 280.
[27]Josephus, AJ 19.280-291.
[28]P. Lond. 1912 (H.I. Bell, Jews and Christians in Egypt (1924), 23ff., plate I); see also the text of the letter and commentary in CPJ II, No. 153.

The Jews, on the other hand, I order not to aim at more than they have previously had[29]. . . . If they disobey, I shall proceed against them in every way as fomenting a common plague for the whole world. [30]

(trans. V. Tcherikover, *CPJ* II, 43).

In the edict sent to Alexandria, Claudius demanded that both Greeks and Jews should take 'the greatest precaution to prevent any disturbance'. In the general edict he states:

I enjoin upon them also by these presents to avail themselves of this kindness in a more reasonable spirit, and not to set at nought the beliefs about gods held by other peoples, but to keep their own laws.

(trans. L. Feldman, *LCL*).

All these documents show Claudius as a clever politician[31] who takes no sides but is keen to restore order and the sane traditions of Augustus' policy, which included the toleration of the Jewish community, with its special and long-established religious rights.[32] There was nothing especially cordial[33] in Claudius' attitude towards Jews.[34]

---

[29]This phrase is rather vague and can be interpreted variously, since it is not clear what the *status quo* of the Jewish community previously was, and whether it, or any part of it, possessed Alexandrian citizenship. See discussion of the legal status of Alexandrian Jews in *LCL ad loc* (Feldman) and Barclay, *Jews in the Mediterranean Diaspora*, 60-71.

[30]The opinion that the word 'plague' was a reference to a nascent Christianity has no justification.

[31]The publication of the letter has helped to change, in the opinion of many scholars, the traditional profile of Claudius as of a slow-witted and shallow person. See discussion in *CPJ* II, 38.

[32]On Claudius' religious policy in general see A. Momigliano, *Claudius the Emperor and His Achievement*, ET (Cambridge: W. Heffer & Sons, Ltd, 1961), 20-38; V.M. Scramuzza, *The Emperor Claudius* (Cambridge, Mass: Harvard University Press, 1940), 145-156; cf. B. Levick, *Claudius* (London: B.T.Batsford Ltd, 1990), 87.

[33]It is argued sometimes that close relations with Agrippa would have prevented Claudius from acting against Roman Jews. It is true that nearly all documents produced by Romans in favour of Jews were a result of personal dealings, but this does not mean that Roman officials were ready to sacrifice the interests of the empire for the sake of friendly connections. On this issue see D. Slingerland, 'Suetonius *Claudius* 25.4' 313, who reminds us that, despite their close friendship, Claudius made Agrippa stop fortifying the walls of Jerusalem. Slingerland rightly observes that 'imperial friendship with individual members of the Jewish aristocracy was one thing, the handling of Jewish masses entirely different'.

[34]See Murphy-O'Connor, *St. Paul's Corinth,*, 137-139; D. Slingerland, 'Suetonius *Claudius* 25.4', 308-312.

Now let us examine the evidence concerning the Jewish expulsion. Suetonius reports that Claudius' expelled those Jews from Rome who were constantly making disturbances at the instigation of Chrestus' (*Iudaeos impulsore Chresto assidue tumultantis Roma expulit*).[35] Suetonius does not give any date for the event. Dio Cassius' testimony (60.6.6) runs as follows:

> Τούς τε Ἰουδαίους πλεονάσαντας αὖθις, ὥστε χαλεπῶς ἂν ἄνευ ταραχῆς ὑπὸ τους ὄχλου σφῶν τῆς πόλεως εἰρχθῆναι, οὐκ ἐξήλασε μέν, τῷ δὲ δὴ πατρίῳ βίῳ χρωμένους ἐκέλευσε μὴ συναθροίζεσθαι.

As for the Jews, who had again increased so greatly that by reason of their multitude it would have been hard without raising a tumult, to bar them from the city, he [sc. Claudius] did not drive them out but ordered them, while continuing their traditional mode of life, not to hold meetings.

(trans. E. Cary, *LCL*)

Neither Suetonius nor Dio gives a date for the action of Claudius. However, from 60.3.2 onwards Dio arranges his narrative in chronological order.[36] He mentions that Claudius gave land to Agrippa I and his brother Herod, the events that Josephus dated in AD 41. After that he gives two chronological references: 'then' (60.8.4) and 'in this year' (60.8.7); after these he completes the narrative of the events of the year in question and begins the next portion with the words 'in the next year' (60.9.1). This allows us to assume with a high degree of confidence that he believed Claudius' action to have taken place in the same year.[37]

Luke in Acts 18:2 mentions that Paul found in Corinth Aquila and Priscilla who had 'recently' (προσφάτως) come to Corinth from Italy because Claudius had ordered all Jews to depart from Rome. At first sight it seems that, since their arrival in Corinth was nearly at the same time as Paul's, the expulsion, mentioned by Luke, has to be dated by the very end of 40s, since it is generally assumed that Paul came to Cor-

---

[35]*Claudius* 25.4 = *GLAJJ* II No. 307. The text of Suetonius can be understood as referring either to the expulsion only of the trouble-makers (which seems to me preferable) or to the expulsion of the whole Jewish community; cf. the translation by J.C. Rolfe, *LCL*: 'Since the Jews constantly made disturbances at the instigation of Chrestus, he expelled them from Rome'.
[36]G. Lüdemann, *Paul, Apostle to the Gentiles: Studies in Chronology* (Philadelphia and London: SCM, 1984), 187, n. 67.
[37]Slingerland, 'Suetonius *Claudius* 25.4', 307f.

inth in AD 51.[38] On the other hand, the text of Acts does not necessarily imply that Aquila and Priscilla came to Corinth directly from Rome. They could have spent several years somewhere else before arriving in Corinth, and thus the early date for the expulsion cannot be ruled out on the basis of traditional Pauline chronology.[39]

Orosius gives the following evidence:

Anno eiusdem nono expulsos per Claudium urbe Iudaeos Iosephus refert, sed me magis Suetonius movet, qui ait hoc modo Claudius Iudaeos impulsore Christo (sic!) adsidue tumultuantes Roma expulit; quod, utrum contra Christum tumultuantes Iudaeos coerceri et conprimi iusserit, an etiam Christianos simul velut cognatae religionis homines voluerit expelli, nequam discernitur.

Josephus reports that Jews were expelled from the city by Claudius in his ninth year, although I am more convinced by Suetonius, who testifies as follows: Claudius expelled the Jews from Rome who were constantly rioting because of the instigator Christ. It is impossible to determine whether he ordered only the Jews who were agitating against Christ to be restrained and supressed, or whether he wanted to expel also Christians as people of related faith.

So much for direct evidence. As for indirect evidence, some remarks in Philo's *Legatio* and in Claudius' Letter to Alexandria can also be interpreted as containing hints about Claudius' action against the Jews in Rome. In the *Legatio*, which was written in the early years of Claudius' principate,[40] Philo discusses Augustus' policy towards Jews. He says among other things that he 'did not expel them from Rome' or 'prevent them from meeting for the exposition of the Law'. These remarks, which are rather strange, make sense only if Philo was aware that an expulsion and prohibition against meetings could possibly take place, or had taken place, and he therefore refers to Augustus' treatment of the Jews as a precedent for Claudius, 'thus making an implicit protest at which the new emperor could not possibly take offence'.[41] The warning in the Letter to Alexandria against 'fomenting a common

---

[38]But see Lüdemann, *Paul*, 170-175, who developed a new Pauline chronology and argued that Paul first stayed in Corinth in AD 41/42.

[39]Leon, *The Jews*, 25; Stern, 'The Jewish Diaspora', *CRINT* 1, 182.

[40]Smallwood, 'The Jews under Roman Rule', 213.

[41]Smallwood, 'The Jews under Roman Rule', 214; cf. also Murphy-O'Connor, *St.Paul's Corinth: Texts and Archaeology* (Wilmington: Michael Goazier, Inc., 1983, Good News Studies, 6), 136f.

plague' can also be seen as a reference to Claudius' irritation with Jews in Rome.

The Scholion to Juvenal 4.117[42] mentions Jews who were expelled from Rome and settled in Aricia. While Momigliano connected this passage with the expulsion of AD 19,[43] Juster and Schürer attributed the expulsion to Claudius' reign;[44] neither connection can be verified.[45]

G. Howard attracts attention to a passage in the Syriac *Doctrine of Addai*, which he interprets as a reflection of the Jewish-Christian clashes under Claudius.[46] The passage in question retells a fantastic story about queen Protonice, the wife of Claudius and a Christian convert, who travelled to Jerusalem and restored to James the possession of Golgotha, the cross and the tomb of Christ which were being withheld from Christians by the Jews. When she returned to Rome and gave Claudius the account of her trip, the latter expelled all the Jews from Italy. Given the non-historical character of the whole composition this evidence should be dismissed.

The questions raised by this contradictory evidence, which has generated a vast body of scholarly literature, can be formulated as follows: (1) Was there an expulsion of Jews under Claudius (Acts, Suetonius, Orosius)? (2) If there was an expulsion, were all the Jews banned from Rome (Acts) or only the rioters (as the evidence of Suetonius could possibly imply)? (3) Were there two events—a ban on meetings (Dio) and an expulsion (Suetonius, Acts, Orosius)—connected with Jews, or do our sources refer to the same event? (4) What was the date of the event? (5) Does Suetonius register the disputes in the Jewish community in Rome and connect them with Christ and the beginning of the Christian mission, or with 'Chrestus', a certain Jewish troublemaker?

Not surprisingly, taking into consideration the contradictory character of our evidence the answers which have been given to these questions are very diverse. Barclay in his survey reasonably reduced the answers to the first four questions to two types of solution. One is to give credence to all four direct sources and to postulate two different

---

[42]Stern, *GLAJJ* II, No. 538.
[43]Momigliano, *Claudius the Emperor*, 30, 96, n. 24.
[44]Juster, *Les Juifs*,1, vol.1, 181, n. 9; Schürer, *Geschichte*, 3, 63.
[45]Cf. remark in Schürer, Vermes, Millar, Goodman, *The History of the Jewish People*, 3, 1, 78, n. 94 that the story might refer to another event, or be fictional.
[46]'The Beginnings of Christianity in Rome: A Note on Suetonius, *Life of Claudius* XXV. 4', *ResQ* 24 (1981), 177.

events which took place during Claudius' reign. The other is to take all sources as referring, even if confusingly and contradictorily, to the same event. Barclay himself supported the first solution and accepted that there was a ban on meetings in AD 41 and a limited expulsion in AD 49.[47] I would rather support the second one.

The evidence of Orosius should be dismissed as secondary and completely unreliable.[48] The date which he suggested cannot stand and must be discarded once and for all; it is quite possible that he actually chose it for apologetic reasons.[49] Those scholars who accept Orosius' dating do so either because they consider it psychologically impossible for Claudius to act at the same time both in favour of and against the Jews (see above), or because they believe that Suetonius refers to Christians, and that a later date would harmonize better with Luke's evidence and the beginning of the Christian mission.[50] Such an approach ignores source criticism and cannot be justified. As Lüdemann quite correctly observes, 'source criticism should be performed before reconstruction of the historical events'.[51]

Suetonius, Dio and Luke refer to measures against Jews taken by Claudius. All three authors know about the tradition of the expulsion, but while Luke accepts it at face value (all Jews were expelled) and Suetonius perhaps with a certain restriction (only those who participated in the disturbances), Dio refutes it completely. The indirect witness of Philo, discussed above, seems to confirm that at the beginning of Claudius' reign two actions—expulsion and a ban on meetings— were rumoured *simultaneously*. We are forced to admit that the contradictory character of our sources does not allow us to restore precisely what actually happened. It is clear, however, that very soon after Claudius came to power he took some actions against Jews in Rome, as a result of which many of them left the capital.

---

[47]Barclay, *Jews in the Mediterranean Diaspora*, 305f.

[48]I wholly support Lüdemann, 164, who insists that 'one should, for reasons of method, in any event *not* proceed on the basis of the date of the Jews' expulsion that he has preserved'.

[49]See Lüdemann, *Paul, Apostle to the Gentiles*, 186f., n. 64, who argues that since Orosius, who collected the references to Christ by secular writers, was sure that Claudius' decree reported by Suetonius was related to Christ's impact in Rome, chronological reasons prevented him from accepting the earlier date.

[50]Cf. for instance V.M. Scramuzza, *The Emperor Claudius* (Cambridge, Mas.: Harvard University Press, 1940), 287, n. 20: 'if Chrestus . . . is to be identified with Christ, Orosius' date is plausible'.

[51]Lüdemann, *Paul, Apostle to the Gentiles*, 167.

The reason for Claudius' discontent with the Jews is explained only by Suetonius. The literature discussing his short phrase is enormous, but is justified by the importance of the issue, i.e. the beginning of Christianity in Rome. The starting point both for those who see in Suetonius' 'Chrestus' a reference to Jesus Christ and for those who vigorously refute this identification is an argument over spelling.

Those who advocate the equation point out that the spellings *Chrestus* and *Christus*, *Chrestiani* and *Christiani* were used interchangeably by Christians themselves. Even in the *codex Sinaiticus* we have three examples of Χρηστιανός.[52] Tertullian, *Apol.* 3.5 explained that, because of the way in which it as commonly pronounced by pagans, the letter *e* was substituted for *i* as a result of popular etymology:

> *Christianus' vero, quantum interpretatio est, de unctione deducitur; sed et cum perperam 'Chrestianus' pronuntiatur a vobis - nam nec nominis certa notitia apud vos -, de suavitate vel benignitate compositum est.*

> But Christian so far as the meaning of the word is concerned, is derived from anointing. Yes, and when it is wrongly pronounced by you 'Chrestianus' (for you do not even know accurately the name [you hate]; it comes from sweetness and benignity.

> (trans. S. Thelwall, *ANF*)

Lactantius *Div. inst.* 4.7.4 witnesses that the name of Christ was also commonly corrupted in the same way as the word 'Christian':

> *Christus non proprium nomen est, sed nuncupatio potestatis et regni . . . sed exponenda huius nominis ratio est propter ignorantiam errorem, qui eum immutata littera Chrestum solent dicere.*

> Christ is not a proper name, but a title of power and dominion . . . . But the meaning of this name must be set forth, on account of the error of the ignorant, who by the change of a letter are accustomed to call him Chrestus.

> (trans. W. Fletcher, *ANF*)

Thus, Suetonius makes a quite common mistake which is not surprising, especially for a pagan author who did not take pains to find out the true history of Christ and the date of his execution,[53] or to get

---

[52] Acts 11:26; 26:28; 1 Pet. 4:16 (all by the first hand). See other examples in F. Blass, 'ΧΡΗΣΤΙΑΝΟΙ - ΧΡΙΣΤΙΑΝΟΙ', *Hermes* 30 (1895), 465-470.

to the heart of Messianic implications of the name. Besides *Chrestus* was a common personal name and, for this reason, the Gentile author would naturally spell the name of Christ with 'e' if he was not instructed otherwise.

Those who deny the identification argue that precisely because Chrestus was a common name we must not be surprised to find a certain Jewish (or Christian) troublemaker in Rome who had this name.[54] They also refer to the fact that Suetonius, as Tacitus before him, knew the correct name of the adherents of 'a new and mischievous superstition'.[55] But is this so?

The reading of the scholarly literature sometimes leaves an impression that we possess manuscripts written by the hand of Suetonius or Tacitus. What we really have are manuscripts produced by Christian scribes[56] who did not hesitate to correct and improve what they thought to have been wrong. The misspellings of the names 'Christ' and 'Christiani' were among the most obvious errors in need of correction. The example of Tacitus' written tradition is instructive. Despite claims that Tacitus knew the correct spelling, the *codex Mediceus* witnesses that the situation is far from being clear. In this manuscript we have the spelling *Chrestiani* which was then corrected either by a scribe or by a later hand.[57] This inevitably leads to the conclusion that in the archetype from which the *codex Mediceus* was derived the name was spelt with *e*.[58] The name *Christus*, however is spelt in the *codex Mediceus* with *i*. This could be a result of correction on the part of the scribe responsible from this manuscript.[59] Alternatively, perhaps Tacitus meant that the Christians were called *Chrestiani* by the Roman *vulgus*,[60] although the name of the *auctor nominis* was Christus,[61] and we have

---

[53]Suetonius' passage in *Nero* 16.2, unlike Tacitus' in *Annales* 15.44 does not reveal any knowledge about the Christ-story. Theoretically it would have been quite possible for a Gentile author to believe, even at the beginning of the second century, that Christ was in Rome at the time of Claudius. The error of Suetonius or his source would have been quite understandable against the background of the transparent meaning of the words in *-iani*: partisans of a certain leader. The extravagant idea that Jesus escaped dying on the cross and went to Rome, where he caused trouble, R. Graves and J. Podro, *Jesus in Rome: A Historical Conjecture* (London: Cassel and Company, 1957), 42, does not warrent discussion.

[54]See the list of candidates in Slingerland, 'Suetonius *Claudius* 25.4', 133f.

[55]Nero, 6.16.2, where manuscripts of Suetonius have *Christiani*.

[56]The earliest manuscript of Suetonius is the *codex Memmianus* of the ninth century with corrections made in the eleventh-twelfth; the famous *codex Mediceus alter* which contains Tacitus' *Annales* XI-XVI was written in the eleventh century.

[57]Fuchs, 'Tacitus über die Christen', *VC* 4 (1950), 70, n. 6.

[58]Fuchs, 'Tacitus über die Christen'.

to read this passage as ironic: they who were hateful because of their abominations were called by the Roman crowd by a name derived from the word 'good'. In the end, we have to conclude that we cannot be sure that Tacitus knew the correct spelling and actual meaning of the name.

The same is true for Suetonius. It is generally assumed that when Orosius quoted Suetonius' passage, it was he who was responsible for the correction of *impulsore Chresto* to *impulsore Christo*, as well as for connecting the expulsion with Christian polemics. This is possible, especially against the background of his apologetic tendency. But it is similarly possible that he found this spelling in his copy of Suetonius. The corruption from *Christus* to *Chrestus* would not be surprising, given the fact that before the copying of pagan literature became an occupation of Christian scribes, it was in the hands of pagans for whom the form *Chrestus* was more familiar and understandable. That the name was not corrected later by Christian scribes can be explained by their belief that Suetonius did not mean Christ. Christian scribes would certainly have corrected the wrong spelling in an obvious context, but in this particular case the situation was reversed: they knew all too well that Christ was not in Rome in the 40s and that he was not the *impulsor*. They would, together with part of our modern scholarly community, rather take Suetonius' Chrestus to be someone else. In the Mediaeval Period, when the manuscripts which are now in our posession were produced, the name Chrestus was still in use, though less common, the correct spelling and meaning of the name of Christ was well established and the puns based on changing one letter had long been abandoned.

I am by no means intending to put forward any definite hypothesis about the textual transmission of Suetonius. All I wish to show is

---

[59]*E.g.* a scribe of the *codex Mediceus* precisely copied the word *Chrestiani* from the manuscript which he had in front of him, then automatically wrote Christus correctly and after that, realizing that there is a contradiction between the two spellings harmonized them by correcting the first word also.

[60]Cf. Taylor, Why were the Disciples', 77: 'The wording presupposes that at Rome in the 60s the common people called the disciples Χρηστιανοί, so followers of Χρηστός, although the educated knew the correct form of the founder's name to be Χριστός'.

[61]Cf. Fuchs, 'Tacitus über die Christen', 74, n. 13: 'Dass aber auch Christus selbst bei Tacitus den Namen *Chrestus* getragen haben müsse . . . ist keine überzeugende Folgerung. Wie die griechischen Kirchenschriftsteller den Namen Χριστός mit χρηστός zusammenzubringen lieben . . ., so war es umgekehrt auch möglich, von dem Worte *Chrestianus* zu *Christus* zurückzuschreiten'.

that the foundation on which we have built is very shaky indeed. We need to abandon the habit of making dogmatic statements about how actually Suetonius or Tacitus spelled the name of Christ or of the adherents of the new religion. We simply do not know.

Leaving aside arguments from the spelling, we have to admit that all other arguments which have been suggested in order to support the identification with Jesus are not decisive and can easily be challenged.[62] On the other hand, there are no arguments to prove that Christian involvement in the Jewish disturbances in Rome under Claudius was historically impossible. The other solution—Chrestus is the name of the otherwise unknown Jewish troublemaker—is also not supported by any additional evidence. Slingerland somewhat misrepresents the situation when he writes that the 'Chrestus event makes perfectly good sense just as it appears in Suetonius, Acts and, provided he was referring to the same occurrence, Dio Cassius',[63] since the 'Chrestus-event' appears only in Suetonius. I wonder along which lines scholarly discussion would have developed if, in our manuscript tradition, we had had a 'Christus-event' in the Suetonius' passage. This returns us to the issue of spelling and to the disappointing conclusion that both solutions are equally unprovable. After all due consideration I would, however, be inclined to support the identification of Christus with Christ and to admit that Suetonius' passage echoes disturbances in Rome's Jewish community provoked by the appearance of the first Christians.[64] This solution seems to me to be more reasonable and economical than the other one.

Nero's reign, which was marked by a most severe persecution of Christians, seems to have been quite placid for Jews.[65] Information about any event connected with the Jewish community in Rome during the years of the Jewish War is absent. The triumphal procession with which the victory over Judaea was celebrated definitely would not have made Roman Jews feel more secure. But though Palestine, as a specifically Jewish homeland, ceased to exist, the privileges of Diaspora Jewry were not abolished. The only really important change

---

[62]These arguments most fully represented in H. Janne, 'Impulsore Chresto', *Annuaire de l'Institut de Philologie et d'Histoire orientales* 2 (1934), 531-553 and most vigorously refuted by by Slingerland, 'Chrestus: Christus?', 137-114.

[63]Slingerland, 'Chrestus: Christus?', 144.

[64]I see no reason why it should not have been possible for Christianity to reach Rome in circa AD 40; cf. Murphy-O'Connor, *St. Paul's Corinth,* 132.

[65]On Nero's consort Poppaea and her possible involvment with Judaism see p. 66.

was the introduction of a poll tax, the so called *fiscus Iudaicus*, which replaced the Temple tax.[66]

Finally, the total number of Jews in Rome in the first century AD has been much debated and the estimates vary between ten thousand and sixty thousand.[67]

II. Epigraphic Evidence

The most important information about the Jewish community of Rome is obtained primarily from the inscriptions[68] found in six Jewish underground cemeteries, which are usually called catacombs: Monteverde (on the Via Portuense), Vigna Randanini, Via Cimarra, Vigna Casilina, Villa Torlonia (two catacombs).[69] These are of the second to fourth centuries AD.[70]

The synagogues of Rome

The inscriptions found in the catacombs reveal the existence of at least eleven synagogues in Rome.

(1) The synagogue of the Agrippesians ('Αγριππησίων)[71] is believed to have been named after Marcus Vipsanius Agrippa, who was

---

[66]See in detail chapter 1.

[67]See references in H. Solin, 'Juden und Syrer im westlichen Teil der römischen Welt, *ANRW* II 29, 2 (1983) 698f., n. 53. For the unreliability of demographic calculations of the Jewish population in the Hellenistic and Roman periods, see p. 23; cf. also L.V. Rutgers, 'Attitudes to Judaism in the Greco-Roman period: Reflections on Feldman's "Jew and Gentile in the Ancient World"', *JQR* 85:3-4 (1995), 365, who especially stresses the unreliability of figures provided by (near) contemporaries (and these are the basis for the demographic calculations for Rome's Jews).

[68]But not excusively: other archaeological remains, such as wall paintings, sarcophagi, gold glasses, pottery lamps and funerary architecture, can also help us to understand the everyday life of Jewish communities; see Rutgers, *The Jews in Late Ancient Rome*, 50-100.

[69]See detailed description in Leon, *The Jews*, 46-66; 351-355; Noy, *JIWE* 2 1-9; 173-181; 332; 337-338; 341-346 (with updated bibliography).

[70]For the brick-stamps in some of the catacombs belong to the first century AD, see detailed study by Frey in *CIJ* I², 211-227. But the gap between the date of the stamp and of the use of the brick may be quite substantial. There are no epitaphs in the catacombs earlier than the second century AD. The majority is datable in the third-fourth century AD.

[71]*CIJ* I² 425, 365, 503, 733e (B) = Noy, *JIWE* 2 130, 170, 549, 562.

the son-in-law of Augustus. Other possible candidates are the Jewish kings Agrippa I or Agrippa II. It is also possible that the name was derived not from a person named Agrippa, but rather from a building or area, for instance from the *Horrea Agrippiana* in *Regio* VIII of Rome.[72]

(2) Six epitaphs mention the synagogue of the Augustesians (Αυγουστησίων).[73] It has been suggested that both the synagogue of the Agrippesians and the synagogue of the Augustesians originally consisted of slaves and freedman of Agrippa and of Augustus.[74] This is not entirely impossible.[75]

(3) The synagogue of the Calcaresians (Καλκαρησίων)[76] used to be reckoned to have been a congregation of the Jewish guild of lime-burners, since the Latin word *calcarenses* (*calcarienses*) seems to have been used in inscriptions to designate a guild of lime-burners (though individuals were usually called *calcariarii*). Leon, however, pointed out that Jews usually had no separate congregations for those who were engaged in the same occupation and suggested that the name was derived from the locality.[77]

(4) The synagogue of the Campesians (Καμπησίων, *Campi*)[78] is generally held to have derived its name from the *Campus Martius*, where its house of prayer could have been situated.[79]

(5) The synagogue of Elaea ('Ελαία, 'Ελέα) is attested in two inscriptions.[80] The name is puzzling. It has been suggested that it was derived from the olive or olive tree. Other interpretations include the name of the prophet Elijah, the name of Velia, a spur of the Palatine, the name of the city from which its members had emigrated (candidates include Elaea in Aeolia, Phoenicia, Bithynia and one in Mysia which was a port of Pergamum, etc.). Each of these interpretations has weak points and none can be regarded as wholly satisfactory.[81]

(6) There are four inscriptions in which the synagogue of the Hebrews ('Εβρέων) is mentioned.[82] In a few inscriptions individuals are

---

[72]Leon, *The Jews*, 140-142; Noy, *JIWE* 2 130, 110.
[73]*CIJ* I² 284, 301, 338, 368, 416, 496 = Noy, *JIWE*,2 547, 96, 169, 189, 194, 542; for the explanation of the name see p. 70.
[74]Cf. the phrase in Phil. 4:22: οἱ ἐκ τηςς Καίσαρος οἰκίας. See also Schürer, Vermes, Millar, Goodman, *The History of the Jewish People*, 3, 1, 96.
[75]Cf. van der Horst, *Ancient Jewish Epitaphs*, 86, n. 3.
[76]*CIJ* I² 304, 316, 384, 504, 537 = Noy, *JIWE* 2 69, 98, 165, 1, 558, 584.
[77]Leon, *The Jews*, 142-144; Noy, *JIWE* 2 69, p. 61.
[78]*CIJ* I² 88, 319, 523 = Noy, *JIWE* 2 288, 560, 577.
[79]Leon, *The Jews*, 144f.; Noy, *JIWE* 2 288, p. 250.
[80]*CIJ* I² 281, 509 = Noy, *JIWE* 2 406, 576.
[81]Leon, *The Jews*, 145-147; Noy, *JIWE* 2 406, p.336.

called Hebrews.[83] It has been suggested that they were members of this synagogue, but this is rather doubtful.[84]

(7) The group of Secenians (Σεκηνῶν)[85] is referred to in one inscription only. The word 'synagogue' is not mentioned, but the genitive case of the name Secenians after the title grammateus fits well to the pattern of the inscriptions which give the names of the congregations and it is reasonable to suppose that in this case we also have the name of the synagogue. The attempts to explain the meaning of the name have given rise to the following theories of its derivation from different place names: (a) a place in Galilee which was called Sogane by Josephus (Vita 265) and was differently spelt in the Talmud. Against this proposition, however, speak both the size of the place (it was only a village) and the fact that it was destroyed rather early, perhaps in the second century AD; (b) Sicininum, a place on the Esquiline; and (c) the harbour town of Scina (Iscina) in North Africa, called locus Iudaeorum Augusti on the Tabula Peutingeriana, a fourth-century map.[86]

(8) The synagogue of the Siburesians (Σιβουρησίων) is attested by six (or, perhaps, seven) inscriptions.[87] The name is generally agreed to derive from the Subura, a district between the Viminal, the Esquiline and the Imperial Fora and the west slope of the Esquiline. The spelling with Sib- is not registered outside Jewish epigraphy.[88]

(9) The synagogue of the Tripolitans (Τριπολειτῶν) is known from one inscription.[89] The name of the congregation is derived from the name of the city from which members of the synagogue came to Rome. Two cities of that name in Phoenicia and in North Africa are considered to be possible candidates.[90]

---

[82]CIJ I² 291, 317, 510, 535 = Noy, JIWE 2 33, 2, 578, 579; for the meaning of the name see pp. 162-184.
[83]CIJ I² 354, 370, 379, 502, 505 = Noy, JIWE 2 44, 112, 108, 561, 559.
[84]Leon, The Jews, 149.
[85]CIJ I² 7 = Noy, JIWE 2 436.
[86]Leon, The Jews, 149-151; Noy, JIWE 2 436, p. 361.
[87]CIJ I² 18, 22, 35a (Prolegomenon), 67, 140, 380=Noy, JIWE 2 428, 452, 527, 452, 338, 557; cf. also 37 = 488, in which most editors have restored the name of this synagogue.
[88]Leon, The Jews, 151-153; Noy, JIWE 2 338, p. 284.
[89]CIJ I² 390 = Noy, JIWE 2 166, cf. also 408 = 113, which is an epitaph of a certain Symmachus εἱεροσάρης (= γερουσιάρχης) Τριπολίτης. There is no reference to a synagogue in the inscription and perhaps the deceased was not an official of the synagogue of the Tripolitans, but was from Tripolis. The possible interpretations are 'gerousiarch of Tripolis' and 'gerousiarch and of Tripolis', Noy, JIWE 2 p. 96).
[90]Leon, The Jews, 153f.

(10) The synagogue of the Vernaclesians (Βερνάκλων, Βερνακλ-
ώρων, Βερνακλησίων)[91] is referred to in four inscriptions. There are two
main theories concerning the meaning of the name. According to one,
the name is derived from the Latin word *verna*, ('house-born', which
was used to designate slaves born in the household as distinguished
from those who were purchased) and the congregation consisted of
Jews of servile origin. According to the other, the name is derived
from *vernaculus*, 'native', 'indigenous' and the congregation originally
consisted of native-born Romans.[92]

(11) The synagogue of Volumnesians (Βολουμνησίων, Βολυμνη-
σίων) is attested by four inscriptions.[93] The name of the synagogue is
considered to derive from the name Volumnius who was identified by
some scholars with the Volumnius, a procurator of Syria in 8 BC and a
friend of Herod. He was mentioned by Josephus several times (*AJ*
16.9,1; 2.280, 283; *BJ* 1.27.2.538; *AJ* 16.II.3.369). Leon strongly objects to
this view, and considers it is better to admit that the identity of the patron or the builder of the synagogue is unknown to us.[94]

Four other Roman synagogues (of the Herodians, [possibly
Rhodians], of Arca of Lebanon, of the Calabrians, of Severus) were
named but the evidence for them is inadequate. The most discussed
one among them is the synagogue of the Herodians, because of the uncertainties of the reconstruction of the name and the impossibility, as
many scholars have seen it, of the notion that a congregation would
have been named after the hated King Herod.[95]

The organisation of Roman synagogues

Literary sources give no information about the organisation of Jewish
communities in Rome. Philo in the *Legatio* 155-157 just mentions the
existence of Jewish prayer-houses and the district on the right bank of
the Tiber as the place where the Jews lived. The book of Acts 28:17
alone refers to the leaders of the Jewish community in Rome, and it
does so without specifying their official titles: τοὺς ὄντας τῶν Ἰουδαίων

---

[91]*CIJ* I[2] 318, 383, 398, 494 = Noy, *JIWE* 2 114, 117, 106, 540.
[92]See detailed discussion in Leon, *The Jews*, 154-157; cf. also Noy, *JIWE* 2 106, p. 90.
[93]*CIJ* I[2] 343, 402, 417, 523 = Noy, *JIWE* 2 167, 100, 163, 577.
[94]Leon, *The Jews*, 157-159.
[95]See detailed discussion in Leon, *The Jews*, 159-165; cf. also Noy, *JIWE* 2 292, p. 253
with updated bibliography, a new reading and a new interpretation (Ἡροδίων as
the personal name).

πρώτους.[96] The inscriptions reveal to us the titles of the officials of the synagogues, but say nothing about their actual role in communal life. This accounts for the abundance of different, and sometimes opposite, interpretations in scholarly literature.

The most important question to be answered concerning the structure of the Jewish community in Rome is whether there existed a central council similar to that in Alexandria, or whether all Roman Jewish communities were completely autonomous? Juster, Krauss, La Piana and Baron were the proponents of the existence of the central body exercising supervision over the entire Jewish community, while Schürer, Frey and Leon held the view that the synagogues were all independent.[97] The latter assumption is now dominant among scholars.[98] It is also generally assumed that the overall pattern for the structure of each congregation was fairly homogeneous.[99]

The titles of the synagogues' officials known from the epitaphs are as follows:

(1) ἀρχισυνάγωγος. This title is mentioned in four or five inscriptions from Rome.[100] The synonymous Hebrew title is *rosh ha-kneseth*, which could in fact be a back-formation from the Greek word.[101] Some scholars view the *archisynagogos* as the president of the congregation, who supervised both the worship and the business of the synagogue,[102] others as an official responsible exclusively for its cultic life.[103] Rajak and Noy argue that the position of *archisynagogos* was

---

[96]Attempts have been made to identify Luke's οἱ ὄντες τῶν Ἰουδαίων πρῶτοι with officials known from the inscriptions. Frey suggested that they should have been *gerousiarchs* (CIJ I, CVI); Penna, 'Les Juifs à Rome', 330, thought that they must have been the *archontes* of each community, but did not exclude the possibility that other officials (*grammateus, gerousiarchesi* and some *presbyteroi*) were also involved. M. Williams, 'The Structure of Roman Jewry Re-considered—Were the Synagogues of Ancient Rome Entirely Homogeneous?', ZPE 104 (1994), 130, warns that no firm identification can be made, since the wording is too imprecise and may not even imply office-holders, but just prominent members of the community.
[97]See discussion and references in Leon, *The Jews*, 167-194.
[98]For a collection of generally held opinions consult W. Wiefel, 'The Jewish Community in Ancient Rome and the Origins of Roman Christianity', *The Romans Debate*,[2] ed. K.P. Donfried (Edinburgh: T & T Clark, 1991), 85-101.
[99]But see Williams, 'The Structure of Roman Jewry', 129-141, who argues that the synagogues of Rome were varied both in their structure and titulature.
[100]CIJ I[2] 265, 282 (?), 383, 336, 504 = Noy, JIWE 2 322, 534 (?), 117, 13, 558; see the list of attestations of the term from the Mediterranean world in NewDocs 4, p. 214-217 and in T. Rajak, D. Noy, '*Archisynagogoi*: Office, Title and Social Status in the Graeco-Jewish Synagogue', JRS 83 (1993), 89-93.
[101]NewDocs. 4, 220; cf. Rajak, Noy, '*Archisynagogoi*'.

mainly honorific. People holding this office were benefactors and patrons of the communities.[104] The *archisynagogoi* are mentioned in Acts
13:15 in a context which implies their important role in the regulation
of the service, but this reference does not help in deciding what their
rôle was outside the service duties.[105]

(2) γερουσιάρχης. The title is attested by fourteen inscriptions.[106]
The generally held opinion is that the *gerousiarch* occupied an important position (perhaps that of a chairman) within the *gerousia* (Council
of Elders, a congregation's governing body), which means that he was
the administrative head of the community.[107] There is also one attestation of the title ἀρχιγερουσιάρχης[108] The meaning of the term is not
clear. The bearer of the title could have been the head of the central
board of all the city synagogues, but the absence of other references to
this official, as well as serious doubts whether such a body existed in
Rome, make this proposition rather questionable.[109]

(3) ἄρχων. This is the most frequently mentioned office—we
have about fifty attestations in Rome.[110] One's interpretation of the title depends upon the position one holds in the debate on the existence
of the central council. Those who believe in the autonomy of the congregations consider *archontes* to have been the members of an executive committee which managed the day-to-day running of each
congregation. Those who maintain that a central administrative body
existed regard them as members of this body, each representing a synagogue.[111] The precise functions of the *archontes* are unknown. A late
Christian homily supplies the information that the *archontes* were
elected in September.[112] From the titles δὶς ἄρχων and (once) τρὶς ἄρχων
it can be deduced that they were appointed for a prescribed time, per-

---

[102]Leon, *The Jews*, 171f.; B.J. Brooten, 'Women Leaders in the Ancient Synagogue'
(Chico: 1982, Brown Judaic Studies, 36), 23f.; Williams, 'The Structure of Roman
Jewry Reconsidered', 135.
[103]Schürer, Vermes, Millar, Black, *The History of the Jewish People*, 2, 434-436; 3, 1,
100; P.W. van der Horst, *Ancient Jewish Epitaphs*, 92.
[104]Rajak, Noy, '*Archisynagogoi*', 84-89.
[105]For a different evaluation of this passage see Williams, 'The Structure', 135; cf.
also Mk 5:22, 35, 36; Lk 8:49; 13:14.
[106]*CIJ* I² 9, 95, 106, 119, 147, 189, 301, 353, 368, 405, 408, 425, 511, 733b = Noy, *JIWE*
2 487, 351, 321, 354, 238, 389 (?), 96, 86, 189, 162, 113, 130, 554, 555.
[107]Leon, *The Jews*, 180f., Schürer, Vermes, Millar, Goodman, *The History of the Jewish
People*, 3, 1, 98.
[108]Noy, *JIWE* 2 521.
[109]Noy, *JIWE* 2 409.
[110]See list in Noy, *JIWE* 2 Index, p. 538.
[111]Leon, *The Jews*, 174f.

haps for a year. On the other hand, six inscriptions indicate the existence of a lifelong *archontes* (διὰ βίου).[113] The latter was possibly honorary.[114]

There are two examples of the title 'child archon' (ἄρχων νήπιος).[115] Here the title was definitely honorary, perhaps as a recognition of the important status of the family in the community. Such a distinction for a child was not uncommon in other communities in antiquity—Italian municipal life supplies us with the parallel of child decurions and Christian communities of child *lectores*.[116]

Two other titles—the archon πάσης τιμῆς and archon *alti ordinis* —are uniquely Roman. Frey understood τιμή as 'price', 'payment' and thought archon πάσης τιμῆς to be a kind of a treasurer, a financial executive of the Jewish community.[117] Leon interpreted the title as an indication of the higher dignity of this official as compared with an ordinary archon. The second title was, in his opinion, the Latin equivalent of the Greek term.[118] However, recently it has been argued that archon *alti ordinis* never existed and that the inscription has been interpreted incorrectly.[119] Williams suggested that the three puzzling titles of the archon διὰ βίου, the archon πάσης τιμῆς, and the archon *alti ordinis* were the designations of the leading officials in different congregations. According to her hypothesis, the synagogues had considerable diversity in their structure, and the variations of descriptions of leaders terms reflected this lack of homogeneity.[120]

In six inscriptions we have the title *mellarchon*.[121] The meaning of the title is clear from the composition of the word: 'archon-to-be'. The

---

[112]The title of the homily is *De Nativitate Sancti Ioannis Baptistae*. It was falsely attributed to John Chrysostom and in the older editions (until that of Montfaucon) was printed under his name; see *CIJ* I², p. LXXXLII; Leon, *The Jews*, 174, n. 2; Schürer, Vermes, Millar, Goodman, *The History of the Jewish People*, 3, 1, 99, n. 43.
[113]*CIJ* I² 266, 398, 416, 417, 480, 503 = Noy, *JIWE* 2 287 (?), 106, 194, 163, 198 (?), 549.
[114]So Leon, *The Jews*, 174; van der Horst, *Ancient Jewish Epitaphs*, 90. Cf., however, Williams, *The Structure*, 133, who claims that, since in the Greek world office holders for life are well attested, there is no difficulty in accepting the existence of the Jewish office διὰ βίου. She suggests that 'the main difference between senior archons like our (*archon*) διὰ βίου too and those of the 'ordinary' variety will have lain in status rather than function'. It is usually believed that civic office-holders for life have earned the title by donating to a fund for the expenses of their office.
[115]*CIJ* I² 88, 120 = Noy, *JIWE* 2 288, 337.
[116]Leon, *The Jews*, 179f.
[117]*CIJ* I, p. LXXXIX f. See the critical evaluation of this interpretation by Leon, *The Jews*, 177.
[118]Leon, *The Jews*, 177f.

age of the deceased who bore this title varies from two years and ten months[122] to thirty eight.[123]

There has been an attempt to explain the title *exarchon*, which is found in two inscriptions[124] as an opposite to an 'archon-to-be'—a 'former archon'.[125] Terms like ἔξαθλος ('past athletic exercise'), ἔξηβος ('past one's youth') seem to support such an interpretation.[126] However, terms with a prefix ἐξ- denoting a former status seem difficult to find in the Greek language.[127] On the other hand, the prefix may be regarded as Latin for the penetration of Latin affixes into the Greek language is not uncommon. But it seems that the meaning 'former' for *ex-* is not registered before the late 360s.[128]

According to another interpretation the term, *exarchon* is the equivalent of *archon*, but, as Leon quite correctly observes, an alternative to such a traditional title seems to be very unlikely.[129] Some see in *exarchon* the supreme head of all Roman Jews,[130] or a president of the

---

[119]I. Di Stefano Manzella, 'L. Maecius Archon, centurio alti ordinis. Nota critica zu *CIL*, VI, 39084 = *CIJ*, I, 470', *ZPE* 77 (1989), 103-112. The key to the interpretation of this inscription is the S-shaped character after the word *archon* and before the word *alti*. Di Stefano Manzella explained this character as a symbol for *centurio*. In this case *Archon* must be taken as a *cognomen* and the inscription is assumed to be a reused pagan one. This interpretation was accepted by Noy, and the inscription appeared in *JIWE* 2 in Appendix 4 (No. 618). Inscriptions not considered to be Jewish, although he noted that the title *centurio alti ordinis* unlike *centurio primi ordinis* is otherwise unattested. The interpretation does not seem to be conclusive to van der Horst, *Ancient Jewish Epitaphs*, 90, n. 18, though he admits that it 'deserves consideration'. It was rejected by Williams, *The Structure*, 133 (without arguments).
[120]Williams, *The Structure*, 136 ff.
[121]*CIJ* I² 85, 284, 325, 402, 457, 483 = Noy, *JIWE* 2 259, 547, 101, 100, 179, 180.
[122]*CIJ* I² 402 = Noy, *JIWE* 2 100.
[123]*CIJ* I² 457 = Noy, *JIWE* 2 179.
[124]*CIJ* I² 317, 465 = Noy, *JIWE* 2 2 4.
[125]Leon, *The Jews*, 189; the idea was put forward by Müller, but did not find support before Leon, who finds this interpretation 'at least a plausible one'.
[126]Leon, *The Jews*, 189; van der Horst, *Jewish Epitaphs*, 90.
[127]See Williams, *The Structure*, 139f. She thinks that the suggested parallels, besides being rare and literary are not apposite, since in both cases advanced age is implied. Williams argues that 'a twenty year old, such as the exarchon Gaius Furfanius Rufus can hardly be described as "past the archonship", when men older than he often held the post'. The rarity of examples makes it difficult to decide (at least in the case of ἔξαθλος) whether it was age or former status that was being emphasized.
[128]Williams, *The Structure*, 139, claims that Latin parallels 'prove curiously elusive'. For a different view cf. Noy, *JIWE* 2, p.12.
[129]Leon, *The Jews*, 189.

synagogal board similar to *gerousiarches* in some other Roman congregations.[131] On the whole, it must be admitted that the term is far from being clear.

(4) γραμματεύς. This title is the second in frequency after archon. We have twenty five instances of grammateus,[132] two of μελλογραμματεύς ('a secretary designate')[133] and three of γραμματεύς νήπιος ('a child secretary').[134] The *grammateus* was a subordinate official, a secretary of the community. The presence of child secretaries may imply that in some families this office was hereditary and that 'there was a presumptive right to this office, as perhaps also to that of archon'.[135]

(5) ὑπερέτης is attested in only one inscription.[136] Frey suggested that a *hyperetes* would be an assistant of an *archisynagogus* (*hazzan*) who took care of the sacred scrolls. Perhaps he also administered punishments.[137] The interpretation is based on the NT usage.[138]

(6) φροντιστής. We know only two *phrontistai* in Rome.[139] Theirs is considered to be a prestigious office, since on both occasions the title is listed at the end of a series of important offices. It looks as though it was an elective post, since in one of the inscriptions the deceased held this office twice. In non-Jewish sources the term is used as equivalent to the Latin *procurator* and quite possibly refers to a kind of manager. This led Frey to conclude that *phrontistes* was the business manager of the synagogue.[140]

(7) προστάτης. The title is known from two inscriptions.[141] Outside the Jewish world the term was used either for the leader of a political body or for the patron or representative of a group. The term is usually used in the second meaning and the Jewish *prostates* is consid-

[130]Juster and Krauss, see Leon, *The Jews*, 189.
[131]Williams, *The Structure*, 140.
[132]*CIJ* I² 7, 18, 24, 31, 36, 53, 67, 99, 102, 122, 125, 142, 145, 146, 148, 149 (bis), 180, 221, 225, 284, 318, 351, 433, 456 = Noy, *JIWE* 2 436, 428, 473, 457(?), 526(?), 484, 452, 255, 250, 262, 344, 263, 257, 256, 253, 223, 255, 266, 249, 547, 114, 188, 1, 85; 502, (not in *CIJ*).
[133]*CIJ* I² 121, 279 = Noy, *JIWE* 2 231, 404.
[134]One inscription has this title, *CIJ* I² 146 = Noy, *JIWE* 2 256, two others mark the child's age (99, 180 = 255, 284 = 547).
[135]Leon, *The Jews*., 186; cf. also van der Horst, *Ancient Jewish Epitaphs*, 92.
[136]*CIJ* I² 172 = Noy, *JIWE* 2 290.
[137]Leon, 'The Jews', 190; van der Horst, *Ancient Jewish Epitaphs*, 93.
[138]Luke 4:20.
[139]*CIJ* I² 337, 494 = Noy, *JIWE* 2 164, 540.
[140]*CIJ* I, XCIf. Leon, *The Jews*, 191, on the whole accepts this interpretation; cf. also the discussion of the term in L. Robert, *RPh* (1958), 36-38.
[141]*CIJ* I² 100, 365 = Noy, *JIWE* 2 373,170.

ered to be the official who defended the interests of the congregation in relations with the political authorities.[142] Williams, in line with her theory of the diversity in the structure and the titulature of the officials in the synagogues of Rome, views the title as an alternative to *archisynagogos*.[143]

(8) πάτηρ (μήτηρ) συναγωγῆς. We have ten attestations of the title *pater* and three of the title *mater* of the synagogue.[144] The generally held opinion is that the title was 'purely an honorary one, probably involving no active duties'.[145] The main ground for such an assumption was the belief that since women could bear the title it could not be anything other. This argument is untenable since the epigraphic evidence testifies to the high position and even leadership of women in many Jewish congregations.[146] Some compare the *pater/mater* of synagogues with the *pater* and *mater* of *collegia*, where the titles were the equivalent of *patronus* and *patrona*.[147] On another hypothesis the title-bearers were in charge of the charitable activities.[148] The *Codex Theodosianus* 16.8.4. includes fathers of the synagogue, along with other officials who serve the synagogues (*qui synagogis deserviunt*), in the group of persons who were granted the immunity from every compulsory service of a corporal nature (*munera corporalia*). This necessarily means that the fathers of the synagogues had some functional rôle since this was implied by the *Codex Theodosianus*.[149] The law is dated in the fourth century and it is difficult to say whether the father of the synagogue was a functionary in the earlier period as well. Van der Horst thinks that: 'the father of the synagogue was possibly a functionary that had something to do with the administration of the synagogue, although our knowledge remains very vague. *The matres synagogarum* were their female colleagues'.[150] Neither of the suggested interpretations of

---

[142]Leon, *The Jews*, 191f.

[143]Williams, *The Structure*, 138f.

[144]*pater*: CIJ I² 88, 93, 271, 319, 494, 508, 509, 510, 535, 537 = Noy, *JIWE* 2 288, 209, 210, 560, 540, 544, 576, 578, 579, 584; *mater*: 166, 496, 523 = 251, 542, 577.

[145]Leon, *The Jews*, 186; cf. Schürer, Vermes, Millar, Goodman, *The History of the Jewish People*, 3, 1, 101.

[146]See the discussion, based on epigraphic data, of the important role of women in the Jewish synagogues in Brooten, *Women Leaders*. For recognition of the same phenomenon in a literary document (*The Testament of Job*) see P.W. van der Horst, *Essays on the Jewish World of Early Christianity*, (Freibourg: Universitäts–Verlag, Göttingen: Vandenhoeck & Ruprecht, 1990), 94-110.

[147]CIJ I², p. XCV, Williams, *The Structure*, 133f.

[148]A. Berliner, *Geschichte der Juden in Rom*, vol. 1 (Frankfurt-am-Main, 1893), 69.

[149]Brooten, *Women Leaders*, 65f.; van der Horst, *Ancient Jewish Epitaphs*, 94.

the title can be proved, but on the whole there is no doubt that the status of the *pater/mater* of the synagogue was very high and very honourable indeed.

(9) ἱερεύς. There are five examples of this title, and one example of ἱερίσσα, among Roman inscriptions. The generally accepted view is that *hiereus* ('priest') is an equivalent of the Hebrew *kohen* in the sense of 'a descendant of Aaron' and that these priests had no official position in the community, 'but because of their hereditary distinction they had a minor part in the cult, especially that of pronouncing certain benedictions'.[151] But no matter how minor their part in the cult was, they must have played some kind of a functional role at least in the fourth century since *Codex Theodosianus* 16.8.4 exempted them, alongside the *archisynagogi, patres synagogarum* and all others who serve the synagogues, from *munera corporalia*.[152]

The organisation of Roman congregations was not unique and the majority of the titles of the officials are known from all over the Mediterranean world. The elaborate structure and titulature of the synagogues echoed to a considerable extent the political organisation of Graeco-Roman cities.[153] Despite this similarity, it is necessary to admit that the meaning of many of the titles in the Jewish context are far from being clear and that reconstructions of the structure of the Jewish congregations in Rome are to a large degree conjectural.

In conclusion: cognizance needs again to be taken of the fact that much of the evidence which has survived is later than the first century. This fact should not, however, compel us to conclude that we know nothing about the first century Jews in Rome or in the Diaspora in general. The references in the New Testament to some Jewish officials in

---

[150]van der Horst, *Ancient Jewish Epitaphs,,* 107.
[151]Leon, *The Jews,* 192; cf. *CIJ,* I², p. C-CI; van der Horst, *Ancient Jewish Epitaphs,* 96.
[152]Cf. an interesting discussion by Brooten, *Women Leaders,* 91f., of two possible explanations for the lawgiver's having included priests in the law. According to the first interpretation, the Christian lawgiver included this general term for an official religious functionary without realising that Jewish priests had no function in the community life. According to the other, the lawgiver was well-informed of the operation of the synagogue, and the law reflected the priests' rôle as functionaries in the fourth century. Though Brooten in the end thinks that 'it seems more prudent simply to let the two explanations both stand as good possibilities', she admits that the second explanation is more convincing. I tend to agree with her (especially given that 'the imperial court writers would certainly not have had an interest in liberating more persons than necessary from the corporal duties').
[153]Cf. van der Horst, *Ancient Jewish Epitaphs,* 96, who thinks that the city possibly served as a model for the Jewish community.

Palestine and in the Diaspora allow us to assume that at least some elements of the synagogue system existed in the time of Paul and Luke. On the other hand, we should not be over-confident that we know a great deal about the Diaspora of the first century. There is always the possibility that an archaeological find from the first century may occur which could provide evidence to enable us to draw further conclusions, or to modify, or even reject our perceptions, which have been arrived at largely by a process of retrojection from later evidence.

CONCLUSION

The relationship of the study of the Jewish Diaspora in the first century to the book of Acts provided the starting point for this volume. In considering epigraphic material in particular, it was found necessary to go outside of the period of the book of Acts and into the second century and beyond in order to draw out certain aspects of Jewish/ Gentile relationships which are nevertheless relevant to the world of Acts. Furthermore, the book has argued that the account given in the book of Acts provides excellent testimony for the ancient historian interested in Jewish/Gentile relations—the case of Timothy is a significant example of this.

Chapter one demonstrates that Luke in Acts accords with other extant sources in recognising the boundary between Jews and friendly Gentiles. Chapters two and three argue that, by an extended analysis of the contentious evidence relating to proselytes, it is by no means strange that the book of Acts shows no awareness of a Jewish mission. Chapter four shows that the 'God–fearers' of Acts whose existence was once thought to be questionable, can be seen from epigraphic evidence particularly from Aphrodisias—further evidence on this is considered in chapter five. The whole notion is seen to be in line with later developments in the Bosporan Kingdom discussed in chapter six. In chapter seven Luke's description of the 'God–fearers' in Acts is considered in the light of the evidence with which Luke's account is shown to be in harmony.

Chapter eight weighs up the evidence of Acts and other sources for the Jewish community in Antioch, and chapters nine and ten do the same for Asia Minor and Macedonia and Achaia. In each case, other epigraphic evidence supports the picture we can obtain from the book of Acts. By the time we reach Rome, the climax of the Book of Acts, the

general pattern is clear, though it must be acknowledged that much of
the evidence we would like to have is not available, and it is not always
easy to identify specific Jewish inscriptions.

Only such a wide–ranging study can hope to illuminate some of
the issues raised in looking at the book of Acts in relation to the Jewish
Diaspora—even then some of them had to be relegated to appendixes.
There is always the exciting expectation for the scholar that further
evidence will come to light which will help us draw more completely
the picture of the book of Acts in its first century Diaspora setting.

APPENDIX 1

SYNCRETISM—THE TERM AND THE PHENOMENON[1]

The history of the use of the term syncretism shows that, apart from being used in a way that is etymologically incorrect, it has acquired vague meanings. Because of the potential scope of its application it has become an expression covering every kind of religious or even cultural contact. Used to describe different religious phenomena, it creates an illusion that each of them is related to the rise of a mixed religion. This pattern of thought was especially popular among scholars of the nineteenth century. It still affects the modern investigations of the Mediterranean religious situation of the Hellenistic and Roman periods.

---

[1]This is a revised part of an article published under the same title in *TynB* 44.1 (1993) 117-128.

A problem of scholarly terminology does not belong to the sphere of purely theoretical speculation. Scientific language possesses an ability to shape our thoughts and to play games with us through words. This can sometimes create confusion. The term *syncretism* epitomises the problem.

If we consult lexicographical definitions in an attempt to determine precisely the meaning of the word *syncretism* the picture that emerges is rather confusing. *The Oxford English Dictionary* defines *syncretism* as 'attempted union or reconciliation of diverse and opposite tenets or practices, esp. in philosophy and religion'. It treats syncretism, firstly as a result and not as a process, and secondly as something man-made and not natural. The German *Die Religion in Geschichte und Gegenwart* suggests a more complicated picture, which also allows for the possibility that religion might coalesce in the natural course of events: 'er bezeichnet einerseits den bewußten Zusammenschluß verschiedener Religionen bzw., einzelnen Elemente in ihnen, anderseits das organische Zusammenwachsen von Religionen oder ihre Anschauungen und Praktiken zu einer Einheit'.

If we turn to more specialised scholarly literature we find the picture even more uncertain. G. van der Leeuw, in his famous book *Phänomenologie der Religion* (published in English under the title *Religion in Essence and Manifestation*), understands syncretism as 'the process leading repeatedly from Polydemonism to Polytheism'.[2] Later in the same book, while trying to 'apprehend its essential nature somewhat more thoroughly', he describes it 'as one form of the *dynamic of religions*'.[3]

For J.H. Kamstra, syncretism means amalgamation, something opposite to an encounter, the word he uses to mean the existential meeting of two religions.[4] He sees syncretism as the 'result of alienation in an existing religion. . . . The criterion for syncretism is therefore alienation, something which either comes in as alien from without or which is alienated from within—whatever it is'.[5] Lastly M. Pye defines syncretism as 'the temporary ambiguous coexistence of elements from

[2]Ch. 19:1 cited here and elsewhere in the English translation by J.E. Turner (London 1964[2]) of the German edition (Tübingen, 1933).
[3]Ch. 93:1.
[4]J.H. Kamstra, *Encounter or Syncretism: The Initial Growth of Japanese Buddhism* (Leiden 1967), 5.
[5]J.H. Kamstra, *Syncretism op de Grens tussen Theologie en Godsdienstfenomenologie* (Leiden 1970) cited in M. Pye, 'Syncretism and Ambiguity', *Numen* 18 (1971), 86.

diverse religious and other contexts within a coherent religious pattern'.[6]

These conflicting definitions reflect a situation where the word, having the status of a technical term, is nevertheless used by different scholars in different ways in the manner of Lewis Carrol's Humpty Dumpty.[7] This makes the process of reading some articles similar to the complexity of solving a crossword.

A survey of the history of this term's use illustrates the same problem. The word συγκρητισμός is a *hapax legomenon*.[8] It was used by Plutarch in his work περὶ φιλαδελφίας (*de fraterno amore* 19). Plutarch mentioned that Cretans, who constantly fought each other, stopped their war and they came to an agreement when threatened by a common enemy καὶ τοῦτ᾽ ἦν ὁ καλούμενος ὑπ᾽ αὐτῶν συγκρητισμός ('and this was called by them "syncretism"'). The etymology and meaning of the word, as it was understood by Plutarch, is absolutely clear, i.e. to be united like Cretans at the time of danger from outside. The verb συγκρητίζειν was mentioned both by the *Suda* and *Etymologicum Magnum*. It was never again used in any Greek literature which has survived.

It was Erasmus who revived the word (in its verbal form) in his letter to Melanchthon in 1519: *aequum est nos quoque synkretizein. Ingens praedium est concordia.* Erasmus used the word in the traditional sense of Plutarch—to come to concord and fight mutual enemies together despite the differences of opinions which existed in the Humanist's camp. His definition was widely adopted and the term was used in a positive sense. However, in the 17th century the situation changed completely. The word began to be used in a negative way and this pejorative, meaning as Rudolph quite rightly stresses, 'ihn bis heute nicht ganz verlassen hat'.[9] This unexpected and abrupt change was

---

[6]Pye, 'Syncretism', 93.

[7]Lewis Carroll, *Through the Looking Glass*, (ch. 5). 'When I use a word', Humpty Dumpty said in a rather scornful tone, 'it means just what I use it to mean—neither more nor less'. 'The question is', said Alice, 'whether you can make words mean so many different things'. 'The question is', said Humpty Dumpty, 'Which is to be master—that's all'.

[8]The history of the term has been discussed at length on several occasions, see esp. A. Pariente, 'ΣΥΓΚΡΗΤΙΣΜΟΣ', *Emerita* 37 (1969) 317; C. Colpe, 'Die Vereinbarkeit historischer und struktureller Bestimmungen des Synkretismus', in A. Dietrich (ed.), *Syncretismus im syrisch-persischen Kulturgebiet* (Göttingen 1975) (Abhandlungen d. Akademie d. Wiss. in Göttingen, Phil.-Hist, Klasse, 3 Folge N 96) 15f.; K. Rudolph, 'Synkretismus—vom theologischen Scheltwort zum religionswissenschaftlichen Begriff', *Humanitas Religiosa, Festschrift f. Harolds Biezais* (Stockholm 1979) 194ff.

connected with the name of George Calixtus, whose attempt to harmonise the different views of Protestants, and subsequently all Christendom,[10] met with universal disapproval. Though still used etymologically in a correct way, the word *syncretism* little by little had undergone a substantial change of meaning—the stress now was put not on unification against a mutual enemy, but on the incompatibility of different forces.[11]

The next development took place in the nineteenth century and was marked by the rejection and complete loss of the etymological meaning of the word. It was used as a term to define a mixture of heterogeneous elements in religions and cults in the Hellenistic period and gradually came to be understood as a derivative from συγκεράννυμι.[12]

The etymological incorrectness of the term does not mean, of course, that it cannot be used. If this were so, too many terms would have to be abandoned. Much more important is the question whether in religion there really exists an autonomous phenomenon, to describe which we need a term *syncretism* and if it exists, what it is.

When it first entered the terminology of the history of religions it was used in a narrow way to depict the religious situation which came into being in the Mediterranean world after Alexander. At that time the population of a vast territory was interacting with Hellenism. Thus, conditions came about which welcomed innovative processes on an unprecedented scale in different religions. But, strictly speaking, all religions are genetically heterogeneous and in this sense syncretistic. To postulate a difference between syncretistic and traditional religions as well as syncretistic and pure ones, is meaningless. All we can do is to direct our attention to the balance between traditional elements (i.e. those which have become traditional) and innovative features, at particular stages. Innovations in religion can take place either as a result of internal development or under external influence. What we actually mean in applying the term *syncretism* to Hellenistic religions is

[9]Rudolph, 'Synkretismus', 195.

[10]Cf. the remark of R.J. Zwi Werblowski: 'Da werde als Synkretismus gescholten, was heute vielleicht von vielen lobend Ökumenismus gennant werden würde' ('Synkretismus in der Religionsgeschichte', *Synkretismus in der Religionen Zentralasiens*. eds. W. Heissig, H. Klimkeit, (1987) 2.

[11]Cf. a good example of such an attitude is in the *Eirenikon Catholicum* by the Jesuit Voit Elber (cited by Rudolph, 'Syncretismus', 95) who stated that the principles advocated by Calixtus meant the union not of people who belonged to different religions, but of different religions.

[12]See p. 200–01. *Excursus*.

that during the Hellenistic period the process of heterogeneous innovations was especially active. This consideration did not escape the
notice of some historians of the religion of this period, and it made
them feel unsure about the correctness of the use of the term. F.C.
Grant, in his book with the characteristic title *Hellenistic Religions: The
Age of Syncretism*, admits that syncretism 'is no late development of the
Hellenistic age'. It was to be found as far back as the history of Greek
and other ancient religions could be traced. 'What distinguished the
syncretism of the Hellenistic age was its vast extent, its thoroughness,
and the remoter origins of some of the cults and deities involved'.[13]

The scale of the process cannot be regarded as sufficient justification for the introduction of a new technical term. The meaning of the
term will be, in this case, incapable of being fixed precisely. There will
be every danger that, instead of being a useful tool, it will turn into a
source of misrepresentation of the material. A further possibility is
that such a term, thanks to its vagueness and universal potential, will
start out on an independent life. All these dangers were realized in the
case of *syncretism* .

Heterogeneous innovations in Hellenistic religions were numerous and complex. As a result, the meaning of the term *syncretism* has
become more and more vague. It has been applied to very different
phenomena such as:

1. *Interpretatio graeca* (or *latina*), when someone else's deities were
   identified with the gods of the Greek (or Roman) pantheon, on
   the basis of similarities in rites, iconography or their place in
   the pantheon.
2. Transmission of a certain cult to another ethnic milieu.
3. Assimilation of such transmitted deities.
4. Translation of a religious work into another language which in-
   troduces new shades of meaning in that language which never
   existed in the original, as happened, for instance, with the LXX.
5. Philosophical speculations in which different deities are treated
   as simply different names for the same deity.
6. Creation of a new cult by means of the amalgamation of different features of different deities.

Using the term *syncretism* to describe all these phenomena creates an illusion that each of them is contributory to the rise of a mixed

---

[13](New York, 1953), XXIf.

religion. The implication of the term is that the features of different religions coalesce. As a consequence, any contact in the religious sphere is seen as sufficient grounds for declaring the existence of religious syncretism. Taking into consideration how various and widespread contacts between religions have been in human history, we cannot be surprised by the fact that many scholars have found it convenient to think in terms of the *syncretistic* character of the religious phenomena they were investigating nor can we be surprised at the expansion of the term beyond the limits of the Hellenistic period.

The fact that the term *syncretism* has been applied to such a variety of religious phenomena, and in its wider sense has become an expression covering any kind of religious, or even cultural contacts,[14] has made the need to clarify the issue very urgent. Some have doubted the very wisdom in keeping the term:

> One might even ask if exact definitions are always useful in the study of religion. After all, terms are labels which we put on phenomena; they are necessary and useful as long as they serve the purpose of clarity and exactitude. But in a case like this . . . it is questionable that the phenomenon under discussion is so homogeneous that it is capable of exact definition.[15]

Another group of scholars decided to harmonise the chaos and create a typology of syncretism. Such typology was proposed, for instance, by P. Lévèque[16] and it is only natural, that it turned out to be a short history of Mediterranean religions from the Creto-Mycenæan period up to Roman times.

C. Colpe suggests that a universal typology of syncretism should be worked out and he sketched a programme for investigating different types of contacts in the sphere of religion and language. He understands syncretism as a universal phenomenon which is manifested in symbios, acculturation and identification, so that any ethno-cultural contact can be treated in terms of syncretism.[17]

---

[14]'Religious syncretism in the wider sense of this term is an expression for cultural contact . . .'. Å. Hultkanz, 'Pagan and Christian Elements in the Religious Syncretism among the Shoshoni Indians of Wyoming', *Syncretism* , ed. S.S. Hartman (Stockholm: Scripta Instituts Donneriani Aboensis, 1969), 15.

[15]Ringgren, 'The Problems of Syncretism', 7. It is worthwhile mentioning that Van der Leeuw used the term *syncretism* only five times in his famous 700 page book. The reason is, to my mind, obvious—he was dealing with the classification of real phenomena and needed precise terms and conceptions.

[16]P. Lévèque, 'Essai de typologie des syncrétismes', *Les syncrétismes dans les religions grecque et romain* (Strasbourg, 1973), 179ff.

A heuristic model of syncretism was suggested by U. Berner.[18] He defines syncretism as a process in the history of religion which manifests itself either at the system level, when two competing systems made contact or at the element level, when such a connection exists only between the elements. Syncretism for Berner expresses a tendency to overcome the competitive character of the systems and to abolish the borders between them. The heuristic model developed by Berner is a masterpiece on its own. Berner suggests a lot of detailed and sophisticated definitions of different types of syncretism (or as I would prefer to say, of religious contacts) such as *absorbierender Synkretismus, agglomerativer Synkretismus, Meta-Synkretismus,* etc. What is interesting to note is that some traditional concrete terms such as, for instance, *identification,* have now become subdivisions of the universal conception of syncretism, though the term *syncretism* in the first place came into being as a duplicate of them, and in some cases is still in this position.

Thus, at the moment we have a rather peculiar situation where, on the one hand, the majority of scholars who work in the field of Mediterranean religions use the term *syncretism* in a vague and indeterminate sense (with one especially delicate point, which many try to avoid—whether Christianity can be called syncretistic), and on the other hand, *syncretism* has become an expression covering any kind of religious development (cf. van der Leeuw's 'dynamic of religions') and as such is seen to constitute an autonomous sphere of knowledge.

---

[17]Colpe, 'Die Vereinbarkeit', 15f.

[18]U. Berner, 'Heuristische Modell der Synkretismusforschung', *Synkretismusforschung, Theorie und Praxis,* ed. G. Wiesner, (Wiesbaden: 1978), 11.

Excursus: Derivation of the word συγκρητισμός.

Pariente, 'ΣΥΓΚΡΗΤΙΣΜΟΣ', made an attempt to prove that Plutarch's συγκρητισμός was actually derived from σύγκρατος and in the long run from συγκεράννυμι (with the root -κρα- in the Ionian form). Thus, from the very beginning, as Pariente supposes, it had the same meaning as it had obtained in the 19th century. The story about the Cretans' federation in the extreme situations, according to Pariente, was invented by Plutarch and represents a classical piece of popular etymology. The Ionic form could be explained by the fact that it was borrowed from technical language where Ionic dialect had a tendency to be preserved just as, for instance, military terms were preserved in their Doric form. The appearance of such a term, as Pariente states, was assisted by the existence of the group κρητισμός, κρητίζω, Κρής. Following I. Wackernagel, *Vorlesungen über Syntax* (Basel: 1920), 301, he insists that if the historic situation described by Plutarch had any chance of being probable, it must be dated to the Creto-Mycenæan period. Forms ending in –ισμός appeared in the Greek language much later. Pariente is convinced that the word συγκρητισμός came into being either in Plutarch's time or just a little earlier and belongs to the class of derivatives ending in –ισμός from the nouns, like ῥοπαλισμός ‹ ῥόπαλον, κεφαλισμός ‹ κεφαλή, σκαρ-ιφισμός ‹ σκάριφος. None of these arguments seems convincing to me. In the third century BC thirty Cretan cities were united in κοινὸν τῶν Κρηταιέων. As M. van der Mijnsbrugge, *The Cretan Coinon* (New York: 1931) 57f., supposes, the origin of this Cretan Koinon is to be sought in the ancient insti-tution of *syncretismus*, though the historical *koinon* was formed without a foreign threat to the independence of the island. R.F. Willetts, *The Civilisa-tion of Ancient Crete* (Berkeley 1977), 181 sees the explanation of the tradition in 'a tribal confederacy of the Dorians formed during their migration into Greece and perpetuated, through necessity and precedent, during their migration over Crete'. The legend reported by Plutarch could have origi-nated in a period when the Cretan Koinon came into being in order to give it the authority of tradition. If we turn to the linguistic arguments of Pari-ente, our attention is drawn to the fact that all three words he adduced to prove his supposition that the words ending in –ισμός were not necessarily derived from verbs, are very rare if not *hapaxes*. Therefore an absence of the appropriate meaning of the verb cannot guarantee that the verb actually had never had a suitable meaning. Besides, one of the examples of Pariente must be abandoned. Pariente's translation of the verb ῥοπαλίζω (which was explained by Hesychius as στρέφει, κίνει ὡς ῥόπαλον) as *herir con una maza* is unjustified. It seems evident that ῥοπαλισμός (*hapax legomenon*, mentioned in the plural form by Aristophanes, *Lys.* 553) is derived from ῥοπαλίζω—the explanation given by Hesychius does not exclude the use of the word in the erotic context. But even if sometimes the words ending in –ισμός were denominative derivatives, the supposed συνκρητισμός ‹ σύγκρατος does not follow this pattern, σύγκρατος being a verbal adjective. It is also worthwhile to remember that glossaries fix the existence of the noun συγκερασμός from συγκεράννυμι with the suffix -σμ-. To sum up, Plutarch's etymology of the word συγκρητισμός is very likely to be correct.

APPENDIX 2

THE MEANING OF ΠΡΟΣΕΥΧΗ

The need to reconsider the criteria for distinguishing Jewish inscriptions, which have been worked out by previous generations of scholars, seems now to be indisputable. Detailed investigation of the terms used in supposedly Jewish inscriptions should be viewed as the first step in re-evaluating the epigraphic evidence. This discussion of the term προσευχή shows that there is no clear evidence that the Gentiles ever borrowed this markedly Jewish term for their place of worship. The Judaizing group of Μασσαλιανοί (Messalians) which, however, can hardly be labelled as Gentile in the conventional sense of the word, may be seen as the only possible exception.

I. Criteria for distinguishing Jewish Inscriptions

This book is primarily based on epigraphic sources and inscriptions which are usually listed as Jewish. But what are the criteria for considering an inscription to be Jewish? This methodological issue has attracted much scholarly attention recently. Previous generations of scholars had worked out the criteria for singling out Jewish inscriptions and although there were some cases where doubts were cast on the attribution of a particular inscription, on the whole we seemed to be standing on more or less safe ground. Kant who has based his study of Greek and Latin Jewish inscriptions on the traditional criteria, summarised them as follows:

> In the inscriptions discussed here, Jewishness has been identified by symbolism (e.g. menorah, loulab, ethrog, ark, shofar), self-identification ("Lucius . . . a Jew"), typical Jewish names (Benjamin, Ananias), reference to Jewish religious customs (e.g. one who follows the law), presence in a Jewish catacomb or cemetery, and the mention of a synagogue or Jewish office (e.g. head of the synagogue). These criteria express characteristics traditionally associated with ancient Jews of the Hellenistic and Roman periods.[1]

Noy said much the same in his important volume on Jewish inscriptions from Italy, Spain and Gaul, which was published as part of the Jewish Inscriptions Project in Cambridge.[2] However, he added a warning remark concerning the use of such symbols as lulab, amphora, Solomon's knot and five- and six-pointed stars, which occur too often in a non-Jewish context to be regarded as indicators of Jewishness. He also pointed out that Jewish names can be seen as a criterion of Jewish provenance only if there are no indications that the inscription is Christian or pagan.[3]

While using the traditional criteria, Kant nevertheless realised 'that they are by no means safe, because this way of determining Jewishness . . . by no means points to a perfectly clear boundary between Jews and non-Jews in the ancient Mediterranean world'.[4] The understanding of the vagueness of this boundary found its most distinct expression in an article by R.S. Kraemer, who challenged the established criteria for Jewish inscriptions and stated that we need first

---

[1]Kant, 'Jewish Inscriptions', 682.
[2]Noy, *JIWE* 1.
[3]Noy, *JIWE* 1, IX.
[4]Kant, 'Jewish Inscriptions', 683.

to reconsider the evidence for the Jewishness of many, if not most inscriptions previously classified as Jewish'.[5] One of the ways to escape the danger of wrong attribution is to apply several criteria, as was recommended by P. van der Horst.[6] The drawback is that this *desideratum* cannot always be fulfilled, since quite often no more than one criterion can be recovered. This was correctly pointed out by A.J.Bij de Vaate and J.W. van Henten, who conclude that it is necessary to re-evaluate the origin of *all* inscriptions from Asia Minor to create a new corpus of Jewish inscriptions, and to admit openly that there are a number of inscriptions where origin cannot be determined which should be labelled 'Jewish or non-Jewish' to show that they are possibly, but not necessarily, Jewish.[7]

The need to re-evaluate the epigraphic Jewish material is indisputable. The first question that must be answered is which inscriptions are to be defined as Jewish. What are the limits of this term? If an inscription employs a Jewish term (e.g. προσευχή), can we label it as Jewish? In the case of the inscriptions from the Bosporan Kingdom discussed in Chapter 6 above, where the terms προσευχή and συναγωγὴ τῶν Ἰουδαίων appear, the manumissions of the slaves in Jewish prayer-houses, which put them under the guardianship of Jewish communities, were not necessarily produced by Jews. It is quite possible that they belong, as I believe they do, to God-fearers, that is formally to Gentiles. Is it right to list them among Jewish documents? How can we after all determine the Jewishness of an inscription? Are we to call a Jewish inscription one which was produced by an ethnic Jew? Or by someone who belongs to the Jewish religion, for instance a proselyte?[8] It was suggested recently that even the term Ἰουδαῖος, which has usually been treated as an unquestionable indicator of Jewish ethnicity (cf. the quotation from Kant above), may indicate geographic origin (that is, Judaean)[9] or, alternatively, pagan adherence to Judaism.[10] The first assumption

---

[5]R.S. Kraemer, 'Jewish Tuna and Christian Fish: Identifying Religious Affiliation in Epigraphic Sources', *HTR* 84:2 (1991), 161.

[6]van der Horst, 'Ancient Jewish Epitaphs', 18.

[7]A.J. Bij de Vaate & J.W. van Henten, 'Jewish or Non-Jewish? Some Remarks on the Identification of Jewish Inscriptions from Asia Minor', *BiO* 53: 1-2 (1996), I am deeply grateful to Prof. van Henten, who kindly sent me a copy of this article before the volume of *BiO* became available.

[8]Cf. the definition of Jewish papyri by V. Tcherikover as 'papyri relating to Jews and Judaism', (*CPJ* I, XIX).

[9]Kraabel, 'The Roman Diaspora', 455.

[10]Kraemer, 'On the Meaning of the Term "Jew"', 35.

seems to me to have very little chance of being true,[11] while the second deserves serious consideration.

If someone under Roman rule openly admitted his or her Jewishness this inevitably had legal implications—Jews, both male and female, including slaves and freedmen, from the age of 3 to 60 or 62, were taxed by the Roman authorities.[12] The taxation can hardly have been carried out without the co-operation of the local communities.[13] Could their members allow anyone to declare himself Jewish, if they did not consider him to be such and without being accused of concealing the exact number of members of their community? Besides, there was a ban on circumcision after Hadrian which, though it seems not to have been obeyed in all parts of the empire,[14] nevertheless is a factor which must be taken into

---

[11]The only argument Kraabel gave in favour of his hypothesis was that such an interpretation of the term would better explain the enigmatic expression οἱ ποτὲ Ἰουδαῖοι of an inscription from Smyrna (CIJ II 742), which is dated to the second century AD. According to the traditional interpretation these words mean 'the former Jews', that is, the Jews who have renounced their religion. Kraabel argued that this proposal did not fit well with the position of this phrase in the middle of a long text which registered donations for public work: 'This is surely an odd way to record one's apostasy!' Kraemer, 'On the Meaning of the Term "Jew"', 35. But if the traditional interpretation is correct, this phrase in this particular inscription need not be taken as a special proclamation of apostasy. It could equally well be the name by which these people were known in the city. The name itself, for instance, could have purely economic connotations: those Jews who previously paid and now, as a result of their new status, have stopped paying the *fiscus Iudaicus*. Cohen, 'Religion, Ethnicity and Hellenism', 221f., n. 5, discussing Kraabel's interpretation of οἱ ποτὲ Ἰουδαῖοι, noted that people from Judaea living in Smyrna would be called not 'the former Judaeans', but simply 'Judaeans'. On the whole, the geographical interpretation of the term needs more serious arguments if it is to hold proof. Cf. Cohen, 'Religion, Ethnicity and Hellenism', 208: '.... In non-formal usage the singular *ho Ioudaios*, and perhaps even the plural *hoi Ioudaioi*, could be used to designate anyone living in the district, even someone who was not a member of the *ethnos*. Unambiguous attestation of this usage, however, is missing'. It must also be explained how it was possible for contemporaries to distinguish between the conventional religious/ethnic meaning of the term and its geographical usage. If the word 'American' is conventionally reduced to the meaning—no matter however incorrect it may be—of 'a citizen of the United States', and if we use this term to speak of a Canadian (which would be geographically correct) without further clarification, are we not likely to be misunderstood?

[12]CPJ I, 81. According to Juster, *Les Juifs*, vol. 2, 286, the tax was in operation till the middle of the third century, and was probably abolished only by Julian. Tcherikover and Fuks traced it until the middle of the second century (CPJ III, No. 460, AD 145/6 or 167/8, Karanis) and doubted if it were possible to establish when, and by whom, the tax was abolished (CPJ I, 81, n. 64); cf. p. 9-10.

[13]L.A. Thompson, 'Domitian and the Jewish Tax', *Historia* 31 (1982), 333.

consideration. Those who resolved to join the Jewish people in such circumstances must have been really devoted to Judaism. If those who designated themselves as Jews in the inscriptions were proselytes, and were accepted by Jewish communities as members, have *we* the right to reject *their* right of self-definition as Jews and to exclude these inscriptions from the category of 'purely' Jewish?

Often the decision to define inscriptions as Jewish depends upon a general perception of what Jews could and could not do. Thus, commenting on a dedication from Brescia to *Iunones* by a certain Annia Iuda, Noy, who understands Iuda as a personal name, writes that it is 'undoubtedly pagan, since Pascal . . . shows that the *Iunones* are local divinities in Cisalpine Gaul'.[15] For Kraemer, however, this does not seem so evident. On Kraemer's hypothesis the epithet *Iuda*, which is treated as a variant of *Ioudaia*, i.e. Jewish, 'may designate a non-Jew who has adopted some degree of Jewish observance'.[16] But Kraemer also does not rule out the possibility that Annia was born Jewish and was a member of a Jewish community when she made her dedication, which would inevitably lead us to conclude, 'that Jewish women were not above making offerings to pagan spirits'.[17] The interpretation of this inscription is important from a methodological point of view. If, on the one hand, the word *Iuda* (no matter whether we understand it as a personal name, with Noy, or as an ethnic designation, with Kraemer) was never used by pagans and Christians and if, on the other, according to the generally accepted view, Jews did not make dedications to pagan spirits, then we have to make a choice: either we accept that *Juda* was on this occasion used by a pagan, or we introduce some corrections into the established picture of Judaism. It seems to me that the last decision is more reasonable, though we risk neglecting the unique piece of evidence of pagan usage of *Iuda* that this inscription may provide. But if we make another choice, we are in danger of violating our sources and reading into them whatever our presuppositions suggest should be there. Only additional evidence of undoubtedly pagan usage could tip the balance. In the field of epigraphy, given the lacunose character of our evidence and our insufficient knowledge of linguistic usage, we can build only on parallels.

---

[14]Cf. Reynolds, Tannenbaum, *Jews and God-Fearers*, 21.
[15]Noy, *JIWE*, 1, 19.
[16]Kraemer, 'On the Meaning of the Term "Jew"', 319.
[17]Kraemer, 'On the Meaning of the Term "Jew"', 318.

The existence of a religious language which was shared by Jews, Christians and Gentiles complicates the picture even more, and makes singling out Jewish inscriptions a particularly difficult task. Some formulae which used to be considered to be exclusively Jewish can occasionally be found not only in Christian inscriptions (which is not surprising and must be expected because of the borrowing of the religious language), but also in Gentile ones. Scepticism about the possibility of distinguishing between these usages is not, on that account, obligatory. For instance, the term εὐλογητός, which occurred in Christian inscriptions, was never used by pagans. So it can safely be interpreted as a Jewish term in the Bosporan inscriptions which belong to the first century AD, i.e. to the period much earlier than the appearance of Christianity in that part of the world.[18] But the fact, that in these inscriptions, there is a concentration of Jewish terms, does not necessarily mean that they were produced by Jews: what we know of religious development in the Bosporan Kingdom shows that these Jewish terms could have been used by God-fearers. In this particular place it can be proved, I believe, that the local population was under strong Jewish religious influence. But does the presence of religious formulae always imply a religious influence—even if we are sure (which is not always the case) that some formulae were originally Jewish and were borrowed from them by the Gentiles? Would it not be reasonable to suppose that sometimes a formula was borrowed just because it seemed to be expressive, or appropriate to a particular situation?

To answer these questions is much more difficult than to raise them, especially given the scanty character of our sources and the accidental character of our information. It seems that the first step in re-evaluating the epigraphic evidence must be a detailed investigation of the terms involved, with special attention to the probability (or improbability) of their having been used independently by different religious groups. An attempt at such a discussion of the term προσευχή is made here.

---

[18]Contrary to de Vaate and van Henten, who do not take into consideration the chronological framework of these inscriptions and the difference between the form εὐλογητός as applied to God and εὐλογεία (εὐλογέω).

II The Meaning of ΠΡΟΣΕΥΧΗ[19]

There is no doubt that the Greek word προσευχή has the meaning 'Jewish prayer-house'. But it is generally assumed that the word was not restricted to this meaning alone, and that it could also refer to a Gentile sanctuary, either as a result of Jewish influence or independently. This assumption is epitomized by the entry in *LSJ*: 'place of prayer, sanctuary, chapel . . . esp. among the Jews'. I shall discuss later two inscriptions which are referred to in *LSJ* as examples of the non-Jewish usage of the term. First, it is worthwhile to recall some basic information about the usage of the word.

The word προσευχή was never used by Gentile authors in its first meaning—'prayer'.[20] Outside the literary sources, I know only two examples of the use of the word by Gentiles.[21] But in Hellenistic Jewish and later Christian circles the word was very popular. To begin with, it occurs 114 times in the Septuagint, where it usually renders the word תְּפִלָּה.[22] As for the secondary meaning—that of 'prayer-house'— it is well attested with reference to Jewish prayer-houses by the epigraphic evidence[23] and by literary testimonia both Gentile[24] and Jewish. Philo employs προσευχή so often that E. Goodenough was able to insist that 'it has made epigraphists in general feel it safe to presume

---

[19]This is an extended version of my article 'A Jewish or Gentile Prayer House? The Meaning of ΠΡΟΣΕΥΧΗ', published in *TynB* 41.1 (1990), 154-159.

[20]According to *TLG*.

[21]One is in a private letter in Egypt from the third century AD (*BGU* IV.1080), another is in an inscription from Epidaurus from the fourth century BC, which will be discussed in detail below. In the Egyptian letter the word προσευχαί is coupled with εὐχαί· κατὰ τὰς κοινὰς ἡμῶν εὐχὰς καὶ προσευχὰς ἐφ᾽ αἷς οἱ θεοὶ τέλ<ε>ιον ἐπα-κούσαντες παρέσχον—'by our common prayers and entreaties which the gods, having listened to them, completely fulfilled'.

[22]προσευχή like תְּפִלָּה has the meaning of both said and sung prayer, see Hengel, 'Proseuche und Synagoge', 161, n. 15.

[23]First of all from Egypt: in ten (or eleven) inscriptions, the earliest from the third century BC, and several times in papyri (see the list in Hengel, 'Proseuche und Synagoge', 158, nn. 1-5, 159, n. 6 and Schürer, Vermes, Millar, Black, *The History of the Jewish People*, 2, 425f). προσευχή is also mentioned in nine inscriptions from the Bosporan Kingdom from the first to the fourth century AD (*CIRB* 64= Appendix 3, I, 1; 70 = App. 3, II, 1; 71 = App. 3, II, 2; 73 = App. 3, II, 4; 985 = App. 3, II, 5; App. 3, II, 6; 1123 = App. 3, II, 7; 1127 = App. 3, II, 9, 1128; in an inscription from Olbia (*IPE* I² 176, the claim that here the word designates a Gentile sanctuary will be discussed later), Rome (*CIJ* I 531 = *JIWE* 2, 602), Delos (*CIJ* I, 728).

[24]Juvenal, *Sat.III, 296*; Cleomedes, *De motu circ. corp. caelest.* II, 1; Artemidorus 3,53,1; 3,53,4; Apion op: Josephus, *Contr. Ap.* II, 10.

that any inscription which uses the word is probably Jewish, unless other evidence contradicts'.[25]

What possible evidence could this be? Schürer put forward three cases where he claimed the term προσευχή designated a Gentile building:[26] an example in Epiphanius' description of the Messalians, an inscription from Olbia,[27] and another inscription from Gorgippia.[28] *LSJ* examples of the non Jewish usage are: the same inscription from Olbia and one from Panticapaeum.[29] But the most serious indications that προσευχή can have the meaning of 'Gentile sanctuary' come from quite different sources: an inscription from Epidaurus from the fourth century BC[30] and one from Amastris (Paphlagonia) from the third century AD.[31] I shall begin with these.

The fact that in the Epidaurian inscription προσευχή is used in its secondary sense of prayer-house is widely accepted.[32] If this intepretation of the term is correct, then the inscription provides a clear case of προσευχή referring to a non-Jewish prayer-house. But the assumption that any kind of prayer house is meant seems to me questionable.

There are large lacunae both immediately before the word in question and soon afterwards: ἐρ[γώναι[18] ...]σ τας ποτευχας καὶ τοῦ βωμο[ῦ] ἐλομένω δραχμᾶς[[45] ...]. The length of the lacunae make it impossible to supplement the lost text with certainty.[33] The Doric form ΠΟΤΕΥΧΑΣ can be understood metonymically, i.e. as a designation of a building, only if we take it to be a genitive singular which is coupled with another genitive τοῦ βωμοῦ.[34] But this is not the only one possible intepretation. ΠΟΤΕΥΧΑΣ might quite well be an accusative plural

---

[25]E. Goodenough, *Jewish Symbols in the Greco-Roman Period*, vol. 2: *The Archaeological Evidence from the Diaspora*, (New York: Pantheon Books, 1953), 86.

[26]The new English translation left this position unaltered: Schürer, Vermes, Millar, Black, *The History of the Jewish People*, 2, 440, n. 61.

[27]*IPE* I² 176=*CIJ* I² 682, Lifshitz, *Prolegomenon*, 682 = DF 11.

[28]*CIRB* 1123=Appendix 3, II, 7; Schürer, Vermes, Millar, Black, 2, 440, n. 61.

[29]*CIRB* 70=Appendix 3, II, 1.

[30]*IG* IV,1, ed. min. 106, 27.

[31]E.Kalinka, 'Aus Bithynien und Umgegend', JÖAI, 28, 1 (1933), Beiblatt, 61, No. 8.

[32]See, for instance, the edition of the inscription and such widely used reference-books as *TDNT* II, 808, *BAGD* and Stern, *s.v. GLAJJ* II, 330, No. 395. For a discussion of whether in this inscription the temple of Aphrodite or of Artemis is meant, see A.Burford, 'Notes on the Epidaurian Building Inscriptions', *ABSA* 62 (1966), 285ff.

[33]See, however, now the tentative restoration of the lost text in accordance with the traditional interpretation, i.e. προσευχή = the temple, by J.G. Vinogradov, reported in *SEG* XLII, 1849.

which depends upon some word standing in the lacuna. In that case the plural form would exclude metonymy.

This grammatical point is not the only consideration that leads me to question the traditional interpretation. This intepretation presupposes a metonymical change of meaning which is highly unlikely, from both the linguistic and the religious point of view, at that place and time when Jewish influence is out of the question. According to the normal development of Greek usage, words like ἀγορά or συναγωγή had the meaning 'gathering' or 'assembly' before they came to refer to a particular place. Nor was prayer a major feature of the activities in a Greek sanctuary.

The inscription from Amastris, cut on a marble altar six centuries later, reads:

        Θεῷ
        ἀνεικήτῳ
        Ἀσβαμεῖ κα[ὶ]
        Γῇ (?) κυρίᾳ προσ-
5   ευχὴ<ν> εὐξά-
        μενος καὶ
        ἐπιτυχὼν
        ἀνέθηκα Αὐ-
        ρήλιος Πρω-
10   τόκτητος
        εὐχαριστή-
        [ρι]ο[ν].

To the invincible god Asbameus and to Ge (?) sovereign, I, Aurelius Protoktetos, having prayed and succeeded, set up [this] thank-offering.

In the reproduction of this inscription by L. Robert the name Ἀσβαμεύς was most unfortunately omitted by error.[35] This mistake was carried over into the collection of B.Lifshitz, who evidently did not consult the *editio princeps*. That was how he was able to register this inscription as a Jewish one.[36] Since Lifshitz, the erroneous reading, and the

---

[34]See, for instance, *TDNT*, II, 808 (L.H. Greeven): 'The use with βωμός indicates a concrete sense, i.e. a "place of prayer"'.

[35]'Les inscriptions greques et latines de Sardes', *Revue Archéologique* 2 (1936), 237f.; reprinted in *Opera minora selecta*, vol. 3 (Amsterdam: Adolf M. Hakkert, 1969), 1610.

[36]*DF* 35, without mentioning that it is inscribed on an altar.

consequent erroneous interpretation of the inscription as the dedication to the Jewish God and to the Jewish community, have become widespread and can be found on the pages of most reference works.[37]

The first editor of this inscription did not exclude the possibility of reading τῆ instead of Γῆ.[38] There are no purely epigraphical grounds for preferring one of these readings over the other. Robert considered τῆ to be correct since, 'l'épithète de κυρία n'est pas appliquée à une déesse, dont il faudrait reconnaître le nom dans Γῆ'. He suggested instead that κυρία should be connected with προσευχή, for which he proposed the meaning 'community': 'La dédicace est faite, comme si souvent à la communauté (τῇ συνόδῳ, τοῖς μύσταις, τῇ συναγωγῇ) en même temps qu'au dieu; et l'association reçoit l'épithète de κυρία'.[39] He also noted that the word προσευχή appeared in the dedication under Jewish influence. This interpretation has become generally accepted.

However Robert's argument can be turned the other way round. The fact is, προσευχή has never been found as a word for community. With this in mind let us consider the possible interpretations. If we follow Robert's construal of the syntactical connections, then we have to decide what meaning was intended—prayer or prayer-house (community being excluded)—when the word προσευχή was used. The metonymical usage seems to be more plausible. It looks as though it can be supported by a close parallel: a third-century dedication, on a column of red marble from north-east Galatia, to the Most High God and to his holy angels and to his revered prayer-house (τῇ προσκυνητῇ αὐτοῦ προσευχῇ).[40] Nevertheless there is a crucial difference between these two inscriptions. Although προσκυνητός is a rare word, there is evidence from the fourth century of its being applied to a physical object.[41] Besides, the pronoun αὐτοῦ leaves no doubt that in this inscription a building was meant. The adjective κύριος, on the other hand, cannot be combined well with words that refer to buildings of some sort, and προσευχή whenever used metonymically means a building. Thus we reach a dilemma. One or other of the two words κυρία and προσευχή must have been used in an unusual way. Which one?

---

[37]See, for instance, Schürer, Vermes, Millar, Goodman,*The History of the Jewish People*, 3, 1, 35 and Kant, 'Jewish Inscriptions', 693; the latter cited this inscription in full as the most representative example of Jewish dedications.
[38]Kalinka, 'Aus Bithynien', 61, No. 8.
[39]Robert, 'Les Inscriptions', 237f.

Robert decided in favour of postulating an exceptional meaning for προσευχή without any supporting argument. The parallels he offered (see above) fail because, unlike ἡ σύνοδος or ἡ συναγωγή, προσευχή had never been used for a community. Kant recognised the difficulty and mentioned specifically that on this occasion προσευχή had an exeptional meaning. Hengel, who printed in his article the correct reading of the inscription and did not count it among Jewish ones,[42] also noted that 'neben der Gottheit wird auch ihr Versammlungsort—der hier eventuell gar die Bezeichnung des Kultvereins selbst bedeutet—geehrt'.[43] Since ascribing an exceptional meaning to a word is methodologically not the best way to solve a difficult problem, let us test the possibility that προσευχή has in this inscription its basic meaning of 'prayer'.

On the new hypothesis the dedication is made to the deity and to the most mighty prayer, i.e. because the prayer was successful. There is no parallel known to me for a dedication with such a content. Thus it seems that this interpretation must be rejected too.

The elimination of the alternative possibilities returns us to the decision of the first editor, who printed Γῆ in the text of the inscription although he offered τῆ as a possibility. The epithet κυρία occurs with the names of different goddesses such as Artemis, Athena, Hera, Hekate, Isis, Nemesis etc.[44] Cases when it is combined with the name

---

[40]*RECAM* II 209b; A.R.R. Sheppard, 'Pagan Cults of Angels in Roman Asia Minor', *Talanta* 12/13 (1980-1981), 94, No. 11, pl. 2. Mitchell (*Anatolia* II, 36) considers the dedication to be 'certainly a Jewish not a pagan text'. Sheppard is more cautious in his conclusions. He sees in it 'some borrowing from Judaism or else an attempt on the part of pagans to give their cult a Jewish veneer'. His verdict is as indecisive as any could be: 'whether such a cult should be regarded as strictly pagan or as Jewish but heterodox is difficult to say' (p. 69). There are also some other dedications to a place of worship. Cf., for instance, an inscription from Panormos Διὶ ὑψίστῳ κ(αὶ) τῷ χώρῳ - to Zeus Most High and to the Place (where *thiasotai* assemble), Cook, *Zeus*, 2.II, 882 with different interpretations of τῷ χώρῳ Such dedications of a stele or of an altar to the god and/or to a place of worship are importantly different from donations to a sanctuary or to a synagogue, though the opening formulae may be similar, cf. *CIJ* II, 754 (donation of a water-basin to the most holy synagogue) or *CIJ* II, 1444 (donation of an ἐξέδρα to the prayer-house).
[41]Sheppard, *Pagan Cults*, 96. He suggests, on these grounds, dating this inscription in the late third century or the early fourth.
[42]Hengel also mentioned in his note ('Proseuche und Synagoge', 179, n. 96) that Lifshitz in *DF* had omitted the name of the god, but, somehow, very little attention has been paid to his warning even by those who have referred to his article.
[43]This difficulty seems to escape the attention of Lifshitz and Sheppard who both understand προσευχή as a prayer-house. Unlike Lifshitz, Sheppard (*Pagan Cults*, 96) gave the correct text of the inscription.

of Ge are unknown to me, as they were unknown to Robert, but she is described by words of similar meaning, though more solemn, like ἄνασσα, πότνια. Ζεὺς Ἀσβαμαῖος, called thus from the name of the spring near Tyana,[45] was the oath-keeping Zeus (Ζεὺς Ὅρκιος),[46] and thus the link between his name and that of Ge, who was mentioned after Zeus in oaths, seems to be not unnatural.[47] On balance an interpretation which presupposes the unparalleled but not impossible combination of the epithet κυρία with the name of the goddess Ge seems more plausible than any interpretation which postulates an exceptional meaning for προσευχή. But before coming down on one side there is a difficulty to meet: how to understand the remaining part of the inscription?

The *figura etymologica* εὐχὴν (εὐχὰς) εὐχόμενος is attested both by literary texts[48] and by inscriptions.[49] The word εὐχή (εὔχομαι) means both 'a vow' ('to make a vow') and 'a prayer' ('to pray'). Since the making of a vow involves a prayer to the god, whereas a successful prayer may stimulate gratitude (such as putting up an altar to the responsive god) even if no vow has previously been made, it is sometimes impossible to distinguish between the two meanings. Thus the inscription on two marble medallions from the church of St. Sophia at Iznik (sixth century AD) which is a close parallel to our inscription because it employs both εὔχομαι and ἐπιτυγχάνω (ἐυξάμενος...

---

[44]See the list in W.H.Roscher, *Ausführliches Lexikon des griechischen und römischen Mythologie*, vol.2 (Leipzig: Teubner, 1890-1897), 1756-1758; the Egyptian material is collected in G.Ronchi, *Lexicon theonymon*, fasc.3, 600-613. As a rule there is a preceding article, but not always, cf. Ἰσιδι κυρία[ι] (*Les inscriptions grecques et latines de Philae*, ed. A. and E.Bernand (Paris, 1969), 75,1.

[45]*RE*, 2, s.v. Ἀσβαμαῖος. The connection between Ζεὺς Ἀσβαμαῖος and θεὸς Ἀσβαμεύς was pointed out by Kalinka. Ammianus Marcellinus called the god Jupiter Asbamaeus (23.6.19). The remark of R. Kahane in his review *BZ* 79,2 (1986), 357 of L. Zgusta *Kleinasiatische Ortsnamen* (1984) that the latter considers Ἀσβαμεύς to be derived from the place-name Ἀσιβα is sheer misunderstanding.

[46]Philostr. *Vit. Apoll.* I.6: ἔστι δὲ περὶ Τύανα ὕδωρ Ὁρκίου Διός, ὥς φασι, καλοῦσι δὲ αὐτὸ Ἀσβαμαῖον ... τοῦτο εὐόρκοις μὲν ἵλεών τε καὶ ἡδὺ ὕδωρ, ἐπιόρκοις δὲ παρὰ πόδας ἡ δίκη. 'Now there is near Tyana a well sacred to Zeus, the god of oaths, so they say, and they call it the well of Asbama .... This water is favourable and sweet to those who keep their oaths, but to perjurers it brings hot-footed justice.' (trans. F.C. Conybeare, *LCL*).

[47]Cf. also the relief from Lycaonia representing a male and a female figure with the inscription above the head of the latter ΙΑΙΑ (Γαῖα). W.H.C. Frend, the editor of this inscription, considers it to represent Zeus and Ge ('Two Finds in Central Anatolia', *Anatolian Studies*, 6 [1956], 95-99, fig.1).

[48]Cf., for instance, Demosth. 19.130; Aeschin. 1.23, 3.18.

[49]*SEG* XXVIII, 888 (Lydia); *Syll.*³ 1003 (Priene).

ἐπέτυχον), was translated by Sevcenko as *'having prayed* unto Thee, O God, I succeeded'[50] and by G.Horsley *'having made my vow* to you, God, I succeeded'.[51] In the above-mentioned private letter from Egypt of approximately the same time as the inscription from Amastris,[52] both εὐχαί and προσευχαί stand together and both have the same meaning, i.e. 'prayers'. It seems not impossible that in this inscription προσευχή took the place of εὐχή as a kind of stylistic embellishment. The loss of the final ν can be explained either by the influence of the preceding datives, or by a tendency to omit the final ν which is well attested in the inscriptions of this period.[53] Another possibility is suggested by the formula with a dative προσευχῇ προσεύχεσθαι used once in the New Testament.[54] Now let us examine the inscription from Olbia.[55]

> [Ἀγαθῆι τύχηι(?). Οἱ]
> περὶ Σ[άτυρον᾿ Ἀρτεμιδώ -]
> ρου τὸ β, Πουρθαῖ[ος τοῦ δεῖνος],
> Ἀχιλλεὺς Δημητ[ρίου],
> 5 Διονυσιόδωρος ῞Ερ[ωτος],
> Ζώβεις Ζώβει ἄρχ[οντες]
> τὴν προσευχὴν ἐ[πε]-
> σκεύασαν τῇ ἑαυ[τῶν]
> προνοίᾳ στεγάσα[ντες]
> 10 ἀπὸ τοῦ----μέχρι

With good fortune (?). Satyros son of Artemidoros(?) II and his colleagues Pourthaios, the son of . . . , Achilleus the son of Demetrios, Zobeis the son of Zobeis, the archons, have restored by their own care the prayer-house from . . . , having roofed it.

In the last line of the inscription Latyshev, who had not seen it (since by his time it had been unfortunately lost), followed Köhler's reading, which was accepted by Boeckh in *CIG*, ἀπὸ τοῦ θεοῦ μέχρι . . . . If this reading was correct, then it would be the one important piece of evidence that would confirm the pagan character of the inscription and thus the fact that the word προσευχή might be borrowed by Gentiles. However E. Köppen read this line differently.[56] L. Stephani

---

[50]*DOP* 17 (1963), 394f.
[51]*NewDocs* 3 (1983), 65.
[52]See n. 21.
[53]See references in Appendix 3, II, 2, commentary to l.3.
[54]James 5:17.
[55]*IPE* I², 176; *CIJ* I², 682; Lifshitz, *Prolegomenon* No. 682; *DF* 11.

pointed out the uncertainty of the reading of the last line and suggested the restoration ἀπὸ τοῦ θεμελίου or θεμέθλου.[57] Given the impossibility of inspecting the stone it would be unsafe to depend on the unreliable line 10. It has to be discounted, and therefore cannot be invoked as evidence that Gentiles used this term.

Latyshev considered this inscription to be pagan since he could not believe that the city magistrates would repair a prayer-house belonging to a foreign cult which was not acknowledged as a state one and which, as he thought, was probably only tolerated.[58] His conclusion has now been weakened by subsequent epigraphic discoveries showing members of the civic governing class with some interest in Jewish institutions.[59]

Another line of interpretation has been proposed by some of those who have accepted for προσευχή the usual meaning of a Jewish prayer-house. The term ἄρχων is well attested in a Jewish milieu to designate a high-ranking officer of the congregation.[60] R.Erlich suggested that the archons in this inscription should not be the city magistrates, but the Jewish officers.[61] The interpretation of the inscription as Jewish was accepted by Frey. This interpretation is completely undermined by two considerations. First, the individuals whose names are given were mentioned in other inscriptions belonging to the same period—one as an *archon*, another as a *strategos*, the third as a president of the collegium of *strategoi*. Secondly, the *collegium* of archons in Olbia consisted of five members, the same number as in this inscription.[62] While great credence has been given to Lifshitz's view it must be said that it is somewhat surprising that he did not pay attention to these crucial details when he suggested his interpretation of this inscription as a dedication made by a Jewish religious guild (sic!) with the restoration of the first lines as [ἡ σύνοδος ἡ] περὶ σ[υναγωγὸν - -] ρον[63] κτλ—'the society under the presidency of (? . . .)', etc.

The third interpretation and restoration of the first lines was propounded by I.I. Tolstoj:[64]

---

[56]See in *CIG* 2079 and *IPE* I² 176.
[57]L. Stephani.
[58]*Studies in History and State System of Olbia* (St. Petersburg, 1897), 273 (*in Russian*).
[59]See, for example p. 123.
[60]Schürer, Vermes, Millar, Black, 2, 435. Cf. also Juster, *Les Juifs*, vol. 1, 443-447; *RE* s.v. Synagoge, 1313 (S.Krauss), *CIJ*, 1², LXXXVI-LXXXIX; see in detail p. 123.
[61]'The Olbian inscription IOSPE I² 176', *Doklady akademii Nauk–V (Proceedings of the Academy of Sciences)* 6 (1928), 124-127 (*in Russian*).

[Θεῶι ὑψίστωι etc. Οἱ (nomen collegii sacralis)]
περὶ σ[υναγωγον Πόθον Θεοδώ]-
ρου τὸ β, Πουρθαῖ[ος Πουρθαίου],
Ἀχιλλεὺς Δημητ[ρίου],
5   Διονυσιόδωρος Ἔρ[ωτος],
Ζώβεις Ζώβει, Ἄρχ[ων Πόθου] κτλ.

To the Most High God, etc. the members of the sacred guild under the presidency of Pothos the son of Theodores II—Pourthaios the son of Pourthaios, Achilleus the son of Demetrius, Zobeis the son of Zobeis, Archon the son of Pothos, etc.

Tolstoj did not insist that his restoration was correct;[65] he suggested it *exempli gratia*. What was important for him was to mark a possible parallel between this inscription and the ones from the Bosporan Kingdom, where Jewish prayer-houses—and he did not doubt that meaning of προσευχή—attracted Gentile Jewish sympathizers, some of whom organized the cult associations venerating the Most High God. His restoration was severely criticized by Latyshev.[66] The most serious objection is that although the name Ἄρχων was quite common, it never occurs in the inscriptions from the northern shore of the Black Sea.

The basic idea of Tolstoj's interpretation was supported by A. Kocevalov. The latter accepted his restoration of the invocation to the Most High God and Latyshev's restoration ἄρχοντες. Kocevalov argued that 'der Kult des θεὸς ὕψιστος in Olbia in späterer Zeit zu einem Staatskult geworden ist'. It seems that to accept this thesis is to

[62]As A. Kocevalov remarks 'Es wäre aber doch wohl kaum anzunehmen, daß zu derselben Zeit in Olbia einerseits 3 Bürger und anderseits 3 Juden, mit denselben Namen und Vatersnamen gewohnt hätten, und daß ein Διονυσιόδωρος Ἔρωτος, ein Archont der Stadt Olbia, mit seinen Kollegen ein Weihgeschenk für Achilleus Pontarches gestiftet habe - und ein anderer Διονυσιόδωρος Ἔρωτος, auch ein Archont, aber nicht der Stadt Olbia, sondern der jüdischen Synagoge, ungefähr zu derselben Zeit mit seinen Kollegen an der Wiederherstellung eines jüdischen Bethauses beteiligt gewesen sei' ('Beitrage zu den euxeinischen Inschriften', *Würzburger Jahreshefte für die Altertumswissénschaft* 3 (1948), 165. Kocevalov made a few mistakes in his references to particular inscriptions, but this does not affect his interpretation.
[63]The final ν of the accusative required by the construction with περί is a mistake: all who saw the inscription while it was still available recorded υ.
[64]*The White Island and Taurica on the Pontos Euxeinos* (Petrograd, 1916), 82f. (*in Russian*).
[65]For example, there is definitely not enough room for a name and a patronymic.
[66]*Izvestiya Rossijskoj Akademii Istorii Material'noj Kul'tury* (*Transactions of the Russian Academy of the History of Material Culture*) 1 (1921), 22f. (*in Russian*).

go much too far beyond what our evidence allows. The repairing of a Jewish prayer-house initiated by the city magistrates does not imply that Judaism became a state religion. It implies good relations between the city authorities and the Jewish community and quite possibly some kind of business relations, e.g. the synagogue could have been repaired as an act of gratitude for some useful service. But no matter how these relations are interpreted, it is clear that the inscription does not support the assertion that a Gentile temple was called in Olbia προσευχή.

Two other inscriptions from the neighbouring Bosporan Kingdom have been referred to as a proof of possible employment of the term προσευχή by the Gentiles. The reference in *LSJ* to *CIRB* 70 (*App.* 3,II,1) involves a misunderstanding since in this act of enfranchisement from Panticapaeum, the freedman is set free on condition that he fulfil his obligations towards the prayer-house under the guardianship of the Jewish community.

Another manumission from Gorgippia (*CIRB* 1123 = *App.* 3,II,7), which was mentioned by Schürer with the proviso that there was Jewish influence here, deserves more serious attention. At the end of it stands the oath-formula ὑπὸ Δια, Γῆν, Ἥλιον, which seems to point to a Gentile rather than to a Jewish context. But the Elephantine papyri show that even a practising Jew could use pagan oath-formulas under pressure of legal necessity;[67] this applies even more to the Gentile Jewish sympathizer who is the most likely author of this manumission.[68] In this case, however, it can be argued that Jewish sympathizers built places of worship of their own to the Jewish God, which they called by the Jewish name προσευχή and where they manumitted slaves (hence the address to the Most High God which is absent from the manumissions in which the Jewish community is mentioned; also absent are conditions of certain obligations towards the Jewish prayer-house under which a slave was set free). This hypothesis seems to be supported by the last example of alleged Gentile borrowing of the term

---

[67]Schürer, Vermes, Millar, Goodman, *The History of the Jewish People*, 3, 1, 37. Pagan formulas utilizing the names of the pagan gods were a part of everyday speech, and, like theophoric names, were readily used by Jews. Josephus relates without any kind of embarrassment that when the representatives of the Jewish community in Alexandria met Ptolemy VI Philometor, they swore by God and the King—ὤμοσαν τὸν θεὸν καὶ τὸν βασιλέα (*AJ* 13.76); he himself did not hesitate to use the expression νὴ Δία (c.*App.* 1.255; 2.263, see S. Luria, *Antisemitism in the Ancient World*, Addenda, 1, No. 21, *in Russian*).

[68]See pp. 108-110.

προσευχή, suggested by Epiphanius' description of the Messalians (Μασσαλιανοί). He regarded them as belonging neither to the Jews, nor to the Christians, nor to the Samaritans, but noted that they called their places of worship προσευχαί.[69] This example was especially pressed by Latyschev who most unfortunately repeated a mistake made by A.Ya Garkavi when he confused Μασσαλιανοί, members of the Massalian sect, and Μασσαλιῶται, citizens of Massalia (Marseilles).[70]

Let us take a closer look at Epiphanius' text. His main concern is to discredit the Christian sect of Messalians which existed in his time. One of the lines of attack is to show the ignoble origin of the sect. He claimed that Christian Messalians originated from an obscure pagan sect of the same name which came into being in the time of Constantine.

According to Epiphanius, these pagan Messalians acknowledged the existence of other gods but worshipped only one, whom they called Almighty: καὶ θεοὺς μὲν λέγοντες, μηδενὶ δὲ <τούτων> προσκυνοῦντες, ἑνὶ δὴ μόνον δῆθεν τὸ σέβας νέμοντες καὶ καλοῦντες Παντοκράτορα. Epiphanius distinguished between different places of worship which Messalians called by different names. The term προσευχή was applied either to buildings or to open spaces which he likened to *fora*: τινὰς δὲ οἴκους ἑαυτοῖς κατασκευάσαντες ἢ τόπους πλατεῖς φόρων δίκην, προσευχὰς ταύτας ἐκάλουν.

Epiphanius then explained that the term προσευχή was originally employed by Jews and, under Jewish influence, by Samaritans, who imitated Jews in everything.[71] Slightly later he wrote that in some places Messalians built τοπάριά τινα[72], which they called both προσευχαί and εὐκτήρια (this term being found in Christian usage). In other places they made for themselves something similar to churches where they gathered at dawn and sunset amid lamps and torches: ἐν ἄλλοις δὲ τόποις φύσει καὶ ἐκκλησίας ὁμοίωμά τι ἑαυτοῖς ποιήσαντες, καθ᾽ ἑσπέραν καὶ κατὰ τὴν ἕω μετὰ πολλᾶς λυχναψίας καὶ φώτων

---

[69]Epiphanius *Pan.* 80, 1,4 (*GCS*, Epiphanius, vol.3, 485).

[70]Latyshev, *op. cit.*, 273; A.Ya Garkavi, *Zapiski Russkogo Arkheologicheskogo obschestva (Transactions of the Russian Archaeological Society)* 2 (1886), CXXXIV (*in Russian*).

[71]On the attempts to distinguish between synagogues proper and unroofed meeting places known as προσευχαί, which were provoked by the remark of Epiphanius that the Jews and Samaritans also had their places of prayer in the open air, see Schürer, Vermes, Millar, Black, 2, 444f.

[72]This reading is in accordance with Petavius' conjecture; mss: τροπάρια.

συνθροιζόμενοι. Epiphanius also mentioned that they were prosecuted by the authorities on the initiative of a certain Λουππικιανὸς ὁ στρατηλάτης ;[73] many of them were killed for their perversion of truth and imitation of the Christian rites although not being Christians; nor did they *originate from Jews* : ἀλλὰ καί τινες τῶν ἀρχώντων ζηλωταὶ πολλοὺς ἐκ τούτων ἀπέκτειναν, διὰ τὸ παραχαράττειν τὴν ἀλήθειαν καὶ ἀντιμιμεῖσθαι ἐκκλησίας τρόπον, μὴ ὄντας χριστιανοὺς μήτε ἐξ Ἰουδαίων ὁρμωμένους. How can we understand the last statement? Why were Messalians prosecuted for not originating from Jews? Was not imitating (or seeming to imitate) the Christian service sufficient reason for non-Christians to be punished? And Epiphanius definitely could not be implying that this was permissible to Jews. It looks as if the last words reveal the main reason of persecution—Messalians adopted too much from Judaism, and among other things Jewish religious vocabulary. Epiphanius stressed particularly the last issue; hence his learned excursus on Jewish and Samaritan prayer-houses. He was well aware of the fact that προσευχή was a Jewish term, and their usurpation of it confirms the illegality of their behaviour. The authorities were not going to tolerate it, since conversion to Judaism was forbidden. Were Messalians seen by these zealous authorities as converts or near-converts? The Christian legislation inherited from the pagan legal tradition prohibitions against converting to Judaism. The latter prohibited primarily circumcision which was equated with castration. The Christian laws added another criterion for conversion, viewing it as consisting in joining the synagogue and the Jewish cult generally.[74] The prohibition related not only to Christians but to the whole population.[75] Did Messalians come too close to a border which they were not allowed to cross, and were they given a lesson to prevent Christians doing the same? We know from John Chrysostom's *Homilies* against the Jews how much he was disturbed by the attractiveness of Judaism for his flock. A quite substantial number of canons from the Council of Laodicea shows that this was a burning issue in the second half of the fourth century.[76] To summarise,

---

[73]M. Kmosco, *Patrologia Syriaca, I, 3,,* CLXXVI, supposed that Λουππικιανός should be Lupicinus who was *magister equitum* in the Orient under Jovian and Valens (Amm. Marc, *Hist.* 26.5,4). Holl, Epiphanius, *GCS* 486, thought that the correct reading should be Λουκιλλιανός and that Epiphanius had in mind Jovian's father-in-law.

[74]Linder, *The Jews in Roman Legislation,* 80f. Linder refers to the laws from AD 329 (Linder, No. 8), from 353 (Linder, No. 12) and from 383 (Linder, No. 16).

[75]Linder,*The Jews in Roman Legislation,* 81; 131, n. 15.

THE MEANING OF PROSEUCHE

Epiphanius' description of the Massalians portrays them as one of the monotheistic Judaizing groups which could hardly be labelled as Gentile or pagan in the conventional sense of these words.[77]

Can we postulate then, that in the first century Gorgippia a similar group of Judaizers emerged, who built their own prayer house alongside the Jewish one and, like Samaritans in Epiphanius' view, imitated Jews in everything: in other words, that Jewish impact gave birth to Judaizing Gentile structures so early? This seems to me to be most unlikely. We know nothing about such groups in this century. *Hypsistarii*, *Massaliani*, and *Caelicolae* appeared on the historical stage much later. To be attracted by Judaism as by something unusual, to frequent Jewish synagogues, at last to become a God-fearer—all these features fit the historical picture of the first century as it is known to us from other sources. But to create a kind of a parallel 'Judaism', with a Jewish name for God and a Jewish name for a place of veneration, and to manumit slaves in these Gentile prayer-houses as in Jewish ones[78] would be without any precedent whatsoever. It seems that a more economical (and a more historically plausible) interpretation of the inscription from Gorgippia is the one I advocated above.

As all the examples put forward as proof of the Gentile usage of the term προσευχή are on closer examination found to be wanting, my conclusion runs as follows.

(1) There is no clear evidence that the Gentiles ever borrowed this specifically Jewish term for their places of worship.

(2) On one occasion it was used by a Judaizing group precisely because the term was markedly Jewish.

---

[76]Simon, *Verus Israel*, 382f. A different interpretation was suggested by Kraabel who, in the course of expounding his belief in the absence of religious involvement of non-Jews in Judaism, argues that there was no 'accommodation between gentile Christians and non-Christian Jews' behind the rulings of the Council of Laodicaea (*Synagoga Caeca*, 54ff.); cf. also Trebilco, 'Jewish Communities', 101f.

[77]The remark in Schürer, Vermes, Millar, Black, 2, 440, n. 61 that 'there *may be* Jewish influence here' seems to me to be misleadingly cautious.

[78]Among all the manumissions from the Bosporan Kingdom, only two are indisputably Gentile (*CIRB* 74; 1021).

APPENDIX 3

INSCRIPTIONS FROM THE BOSPORAN KINGDOM

(in collaboration with S.R.Tokhtas'ev)

EPIGRAPHIC CONVENTIONS

In this appendix we use the system of critical signs advocated by H.Krummrey and Silvio Panciera ('Criteri di edizione e segni diacritici', *Tituli* 2 (1980), 205-215).

Brackets:
( ) enclose the resolution of an abbreviation.
[ ] enclose a restoration; a question mark shows that the restoration is tentative.
< > enclose a letter mistakenly omitted on the stone and added by the editor.
{ } enclose a superfluous letter.
⌐ ¬ enclose a correction by the editor.

[...] shows lost letters when their number can be calculated without doubt; each dot stands for a letter.
[- ³ -] shows lost letters when their number can be roughly conjectured.
[---] shows lost letters when their amount is unknown.
------ shows a lacuna either at the beginning or at the end of the inscription when the area lost is unknown.

+ shows a letter of which only traces can be discerned and which cannot be identified even tentatively; each cross stands for a letter.

vac. or vac.c.2 or vac.3 shows an uninscribed space in the inscription with an approximate calculation of its size.

Underdotting marks a letter incompletely preserved.

Measurements are all in meters, they are given in the order height x width x depth.

Inventory numbers are given for the Bosporan inscriptions whenever they are available; the Cyrillic letters preceding these numbers are transliterated into Latin letters.

We offer here a selection of inscriptions from the Bosporan Kingdom, illustrating some of the assertions of this book. All have already been published, but the texts of the majority differ from those in the pre-existing publications as a result of fresh collation with the stones. The commentaries are reduced to the minimum essential for this book. In their full form they will be published in the *Addenda and Corrigenda to Corpus Inscriptionis Regni Bosporani (CIRB)* now in preparation by the authors of this Appendix. All photographs of the inscriptions with the exception of 3,II,2, 3,II,6, 3,II,7 are published for the first time. We have not commented on spelling or other linguistic usages which are standard in Hellenistic times although deviating from the usage of the Classical period. Personal names that are not of Greek and Latin derivation are normally left unaccented. The references to earlier editions of the inscriptions are limited to the main, easily available, *corpora*. The first reference is always to *CIRB*, where the references to the *editiones principes* can be found.

I. Dedications

Panticapaeum

1. *CIRB* 64; *IGRR* I, 873

Found in 1901-1903 in Kertch, where it had been used for more than forty years as a threshold lying face downwards. Now in the *Kertchensky istorico-kulturny zapovednik* (historico-archaeological museum of Kertch), inventory no. KL 260.

A rectangular grey marble slab (1.03 x 0.30 x 0.10), inscribed on one face. At the top above the inscription the stone has been trimmed back to leave a triangular gable in relief. Letters: 0.018-0.022. Lunate *omega* and *epsilon; sigma* mostly lunate, but occasionally rectangular. The abbreviation in l.3 is marked by an apostrophe. Guide-lines visible, one above and one below each line of letters. 306 AD.

     Θεῷ ὑψίστῳ
     ἐπηκόῳ εὐ- vac.2
     χήν. Αὐρ(ήλιος) Οὐαλέ-
     ριος Σογους Ὀ- vac.1
5   λύμπου, ὁ ἐπὶ vac.1

τῆς Θεοδοσίας
σεβαστόγνω- vac.1
στο⌐ς⌐, τειμηθεὶς ὑ-
πὸ Διοκλητ vac.1 ια-vac.1
10   νοῦ καὶ Μαξιμιανοῦ,
ὁ καὶ Ὀλυμπιαν vac.1 ὸς
κληθεὶς ἐν τῷ vac.1 ἐ-
παρχείῳ, ὁ πολλὰ
ἀποδημήσας καὶ
15   ἀποστατήσας ἔτη
δέκα ἓξ καὶ ἐν πολ-
λοῖς θλίψεις γενό-
μενος, εὐξάμενος,
ἐκ θεμελίου οἰκο-
20   δομήσας τὴν προσ-
ευχὴν ἐν τῷ γχ΄.

To the Most High God, who listens, in fulfillment of a vow. Aurelius Valerius Sogus, the son of Olympus, the imperial governor of Theodosia, [a man] known to the Emperors, honoured by Diocletian and Maximian, who was also called in the province Olympianos, who was absent from home for a long time and spent sixteen years away, and who suffered from many afflictions, having made a vow, built the prayer-house from the foundation in the year 603.

6. ΘΕΟΔΟΣΙΑΣ with rectangular *sigma* (not *iota*, as in *CIRB*) at the end (cf. 1.11). Theodosia which was an important ice-free harbour (according to Strabo VII.4.4 it could accommodate a hundred ships) was incorporated into the Bosporan Kingdom under the King Leucon I (389/8 - 349/8 BC); the name of the city became part of the official title of the Bosporan rulers. - **7-8.** ΣΕΒΑΣΤΟΓΝΩΣΤΟΝ cut in error. The title is known in nearby Olbia (*IPE* II, 24) and in Prusias on the Hypius in Bithynia (*BCH* 25 (1901), 62ff.). - **10.** According to V. Latyshev, 'Inscriptions trouvées dans la Russie méridionale en 1901-1903 (avec 100 facsimiles)', *IAK* 10 (1904), 28 (*in Russian*) Maximian is *Aurelius Valerius Maximianus (Herculius)*; B. Nadel, 'Studies in the Political History of the Bosporan State in the Crimea at the Beginning of the Fourth Century AD', *AAntASH* 9 (1961), 235 (*in Russian*) argues that he is most probably *Galerius Valerius Maximianus*. - **11.** Ὀλυμπιανός, the Greek transliteration of Latin *Olympianus* = (ὁ)Ὀλύμπου of 1.4/5. - **12-13.** ἐν τῷ ἐπαρχείῳ: τὸ ἐπαρχεῖον is a *hapax*, the reference in *LSJ* s.v. is a mistake, corrected in the *Supplementum*.

The suffix -ειον suggests that the word should have the meaning 'the residence of the ἔπαρχος' (cf. βασίλειον, πρυτανεῖον etc.). Metonymically it could probably have designated the region administered by an *eparchos*. (cf. *CIRB* 67) ἐπαρχεῖον must be correlated with Sogus' title ὁ ἐπὶ Θεοδοσίας in l.5/6. - **16-17.** ἐν πολλοῖς θλίψεις for ἐν πολλαῖς θλίψεσι.

II. Manumissions

Panticapaeum

1. *CIRB* 70; *CIG* II, add., p. 1005 (copy of F. Dubois de Montpéreux); *IPE* II, 52; *IGRR* I, 881; *CIJ* I, 683.
The illustration shows only the upper part of the inscription (ll. 1-12). Found in Kertch in 1832. Now at the Hermitage Museum, St.Petersburg, inventory no. P.1832.34.
A slab of white marble, broken in two pieces (0.64 x 0.27-0.29 x 0.08-0.09). Above is a gable in relief with three acroteria in the form of palmets (the central one lost) and a circular feature in the centre; the gable rests on a moulding; the inscription is cut on the face below. Guide-lines visible, one above and one below each line of letters. In l.4 dot for stop. In l.5 the lettering towards the right end is more broadly spaced than normally. Letters: 0.014. Rectangular *sigma*.
81 AD.

```
   Βασιλεύοντος βασιλέως Τιβε-
   ρίου Ἰουλίου Ῥησκουπόριδος φιλο-
   καίσαρος καὶ φιλορωμαίου, εὐσε-
   βοῦς • ἔτους ζοτ΄ μηνὸς Περει[τί]-
5  ου ιβ΄, Χρήστη γυνὴ πρότε-
   ρον Δρούσου ἀφείημι ἐπὶ τῆς πρ[ο]-
   σευχῆς θρεπτόν μου Ἡρακλᾶν
   ἐλεύθερον καθάπαξ κατὰ εὐχή[ν]
   μου ⌐ἀ⌐νεπίληπτον καὶ ἀπαρενό-
10 χλητον ἀπὸ π⌐α⌐ντὸς κληρονόμου
   [τ]ρέπεσ⌐θ⌐αι αὐτὸν ὅπου ἂν βού-
   λη[τ]αι ἀνεπικωλύτως καθὼς ηὐ-
   ξάμην, χωρὶς ἱς τ[ὴ]ν προσευ-
```

χὴν θωπείας τε καὶ προσκαρτε-
15 ρήσεως, συνεπινευσάντων δὲ
καὶ τῶν κληρ⸢ο⸣νόμων μου ˙ Ἡρα-
κλείδου καὶ ˙ Ἑλικωνιάδος,
συνεπ[ιτ]ροπευούσης δὲ καὶ τῆς
συναγωγῆς τῶν Ἰουδαίων.

In the reign of the king Tiberius Iulius Rhescuporis, friend of the Emperor and friend of the Romans, pious, in the year 377, on the 12th of Pereitios, I, Chreste, formerly the wife of Drusus, set free in the prayer-house my house-bred slave Heraclas once and for all in fulfillment of a vow to move without let or hindrance from any of my heirs wherever he wants unimpededly, in accordance with my vow, on condition that he honours the prayer-house and is conscientious in his attendance there, with the agreement of my heirs Heraclides and Heliconias and also under the joint gardianship of the Jewish community.

9. ΑΝΕΠΙΛΗΠΤΟΝ on the stone, *cf.* l. 10. **10.** ΠΛΝΤΟΣ on the stone. - **11.** ΡΕΠΕΣΤΑΙ on the stone, corrected by V.Latyshev. For other examples of confusion of θ and τ in the Bosporan inscriptions see *CIRB*, p.808f. - **13-15.** - χωρὶς κτλ. with small variations is a standard formula in the Panticapaean manumissions in the prayer-house (*CIRB* 71, 73, probably 72=App. 3,II, 2, 4, 3; cf. also App. 3,II,6 and *CIRB* 985=App. 3, II, 5 from Phanagoria). The article after χωρὶς is omitted also in *CIRB* 73=App. 3, II, 4 and App. 3,II,6. θωπεία which normally means 'flattery' seems to be used with a special meaning of some kind of devotion to the prayer-house in the acts of enfranchisement in the Jewish prayer-house in the Bosporan Kingdom. The meaning of προσκαρτέρησις is disputable (see discussion in *CIRB* and *CIJ*). We agree with the interpretation of B. Nadel who considered that the freedmen was under obligation to do some work for the prayer-house (B.Nadel, *Vestnik Drevnej Istorii (The Journal of Ancient History)*, No. 1 (1948), 203-206 (*in Russian*); id., *Vestnik Drevnej Istorii* , No. 1 (1958), 139-141 (*in Russian*); id., 'O starogreckich napisach dotyczacych Zydow z rejonu Morza Czarnego' *Biuletyn Zydowskiego Instytutu Historycznego* 33 (1960), 79-82 (*in Polish*); id., 'Actes', 276, n. 27), cf, also pp. 109-110.

2. *CIRB* 71; Lifshitz, *CIJ* I², Prolegomenon , 683a.
Found in Kertch in 1928. It is reported in *CIRB* to be in the Kertch museum, but neither the stone nor the inventory no. in the Kertch

museum inventory was found by us. We have not therefore been able to make a new reading except from photographs.
A slab of white marble, broken at the top (0.32 x 0.37 x 0.07-0.11), inscribed on one face. The middle part has been damaged by some sharp instrument. Whole surface worn; many letters are very faint. Letters: 0.011-0.017. I century AD.
The text and translation see on p. 74.

2. κου, as suggested by V. Yajlenko, 'Studies in Bosporan Epigraphy', *The Inscriptions and the Languages of Ancient Asia Minor, Cyprus and Ancient North Black Sea Shore* (Moscow: Academy of Sciences, Institute of History, 1987, *in Russian*), 57, No. 38 could be the ending of the patronymic of the manumittor. - **3.** The editors of *CIRB*, following J. Marti read: ᾿Ελπία[ν]---α. τῆς θρεπτ[ῆς]. They argue that the traces of the letter of quadrangular form can be discerned at the end of the line. It seems that the photographs do not support this view. We follow the reading that was suggested by I. Tolstoi (*CIRB*, 71, commentary), which was also proposed by S. Luria and accepted by B. Nadel ('Actes', 270, cf. *id.*, 'Zydowskie dokumenty prawne ze starozytnego Nadczarnomorza', *Biuletyn Zydowskiego Institutu Historychnego*, 27 (1958), 12-13, No. 5 (*in Polish*]). Nadel, in fact, later changed his view and (in 'Slavery and Related Forms of Labor on the North Shore of the Eusine in Antiquity', *Actes du colloque 1973 sur l'esclarage* [Paris, 1976, Annales littéraires de l'Université de Besançon,182], 229, n. 166) accepted the reading of Lifshitz who ('Notes', 95; *Prolegomenon*, 683a) offered ᾿Ελπία[ν ἐμ]α[υ]τῆς θρεπτ[ῆς ?], but this is too long for the space (there can only be two letters between ΕΛΠΙΑ and Α). H. Bellen, Συναγωγὴ τῶν ᾿Ιουδαίων καὶ Θεοσεβῶν. Die Aussage einer bosporanischen Freilassunginschrift (*CIRB* 71) zum Problem der 'Gottesfürchtigen', *JAC* 8/9 (1965-1966), 174, considered that the letter E could be discerned after ΕΛΠΙΑ; this is not justified by the photographs of the stone. The emendation ᾿Ελπί<δ>α ἐ[μ]α[υ]τῆς θρεπτ[ήν], that he proposed is much less probable that the omission of the final ν, which is well attested in the Greek inscriptions of the Roman period, cf. examples from Panticapaeum *CIRB* 81 Μαστου<ν>, *CIRB* 82 Παπα<ν>, *CIRB* 89 Ζοτουμα<ν> (Yajlenko, 'Studies' 61f. No. 47, *de visu* discloses the absence of the final ν on the stone), *CIRB* 103 ᾿Εκτᾶ<ν>. For the omission of the final ν see K. Dieterich, *Untersuchungen zur Geschichte der griechischen Sprache von der Hellenistischen Zeit bis zum 10. Jahrh. n. Chr.* (Leipzig: Teubner, 1898,), 89ff.; A.Thumb, *Die griechische Sprache* *im Zeitalter des Hellenismus. Beiträge zur Geschichte und Beurteilung der KOINH* (Strassburg: Verlag von Karl J.Trübner, 1901), 173; G.Mihailov, *La langue des inscriptions grecques de Bulgarie* (Sofia, 1943), 74; L.Threatte, *The Grammar of Attic Inscriptions*, vol.1 (Berlin, New York: De Gruyter, 1980), 636f. - **9-10**. Those who saw the stone reported final ν at the end of l.9; on the photograph it is not so obvious. The emendation suggested by Bellen and Lifshitz (see in detail p. 75), which supposes the appearance of the superfluous ν at the end of the line inside the composite θεοσεβῶν is not without an epigraphic parallel: *CIJ* I 712 ΘΕΟΝ I ΚΤΙΣΤΟΥ instead of Θεοκτίστου. Nevertheless, for reasons that are explained on p. 75. it seems to us unacceptable.

3. *CIRB* 72; Lifshitz, Prolegomenon,*CIJ* I² 683a.
Found in Kertch in August 1912.
Now at the Kertch museum, inventory no. Kl 933.
Lower right corner of a marble slab (0.15 x 0.11 x 0.05). Letters poorly cut, rectangular *sigma*. Letters: 0.015-0.018. The end of the first - the beginning of the second century AD.

　　　- - - [συνεπι-]
　　　[τροπευού]σης δὲ κα[ὶ]
　　　[τῆς συναγω]γῆς τῶν
　　　['Ιουδα]ίων.

Under the joint guardianship also of the Jewish community.

4. *CIRB* 73; *CIG* II, add., p. 1004 (copy of F. Dubois de Montpéreux); *IPE* II, 53; *CIJ* I, 684.
No illustration.
Non vidimus.
Found in Kertch. Now at the Museum of Simferopol.
A slab of white marble, chipped at the upper right and lower left corners (0.47 x 0.28 x 0.05), inscribed on one face. The surface is very worn and the inscription is damaged. Letters: 0.018. First half of the second century AD.

　　　[Βασιλεύοντος βασιλέως- - -]
　　　[- - -φιλοκαίσαρος καὶ φιλο-]
　　　[ρωμαίου, εὐσεβοῦς, ἔτους- - -]
　　　[μηνὸς] Ἀρτ[εμ]ι[σίου - - -]

5   [ἀφ]ίημι τοὺς ἐ[μοὺς θρεπτοὺς ἐν τῇ]
     [π]ροσευχῇ κατ᾽ [εὐχὴν ἐλευθέρους]
     [καθάπαξ ?], σώμα[τα ἀνδρεῖα?- - -]
     [- - -]καὶ Ἑρμᾶν, [ἀνεπιλήπτους]
     [καὶ ἀπα]ρ⌐ε¹νοχλήτο[υς ἀπὸ τ᾽ ἐμοῦ]
10   [καὶ πα]ντὸς κληρονόμ[ου - - - ἐπὶ]
     [παραμ]ονῇ μέχρι τῆς ζωῆ[ς μου---]
     [- - -]εὐάρεστοι τῇ μ[ητρὶ μου ?]
     [- - -]ιταδι, καὶ πάντα ὥσ[περ ? - c.2 -]
     [- - -]καὶ τελευτήσαντός μου
15   [- - -]ε ποιήσουσιν πάν[τα - c.2 -]
     [μετὰ δὲ τὴν] τελευτὴν εἶν[αι αὐτοῖς]
     [τρέπεσθαι ἀν]επικωλύτως ἄν[ευ]
     [πάσης ἀμφισ]βητήσε⌐ω¹ς, κατ᾽ [εὐχήν]
     [μου , ὅπου ἂ]ν γῆς βούλ⌐ω¹νται, χ[ωρὶς]
20   [εἰς τὴν] προσευχὴν θωπείας τε καὶ προσ-
     [καρτ]ερήσε⌐ω¹ς, συνεπιτροπε[υούσης]
     [δὲ] καὶ τῆς συναγωγῆς τῶν
     Ἰουδαίων.

In the reign of the king . . . the friend of the Emperor and the friend of the Romans, pious, . . . in the year . . ., in the month of Artemisios . . . . I set free in the prayer-house once and for all (?) in fulfillment of a vow my male house-bred slaves (?), . . . and Hermas, without let and hindrance from me and from any of my heirs, on condition that they remain with me till the end of my life . . .well-pleasing to my mother (?) . . . and everything as (?) . . . and when I die . . . they shall do everything . . . after my death they are to have an undisputed right to move unimpededly in accordance with my vow wherever they want, on condition that they honour the prayer-house and are conscientious in their attendance there under the joint guardianship also of the Jewish community.

We have not re-read this inscription from the stone, but have reconsidered the text in the light of the copy made by F. Dubois de Montpéreux (whose copies of the inscriptions are usually of outstanding quality and must be very carefully studied), in the Archive of the Russian Academy of Sciences (St. Petersburg), f.68, op. 1, d.2, 1.190 verso - 191. We concluded that in some cases his readings are preferable to those of other editors, since unlike them he saw it before so much damage had occurred to the two side margins.

1-3. The tentative restoration of the first lines was made by V.Latyshev. - **5.** Latyshev's copy shows that some traces of E and M can be discerned. - **6.** The reading follows that in Dubois' copy. **6-7.** We follow Latyshev's restoration though the traces of letters before ΣΩΜΑ in Dubois' copy do not support it. - **9.** B. Nadel, *Vestnik drevnej istorii*, No 1 (1958), 142, proposed that the form ἀπαρανοχλή[τους] which stands on the stone should be accepted as a derivation from the verb ἀνοχλέω, but there are no obvious parallels, and the meaning would be rather unsuitable, while ἀπαρενόχλητος is common in the acts of enfranchisement (cf. *CIRB* 70, 71); so we prefer to emend. - **12.** We accept Latyshev's restoration. S. Luria suggested [παρ᾽ ἐμοὶ καὶ συν]ευαρεστο[ύσ]η μ[οί] (reported by B. Nadel, *ibid.*, 143, also in *CIRB*, *app. crit.*). -**13.** ΙΤΑΔΙ - Dubois, the copy by Latyshev shows traces of Ι. τάδε - *C I J* without grounds. Luria reads τὰ δίκαι(α) πάντα ὥς (reported by Nadel, *ibid.*).- **18-19.** Latyshev restored καθὼς ηὐξάμην but it is not supported either by his own copy, or by that of Dubois: ΚΑΤ[- -³⁻⁴- -]F. For the restoration of Nadel, 'Actes', 275 κα[ὶ πάσης δίκης ?] there is not enough room. We suggest κατ᾽ εὐχήν, though this formula is not usually repeated twice in the Bosporan inscriptions. - **20-23.** The readings are those of Dubois.

Phanagoria

5.   *CIRB* 985; *IPE*, II, 364; *IGGR* 906, *CIJ* 691, Lifshitz, *CIJ* I², Prolegomenon , 691.
Found on the shore of the Taman gulf in the territory of ancient Phanagoria. Now at the Hermitage Museum in St. Petersburg, inventory no. T 1880.7.
A slab of white marble (0.56 x 0.24 x 0.17), inscribed on one face. The surface is so badly worn that part of the inscription is completely lost. Letters: 0.013. 16 AD.

> [Β]ασιλεύοντος [βα-]
> [σ]ιλέως Ἀσπούργο[υ]
> φιλορω{ι}μαίου, ἔτους
> γιτ, μηνὸς Δαισίου ζ.
> 5   [Φ]οδακος Πόθωνος [ἀ-]
> [ν]ατίθησι τὸν ἑαυτοῦ
> [θρεπτὸ]ν Διονύσιον

[τ]ὸν κ[α]ὶ Λογ[γ ?]ι (?)ωνα ἐ-
π[ὶ τῆς προσευχῆς] ΑΠΟΛ-
10   [- - - - - - - -] ΟΛΗ
     [- - - - - - - - -] ΑΣ
     [- - - - - - - -]ΤΗ [---]
     [- - - - - - - - - - - - -]
     [- - - - - - - - - - - - -]
15   [- - - - - - - - - - -]ΑΝ
     [- c.5 -]Ο[- c.4 -]ΥΣ[.]
     [- - - - - - - - - - -]ΝΘΕ.
     [- - - - - - - - -]ης θω-
     πεί[ας ἕνεκα καὶ] προσ-
20   καρ[τερ]ήσεως.

In the reign of the king Aspurgus, the friend of the Romans, in the year 313, on the 7th of the month Daisios, Phodacos the son of Pothon dedicates his house-bred slave Dionysios, who is also (called) Longion (?) in the prayer-house (?) . . . on condition that he honours [the prayer house] and is conscientious in his attendance there.

9-10. It is doubtful that the stone has enough room for the proposed restoration τῆς προσευχῆς. Latyshev suggested Ἀπόλλ[ωνι], a restoration which has led to the widely circulated view that the text recorded 'the prayer-house of Apollo'. That conflicts with the normal usage of προσευχή.

6. D.I. Danshin, 'Phanagorian Community of Jews', *Vestnik Drevnej Istorii* No. 1 (1993), 59-72; I.A. Levinskaya, S.R. Tokhtas'ev, 'The New Jewish Manumission from Phanagoria', *Bulletin of Judaeo-Greek Studies* No. 13 (Winter 1993), 27-28.
Found in 1989 in the Mediaeval wall during the excavations at Phanagoria. Now in the collection of the Phanagorian expedition of the Institute of Archaeology of the Russian Academy of Sciences (Moscow).
A block of light yellow marble (0.358 x 0.229 x 0.108-0.121), several times reused. It was originally part of an architectural decorative feature, roughly recut with the face smoothed to carry an inscription, and finally in the Mediaeval period reused as building material. Rectangular *sigma*, diamond-shaped *theta, omicron, omega*. Letters: 0.08-001 (in ll. 1-9), 0.01-0.018). In places visible guide-lines above and below the lettering. Between 45 and 52 AD, most probably 51 AD.

[Β]ασιλε<ύ>ον[τος]βα-
σιλέως Κότυος
ἔτους ʼηʼμτʼ μηνὸς
Ξανδικοῦ αʹ. Ψυχα-
5　ρίων, Σογος, Ανος
[ο]ἱ τούτο<υ> υεἱοί. Καρ-
σανδανος καὶ Καρ-
αγος καὶ Μετρό-ᵛᵃᶜ·ᶜ·²
τειμος ἄφετοι τῇ
10　προσευχῇ, ἀνεπίλ<η>-
πτοι, ἀνεπικόλυ-
τοι, χωρὶς εἰ τὴν
προ<σ>ευχὴν προσκαρ-
τερήσεως καὶ θωπία-
15　ς καὶ ἔσταν ἄφετ[ο-]
[ι] συνεπιτροπε<υ>ούσ-
ης τῆς συναγω[γῆ-]
[] τῶν Ἰουδαί-
ων.

In the reign of the king Cotys, on the 1st day of the month Xandikos,
Psycharion and his sons Sogos and Anos. Karsandanos and Karagos
and Metroteimos are set free for (in?) the prayer-house without let
or hindrance on condition that they are conscientious in their
attendance to prayer-house and honour it and they became free also
under the joint guardianship of the Jewish community.

2. Cotys I reigned from 45 to 67 AD, which determines the lower date
(=342 of the Bosporan era) of the inscription. - **3.** The first letter of the
figure has been mistakenly inscribed as N; the correction to H was
suggested by the first editor and gives the date 348 of the Bosporan
era (=51 AD). In any case, given the other two figures of the date, the
inscription cannot be later than 52 AD (=349 of the Bosporan era). - **6-
8.** Καρ both in l.6 and in l.7 was interpreted by the first editor as an
ethnic. This is hardly possible: first, the normal position of the ethnic
was after and not before the name, second, there is, to the best of our
knowledge, no epigraphical evidence from the Roman period for the
use of Κάρ as an ethnic, third, the repetition of an ethnic would be
strange, especially in a text which is strikingly laconic elsewhere, cf.
the omission of the titles of king Cotys, his Roman *nomen* and
praenomen and his patronymic (cf. *CIRB* 958, 41, 42). We suggest that

we have two names beginning Καρ-, both belonging to the group of Iranian names given to the local slaves of Scytho-Sarmatian origin. For instance, the Iranian form of Καρσαδανος could be restored as *Karš-ant-āna- (patronymic from *Karš-ant(a)- and compared with ancient Persian or Median names *Karš-aina- (W.Hinz, *Altiranische Sprachgut der Nebenüberlieferungen* (Wiesbaden, 1975), 149); another possible Iranian explanation of this name can be given by comparing with the Avestan name Kərəsa-oxšan- and similar, and the Iranian names from Tanais in the Bosporan Kingdom Ασπ-ανδανος (*CIRB* 1279,14) and Ιασ -ανδαν-ακος (*CIRB* 1287,30). The name of the second freedman, Καραγος, corresponds to the Persian or Median name from Persepolis *Kāraka- (Hinz, *Altiranische Sprachgut*, 148). **9-10.** There is here a mixture of two formulae, one from Greek sacral manumissions in the form of donation of a slave to a deity, which utilizes the verb ἀνατίθημι, and another from the civil mode of enfranchisement using the verb ἀφίημι. See Appendix 3 ,II, 7. - **15.** ἔσταν probably for ἔστησαν; cf. the examples of contraction, notably κατέσεν for κατέστησεν, cited by E. Nachmanson, 'Die schriftliche Kontraktion auf den griechischen Inschriften', *Eranos* 10 (1910), 130. - **17-19.** This is the earliest mention of the Jewish community (cf. *CIRB* 985=App. 3, II, 5 where the Jewish prayer-house may have been mentioned).

Gorgippia

7. *CIRB* 1123 ; *IPE* II 400, *CIJ* 690, Lifshitz, *CIJ* I². Prolegomenon, 690.
Found in Anapa. Now at the Hermitage Museum, St. Petersburg, inventory no. Gp 20.
A slab of white marble (0.29 x 0.21 x 0.08), inscribed on one face. The surface is badly worn, with serious damage to some letters which have been overcut in modern times by someone who did not always understand the text and wrongly interpreted some letters. Guidelines visible, one above and one below each line of letters. Letters: 0.012. 41 AD.

      Θεῶι ὑψίστωι παντο-
      κράτορι εὐλογητῷ, βα-
      σιλεύοντος βασιλέ-
      ως [Μιθρ]ιδάτου φιλο-
5   ΓΕΡΜΑΚΟΥ καὶ φιλοπάτ-

ριδος ἔτους ηλτ, μη-
νὸς Δείου, Πόθος Στ-
ράβωνος ἀνέθηκεν
τῆι προσευχῆι κατ᾿ εὐχὴ-
10   ν θ[ρ]επτὴν ἑαυτοῦ, ᾗ ὄνομα Χρύσα, ἐφ᾿ ᾧ ᾗ ἀνέπα-
φος καὶ ἀνεπηρέαστος
ἀπὸ παντὸς κληρον[όμ]-
ου ὑπὸ Δία, Γῆν, Ἥλιο[ν].

To the Most High God, Almighty, blessed, in the reign of the king
Mithridates, the friend of ? and the friend of the fatherland, in the
year 338, in the month Deios, Pothos, the son of Strabo, dedicated to
the prayer-house in accordance with the vow his house-bred slave-
woman, whose name is Chrysa, on condition that she should be
unharmed and unmolested by any of his heirs under Zeus, Ge,
Helios.

4. V. Latyshev suggested the restoration φιλογερμα(νι)κοῦ, which is,
however, unparalleled; L. Stephani, *Mélanges gréco-romains tirés du
Bulletin hist.-philologique de l'Académie impériale des sciences* II (1866),
200, who is said to have seen the text before the modern overcutting,
read ΦΙΛΟΙ.ΜΑΙΟΥ - φιλο[ρω]μαίου; which makes sense, but does not
conform to what we can see on the stone; A.I. Boltunova, *Vestnik
drevnej istorii* No. 1 (1954), 170f., proposed φιλοσυμμάχου which does
not correspond with the traces. Inspection of the stone confirms the
reading of Latyshev ΓΕΡΜΑΚΟΥ. - **7-8.** Στράτωνος in *CIJ* 691 is a
mistake, made by Latyshev, and repeated by Lifshitz in *Prolegomena*
691. **8-9.** The different formula can probably be explained by the
influence of the pagan manumissions of the type in which the
freedman was dedicated to a certain deity (*CIRB* 74, 1021). For a list
of Talmudic references to the consecration of slaves to the Temple see
B. Nadel, 'Slavery', 218. Cf. also App. 3, II, 6, where both formulae
are mixed.

8. *CIRB* 1124 ; Lifshitz, *CIJ* I², *Prolegomenon*, 690b.
Found in Duzu-Kale, to the south-east of Dzhubga and most
probably from Gorgippia. Moulding above (badly damaged). Now
at the Hermitage Museum, St. Petersburg, inventory no. A 1087.
A fragment of a slab of white marble with moulding above, now
badly damaged (0.18 x 0.11 x 0.05), inscribed on one face. Letters:
0.01. Superscript bars above the figures. 59 AD.

[Βασιλ]ε<ύ>οντος βασι[λέως Κότυος φι-]
[λοκαί]σαρος καὶ φιλο[ρωμαίου, εὐσε-]
[βοὺς, ἔ]τους ϛντ΄, μηνὸ[ς - - -]
[Φιλότ]ειμος (?) Γαδειος [- - -]
5   [- - -]ον γυναικὸς α[ὐτοῦ - - -]
[- - -εὐξ]αμένης αὐτῆ[ς - - -]
[- - -]ς καὶ τῆς γυνα[ικὸς - - -]
[Καλλισθ]ενείας, ἀφί[ησι τὸν θρεπτὸν ?]
[- - -]ν μετὰ γυνα[ικὸς αὐτοῦ - - -]
10   [τὸ γένο]ς (?) Ἰουδαίου[ς - - -]

In the reign of the king Cotys, the friend of the Emperor and the
friend of the Romans, pious, in the year 356, in the month . . .
Philoteimos (?), the son of Gadeis . . . of his wife, according to her
vow (?) . . . and of the wife of . . . Callistheneia, set free the house-
bred slave (?) with his wife . . . Jews by descent(?).

4. For the patronymic of the manumittor a semitic etymology can be
proposed. Γαδεις may be derived from Heb. *Gaddi* or Aram.* *Gad(d)e;*
see Levinskaya, Tokhtas'ev, 'The Jewish Names', 121f. - **6.** Restoration by Lifshitz, 'Notes d'épigraphie grecque', *RB* 76 (1969) No. 8, p.
97, cf. also *Prolegomenon.* - **10.** It is the only example of an ethnic for a
slave in Bosporan manumissions; see App. 3, II, 6, *app. crit.*, 6-8.

9. *CIRB* 1127.
Bought in Anapa. Now lost. Re-read from a drawing by N.I.
Veselovsky.

The left lower corner of a marble slab (0.14 x 0.24 x 0.24), inscribed on
one face. Letters: 0.015. Lunate *sigma* and *epsilon.* Letters: 0.015. The
first half of the second century AD.

- - - - - - - - - - - - - - ἦ ὄνο[μα]
[.]+++νωμη, ἐ{α}φ᾽ ᾧ τε ἦ ἀ[νέ-]
παφος καὶ ἀνεπηρέαστος ἀ[πό]
τε ἐμοῦ καὶ παντός μο[υ]
5   κληρονόμου, προσμέ[νου-]
σα τῇ προσευχ[ῇ]

whose name is ... on condition that she should be unharmed and unmolested both by me and by any of my heirs, remaining attached to the prayer-house.

III Religious associations

Tanais

1. *CIRB* 1260; *IPE* II, 438.
Found in Nedvigovka in 1869-1870. Now at the Hermitage Museum, St. Petersburg, inventory no. Tn. 320.
A marble slab reconstructed from 21 pieces (0.98 x 0.62 x 0.11), inscribed on one face. The inscription is cut within a moulded panel; above it a gable in relief with central acroterion (the two side corners are lost) encloses an image of an eagle with his head turned to the left and with swags on either side. The first line of the inscription is on the cornice of the gable; between the words is a big space with something, perhaps an ivy leaf, incised centrally. Between the gable and the inscribed area there is a swag upheld by eagles (only the left one survives) with three more lines of inscription in the space between the wings of the eagles and the swag. Letters irregular; some show cursive influence. Letters: 0.012-0.02. 155 AD.

```
      [ Ἀγ]αθῆι  vac. τύ[χηι]
      Θεῷ
      ὑψίστῳ ἐπη-
      κόῳ εὐχή.
5     Βασιλεύον[τ]ος βασιλέως [Τιβερίου]
      Ἰουλίου Εὐπ[άτ]ορος, φιλοκ[αίσαρος]
      καὶ φιλορωμα[ίου, ε]ὐσεβοῦς, [ἐν τῷ ἔτει]
      βνυʹ [κ]αὶ μηνὶ [- - - Ἡ σύνοδος]
      ἡ π[ερὶ ἱ]ερέα Φά[ννην Στρατονείκου]
10    [καὶ συνα]γωγὸν [- - - ]
      [- c.6 -]κου[ - - - ]
      [- - - Ἰο]υλιάδ[ην]
      [ Ἡρακ]λείδ[ου καὶ οἱ λ]οιποὶ θια-
      σ[ῶ]ται.  vac.
```

15   [Δα]δας β΄[- - -]ων Ἀμαρθαστου
     [Δ]ημήτριος β΄ [- - -]ακος Χ[α]ρίτωνος,
     Παρβας Ζαβα[ργου ?, Ἀμ]αρθαστος β΄,
     [Δ]αδας Θεαγ[γέλο]υ, Αρδαρος Μύρωνος,
     [Α]θηνόδωρος Μη[νοφί]λου, Ἔρως Παρθενοκλέους,
20   [Α]χαιμένης Θ[εαγγέ?]λου Ομψαλακος Φιδα,
     [Συν]έκδημος Ἀρ[- - -]υ, Μυρεῖγος β΄,
     [Βα]σιλείδη[ς - - -]   Φάννης Στ[ρα-]
     [- - -]λ [- - - Χα]ρίτω-   τονείκου ἱε-
     [νος, ὁ δεῖνα - - -]κου,   [ρ]εὺς εὐξ[ά]-
25   [- - -]ος Φιλ[ώ]του   μενος ἀπε-
     [- - -]ος Πάπ[π]ου,   κατέστησε τ[ὸν]
     [Μενέ?]στρατος β΄,   τελαμῶνα
     [Ζήνω?]ν Φάννεως.   ἐκ τῶν ἰδίω[ν].

With good fortune. To the Most High God, who listens, the vow. In
the reign of the king Tiberius Iulius Eupator, the friend of the
Emperor and the friend of the Romans, pious, in the year 452, in the
month . . . . The association under the presidency of the priest
Phannes the son of Stratoneikos and the convener . . . Iulianos and
other members of the association (the list of the names). Phannes
the son of Stratoneikos, the priest, in fulfilment of the vow restored
this stele at his own expense.

9. Restored by V. Latyshev who reasonably argued that the priest of
this line and the priest of the line 22 is one and the same person.

2. *CIRB* 1280 ; *IPE* II, 448.
The photograph shows a reconstruction made in the 1960's when the
fragments recognised as belonging to this text were collected and set
in plaster. Since the plaster cannot easily be removed, fragments
subsequently recognised as belonging cannot be combined with them
for photography and are not shown in the illustration.
Found in the southern part of ancient Tanais during the building of
the railway in 1869-1870. Now in the Hermitage Museum,
St.Petersburg, inventory no. Tn. 322.
A slab of white marble reconstructed from eighty–one pieces (1.57 x
0.83 x 0.03), inscribed on one face. Letters: 0.25-0.035. Lunate *sigma*
and *epsilon*. 225 AD.

     Ἀγαθῆι vac.2 τύχη[ι]
     Θεῷ ὑψίστωι ἐπηκόωι ἡ σύ[ν]ο-

δος ἡ περὶ θεὸν ὕψιστον καὶ ἱερέ-
α Καλλισθένην Πάππου, ὁ [κ]αὶ
5   Θυλογανος, καὶ συναγωγὸν Ψυχαρί-
ων Φιδανοι καὶ φιλάγαθον [Ἀσ]κληπι-
άδην Οὐαλερίου καὶ παρα[φιλά]γαθον
Χαρακστον Ομρασμακου καὶ [ν]ιανισκά[ρ-]
χ[η]ν Φάννην β΄ και γυμνασιάρχην Ἡρακλεί-
10   δην β΄ καὶ οἱ λοιποὶ θιασῶται·
The list of the names for 21.5 lines.
[Εν τῷ] βκφ΄ ᵛᵃᶜ· 1 ἔ[τει καὶ μ]ηνὶ Περειτ[ίῳ - - -]

With good fortune. To the Most High God, who listens, the
association under the presidency of the Most High God and priest
Kallisthenes the son of Pappos, who is also called Thyloganos, and
convener Psycharion the son of Phidanus and promoter of goodness
Asklepiades, the son of Valerius, and the deputy promoter of
goodness Charakstos, the son of Omrasmakos and supervisor of the
youth Phannes II, and the director of the gymnasium Herakleides II,
and the other members of the association (the list of the names). In
the year 522, in the month of Pereitios ...

5. For the distribution and meaning of the title φιλάγαθος see E.
Ziebart, *Das griechische Vereinswesen* (Leipzig: S. Hirzel, 1896,
Preisschriften gekrönt und herausgegeben von der Fürstlichen
Jablonowski'schen Gesellschaft, 34), 155; F. Poland, *Geschichte des
griechischen Vereinswesens* (Leipzig: S.Hirzel, 1909, Preisschriften v.
Jablonowski'schen Gesellschaft, 38), 413. - **7.** a title παραφιλάγαθος is
known only from the Bosporan inscriptions. - **10.** For the duty of a
γυμνασιάρχης see F. Quass, *Die Honoratiorenschicht* (Stuttgart, 1993),
317-323; Poland, *Geschichte*, 401-402.

3. *CIRB* 1281; *IPE* II, 449, IV, add., p.293.
Found in Nedvigovka in 1869-1870. Now at the Hermitage Museum,
St. Petersburg, inventory no. Tn. 319.
A marble slab, partly reconstructed from twenty four pieces (0.88 x
0.05 x 0.02), inscribed on one face. Nearly all the right part is lost. On
the upper part of the slab two images of eagles were incised on the
either side of a wreath. Only the left one, part of the wreath and the
tail of the right one remain, rectangular *sigma* and *epsilon*, diamond
shaped *theta*, *omicron* and *phi*, triangular bowls for *beta* and partly for
rho. Letters: 0.02-0.025. First quarter of the third century AD.

Θεῶι [ὑψίστωι]
Βασιλεύοντος β[ασιλέως Τιβερίου]
Ἰουλίου˙ Ρησκουπό[ριδος φιλοκαί-]
σαρος καὶ φιλορωμ[αίου, εὐσεβοῦς],
5   ἱσποιητοὶ ⌜ἀ⌝δελφο̣[ὶ σεβόμενοι]
[θε]ὸν ὕψιστον ἀγ[έστησαν τὸν]
τελ⌜α⌝μῶνα ἐνγ[ράψαντες ἑαυτῶν]
τὰ ὀνόματα˙ vac. [- - - ?]
The list of the names for 13 lines.
22   [Ἐν - - -] ἔτι κ̣[αὶ μηνὶ Δα]ισίου α´.

To the Most High God. In the reign of the king Tiberius Iulius
Rheskuporis, the friend of the Emperor and the friend of the
Romans, pious, those adopted as brothers worshipping the Most
High God set this stele, having written their names (the list of the
names). In the year... on the 1st day of the month of Daisios.

5. ΛΔΕΛΦΟ on the stone. - **5-6.** R. Reitzenstein *Die hellenistischen
Mysterienreligionen* (Leipzig: Teubner, 1927[3]), 99, proposed that the
adopted brothers in Tanais were contrasted with γνήσιοι. S.A.
Zhebelev *The Nothern Black Sea Shore* (Moscow-Leningrad, 1953), 300f.
(*in Russian*), developed this thesis and argued that those adopted
brothers were sons of those who had not been members of the
associations while *thiasotai* were sons of the members. - **7.**
ΤΕΛΛΜΩΝΑ on the stone. - **22.** Latyshev's restoration [μηνὸ Δα]ισίου
seems to be ruled out by the traces of Κ before lacuna.

4. *CIRB* 1283; *IPE* II, 452
The photography does not include all the known fragments for the
same reason as 3, III, 2.
Found in Nedvigovka in 1869-1870 during the building of the
railroad. Now at the Hermitage Museum, St. Petersburg, inventory
no.Tn. 317.
A marble slab, reconstructed from sixty-eight pieces (0.76 x 0.60 x
0.02). Letters irregular, lines 2-6 were cut more carefully than the
rest, with some spaces between the words. In line 1, the second half
of line 18 and line 19, the letters are half the size of those in the other
lines. Rectangular *sigma* , diamond-shaped *theta, omicron, omega*.
Letters: 0.03-0.015. 228 AD.

[Ἀγαθ]ῆι vac. τύχη.

Θεῷ ^{vac.} [ὑ]ψίστῳ [εὐ]χή.
Βασιλεύοντ[ο]ς βασιλέως [Τιβερίου]
Ἰουλίου Κότυος φιλοκα[ίσαρο]ς καὶ φι-
5 [λορωμαί]ου, εὐσεβοῦς, ^{vac.1} εἰσποιητοὶ
ἀδ[ελφοὶ] σεβόμενοι θεὸν ^{vac.1} ὕψιστον,
ἐνγρά[ψαντ]ε̄ ἑαυτῶν τὰ ὀνόματα
περὶ πρεσβύτερον Μ[- ^{c.4} -]β΄.
The list of the names for 10.5 lines.
Ἐν τῷ ^{vac. 1} εκφ΄ ^{vac. 1} ἔτει, ^{vac. 3} Γορπιαίου α΄.

With good fortune. To the Most High God the vow. In the reign of
the king Tiberius Iulius Cotys, the friend of the Emperor and the
friend of the Romans, pious, those adopted as brothers worshipping
the Most High God, having written their names, under the
presidency of the elder M . . . II (the list of the names) in the year
525, on the 1st of Gorpiaios.

Select Bibliography

Alfoldi, A. 'Redeunt Saturnia regna, II: An Iconographical Pattern', *Chiron* 3 (1973), 131-42.
Allen, W.C. 'On the Meaning of προσήλυτος in the Septuagint.' *Expositor IV* (1894), 264-275.
Allen, W.C. *A Critical and Exegetical Commentary on the Gospel according to St. Matthew*. New York: 1907.
Alessandri, S. 'La presunta cacciata dei Giudei da Roma nel 139 a.Cr.' *Studi Class. e Orient. 17* (1968), 187-198.
Altaner, B. *Patrology*. ET, Freiburg-Edinburgh-London: Herder/Nelson, 1960.
Attridge, H.W., J.J. Collins, Th.H. Tobin, eds. *Of Scribes and Scrolls. Studies on the Hebrew Bible, Intertestamentary Judaism, and Christian Origins presented to John Strugnell on the occasion of his sixtieth birthday*. 1990, vol. 5.
Attridge, H.W. and G. Hata, eds. *Eusebius, Christianity and Judaism*. Detroit: Wayne State University Press, 1992.
Aupert, P. and O. Masson, 'Inscriptions d'Amathonte, I'. *BCH 103* (1979): 361-388.
Bagatti, B. *The Church from Circumcision. History and Archaeology of Judaeo-Christians*, The Studium Biblicum Franciscanum, Smaller series, 2, *ET by* E.Hoacle Jerusalem: Franciscan Printing Press, 1971, 237-239 (first published in French in 1965 also as *Studium Biblicum Franciscanum*, Collectio Minor, 2).
Bagatti, P.B. and J.T. Milik, *Gli scavi del 'Dominus Flevit'* (*Monte Oliveto - Gerusalemme*) I. Jerusalem: Franciscan Press, 1958.
Bamberger, B.J. *Proselytism in the Talmudic Period*. 2nd ed., New York: Ktav, 1968.
Barclay, J.M.C. *Jews in the Mediterranean Diaspora from Alexander to Trajan (323 BCE— 117 CE)*. Edinburgh: T. & T. Clark, 1996.
Baron, S.W. *A Social and Religious History of the Jews*, vol. 1-2. New York: Columbian University Press, 1952.
Barrett, C.K. *A Critical and Exegetical Commentary on The Acts of the Apostles, vol.1*. Edinburgh: T & T Clark, 1994.
Bauman, R.A. 'Tertullian and the Crime of Sacrilegium.' *The Journal of Religious History*, 4 (1966-1967) 175-183.
Bauman, R.A. *Impietas in Principem: A Study of Treason against the Roman Emperor with Special Reference to the First Century A.D*. Munich: Beck'sche, 1974, Münchener Beiträge zur Papyrforschung und Antiken Rechtsgeschichte, 67.
Bauman, R.A. *The Crimen Maiestatis in the Roman Republic and Augustan Principate*, Johannesburg: Witwatersrand University Press, 1967.

Bean, C. 'Notes and Inscriptions from Pisidia.' *Anatolian Studies* 10 (1960), 43-82.

Beare, F.W. *The Gospel According to Matthew, A Commentary.* Oxford: Basil Blackwell, 1981.

Bechtel, F. *Die historischen Personennamen des griechischen bis zur Kaiserzeit.* Halle: Niemeyer, 1917.

Bellen, H. 'Συναγωγὴ τῶν 'Ιουδαίων καὶ Θεοσεβῶν. Die Aussage einer bosporanischen Freilassunginschrift (CIRB 71) zum Problem der "Gottfürchtigen".' *JAC 8/9* (1965-1966), 171-176.

Bell, H.I. *Jews and Christians in Egypt: the Jewish troubles in Alexandria and the Athanasian Controversy.* London: British Museum, 1924.

Berliner, A. *Geschichte der Juden in Rom von der ältesten Zeit bis zur Gegenwart*, vol. 1. Frankfurt-am-Main, 1893. *Les inscriptions grecques et latines de Philae*, ed. A. and E. Bernard. Paris, 1969.

Bernard, A. *Le Paneion d'El Kanais: les inscriptions grecques.* Leiden: Brill,1972.

Bernays, J. 'Die Gottesfürchtigen bei Juvenal', *Gesammelte Abhandlungen* 2, ed. Usener, H. 1885. Reprint, Hildesheim: Georg Olms, 1971.

Berner, U. 'Heuristische Modell der Synkretismusforschung', *Synkretismusforschung, Theorie und Praxis.* G. Wiesner, ed. Wiesbaden, 1978.

Bertholet, A. *Die Stellung der Israeliten und der Juden zu den Fremden.* Freiburg, Leizig: Mohr, 1896.

Bertram, G. 'θεοσεβής', *Theological Dictionary of the New Testament, vol. 3.* ed. G. Kittel. ET, Grand Rapids: Eerdmans, 1965. 123-128.

Betz, H.D. *Galatians.* Philadelphia: Fortress Press, 1979.

Bialoblocki, S. *Die Beziehungen des Judentums zu Proselyten.* Vortrag gehalten bei dem wissenschaftlichen Kursus der Rabbiner der süddeutschen Landesverbände in Mainz am 17.XII.1929. Berlin: n.p., 1930.

Bickerman, E.J. 'The Name of Christians.' *HTR* 42 (1949), 109-124 (reprinted in *Studies in Jewish and Christian History*, vol. 3, 1986), 139-151.

Bickerman, E.J. 'Les privilèges juives', *Mélanges Isidore Levy*, 1953. Bruxelles: Secretariat des Editions de l'Institut, 1955, Annuaire de l'Institute de Philologie et d'Histoire Orientales et Slaves XIII. 11-34.

Bickerman, E.J. 'The Altars of Gentiles: A Note on the Jewish "ius sacrum"'. *Studies in Jewish and Christian History* vol. 2. Leiden: Brill 1980, 324-346.

Bij de Vaate, A. and J.W. van Henten, 'Jewish or Non-Jewish? Some Remarks on the Identification of Jewish Inscriptions from Asia Minor', *Bibliotheca Orientalis*, 53: 1-2, (1996), 16-28.

Bilde, P., T. Engberg-Pedersen, L. Hannestad, J. Zahle, eds.,*Religion and Religious Practice in the Seleucid Kingdom.* Aarhus University Press, 1990, Studies in Hellenistic Civilization, 1.

Blass, F. 'ΧΡΗΣΤΙΑΝΟΙ - ΧΡΙΣΤΙΑΝΟΙ'. *Hermes* 30 (1895), 465-470.

Blawatsky, V. and Kochelenko, G. *Le culte de Mithra sur la côte septentrionale de la mer noire.* Leiden, 1966.

Blommerde, M. 'Is There an Ellipsis between Gal 2,3 and 2,4?' *Bib* 56 (1975), 100-102.

Bormann, L., K. Del Tredici, and A. Stadhartinger. eds.*Religious Propaganda and Missionary Competition in the New Testament World: Essays Honoring Dieter Georgi.* Leiden, New York, Köln: E.J. Brill, 1994.

Braude, W.G. *Proselytizing in the First Five Centuries of the Common Era, the Age of Tannaim and Amoraim.* Providence: Brown University Press, 1940.

Brooten, B.J. *Women Leaders in the Ancient Synagogue: Inscriptional Evidence and Background Issues.* Chico: Scholars Press, 1982. BJS, 36.

Brooten, B.J. 'The Gender of ʹΙαηλ in the Jewish Inscription from Aphrodisias', *Scribes and Scrolls. Studies on the Hebrew Bible, Intertestamentary Judaism, and Christian Origins presented to John Strugnell on the occasion of his sixtieth birthday*, eds. H.W. Attridge, J.J. Collins, Th.H. Tobin. Lanham: University Press of America, 1990. Resources in Religion vol. 5, 163-173.

Bruce, F.F. *The Acts of the Apostles, Greek Text with Introduction and Commentary*. 3rdrevised and enlarged edition, Grand Rapids/ Leicester: Eerdmans/ Apollos, 1980.

Bruce, I.A.F. 'Nerva and the *Fiscus Iudaicus*.' *PEQ* 96 (1964), 254-334.

Bruchman, C.F.H. *Epitheta deorum quae apud poetas graecos leguntur*. Leipzig: Teubner, 1893. Ausführliches Lexikon des griechischen und römischen Mythologie: Supplement.

Bruner, D. *Matthew, The Churchbook: Matthew 13-28*, 2. Dallas, London, Vancouver, Melbourne: Word Publishing, 1990.

Buckler W.H. and W.M. Calder, eds. *Anatolian Studies Presented to Sir William Mitchell Ramsey*. Manchester: University Press, 1923.

Burford, A. 'Notes on the Epidaurian Building Inscriptions'. *ABSA* 61 (1966), 254-334.

Burton, E. *Galatians: The International Critical Commentary*. Edinburgh: T. & T.Clark, 1921.

Cameron, A. *Circus Factions: Blues and Greens at Rome and Byzantium*. Oxford: Clarendon Press, 1976.

Caquot, A. and M. Philonenko, eds. *Hommages à André Dupont-Sommer*. Paris: Libraire d'Amérique et Orient Adrien-Maisonneuve, 1971.

Chantraine, P. *La formation des noms en grec ancien*. Paris: Librarie ancienne Honoré Champion, éditeur Édouard Champion, 1933.

Cohen, S.J.D. 'Was Timothy Jewish (Acts 16:1-3)? Patristic Exegesis, Rabbinic Law, and Matrilineal Descent'. *JBL* 105:2 (1986), 251-268.

Cohen, S.J.D. 'Respect for Judaism by Gentiles According to Josephus'. *HTR* 80:4(1987), 409-430.

Cohen, S.J.D. 'Crossing the Boundary and becoming a Jew.' *HTR* 82 (1989), 13-33.

Cohen, S.J.D. 'Religion, Ethnicity, and "Hellenism", in the Emergence of Jewish Identity in Maccabean Palestine', *Religion and Religious Practice in the Seleucid Kingdom*, eds. P. Bilde, T. Engberg-Pedersen, L. Hannestad, J. Zahle. Aarhus University Press, 1990, Studies in Hellenistic Civilization, 1. 204-223.

Cohen, S.J.D. 'Adolf Harnack's "The Mission and Expansion of Judaism": Christianity Succeeds where Judaism Fails", *The Future of Early Christianity: Essays in Honour of Helmut Koester*, eds. B.A. Pearson, A.T. Kraabel, G.W.E. Nickelsburg and N.R. Peterson. Minneapolis: Fortress, 1991, 163-169.

Cohen, S.J.D. 'Was Judaism in Antiquity a Missionary Religion?', *Jewish Assimilation, Acculturation and Accommodation: Past Traditions Current Issues and Future.*

Prospects, ed. M. Mor. Lanham, New York, London: University Press of America, 1992, 14-23.

Cohen, S.J.D. and E.S. Frerichs, eds. *Diasporas in Antiquity*. Atlanta: Scholars Press,1993.

Colpe, C. 'Die Vereinbarkeit historischer und struktureller Bestimmungen des Synkretismus', *Synkretismus im syrisch-persischen Kulturgebiet*, Dietrich, A. ed., Göttingen, 1975 (Abhandlungen d. Akademie d. Wiss. in Göttingen, Phil.-Hist, Klasse, 3 Folge No. 96), 15-37.

Conzelmann, H. *Acts of the Apostles*. Philadelphia: Fortress, 1987, Hermeneia.
Conzelmann, H. *Gentiles - Jews - Christians: Polemics and Apologetics in the Greco-Roman Era*. ET, Minneapolis: Fortress Press, 1992.
Cook, A.B. *Zeus: A Study in Ancient Religion,* 2, II. Cambridge: CUP, 1925.
Couchoud, P.L. and R. Stahl, 'Les deux auteurs des Actes des Apôtres'. *RHR* 97 (1928), 6-52.
Cumont, F. 'Les mystères de Sabazius et le judaïsme'. *CRAIBL* (1905), 63-79.
Cumont, F. 'A propos de Sabazius et de judaïsme.' *Musée Belge* 14 (1910).
Cumont, F. "Ὕψιστος.' *RE* 9, 444-450.
Cumont, F. 'L'aigle funéraire des Syriens et l'apothéose des empereurs.' *RHR* 62 (1910), 119-164.
Cumont, F. *The Oriental Religions in Roman Paganism*. ET, Chicago: The Open Court Publishing Co, 1911.
Cumont, F. 'Un *ex-voto* au Theos Hypsistos.' *BullAcadBelg* (1912), 251-253.
Dalbert, P. *Die Theologie der hellenistisch-jüdischen Missionsliteratur unter Ausschluss von Philo und Josephus*. Hamburg-Volksdorf: Herbert Reich, 1954.
Datema, C. *Asterius of Amasea, Homilies I-XIV. Text, Introduction and Notes*. Leiden: Brill, 1970.
Davies, P.R. and R.T.White, eds. *A Tribute to Geza Vermes*. Sheffield: JSOT Press.
de Lange, N. *Origen and the Jews*. Cambridge, London, New York, Melbourne: CUP, 1978, University of Cambridge, Oriental Publications, 25.
Deissmann, A. *Light from the Near East*. ET: London: Hodder & Stoughton, 1927.
Derenbourg, J. *Essai sur l'Histoire et la Géographie de la Palestine*. Paris: 1867; republished: Westmead: Gregg International Publishers Limited, 1971.
Detschev, D. 'Antichny nadpisi.' *Godishnik na norodniya muzei v Sofia,* 5 (1926-1931), 153-167.
Diatroptov, P.D. 'The Spread of Christianity in the Chersonese in the Fourth-Fifth Century', *Antichnaya grazhdanskaya obshchina*. Moscow, 1986. 127-150 (*in Russian*).
Diatroptov, P.D. 'The Spread of Christianity along the Northern Shore of the Black Sea', Synopsis of dissertation. Moscow, 1988, *in Russian*.
Dietrich, A. ed., *Syncretismus im syrisch-persischen Kulturgebiet*. Göttingen, 1975 (Abhandlungen d. Akademie d. Wiss. in Göttingen, Phil.-Hist, Klasse, 3 Folge 96).
Dittenberger, W. *Orientis Graecis inscriptiones Selectae,* 1-2, Leipzig: S. Hirzel, 1903-05.
Doutreleau, L., A. Gesche and M. Gronewald, eds. *Papyrologische Texte und Abhandlungen: Didymos der Blinde. Psalmenkommentar (Tura-Papyrus) Teil I.Kommentar zur Psalm 20-21*, vol. 7. Bonn: Rudolf Habelt Verlag, 1969.
Donfried, K.P. ed., *The Romans Debate*. (revised and expanded) Edinburgh: T & T Clark, 1991.
Downey, G. *A History of Antioch in Syria from Seleucus to the Arab Conquest*. Princeton: Princeton University Press, 1961.
Drew-Bear, T. 'Local Cults in Graeco-Roman Phrygia.' *GRBS* 17 (1976), 247-268.
Dunbabin, K.M.D. 'Ipsa deae vestigia... Footprints divine and human on Greco-Roman Monuments.' *JRA* 3 (1990), 85-109.
Dunn, J.D.G. 'The Incident at Antioch (Gal. 2:11-18)', *JSNT* 18 (1983), 3-57.
Dunn, J.D.G. ed., *Jews and Christians: The Parting of the Ways AD 70 to 135*. Tübingen: Mohr-Siebeck, 1992.
Dupont, J. *The Sources of Acts*. ET, London: Darton, Longman & Todd, 1964.
Dussaud, R. 'Voyage en Syrie. Notes archéologiques'. *Revue archéologique,* ser.3, 28 (1896), 299-336.

Engelmann, H. and D.Knibbe, 'Aus ephesischen Skizzenbüchern.' *JÖAI* 52 (1978-80) 19-61.

Erlich, R. 'The Olbian inscription IOSPE I² 176', *Doklady akademii Nauk - V (Proceedings of Academy of Sciences)* 6 (1928), 124-127, *in Russian*.

Feissel, D. *Recueil des inscriptions chrétiennes de la Macédonie du IIᵉ au VIᵉ siecle*. Paris: Ecole française d'Athe;nes, BCH, Supplevment VIII, 1983.

Feissel, D. and M. Sève, 'Inscriptions de Macédoine'. *BCH* 112 (1988), 449-466.

Feldman, L.H. 'Jewish "Sympathizers" in Classical Literature and Inscriptions' *TAPA 81* (1950), 200-208.

Feldman, L.H. 'Proselytes and "Sympathizers" in the Light of the New Inscriptions from Aphrodisias'. *REJ* 148 (1989), 265-305.

Feldman, L.H. 'Jewish Proselytism', *Eusebius, Christianity and Judaism*, eds. H.W. Attridge, G. Hata. Detroit: Wayne State University Press, 1992, 372-408.

Feldman, L.H. 'Proselytism by Jews in the Third, Fourth, and Fifth Centuries', *JSJ* 24,1 (1993), 372-408.

Feldman, L.H. *Jew and Gentile in the Ancient World*. Princeton: Princeton University Press, 1993.

Figueras, P. *Decorated Jewish Ossuaries*. Leiden: Brill, 1983.

Figueras, P. 'Epigraphic Evidence for Proselytism in Ancient Judaism', *Immanuel* 24/25 (1990), 196-201.

Finegan, J. *The Archaeology of the New Testament. The life of Jesus and the Beginning of the Early Church*. Princeton: Princeton University Press, 1969.

Finn, Th.M. 'The God-fearers Reconsidered.' *CBQ* 47 (1985), 75-84.

Flowers, H.J. 'Matthew XXIII. 15.' *Exp* 73 (1961), 67-69.

Fox, R.I.. *Pagans and Christians*. Viking, 1986.

Frend, W.H.C. 'Two Finds in Central Anatolia', *Anatolian Studies*, 6 (1956), 95-100.

Friedlaender, M. *Die religiösen Bewegungen innerhalb des Judentums im Zeitalter Jesu*. Berlin, 1905.

Fuchs, H. 'Tacitus über die Christen'. *VC* 4 (1950), 65-93.

Furnish, V. *II Corinthians*. Garden City, New York: Doubleday and Company, 1984, The Anchor Bible.

Garkavi, A.Ya. *Zapiski Russkogo Arkheologicheskogo obschestva (Transactions of the Russian Archaeological Society)* 2 (1886), CXXXIX *(in Russian)*.

Gasque, W. *A History of the Criticism of the Acts of the Apostles*. Tübingen: Mohr-Siebeck, 1975.

Georgi, D. *The Opponents of Paul in Second Corinthians*. Philadelphia: Fortress Press, 1986.

Gerov, B. *Godishnik na Sofijskiya universitet*. Sofia 1968 *(in Bulgarian)* 119-247, Faculty of Western Philology, 62, 2.

Goodenough, E.R. with A.T. Kraabel, 'Paul on the Hellenization of Christianity', *Religion in Antiquity: Essays in memory of Erwin Ramsdell Goodenough*, ed. J. Neusner. Leiden: Brill, 1968, 14. 23-68, Supplements to *Numen*.

Goodenough, E.R. 'The Bosporus Inscriptions to the Most High God.' *JQR* 47 (1956-1957), 221-244.

Goodenough, E.R. *Jewish Symbols in the Greco-Roman Period*, 13 vols. New York: Pantheon Books, 1953-1968.

Goodman, M. 'Who was a Jew?' Oxford: The Oxford Centre for Postgraduate Hebrew Studies, 1989.

Goodman, M. 'Nerva, The *Fiscus Judaicus* and Jewish Identity', *JRS* 79 (1989), 40-44.

Goodman, M. 'Proselytising in Rabbinic Judaism', *JJS* 38 (1989), 175-185.

Goodman, M. 'Diaspora Reactions to the Destruction of the Temple', *Jews and Christians: The Parting of the Ways AD 70 to 135*, ed. J.D.G. Dunn, (Tübingen: Mohr-Siebeck, 1992), 27-38.

Goodman, M. 'Jewish Proselytizing in the First Century', *The Jews among Pagans and Christians in the Roman Empire*, eds. J. Lieu, J. North and T. Rajak. Lon don and New York: Routledge, 1992. 53-78.

Goodman, M. *Mission and Conversion: Proselytizing in the Religious History of the Roman Empire*. Oxford: Clarendon Press, 1994.

Goodman, M. 'Jews and Judaism in the Mediterranean Diaspora in the Late-Roman Period: the Limitations of Evidence'. *Journal of Mediterranean Studies*, 4,2 (1994), 208-224.

Goodman, M. 'Kosher Olive Oil in Antiquity', *A Tribute to Geza Vermes*, eds. Davies, P.R. and R.T.White. Sheffield: JSOT Press 1990. 227-245.

Graetz, H. 'Der Vers in Matthäus-Evangelium: einen Proselyten Machen.' *Monatsschrift für Geschichte und Wissenschaft des Judentums*, 18 (1869),169-170.

Graetz, H. *Die jüdischen Proselyten im Römerreiche unter den Kaisern Domitian, Nerva, Trajan, und Hadrian*. Breslau, 1884.

Grant, F.C. *Hellenistic Religions: The Age of Syncretism*. New York: Liberal Arts, 1953.

Graves, R. and J. Podro, *Jesus in Rome: A Historical Conjecture*. London: Cassel and Company, 1957.

Gressman, H. 'Die Aufgaben der Wissenschaft des nachbiblischen Judentums'. *ZAW* 43 (1925), 1-32.

Groag, E. 'Notizen zur Geschichte kleinasiatischen Familien'. *JOAI* 10 (1907), 282-299.

Guarducci, M. *Epigraphia Graeca*, vol. 3, Epigrafi di carattere privato, Rome; Instituto poligrafica dello stato, 1974, 4, Epigrafi sacre pagane e christiane, Rome, 1978.

Gundry, R.H. *Matthew. A Commentary on his Literary and Theological Art*. Grand Rapids: Eerdmans, 1982.

Gutmann, J. ed., *Tradition und Glaube: Festgabe für K.G. Kuhn*. Göttingen, 1971.

Gutmann, J. ed., *Ancient Synagogues: The State of Research*. Ann Arbor: Scholars Press, 1981 (*BJS*, 22).

Habicht, Ch. *Gnomon* 46 (1974), 484-492.

Haenchen, E. *The Acts of the Apostles*: A Commentary. ET, Oxford: Basil Blackwell, 1971.

Hall, A.S. 'The Klarian Oracle at Oenoanda'. *ZPE* 32 (1978), 264-267.

von Harnack, A. *The Mission and Expansion of Christianity in the First Three Centuries*. 2 vols. London: Williams & Norgate, 1904-5.

Harrill, J.A. *The Manumission of Slaves in Early Christianity*. Tübingen: Mohr-Siebeck, 1995.

Hartman, S.S. ed., *Syncretism*. Stockholm, 1969, Scripta Instituti Donneriani Aboensis, 3.

Hefele, C.J. *A History of the Councils of the Church* 2. *AD 326 to AD 429*. Edinburgh: T. & T. Clark, 1876.

Heissig, W. and H. Klimkeit, eds., *Synkretismus in der Religionen Zentralasiens*. 1987.

Hemer C.J.*The Book of Acts in the Setting of Hellenistic History*. Tübingen Mohr-Siebeck, 1989, *Wissenschaftliche Untersuchungen zum Neuen Testament*, 49.

Hemer, C.J. 'The Edfu *Ostraka* and the Jewish Tax'. *PEQ*, 104-105 (1972-1973), 6-12, 199 n. 10.

Hemer, C.J. 'Reflections on the Nature of New Testament Greek Vocabulary'. *TynB* 38 (1987), 65-92.

Hengel, M. 'Proseuche und Synagoge: Jüdische Gemeinde, Gotteshaus und Gottesdienst in der Diaspora und in Palästina', *Tradition und Glaube: Festgabe für K.G. Kuhn* (Göttingen,1971), 157-183 = *The Synagogue, Studies in Origins, Archaeology and Architecture*, Gutmann, J. ed. New York: Ktav, 1975. 27-54.

Hengel, M. 'Die Synagogeninschrift von Stobi'. *ZNW* 57 (1966), 145-183 (reprinted in *The Synagogue Studies in Origin, Archaeology and Architecture*, ed. J. Gutmann, New York (1975).

Hengel, M. *Acts and the History of Early Christianity.* ET, Philadelphia: Fortress, 1979.

Hengel, M. *Judaism and Hellenism: Studies in their Encounter in Palestine during the Early Hellenistic Period.* ET, London: SCM Press, 1991.

Heraeus, W. 'Die Sprache des Petronius und die Glossen'. *Kleine Schriften zum 75 Geburstag.*, ed. J.B. Hofmann. Heidelberg: Carl Winter's Universitats-Buchhandlung, 1937. 92-94.

Hillard, T., A. Nobbs and B. Winter, 'Acts and the Pauline Corpus I: Ancient Literary Parallels', *The Book of Acts in Its First Century Setting*, vol. 1, *The Book of Acts in its Ancient Literary Setting*, eds. B.W. Winter and A.D. Clarke. Grand Rapids/Carlisle: Eerdmans/Paternoster, 1993. 183-213.

Hofmann, J.B., ed. *Kleine Schriften zum 75 Geburstag.* Heidelberg: Carl Winter's Universitäts-Buchhandlung, 1937.

Hommel, H. 'Juden und Christen im kaiserzeitlichen Milet.' *IM* 25 (1975), 167-195.

Hommel, H. 'Pantokrator'. *Theologia Viatorum* 5 (1953-1954), 322-378 = id. Schöpfer und Erhalter, (1956) 81-137 = Sebasmata. Studien zur antiken religionsgeschichte und zum frühen Christentum I, WUNT 31, Tübingen: Mohr -Siebeck, 1981, 131-171.

Horbury, W. and Noy D. *Jewish Inscriptions of Graeco-Roman Egypt*, Cambridge: Cambridge University Press, 1992

Horsley, G.H.R. *New Documents illustrating Early Christianity.* The Ancient History Documentary Research Centre, Macquarrie University, 1981.

Howard, G. 'The Beginnings of Christianity in Rome: A Note on Suetonius, *Life of Claudius* XXV 4'. *ResQ* 24 (1981), 175-177.

Janne, H. 'Impulsore Chresto'. *Annuaire de l'Institut de Philologie et d'Histoire orientales* 2 (1934), 531-553.

Jeffreys, E. 'Malalas' sources', *Studies in Malalas.* Sydney: Australian Association for Byzantine Studies, 1990, Byzantina Australiensia, 6. 167-216.

Jeremias, J. *Jesus' Promise to the Nations.* ET, London: SCM, 1958 (SBT, 24).

Johnson, Sh.E. 'The Present State of Sabazios Research', *ANRW* II 17,3, Berlin, New York: De Gluyten 1583-1613.

Judge, E.A. 'Judaism and the Rise of Christianity: a Roman Perspective.' *TynB* 45.2 (1994), 355-368.

Juster, J. *Les Juifs dans l'empire romain*, Vols. 1&2. Paris: Geuthner, 1914.

Kajanto, J. *Onomastic Studies in the Early Christian Inscriptions of Rome and Carthago* Helsinki, 1963. Acta instituti Romani Finlandiae Vol. II:1.

Kalinka, E. 'Aus Bithynien und Umgegend', *JÖAI* 28,1 (1933), 45-112.

Kamstra, J.H. *Encounter or Syncretism: The Initial Growth of Japanese Buddhism.* Leiden: Brill, 1967.

Kamstra, J.H. *Syncretism op de Grens tussen Theologie en Godsdienstfenomenologie.* Leiden: Brill, 1970.

Kant, L. 'Jewish Inscriptions in Greek and Latin.' *ANRW* II 20, 2. Berlin, New York: De Gruyter, 1987. 671-713.

Kasher, A. *The Jews in Hellenistic and Roman Egypt.* Tübingen: Mohr-Siebeck, 1985.

Keil, J. 'Die Kulte Lydiens', *Anatolian Studies Presented to Sir William Mitchell Ramsay*. edd. W.H. Buckler & W.M. Calder. Manchester, 1923. 239-265.

Kittel, G., ed., *Theological Dictionary of the New Testament*. Translated by Geoffrey W. Bromiley. Grand Rapids: Eerdmans, 1966.

Kmosco, M., ed. *Patrologia Syriaca*, part I, vol. 3. Paris: Firmin-Didot, 1926.

Kocevalov, A. 'Beiträge zu den euxeinischen Inschriften'. *Würzburger Jahreshefte für die Altertumswissenschaft* 3 (1948). 163-174.

Konikoff, A. *Sarcophagi from the Jewish Catacombs in Rome*. Stuttgart: Franz Steiner, 1986.

Kraabel, A.T. '"Ύψιστος and the Synagogue at Sardis'. *GRBS* 10 (1969), 81-93.

Kraabel, A.T. 'The Diaspora Synagogue: Archaeological and Epigraphic Evidence since Sukeni'. *ANRW* II 19.1 Berlin, New York: De Gruyten (1979), 477-510.

Kraabel, A.T. 'The Roman Diaspora: Six Questionable Assumptions'. *JJS* 33 (1982), 450-456.

Kraabel, A.T. 'Synagoga Caeca: Systematic Distortion in Gentile Interpretations of Evidence for Judaism in the Early Christian Period', *'To See Ourselves as Others See Us': Christians, Jews, 'Others' in Late Antiquity*, eds. J.Neusner & E.S. Frerichs. Chico: Scholars Press, 1985. 219-246. Reprinted in *Diaspora Jews and Judaism: Essays in Honor of, and in Dialogue with, A. Thomas Kraabel*. University of South Florida, 1992, South Florida Studies in the History of Judaism, 41.

Kraabel, A.T. 'The God-fearers Meet the Beloved Disciple', *The Future of Early Christianity: Essays in Honor of Helmut Koester*, ed. B.A. Pearson, A.T. Kraabel, G.W.E. Nickelsbourg and N.R. Peterson. Minneapolis: Fortress Press, 1991, 276-284.

Kraabel, A.T. 'The Disappearance of the "God-Fearers"'. *Numen* XXVIII,2 (1981) 113-126.

Kraabel, A.T. with R.S. MacLennan, 'The God-Fearers—A Literary and Theologi cal Invention'. *Biblical Archaeology Review* (Sept.- Oct. 1986), 47-53.

Kraabel, A.T. 'Immigrants, Exiles, Expatriates, and Missionaries', *Religious Propaganda and Missionary Competition in the New Testament World: Essays Honoring Dieter Georgi*, eds. L. Bormann, K. Del Tredici, A. Stadhartinger. Leiden, New York, Köln: Brill, 1994, 71-88.

Kraemer, R.S. 'On the Meaning of the Term 'Jew' in Graeco-Roman Inscriptions', *HTR* 82.1 (1989), 35-53 (reprinted in: *Diaspora Jews and Judaism*, 311-329).

Kraemer, R.S. 'Jewish Tuna and Christian Fish: Identifying Religious Affiliation in Epigraphic Sources'. *HTR* 84:2 (1991), 141-162.

Kraeling, C.H. 'The Jewish Comunity at Antioch'. *JBL* 51 (1932), 130-160.

Krshanovsky, V.A. 'The Excavations of Kitei Necropolis', *Archaeological Researches in the Crimea*. Simferopol: Tavria, 1994, 262-266 *(in Russian.)*

Kuhn, K.G. 'προσήλυτος'. *TDNT* 6 (1968), 727-744.

Kuhn, K.G. "Ισραήλ'. *TDNT* 3 (1968), 356-169.

Lake, K. 'Proselytes and God-fearers.' *BC* 5, 74-96.

Lampe, G.W.H. *A Patristic Greek Lexicon*. Oxford: Clarendon Press, 1961.

Lane, E.N. 'Sabazius and the Jews in Valerius Maximus: a Re-examination'. *JRS* 69 (1979), 35-38.

La Piana, G. 'Foreign Groups in Rome during the First Centuries of the Empire'. *HTR* 20 (1927), 183-403.

Latyshev, V. *Izvestiya Archeologicheskoj Komissii* 14 (1905), 94-137. *(in Russian)*

Latyshev, V. 'Inscriptions trouvees dans la Russie meridionale en 1901-1903 (100 facsimiles).' *Izvestiya Archeologicheskoj Komissii* 10 (1909), 1-91. *(in Russian)*

Latyshev, V. *Izvestiya Rossijskoj Akademii Material'noj Kul'tury (Transactions of the Russian Academy of the History of Material Culture)* I (1921), *(in Russian)*.

Leon, H.J. *The Jews of Ancient Rome*. Philadelphia: The Jewish Publication Society of America, 1960. Revised edition: Peabody: Hendrickson Publishers, 1995.

Leumann, M. *Lateinische Laut- und Formen-Lehre*. Munich, 1977.

Léveque, P. 'Essai de typologie des syncrétismes', *Les syncrétismes dans les religions grecque et romain. Colloques de Strasbourg 9-11 juin 1971*. Strasbourg 1973. 179-188.

Levi, I. 'Le proselytisme juif.' *REJ* 50 (1905), 1-9. *REJ* 51 (1906), 29-31.

Levick, B.M. *Roman Colonies in Southern Asia Minor*. Oxford: Clarendon, 1967.

Levick, B.M. *Claudius*. London: B.T. Batsford, 1990.

Levinskaya, I.A. 'The Inscription from Aphrodisias and the Problem of God-fearers.' *TynB* 41,2 (1990), 312-318.

Levinskaya, I.A. and S.Tokhtas'ev,' The Jewish Names in the Bosporan Kingdom' *Acta Associationis internationalis. Terra Antiqua Balcanica*. Serdica, 1991, 118-128 *(in Russian)*.

Levinskaya, I.A. *The Cult of the Most High God*, forthcoming *(in Russian)*.

Lewis, D.M. 'The First Greek Jew.' *JSS* 2 (1957), 264-266.

Lieu, J., J. North and T. Rajak, eds. *The Jews among Pagans and Christians in the Roman Empire*. London and New York: Routledge, 1992.

Lifshitz, B. 'Inscriptions grecques de Césarée en Palestine (Caesarea Palaestinae'. *RB* 68 (1961), 115-126.

Lifshitz, B. 'La vie de l'au delà dans les conceptions juives'. *RB* 68 (1961), 401-411.

Lifshitz, B. *Zeitschr. des Deutschen Palästina - Vereins* 78 (1962), 64-88.

Lifshitz, B. 'L'origine du nom des chrétiens', *VC* 16 (1962), 65-70.

Lifshitz, B. 'Notes d'épigraphie grecque', *RB* 70 (1963), 255-265.

Lifshitz, B. *Donateurs et fondateurs dans les synagogues juives*. Paris: Gabalda, 1967. Cahiers de la Revue Biblique, 7.

Lifshitz, B. and J. Schiby, 'Une synagogue samaritaine à Thessalonique.' *RB* 75 (1968), 368-378.

Lifshitz, B. 'Notes d'épigraphie grecque.' *RB* 76 (1969), 92-98.

Lifshitz, B. *Prolegomenon CIJ I²*. New York: Ktav, 1975.

Linder, A. *The Jews in Roman Imperial Legislation, edited with Introductions, Translations and Commentary*. ET, Detroit: Wayne State University Press, 1987.

Ljungvik, H. 'Aus der Sprache des Neuen Testaments'. *Eranos* 66 (1968), 30-34.

Lüdemann, G. *Paul, Apostle to the Gentiles. Studies in Chronology*. Philadelphia and London: SCM, 1984.

Lüderitz, G. *Corpus jüdischer Zeugnisse aus der Cyrenaika mit einem Anhang von Joyce M.Reynolds*. Wiesbaden: Dr.Ludwig Reichert Verlag, 1983. N12 (Cyrenaica).

Lüderitz, G. 'What is the Politeuma?', *Studies in Early Jewish Epigraphy*, eds. J.W. van Henten, P.W. van der Horst. Leiden-New York-Köln, 1994, Arbeiten zur Geschichte des antiken Judentums und des Urchristentums, 21, 183-225.

Luria, S. *Antisemitism in the Ancient World* (Petrograd, 1922), Addenda (Petrograd, 1923).

MacLennan, R.S. *Early Christian Text on Jews and Judaism*. Atlanta: Scholars Press, 1990, Brown Judaic Studies.

Manzella, I. Di S. 'L.Maecius Archon, *centurio alti ordinis*. Nota critica zu *CIL*, VI, 39084 = *CII*, I, 470'. *ZPE* 77 (1989), 103-112.

Marcus, R. 'Σεβόμενοι in Josephus'. *JSS* 14 (1952), 247-250.

Marshall, A.J. 'Flaccus and the Jews of Asia (Cicero *Pro Flacco* 28.67-69)'. *Phoenix*, 29:2 (1975), 139-154.

Marshall, I.H. *Luke: Historian and Theologian*. Exeter: Paternoster, 1970.

Marti, J.J. 'Novye epigraficheskiye pamyatniki Bospora'. *Izvestiya GAIMK* 104 (1935), 57-89.

Mattingly, H.B. *Coins of the Roman Empire in the British Museum* III *Nerva to Hadrian*. London: The Trustees of the British Museum, 1936.

Mattingly, H.B. 'The Origin of the Name *Christiani*'. *JTS* n.s. 9 (1958), 26-37.

Mazur, B. *Studies in Jewry in Greece*. Athens: Hestia, 1935.

McEleney, N.J. 'Conversion, Circumcision and the Law'. *NTS* 20 (1974), 319-341.

McKnight, S. *A Light Among Gentiles: Jewish Missionary Activity in the Second Temple Period*. Minneapolis: Fortress Press, 1991.

Meek, Th.J. 'The translation of Ger in the Hexateuch and Its Bearing on the Documentary Hypothesis'. *JBL* 49 (1930), 172-180.

Meeks, W.A. and R.L.Wilken, *Jews and Christians in Antioch in the First Four Centuries of the Common Era*. Missoula: Scholars Press, 1978, SBLSBS, 13.

Meeks, W.A. *The First Urban Christians*. New Haven, London: Yale University Press, 1983.

Merrill, E.T. *Essays in Early Christian History*. London: Macmillan, 1924.

Michaelis, W. 'παντοκράτωρ' *TDNT*, 1965. 914-915.

Metzger, B.M. *A Textual Commentary on the Greek New Testament. A Companion Volume to the United Bible Societies' Greek New Testament*. Stuttgart: United Bible Society, 1994².

Millar, F. *The Roman Near East*. Cambridge, Mass./London: Harvard University Press, 1994.

Minns, E.H. *Scythians and Greeks*. Cambridge, 1913.

Mitchell, S., *RECAM II: The Ankara District: The Inscriptions of North Galatia*. British Institute of Archaeology at Ankara Monograph No. 4, B.A.R. International Series 135, Oxford: British Archaeological Reports, 1982.

Mitchell, S. *Anatolia: Land, Men and Gods in Asia Minor, vol. 2*. Oxford: Clarendon Press, 1993.

Moehring, H.R. 'The *Acta Pro Judaeis* in the *Antiquities* of Flavius Josephus. A Study in Hellenistic and Modern Apologetic Historiography', *Christianity, Judaism and Other Graeco-Roman Cults: Studies for Morton Smith at Sixty*. ed. J.Neusner, Part 3. Leiden: Brill, 1975, SJLA, 12. 124-158.

Momigliano, A. 'I nomi delle prime "synagoghe" romane e la condizione giuridica delle communità in Roma sotto Augusto'. *Rassegna Mensile di Israel* 6 (1931-1932), 283-292.

Momigliano, A. *Alien Wisdom: The Limits of Hellenization*. Cambridge: CUP, 1976.

Momigliano, A. *Claudius the Emperor and His Achievement*. ET, Cambridge: W. Heffer & sons, Ltd, 1961.

Montevecchi, O. 'Pantokrator', *Studi in onore di Aristide Calderini e Roberto Paribeni* (Milan, 1957), 401-432.

Moore, G.F. *Judaism in the First Centuries of the Christian Era: The Age of the Tannaim*. Cambridge, Mass., 1927.

Mor, M., ed. *Jewish Assimilation, Acculturation and Accomodation: Past Traditions Current Issues and Future Prospects*. Lanham, New York, London: University Press of America, 1992.

Moreau, J. 'Le nom des chrétiens'. *La nouvelle Clio* 1/2 (1949-1950), 190-192.

Munck, J. *Paul and the Salvation of Mankind*. London: SCM, 1959.

Murphy-O'Connor, J. *St. Paul's Corinth: Texts and Archaeology*. Wilmington: Michael Goazier, Inc., 1983, Good News Studies, 6.

Murphy-O'Connor, J. 'Lots of God-Fearers? *Theosebeis* in the Aphrodisias Inscription.' *RB*, 99-2 (1992), 418-424.

Mussies, G. 'Jewish Personal Names in Some Non-Literary Sources', *Studies in Early Jewish Epigraphy*, Arbeiten zur Geschichte des antiken Judentums und des Urchristentums, XXI, ed. J.W. van Henten and P.W. van der Horst. Leiden-New York-Köln: E.J. Brill, 1994. 124-158.

Mussies, G. Review of JIGRE, *BiO* 52 No. 5/6 (1995), 774-776.

Nadel, B. 'Actes d'affranchissement des esclaves du Royaume du Bosphore et les origines de la *manumissio in ecclesia'*. *Symposion, 1971: Vorträge zur griechischen und hellenistischen Rechtgeschichte*. ed. H.J. Wolff. Köln/Wien: Böhlau Verlag, 1975. 265-291.

Nadel, B. *The Bosporan Manumissions*. PhD Thesis, Leningrad, 1947. *(in Russian)*.

Nadel, B. 'The Bosporan Manumissions and Greek Law'. *Listy filologické* 91:3 (1968), 252-278. *(in Russian)*

Naveh, J. *On Stone and Mosaic: The Aramaic and Hebrew inscriptions from Ancient Synagogues*. Tel Aviv, 1978.

Neusner, J. 'The Conversion of Adiabene to Judaism', *JBL* 83:1 (1964), 60-66.

Neusner, J., ed. *Christianity, Judaism and Other Graeco-Roman Cults: Studies for Morton Smith at Sixty*, Part 3. Leiden: Brill, 1975, SJLA, 12.

Neusner, J. and E.S.Frerichs, eds. *'To See Ourselves as Others See Us': Christians, Jews, 'Others' in Late Antiquity*. Chico: Scholars Press, 1985.

Neusner, J., W.S. Green and E. Frerichs, eds. *Judaisms and Their Messiahs at the Turn of Christian Era*. Cambridge: CUP, 1987.

Niese, B. 'Bemerkungen über die Urkunden bei Josephus Archaeol. B. XIII.XIV.XVI.' *Hermes* 2 (1876), 466-488.

Nigdelis, P.M. 'Synagoge(n) und Gemeinde der Juden in Thessaloniki: Fragen aufgrund einer neuen jüdischen Grabinschrift der Kaiserzeit', *ZPE* 102 (1994), 297-306.

Nilsson, M.P. *Geschichte der griechischen Religion*, vol. 2, II. Munich, 1961^2.

Nock, A.D. *Conversion*. Oxford: Clarendon Press, 1933; reprinted 1972.

Nock, A.D., C. Roberts and T.C. Skeats 'The Guild of Zeus Hypsistos.' *HTR* 29 (1936), 39-88; reprinted with omission of Introduction, Greek text, detailed commentary, and plate in: A.D. Nock, *Essays on Religion and the Ancient World*, vol. 1, ed. Z. Steward. Oxford: Clarendon, 1972. 414-443.

Nolland, J. 'Proselytism or Politics in Horace Satires I, 4, 138-143?' *VC* 33 (1979), 347-355.

Nolland, J. 'Uncircumcised Proselytes?' *JSJ* 12:2 (1981), 173-194.

Noy, D. *Jewish Inscriptions of Western Europe*. Vol. 1: *Italy (excluding the City of Rome), Spain and Gaul*. Cambridge: CUP, 1993.

Noy, D. 'The Jewish Communities of Leontopolis and Venosa', *Studies in Early Jewish Epigraphy*. ed. by J.W. van Henten and P.W. van der Horst. Leiden, New York, Köln, 1994, *Arbeiten zur Geschichte des antiken Judentums und des Urchristentums*, 21, 162-188.

Nutton, V. 'Archiatri and the Medical Profession'. *PBSR* 45 (1977), 191-226.

Orchard, B. 'The Ellipsis between Gal 2:3, 2:4'. *Bib* 54 (1973), 469-481.

Orlandos, A.K. *Ἀρχαιολογικὸν Δελτίον*, 2 (1916).

Overman, J.A. 'The Diaspora in the Modern Study of Ancient Judaism', *Diaspora Jews and Judaism: Essays in Honor of, and in Dialogue with, A. Thomas Kraabel*. eds. J.A. Overman, R.S. MacLennan. University of South Florida, 1992. 64-78.

Overman, J.A. and R.S. MacLennan, eds. *Diaspora Jews and Judaism: Essays in Honor of, and in Dialogue with, A.Thomas Kraabel*. University of South Florida, 1992.

Pallas, D.I. and St.P. Dantes, *Ἀρχαιολογικὸν Ἐφέμερις* (1977).

Pariente, A. 'ΣΥΓΚΡΗΤΙΣΜΟΣ'. *Emerita* 37 (1969), 317-321.

Paton, W.R. and E.L. Hicks, *The Inscriptions of Cos*. Oxford, 1891.

Pelecides, S.' Ἀνασκαφὴ 'Εδέσσης', 'Αρχαιολογικὸν δελτίον 8, 1923 (1925).
Penna, R. 'Les juifs à Rome au temps de l'apôtre Paul.' NTS 28 (1982), 321-347.
Peterson, E. 'Christianus', Miscellanea Giovanni Mercati, vol I. Biblioteca Apostolica
    Vaticana, 1946, 355-372.
Petzl, G. 'Die Beichtinschriften Westkleinasiens'. Epigraphica Anatolica 23 (1994).
Pfuhl E. and H. Mobius, Die ostgriechischen Grabreliefs. Mainz am Rhein: Verlag
    Philipp von Zabern, 1979.
Pines, S. 'The Iranian Name for Christians and the 'God-fearers". Proceedings of the
    Israel Academy of Sciences and Humanities 2 (1968), 143-152.
Plummer, A. An Exegetical Commentary on the Gospel according to St. Matthew. New
    York, 1909.
Poland, F. Geschichte des griechischen Vereinwesens. Leipzig, 1909.
Powell, B. 'Greek Inscriptions from Corinth', AJA Second Series 7. 1903.
Purvis, J.D. 'The Palaeography of the Samaritan Inscriptions from Thessalonica'.
    BASOR 221 (1976), 121-123.
Rabello, A.M. 'The Legal Condition of the Jews in the Roman Empire'. ANRW II,
    13 (1980), 662-762.
Rajak, T. 'Jews and Christians as Groups in a Pagan World', To See Ourselves as
    Others See Us': Christians, Jews, `Others' in Late Antiquity. eds. J. Neusner &
    E.S. Frerichs. Chico: Scholars Press, 1985, 247-262.
Rajak, T. 'Roman Intervention in a Seleucid Siege of Jerusalem?' GRBS 22 (1981),
    65-81.
Rajak, T. 'Was there a Roman Charter for the Jews?' JRS 74 (1984), 107-123.
Ramsay, W.M. The cities of St.Paul. London: Hodder & Stoughton, 1907; reprinted,
    Baker, 1979.
Reinhardt, W. 'The Population Size of Jerusalem and the Numerical Growth of the
    Jerusalem Church', The Book of Acts in Its First Century Setting, vol. 4:
    Palestinian Setting. ed. R. Bauckham. Grand Rapids/Carlisle: Eerdmans/
    Paternoster, 1995) Ch 8.
Reynolds J. and R. Tannenbaum, Jews and God-fearers at Aphrodisias. Cambridge:
    The Cambridge Philological Society, 1987, Proceedings of the Cambridge
    Philological Society, Supplementary Volume 12.
Ringgren, H. 'The Problems of Syncretism', Syncretism, ed. S.S.Hartman.
    Stockholm, 1969, Scripta Instituti Donneriani Aboensis III, 7-14.
Robert, L. 'Les Inscriptions grecques et latines de Sardes.' Revue Archevologique 2
    (1936), 237-240 = id. Opera Minora Selecta, vol. 3. Amsterdam: Adolf M.
    Kakkert, 1969. 1606-1613.
Robert, L. Etudes anatoliennes: recherches sur les inscriptions grecques de l'Asie
    Mineure. Paris, 1937.
Robert, L. Nouvelle inscriptions de Sardes. Paris: Librairie d'Amérique et d'Orient,
    1964.
Robert, L. 'Documents d'Asie Mineure'. BCH 107 (1983), 498-599.
Romaniuk, K. 'Die "Gottesfürchtigen" im Neuen Testament: Beitrag zur neutesta-
    mentlichen Theologie der Gottesfurcht.' Aegyptus 44:1-2 (1964), 66-91.
Ronchi, G. Lexicon theonymon rerumque sacrarum et divinarum ad Aegyptum
    pertinentium quae in papyris, titulis, Graecis Latinisque in Aegypto repertis
    laudantur. Milan, 1977, Testi e Documenti per lo studio dell'Antichita XLV.
Roscher, W.H. Ausführliches Lexikon des griechischen und römischen Mythologie, vol.2.
    Leipzig: Teubner, 1890-1897. 1756-1758.
Rosenbloom, J.R. Conversion to Judaism: From the Biblical Period to the Present.
    Cincinatti: Hebrew Union College Press, 1978.

Rostovtzeff, M. 'The Iranian Rider-God and the South of Russia' in *Vestnik drevnej istorii*, 2 (1990), N 5, 192-200 *(in Russian)*. German translation in M.Rostowzew, *Skytien und der Bosporus. Bd.II: Wiederendeckte Kapitel und Verwandtes*, ed. and trans., H. Heinen. Stuttgart: Franz Steiner Verlag, 1993. 153-168.

Rostovtzeff, M. *Iranians and Greeks in South Russia*. Oxford, 1922.

Rudolph, K. 'Synkretismus—vom theologischen Scheltwort zum religionswissenschaftlichen Begriff', *Humanitas Religiosa, Festschrift f. Harolds Biezais*. Stockholm 1979, 194-212.

Rutgers, L.V. 'Attitudes to Judaism in the Greco-Roman Period: Reflections on Feldman's Jew and Gentile in the Ancient World', *JQR* 85: 3-4 (1995).

Rutgers, L.V. *The Jews in Late Ancient Rome: Evidence of Cultural Interaction in the Roman Diaspora*. Leiden-New York-Köln: Brill, 1995, Religions in the Greco-Roman World, 126.

Safray, S. 'Relations between the Diaspora and the Land of Israel', *CRINT* 1, 201f.

Salac, A.'At the Estuary of the Quiet Don', *Prazska universita Moskovske universite. Sbornik k vyroci 1755-1955*. Prague, 1955. 213-230, *in Russian*.

Saldarini, A.J. *Matthew's Christian-Jewish Community*. Chicago and London: The University of Chicago Press, 1994.

Sanders, E.P. *Jewish Law from Jesus to the Mishnah*. London: SCM Press, 1990.

Sanders, J.T. *Schismatics, Sectarians, Dissidents, Deviants. The First One Hundred Years of Jewish-Christian Relations*. London: SCM,1993.

Sandmel, S. *The First Christian Century in Judaism and Christianity. Certainties and Uncertainties*. New York: Oxford University Press, 1969.

Schürer, E. 'Die Juden im bosporanischen Reiche und die Genossenschaften der σεβόμενοι θεὸν ὕψιστον ebendaselbst'. *SPAW* XII-III (1897), 200-225.

Schürer, E. *Geschichte des jüdischen Volkes im Zeitalter Jesu Christi*, 3 (Leipzig, 1909⁴), ET: *The History of the Jewish People in the Age of Jesus Christ*, A New English Version, revised and edited by G. Vermes, F. Millar, M. Black (vol. 2. Edinburgh: T.&T. Clark, 1979); by G. Vermes, F. Millar, M. Goodman (vol. 3. Edinburgh: T.&T. Clark, 1986).

Schwabe, M. and B.Lifshitz, *Beth She'arim*. Vol.2: *The Greek Inscriptions*. New Brunswick: Rutgers University Press, 1974.

Schwabe, M. *Tarbitz* 21 (1950), 112-123 *(in Hebrew)*.

Schwyzer, E.A. *Griechische Grammatik, vol. I*. Munich, 1953.

Scramuzza, V.M.*The Emperor Claudius*. Cambridge, Mass.: Harvard University Press, 1940.

Sevcenko, I. 'The Moses Cross at Sinai'. *DOP* 17 (1963) 391-398.

Shelov, D.V. *Tanais and the Lower Don in the First Centuries of the Common Era*. Moscow: Nauka, 1972. *(in Russian)*

Shkorpil, V.V. *Isvestiya Archeologicheskoj Komissii* 27 (1908), 68-74. *(in Russian.)*

Sheppard, A.R.R. 'Pagan Cults of Angels in Roman Asia Minor'. *Talanta* 12/13 (1980-1981), 77-101.

Siegert, F. 'Gottesfürchtige und Sympathizanten.' *JSJ* 4,2 (1973), 109-162.

Simon, M. *Verus Israel*. ET, Oxford: OUP, 1986.

Simon, M. 'Theos Hypsistos', *Ex orbe religionum*. Leiden, 1972. 372-385 = id., *Le Christianisme antique et son contexte religieux. Scripta Varia*, vol. 2. Tübingen: Mohr–Siebeck, 1981. Wissenschaftliche Untersuchungen zum Neuen Testament, 23. 495-508.

Simon, M. *Le Christianisme antique et son contexte religieux. Scripta Varia*, vol. 2. Tübingen: Mohr–Siebeck, 1981. Wissenschaftliche Untersuchungen zum Neuen Testament, 23.

Slingerland, D. 'Suetonius *Claudius* 25.4 and the Account in Cassius Dio'. *JQR* 79:4 (1989), 305-322.

Slingerland, D. 'Chrestus: Christus?', *New Perspectives on Ancient Judaism*, vol.4. *The Literature on Early Rabbinic Judaism: Issues in Talmudic Redaction and Interpretation*. ed. A.J. Avery-Peck. Lanham/New York/London: University Press of America, 1989, 133-144.

Smallwood, E.M. *The Jews under Roman Rule. From Pompey to Diocletian*. Leiden: E.J.Brill, 1981², SJLA 20.

Smallwood, E.M. 'Some Notes on the Jews under Tiberius'. *Latomus* 15 (1956), 324-329.

Smallwood, E.M. 'The Alleged Jewish Tendencies of Poppaea Sabina'. *JThSt* 10 (1959), 325-335.

Smallwood, E.M. *Philonis Alexandrini Legatio Ad Gaium*. Edited with an Introduction, Translation and Commentary. Leiden: Brill, 1961.

Solin, H. 'Juden und Syrer im westlichen Teil der römischen Welt: Eine ethnisch-demographische Studie mit besonderer Berucksiehtung der sprachichen Zustande', *ANRW* II 29,2 (1983), 587-789, 1222-1249.

Sordi, M. *The Christians and the Roman Empire*. ET, London and New York: Routledge, 1994.

Spicq, C. 'Ce que signifie le titre de chrétien', *Stud. Theol.* 15 (1961), 68-78.

Stephani, L. 'Parerga archaeologica'. *Mélanges gréco-romains tirés du Bulletin hist.-philologique de l'Académie impériale des sciences, II*. St. Petersburg, 1866. 232-239.

Stern, M. 'The Jewish Diaspora', *The Jewish People in the First Century: Historical Geography, Political History, Social, Cultural and Religious Life and Institutions*, eds. S. Safrai and M. Stern, vol. 1 (Assen: Van Goreum, 1974, *CRINT*, I. 117-183.

Stern, M. *Greek and Latin Authors on Jews and Judaism, edited with Introductions, Translations and Commentary. Vols. 1-3*. Jerusalem: The Israel Academy of Sciences and Humanities, 1976-1987.

Tacheva-Hitova, M. 'Dem Hypsistos geweihte Denkmäler in Thrakien'. *Thracia* 4 (1977), 271-301.

Tacheva-Hitova, M. *Eastern Cults in Moesia Inferior and Thracia*. Leiden: Brill, 1983, EPRO 95.

Taylor, J. *Christians and Holy Places. The Myth of Jewish-Christian Origins*. Oxford: Clarendon Press, 1993.

Taylor, J. 'Why were the Disciples First Called "Christians" at Antioch? (Acts 11:26)' *RB* 101:1 (1994), 75-94.

Tcherikover, V. 'The Sambathions'. *Scripta Hierosolymitana* 1 (1954), 78-98; *CPJ* III, 43-56.

Tcherikover, V. 'Jewish Apologetic Literature Reconsidered'. *Eos* 48,3 (1956), 169-193.

Thompson, L.A.'Domitian and the Jewish Tax'. *Historia* 31 (1982), 329-342.

Tolstoj, I.I. *The White Island and Taurica on the Pontos Euxeinos*. Petrograd, 1916 *in Russian*.

Tracey, R. 'Syria', *The Book of Acts in Its Graeco-Roman Setting*. D.W.J. Gill and C. Gempf, eds. Grand Rapids/Carlisle: Eerdmans/Paternoster, 1994. 223-278.

Trebilco, P. 'Paul and Silas - "Servants of the Most High God" (Acts 16.16-18)'. *JSNT* 36 (1989), 51-73.

Trebilco, P. *Jewish Communities in Asia Minor*. Cambridge: CUP, 1991.

Trebilco, P. 'Asia', *The Book of Acts in Its Graeco-Roman Setting*. D.W.J. Gill and C. Gempf, eds. Grand Rapids/Carlisle: Eerdmans/Paternoster, 1994. 291-362.

Urdahl, L.B. 'Jews in Attica'. *Symbolae Osloensis* 43 (1968), 39-46.

Ustinova, Ju. 'The *Thiasoi* of *Theos Hypsistos* in Tanais'. *History of Religions* 31 (1991), 152-180.
van der Horst, P.W. *Essays on the Jewish World of Early Christianity*. Fribourg: Universitäts-Verlag / Göttingen: Vandenhoeck & Ruprecht, 1990.
van der Horst, P.W. 'Jews and Christians in Aphrodisias in the light of their Relations in other cities of Asia Minor'. *Nederlands Theologisch Tijdschrift* 43:2 (1989), 106-121.
van der Horst, P.W. *Ancient Jewish Epitaphs: An Introductory Survey of a Millenium of Jewish Funerary Epigraphy (300 BCE - 700 CE)*. Kampen: Kok Pharos Publishing House, 1991.
van der Horst, P.W. 'A New Altar of a Godfearer?' *JJS* 43 (1992), 32-37.
van der Leeuw, G. *Phänomenologie der Religion*. Tubingen: 1933. ET: *Religion in Essence and Manifestation*. London, 1964².
van der Mijnsbrugge, M. *The Cretan Koinon*. New York 1931.
van Henten, J.W. and P.W. van der Horst, eds. *Studies in Early Jewish Epigraphy*. Leiden and New York: Köln, 1994, Arbeiten zur Geschichte des antiken Judentums und des Urchristentums, XXI.
van Minnen, P. 'Drei Bemerkungen zur Geschichte des Judentums in der griechisch-romischen Welt.' *ZPE* 100 (1994), 255-257.
van Straten, F.T. 'Gifts for the Gods. Appendix. Votive Offerings Representing Parts of the Human Body (the Greek World)', *Faith, Hope and Worship. Aspects of Religious Mentality in Ancient World*. ed. H.S. Versnel. Leiden: Brill, 1981, Studies in Greek and Roman Religion, 2, 105-151.
Vasmer, M. Untersuchungen über die ältesten Wohnsitze der Slaven, vol.I. Leipzig 1923.
Vinogradov, Y.G. 'Polis at the North Black Sea Shore'. *Antichnaya Grecia*, vol. I. Moscow, 1983. 366-420, *(in Russian)*.
von Domaszewski, A. 'Griechische Inschriften aus Moesien und Thrakien.' *AEM* 10 (1886), 238-244.
von Gerkan, A. *Synagogue in Milet* (1921).
Versnel, H.S., ed. *Faith, Hope and Worship. Aspects of Religious Mentality in Ancient World*. Leiden: Brill, 1981.
Vulpe, R. 'Le sanctuaire des Zeus Casios de Serêmet et le problème d'un vicus cassianus.' *Epigraphica - Travaux dédiés au VIIe Congrès d'epigraphie grecque et latine*. Bucarest, 1977. 113-130.
Wackernagel, I. *Vorlesungen über Syntax*. Basel 1920.
Walker, W.O. 'The Timothy-Titus Problem Reconsidered.' *ExpT 92* (1980/81), 231-235.
Wiefel, W. 'The Jewish Community in Ancient Rome and the Origins of RomanChristianity', *The Romans Debate*, revised and expanded edition, ed. K.P.Donfried. Edinburgh: T & T Clark, 1991. 85-101.
Wiesner, G., ed. *Synkretismusforschung, Theorie und Praxis*. Wiesbaden 1978.
Wilcox, M. 'The "God-Fearers" in Acts - a Reconsideration', *JSNT* 13 (1981), 102-122.
Will, E. and C. Orrieux, *'Prosélytisme juif?' Histoire d'une erreur*. Paris: Les Belles Lettres, 1992.
Willetts, R.F. *The Civilisation of Ancient Crete*. Berkeley 1977.
Williams, M.H. 'Θεοσεβὴς γὰρ ἦν - the Jewish Tendencies of Poppaea Sabina'. *JTS* 39 (1988), 97-111.
Williams, M.H. 'Domitian, the Jews and the 'Judaizers' - a Simple Matter of Cupiditas and Maiestas?' *Historia* 34:2 (1990), 196-211.

Williams, M.H. 'The Jews and Godfearers Inscription from Aphrodisias—a Case of Patriarchal Interference in Early 3rd Century Caria?' *Historia* 51:3 (1992) 297-310.

Williams, M.H. 'The Organisation of Jewish Burials in Ancient Rome'. *ZPE* 101 (1994), 165-182.

Williams, M.H. 'The Structure of Roman Jewry Re-considered - Were the Synagogues of Ancient Rome Entirely Homogeneous?' *ZPE* 104 (1994), 129-141.

Winter, B.W. and A.D.Clarke, eds. *The Book of Acts in Its First Century Setting*, vol.1, *The Book of Acts in its Ancient Literary Setting*. Grand Rapids/Carlisle: Eerdmans/Paternoster, 1993.

Woodward, A.M. 'Excavations at Sparta 1924-1925'. *BSA* 26 (1924-1925), 222-224. *BSA* 29 (1927-1928), 49-50.

Zgusta, L. *Kleinasiatische Personennamen*. Prague: Tschechoslovakischen Akademie der Wissenschaften, 1964.

Zgusta, L. *Die Personennamen griechischer Städte der nordlichen Schwarzmeerkuste*. Praha, 1955.

Zgusta, L. *Kleinasiatische Ortsnamen*. Prague, 1984.

Zwi Werblowski, R.J., W. Heissig and H. Klimkeit, eds. 'Synkretismus in der Religionsgeschichte', *Syncretismus in der Religionen Zentralasiens*. 1987. 1-7.

Index of Greek Words used in the Inscriptions – Appendix 3

Names, Place-names and Ethnics

Ἀθηνόδωρος	3, III, 1
Ἀμαρθαστος	3, III, 1 (twice)
Ανος	3, II, 6
Αρδαρος	3, III, 1
Ἀσκληπιάδης	3, III, 2
Ἀσποῦργος	3, II, 5
Αὐρήλιος	3, I, 1
Ἀχαιμένης	3, III, 1
Βασιλείδης	3, III, 1
Γαδεις	3, II, 8
Δαδας	3, III, 1 (twice)
Δημήτριος	3, III, 1
Διοκλητιανός	3, I, 1
Διονύσιος	3, II, 5
Δροῦσος	3, II, 1
Ἑλικωνιάς	3, II, 1
Ἐλπίας	3, II, 2
Ἑρμᾶς	3, II, 4
Ἔρως	3, III, 1
Εὐπάτωρ	3, III, 1
Ζαβαργος	3, III, 1
Ζήνων	3, III, 1 (?)
Ἡρακλᾶς	3, II, 1
Ἡρακλείδης	3, II, 1; 3, III, 1; 3, III, 2
θεάγγελος	3, III, 1 (twice?)
θεοδοσία	3, I, 1
θυλογανος	3, III, 2
Ἰουδαῖος	3, II, I; 3, II, 2; 3, II, 3; 3, II, 4; 3, II, 6; 3, II, 8
Ἰουλιάδης	3, III, 1
Ἰούλιος	3, II, 1; 3, III, 1 3, III, 3; 3, III, 4
Καλλισθένεια	3, II, 8
Καλλισθένης	3, III, 2
Καραγος	3, II, 6
Καρσανδανος	3, II, 6

Κότυς	3, II, 6; 3, II, 8; 3, III, 4
Λογγίων	3, II, 5 (?)
Μαξιμιανός	3, I, 1
Μενέστρατος	3, III, 1 (?)
Μετρότειμος	3, II, 6
Μηνόφιλος	3, III, 1
Μιθριδάτης	3, II, 7
Μυρείνος	3, III, 1
Μύρων	3, III, 1
Ὀλυμπιανός	3, I, 1
Ὄλυμπος	3, I, 1
Ομρασμασκος	3, III, 2
Ομψαλακος	3, III, 1
Οὐαλέριος	3, I, 1; 3, III, 2
Πάππος	3, III, 1; 3, III, 2
Παρβας	3, III, 1
Παρθενοκλῆς	3, III, 1
Πόθος	3, II, 7
Πόθων	3, II, 5
Ῥησκούπορις	3, II, 1; 3, III, 3
Συγος	3, II, 6
Σογους	3, I, 1
Στράβων	3, II, 7
Στρατόνεικος	3, III, 1 (twice)
Συνέκδημος	3, III, 1
Τιβέριος	3, II, 1; 3, III, 1; 3, III, 3; 3, III, 4
Φαννης	3, III, 1 (three times); 3, III, 2
Φιδανους	3, III, 2
Φιδας	3, III, 1
Φιλότειμος	3, II, 8
Φιλώτας	3, III, 1
Φορδακος	3, II, 5
Χαρακστος	3, III, 2
Χαρίτων	3, III, 1 (twice)
Χρήστη	3, II, 1
Χρύσα	3, II, 7
Ψυχαρίων	3, II, 6; 3, III, 2

Selected Greek Words in the Texts

ἀγαθός	3, III, 1; 3, III, 4
ἀδελφός	3, III, 3; 3, III, 4
ἀμφιβήτησις	3, II, 4
ἀνατίθημι	3, II, 7
ἀνδρεῖος	3, II, 4 (?)
ἀνέπαφος	3, II, 7; 3, II, 9
ἀνεπηρέαστος	3, II, 7; 3, II, 9
ἀνεπικόλυτος	3, II, 6
ἀνεπικωλύτως	3, II, 1; 3, II, 4
ἀνεπίληπτος	3, II, 1; 3, II, 2;
	3, II, 4; 3, II, 6
ἀνίστημι	3, III, 3
ἀπαρενόχλετος	3, II, 1; 3, II, 2;
	3, II, 4
ἀποδημέω	3, I, 1
ἀποκαθίστημι	3, III, 1
ἀποστατέω	3, I, 1
ἄφετος	3, II, 6
ἀφίημι	3, II, 1; 3, II, 2;
	3, II, 4; 3, II, 8
βασιλευς	3, II, 1; 3, II, 4;
	3, II, 5; 3, II, 6;
	3, II, 7; 3, II, 8;
	3, III, 1; 3, III, 3;
	3, III, 4
βασιλεύω	3, II, 1; 3, II, 4; 3,
	II, 5; 3, II, 6; 3,
	II, 7; 3, II, 8; 3,
	III, 1; 3, III, 3; 3,
	III, 4
βούλομαι	3, II, 1; 3, II, 4
γένος	3, II, 8 (?)
Γης	3, II, 7
γης 3, II, 4	
γίγνομαι	3, I, 1
γυμνασιάρχης	3, III, 2
γυνή	3, II, 1; 3, II, 8
	(twice)
ἐγγράφω	3, III, 3; 3, III, 4
εἰμι	3, II, 4
εἰσποιητός	3, III, 3; 3, III, 4
ἐλεύθερος	3, II, 1; 3, II, 4
ἐπαρχεῖον	3, I, 1
ἐπιτροπεύω	3, II, 2
ἔτος	3, I, 1; 3, II, 1; 3,
	II, 4; 3, II, 5; 3,
	II, 6; 3, II, 7; 3,

	II, 8; 3, III, 1; 3,
	III, 2; 3, III, 3; 3,
	III, 4
εὐάρεστος	3, II, 4
εὐσεβής	3, II, 1; 3, II, 4;
	3, II, 8; 3, III, 1;
	3, III, 3; 3, III, 4
εὐχή	3, I, 1; 3, II, 1; 3,
	II, 4 (twice); 3,
	II, 7;
	3, III, 1; 3, III, 4
εὔχομαι	3, I, 1; 3, II, 1; 3,
	II, 8; 3, III, 1
Ζεύς	3, II, 7
ζωή	3, II, 4
Ἥλιος	3, II, 7
θεμέλιον	3, I, 1
θεός	3, II, 2
ἐπήκοος	3, I, 1; 3, III, 1;
	3, III, 2
ὕψιστος	3, I, 1; 3, II, 7; 3,
	III, 1; 3, III, 2
	(twice);
	3, III, 3 (twice);
	3, III, 4 (twice)
παντοκράτωρ	3, II, 7
εὐλογητός	3, II, 7
θιασώτης	3, III, 1; 3, III, 2
θλῖψις	3, I, 1
θρεπτή	3, II, 2; 3, II, 7
θρεπτός	3, II, 1; 3, II, 4; 3,
	II, 5; 3, II, 8 (?)
θωπεία	3, II, 1; 3, II, 4;
	3, II, 5; 3, II, 6
ἴδιος	3, III, 1
ἱερεύς	3, III, 1 (twice);
	3, III, 2
ἵστημι	3, II, 6
καθάπαξ	3, II, 1;
	3, II, 4 (?)
καλέω	3, I, 1
κληρονόμος	3, II, 1; 3, II, 4;
	3, II, 7; 3, II, 9
λοιπός	3, III, 1; 3, III, 2
μήν 3, II, 8; 3, III, 1	
Ἀρτεμίσιος	3, II, 4
Γορπιαῖος	3, II, 4
Δαίσιοσ	3, II, 5; 3, III, 3
Δεῖος	3, II, 7
Περιέτιος	3, III, 2
Ξανδικός	3, II, 6
μήτηρ	3, II, 4 (?)
νιανισκάρχης	3, III, 2

οἰκοδομέω   3, I, 1
ὄνομα   3, II, 7; 3, II, 9;
                   3, III, 3; 3, III, 4
παραμονή   3, II, 4
παραφιλάγαθος   3, III, 2
πᾶς 3, II, 1; 3, II, 2;   3, II, 4 (twice);
                   3, II, 7; 3, II, 9
ποιέω   3, II, 4
πολύς   3, I, 1 (twice)
πρεσβύτερος   3, III, 4
προσευχή   3, I, 1; 3, II, 1;
                   3, II, 2 (twice); 3,
                   II, 4; 3, II, 5;
                   3, II, 6 (twice);
                   3, II, 7; 3, II, 9
προσκαρτερέω   3, II, 2
προσκαρτέρησις   3, II, 1; 3, II, 4;
                   3, II, 5; 3, II, 6
προσμένω   3, II, 9
σεβαστόγνωστος   3, I, 1
σέβω   3, II, 2; 3, III, 3;
                   3, III, 4
συναγωγή   3, II, 1; 3, II, 2;
                   3, II, 3; 3, II, 4;
                   3, II, 6

συναγωγός   3, III, 1; 3, III, 2
συνεπινεύω   3, II, 1
συνεπιτροπεύω   3, II, 1; 3, II, 3;
                   3, II, 4; 3, II, 6
σύνοδος   3, III, 1; 3, III, 2
σῶμα   3, II, 4
τελαμών   3, III, 1; 3, III, 3
τελευτάω   3, II, 4
τελευτή   3, II, 4
τειμάω   3, I, 1
τρέπω   3, II, 1; 3, II, 4
τύχη   3, III, 1; 3, III, 4
υἱος   3, II, 6
φιλάγαθος   3, III, 2
φιλόκαισαρ   3, II, 1; 3, II, 4;
                   3, II, 8; 3, III, 1;
                   3, III, 3; 3, III, 4
φιλόπατρις   3, II, 7
φιλορώμαιος   3, II, 1; 3, II, 4;
                   3, II, 5; 3, II, 8;
                   3, III, 1; 3, III, 3;
                   3, III, 4

Index of Ancient Authors

Biblical references

Leviticus
19:33-34	33
25:23	33

Numbers
6:22-27	156

Deuteronomy
4:39	99
5:14	22
10:18-19	33
16:9-14	22
16:10	22
16:13	22
17:15	33

Psalms
45:8, 12	155

Isaiah
49:6	40
54:15 (LXX)	40

Matthew
19:21	91
23:14	39
23:15	35, 36, 46

Mark
10:21	91
12:40	39

Luke
18:22	91
20:4	39

Acts
2:10	36
2:11	46
2:9-11	24
5:1-5	43
6:1	163
6:5	36, 46
8:27-39	121
10	79, 120
10:1-2	53
10:2	11, 121
10:7	76
10:22	11, 53, 80, 121
10:45	11, 121
11:1	121
11:2	11
11:18	122
11:26	91, 178
13:2	120
13:15	187
13:16	53, 120, 122
13:26	47, 53, 122
13:43	35, 36, 49, 53, 120, 123
13:46	122, 143
13:50	117, 120, 122
14:1	143
15:4-29	13
16:1-3	12, 14, 16
16:14	53, 120
16:16-18	83
17:1	143, 154
17:4	53, 120
17:10	143, 154
17:17	53, 120, 124, 143, 154
17:28	100
18:1-8	42

18:2   29, 174
18:4, 7   154
18:6   143
18:6-7 53, 120
18:12-17   166
18:19   143
21:21   16
26:28   178
28:17   185

Romans
2:25-29   14

1 Corinthians
7:18,19   16
9:20   14

2 Corinthians
11:22   163

6:15   14

Philippians
3:5   163

Colossians
4:11   11

2 Timothy
3:15   15

Titus
1:10   11

1 Peter
4:16   178

James
5:17   219

Galatians
2:3-4   12
2:4   13
2:4-8   13
5:2-4   14
5:6   14

Ancient Authors

Aristophanes
Lysistrata
553   204

Arrian
Dissertationes
2.9.19-20   119

Artemidorus
3.53.1 213
3.53.4 213

Asterius
Homily VIII
7.1   43
15.2   42
25.4   42
27.6   43
29.1   43

Augustinus
Confessionum
8.6   160
I.13.22   159
De Civitate Dei
VI, 11   27
De Consensu Evangelistarum
I.22.30   93, 99
Letters
44.6.13   103

Chrysostom
Adversum Iudaeos
1.3   134
1.6   135
5.3   134
6.5   134
8.6   134
Hom. 14
on Acts 6:1   163

Cicero
ad Familiares
IX.18.4   161
Pro Cluentio
139   168
Pro Flacco
28.66-69   168
28.67   145

Clement of Alexandria
Stromata
7,14   43

Cleomedes
De Motu Circ. Corp. Caelest.
II.1   213

Codex Justinianus
1.9.12 103

Codex Theodosianus
16.5.43   103
16.8.4 192
16.8.19   103

Cyril of Alexandria
De adoratione in spiritu et veritate
                      102

Didymus the Blind
Commentary on
Psalm 21:31   41

Dio Cassius
37.17.1   65
57.18.5a   30
60.3.2 174
60.8.4 174
60.8.7 174
60.9.1 174

65.7.2   10
66.5.4   16
67.14.1-3   5
67.14.2   123
68.1.2   5

Epiphanius
Adversus Haereses
42.1 114
Pan.
80.1-3 102

Eusebius
Historia Ecclesiastica
II.5.6-7   30
II,5.7   171
Praeparatio Evangelica
13.12.7   100

Gregory of Nazanzus
Orations
18.5   101

Gregory of Nyssa
Eun.
2   101

Horace
Satires
1.4.142-3   27

Joannes Lydus
De Mens.
4.53   96

Josephus
Jewish Antiquities
1.146   163
1.36, 146   163
2.280, 283   185
3.15.3, 318-319 119
3.8.9, 217   119
5.323   163
9.20   163
10.8   163
11.25   138
12.119   128
12.120   129
12.125   143
13.356-364   130

14.115   24
14.185-216   170
14.185-267   139, 141
14.188   140
14.215-216   170
14.223-227   144
14.228-229   144
14.231-232   144
14.235   141
14.244-246   148
14.247-255   141
14.256-258   141
14.261   141
14.262-264   144
14.265-267   140
14.7.2 110   120
16.160-17   139
16.162-165   141, 170
16.163   96
16.167-168   146
16.172-173   146
16.2.3, 369   185
16.9,1 185
18.8   123
18.81-84   31
19. 286-291   171
19.280-291   172
20.195   66
20.2.3, 34   119
20.2.4, 41   119
20.34-48   33
20.8.11, 195   119
234   144
237-240   144

Jewish Wars
1.27.2, 538   185
2 8,7 (142)   39
2.17.10, 454   119
2.18.2, 46   119
2.20.2, 560   119
2.398   24
2.462-463,
   479   132
6.96   163
7.3.3, 45   119
7.43   24, 128
7.44   128, 134
7.44-45   130

7.45 124, 135
7.46-52 132
7.54-60 133
7.100-111 133
7.110 130
7.218 5, 10

contra Apionem
1.22 138, 176-182
2 143
2.10 213
2.39 128
2.148 7
2.282 29

Julian
Contra Galilaeos
43B 7

Justin
Dialogus cum Tryphone
12 40
23.3 45
28.2 40

Juvenal
Satires
3.296 213
4.117 (Sch.) 176
14.96 118

Letter of Aristeas
15-16 99

Livy
39.8.5 32
39.8 32
39.15 32

Malalas
Chronographia
10.20 132
10.45 133, 134
15.15 131
Excerpta de insidiis
35 131

Or. Sib.
III 271 24

Origen
Contra Celsum
I,24 99

Pausanius
II.2,8 84
V.15,5 84
IX.8,5 84

Philo
Commentary
on Gen. 14:18 98

De Cherubim
108 33
119 33

De Conf. Ling.
129 163

De Somniis
II, 273 33

De Specialibus Legibus
I.9 38
I.51 33
I.308 33

In Flaccum
45-6 24

Leg. All.
3.82 99

Legatio
155-157 185
157 170
157, 317 96
157-158 169
158 170
159-161 30
160 171
160-161 171
161 142
203 171
245 138
281 154
281-2 24
282 138
315 146
349-367 171

Plato
Ion
536a   160

Pliny the Younger
Epistulae
10.96.9   114

Pliny the Elder
Naturalis Historia
XXIV,5   29

Plutarch
De Fraterno Amore
19   199
Quaest. Conv.
IV,6,1-2   100

Porphyry
Adversum Christianos
I.3   7

Procopius of Gaza
PG 87, 2544D 41

Ptolemy
Apotelesmatica
II, 3.66   7

Seneca
Epistolae Morales
XCV.47   28

Sophocles
Trachiniae
127   109

Suetonius
Julius
42.3   170
Augustus
32.1   170
Tiberius
36.1   31
Claudius
25.4   29, 174
Nero
6.16.2 179
16.2   179
Domitianus
12.2   4

13.2   8
15.1   7
Vespasianus
8,4   140

Tacitus
Annales
1.73.2ff.   7
2.85.4 31
3.24.2f.   7
15.28.3   10
15.44   179

Historiae
V.5.5   100

Tertullian
Apologia
3.5   178
18.6.   163
21.1   6

Testament of Job
               191

Theodoret of Cyrus
PG 81, 445   41

Valerius Maximus
Facta et Dicta Memorabilia
1.3.2   168
1.3.3   29

Xenophon
Anabasis
I.7.2   120

Index of Modern Authors

A
Alessandri, S. 168
Allen, W.C. 22, 37
Altaner, B. 172
Attridge, H.W. 22, 73
Aupert, P. 85
B
Bagatti, B. 45
Bagatti, P.B. 25, 45
Bamberger, B.J. 20, 36
Barclay, J.M.G. 128-29, 130, 135, 140,
    168-69, 173, 176
Baron, S.W. 23, 156, 186
Barrett, C.K. 47, 52, 121-22
Bauman, R.A. 6-8
Bean, C. 96
Beare, F.W. 38
Bechtel, F. 92
Bees, N.A. 162
Bell, H.I. 172
Bellen, H. 60, 75
Berliner, A. 191
Bernard, A. 94-95, 218
Bernays, J. 118
Berner, U. 203
Bertholet, A. 20, 22
Bertram, G. 64
Betz, H.D. 13
Bialoblocki, S. 20
Bickerman, E.J. 30, 60, 91-92, 139
Bij de Vaate, A.J. 109, 209
Bilde, P. 11
Black 146, 187
Blass, F. 178
Blawatsky, V. 108
Blommerde, M. 13
Boeckh, 219
Bormann, L. 56
Bowersock, G.W. 71-73
Braude, W.G. 20
Brixhe, C. 72
Brooten, B.J. 25, 73, 187, 191-92

Bruce, F.F. 13, 47, 121
Bruce, I.A.F. 4, 10
Bruchman, C.F.H. 85
Bruner, D. 20
Buckler, W.H. 85
Burford, A. 214
Burton, E. 13
C
Calder, W.M. 85
Calixtus, G. 200
Cameron, A. 131
Capper, B. 3
Caquot, A. 20
Carrol, L. 199
Cary, E. 5, 10, 30, 65
Chantraine, P. 91
Choroshevsky, V.A. 114
Clarke, A.D. 52
Cohen, S.J.D. 11, 13-14, 16-17, 21-22,
    26, 56-57, 75-77, 79, 119, 124, 210
Collins, J.J. 73
Colpe, C. 199, 202-3
Conybeare, F.C. 218
Conzelmann, H. 7, 15, 47, 121
Cook, A.B. 85, 87-88
Cumont, F. 29, 84, 86-88, 90, 94
Cunningham, J.G. 103
D
Dalbert, P. 20
Dantes, St. P. 165
Datema, C. 42
Davies, P.R. 129
de Lange, N. 61, 163
de Rossi, J.B. 68
de Vaate, 212
de Waele, V.J.M. 163
Deissmann, A. 60, 64, 96, 148-49, 162
Derenbourg, J. 36
Detschev, D. 89
Diatroptov, P.D. 116
Diehl, E. 69
Dietrich, A. 199

Dittenberger, G. 94
Donfried, K.P. 186
Doutreleau, L. 41
Downey, G. 128-29, 131-34
Drew-Bear, T. 97
Dunbabin, K.M.D. 87
Dunn, J.D.G. 3, 148
Dupont, J. 54
Dussaud, R. 87
E
Elber, V. 200
Engberg-Pedersen, T. 11
Engelmann, H. 146
Erlich, R. 220
F
Fairclough, R. 27
Feissel, D. 149, 155-57
Feldman, L.H. 22-23, 33, 48, 53, 55, 59, 60, 68, 71-73, 114, 116, 120, 173, 182
Figueras, P. 25-26, 45
Finegan, J. 45
Finn, Th.M. 57
Flowers, H.F. 38
Fox, R.L. 102
Frend, W.H.C. 218
Frerichs, E.S. 21, 56, 64, 77
Frey, J.-B. 46, 59-60, 64, 68, 70, 94, 147, 150, 162, 182, 186, 188, 190, 220
Friedlaender, M. 36
Fuchs, H. 179-80
Fuks, A. 210
Furnish, V.P. 163
G
Gasque, W. 14
Gempf, K. 121
Georgi, D. 20, 56
Gerov, B. 89
Gesche, A. 41
Goodenough, E.R. 52, 97, 111-12, 114, 213-14
Goodman, M. 2-3, 6, 11-12, 20-24, 29-32, 33, 35, 38-40, 54, 58, 75, 77, 79, 100, 114, 125-26, 129, 138, 143-44, 146, 148, 150-51, 154-55, 157-58, 168, 172, 176, 183, 187-88, 191, 222
Graetz, H. 36
Grant, F.C. 201

Graves, R. 179
Green, G. 155
Green, W.S. 77
Greeven, L.H. 215
Gressman, H. 87
Groag, E. 65
Gronewald, M. 41
Guarducci, M. 45, 94
Gundry, R.H. 36, 38
Gutmann, J. 57, 96, 154
H
Habicht, Ch. 155
Haenchen, E. 14, 46-47, 52, 54, 121, 123
Hakkert, A.M. 93
Hall, A.S. 87
Hannestad, L. 11
Harnack, A. 20, 23
Harrill, J.A. 110
Hartman, S.S. 107
Hata, G. 22
Hefele, C.J. 44
Heinen, H. 106
Heissig, W. 200
Hemer, C.J. 4, 5, 9, 60, 121
Hengel, M. 3, 14, 95-96, 99-100, 154, 165, 213, 217
Heraeus, W. 160-61
Hicks, E.L. 62
Hill, E. 159
Hillar, T. 52
Hoacle, E. 45
Hofmann, J. 160
Holl, K. 102, 224
Hommel, H. 64-65, 68, 75, 109
Horbury, W. 94, 96-97
Horsley, G.H.R. 147, 219
J
Janne, H. 181
Jeffreys, E. 131-32
Jellinek, A. 36
Jeremias, J. 20, 36, 39
Johnson, S.E. 29, 88
Judge, E.A. 91
Juster, J. 23, 141, 144, 176, 186, 190, 210, 220
K
Kajanto, J. 113
Kalinka, E. 214, 216, 218

Kamstra, J.H. 198
Kant, L.H. 68, 74, 76, 95, 97, 113, 208, 209, 216-17
Kasher, A. 128
Keil, J. 85
Klaffenbach, G. 158
Klimkeit, H. 200
Kmosco, M. 102, 224
Knibbe, D. 146
Kocevalov, A. 221
Kochelenko, G. 108
Koester, H. 73
Köhler 219
Konikoff, A. 156
Köppen, E. 219
Kraabel, A.T. 21, 52, 56-57, 78-80, 84-85, 95, 125, 138, 149-50, 154, 209-10, 225
Kraeling, C.H. 128-29, 130, 132-34
Kraemer, R.S. 26, 46, 95, 154, 208-9, 211
Krauss, S. 186, 190, 220
Kroll, J.H. 62
Kuhn, K.G. 20, 37, 47, 96, 163
L
La Piana, G. 156, 165, 186
Lake, K. 20, 53, 55, 70, 120
Lampe, G.W.H. 102
Lane, E.N. 29
Latyshev, V. 110, 219-21, 223
Leon, H.J. 5, 26, 59, 68, 123, 164-65, 169, 175, 182-92
Leumann, M. 91
Leveque, P. 202
Levi, I. 120
Levick, B. 150, 173
Levinskaya, I.A. 76, 108, 112
Lewis, D.M. 154
Lieu, J. 22, 38
Lifshitz, B. 25, 45, 60, 62-65, 75, 91, 96-97, 134, 154, 156-58, 214-15, 217, 220
Linder, A. 103, 224
Ljungvik, H. 13
Lüdemann, G. 14, 174-75, 177
Lüderitz, G. 25-26, 129
Luria, S. 112
M
MacLennan, R.S. 56, 58, 77

Manzella, I. Di S. 189
Marcus, R. 120, 128-29, 138, 140, 142, 144
Marshall, A.J. 145, 168-69
Marti, J.J. 75
Mason, S. 3
Masson, O. 85
Mattingly, H. 3, 91
Mazur, B.D. 57, 96
McEleney, N.J. 11, 119
McKnight, S. 21-23, 37, 39
Meek, Th. J. 22
Meeks, W.A. 129, 132-34, 162, 165
Meritt, B.D. 162
Merrill, E.T. 8, 9
Metzger, B.M. 39, 124
Michaelis 109
Milik, J.T. 25, 45
Millar, F. 20, 22, 24, 65, 75, 100, 114, 129, 138, 141, 143-44, 146, 148, 150-51, 154-55, 157-58, 168, 172, 176, 183, 187-88, 191, 213-14, 216, 220, 222-23
Minns, E.H. 106
Mitchell, S. 57, 97, 102, 122-23, 150
Mitsos, M.T. 158
Mobius, H. 67
Moehring, H.R. 139-40, 143
Momigliano, A. 164, 173, 176
Montevecchi, O. 109
Moore, G.F. 22, 52
Mor, M. 21
Moreau, J. 91
Muller, 189
Munck, J. 35, 36, 38
Murphy-O'Connor, J. 56, 71, 77-78, 173, 175, 181
Mussies, G. 72, 73, 95, 113
N
Nadel, B. 76, 108, 110
Naveh, J. 25
Neusner, J. 21, 33, 56, 64, 77, 139
Nickelsbourg, G.W.E. 21, 56
Niese, B. 141
Nigdelis, P.M. 155
Nillsson, M.P. 84
Nobbs, A. 52
Nock, A.D. 85, 87-88, 93, 96, 109
Nolland, J. 11, 27, 119

North, J. 22, 38
Noy, D. 25, 57, 67-70, 94, 96-97, 147, 155, 163-64, 168, 182-89, 191, 208
Nutton, V. 147
O
Oldfather, W.A. 119
Orchard, B. 13
Orlandos, A.K. 157
Orrieux, C. 22
Overman, J.A. 77
P
Pallas, D.I. 165
Panayotou, A. 72
Pariente, A. 199, 200
Paton, W.R. 62
Pearson, B.A. 21, 56
Pelekidis, S. 85, 156
Penna, 186
Peterson, E. 91
Peterson, N.R. 21, 56
Petzl, G. 109
Pfuhl, E. 67
Philonenko, M. 20
Pines, S. 115
Plummer, A. 37
Podro, J. 179
Poland, F. 90
Powell, B. 162
Purvis, J.D. 156
Pye, M. 198, 199
R
Rabello, A.M. 141
Rajak, T. 22, 38, 64, 75, 139, 141, 142, 143, 170, 186
Ramsay, W.M. 85, 150
Reinhardt, W. 3, 23
Reynolds, J. 25, 65, 67, 70, 72, 74, 75, 76, 78, 211
Riesner, R. 3
Ringgren, H. 107, 202
Robert, J. 87, 90, 97, 158, 161, 165
Robert, L. 54-55, 60-65, 87, 90, 93, 95, 97, 147-48, 150, 156-58, 161, 165, 190, 215-18
Roberts, C. 85, 93, 96, 109
Rolfe, J.C. 4, 170, 174
Romaniuk, K. 48, 55
Ronchi, G. 93, 109, 218
Roscher, W.H. 218

Rosenbloom, J.R. 23
Rostovtzeff, M. 106, 108
Rudolph, K. 199
Rutgers, L.V. 23, 77, 164, 182
S
Safray, S. 148
Salac, A. 108
Saldarini, A.J. 37
Sanders, E.P. 77, 148
Sanders, J.T. 45
Sandmel, S. 20
Santoro, M. 85
Schiby, J. 156
Schkorpil, V.V. 115
Schürer, E. 20, 24, 59, 61, 64-65, 75, 85, 96, 100, 111-14, 129, 138, 141, 143-44, 146, 148, 150-51, 154-55, 157-58, 168, 172, 176, 183, 186-88, 191, 214, 216, 220, 222-23, 225
Schwabe, M. 134, 158, 161
Schwyzer, E.A. 91
Scott, R. 132
Scramuzza, V.M. 173, 177
Selden, J. 118
Sevcenko, 219
Seve, M. 155
Shelov, D.V. 108
Sheppard, A.R.R. 217
Siegert, F. 53, 59, 62, 68-70, 75, 120, 122, 124
Simon, M. 20-21, 98, 100, 225
Skeat, T.C. 85, 93, 109
Slingerland, D. 172-74, 179, 181
Smallwood, E.M. 4, 7, 30, 32, 66, 139, 141, 144-46, 164, 168-69, 171, 175
Smith, M. 139
Solin, H. 182
Sordi, M. 4, 8
Spicq, C. 91
Stadhartinger, A. 56
Stegemann, H. 20
Stephani, L. 111, 219
Stern 7, 11, 16, 27, 29-31, 99, 119, 138, 143-44, 151, 176
Stern, M. 4, 5, 69, 93, 118
T
Tacheva-Hitova, M. 86-87, 89
Tannenbaum, R. 25, 65, 67, 70, 72, 74-76, 78, 131, 211

Taylor, J. 45, 91, 132, 180
Tcherikover, V. 112-13, 173, 209, 210
Thackeray, H.St.J. 29, 128, 130
Thompson, L.A. 9, 10, 202, 210
Tobin, Th.H. 73
Tokhtas'ev, S. 112
Tolstoj, I.I. 220-21
Tracey, R. 128
Trebilco, P. 53, 61-66, 75, 82, 84, 86,
    88, 95, 96, 99, 100, 138, 141-43,
    151, 225
Tredici, K.D. 56
Turner, J.E. 198
U
Urdahl, L.B. 158
Usener, H. 118
Ustinova, Ju. 108
V
van der Horst, P.W. 25-26, 68, 72, 81,
    115-16, 125, 129, 183, 187-92, 209
van der Leeuw, G. 198, 202-3
van der Mijnsbrugge, M. 204
van Henten, J.W. 68, 72, 109, 129,
    209, 212
van Minnen, P. 72
van Straten, F.T. 85
Vasmer, M. 113
Vermes, G. 20, 24, 65, 75, 100, 114,
    129, 138, 141, 143-44, 146, 148,
    150-51, 154-55, 157-58, 168, 172,
    176, 183, 187-88, 191, 213-14, 216,
    220, 222-23
Versnel, H.S. 85
Vinogradov, Y.G. 107
von Domaszewski, A. 88-90
von Gerkan, A. 149
Vulpe, R. 90
W
Wackernagel, I. 204
Walker, W.O. 13
Watts, W. 159
Whitaker, G.H. 99
White, H.G.E. 159
White, R.T. 129
Wiefel, W. 186
Wiesner, G. 203
Wilcox
Wilcox, M. 47, 48, 53, 55, 60, 123, 124
Wilken, R.L. 129, 132-34

Wilkinson, 134
Will, E. 22
Willetts, R.F. 204
Williams, M.H. 5, 8-9, 66, 72-73, 78,
    156, 186, 188-89, 191

Winter, B.W. 52, 166
Woodward, A.M. 85
Y
Ya Garkavi, A. 223
Z
Zahle, J. 11
Zgusta, L. 92, 113, 218
Zwi Werblowski, R.J. 200

Subject Index

Acmonia 123
acts of enfranchisement 111-3
Adiabene 3, 17, 33, 36
Aeolia 183
Agrippa, Marcus 146
Agrippa I 121, 154, 172-174, 183
Agrippa II 183
Agrippas 59
Alexander 200
Alexandria 131, 171, 173, 175, 186
almsgiving 121
altars 29
Anania 33
Ananias and Sapphira 43
Antioch 47, 102, 122, 128-32, 135, 158
aristocracy 122
Antiochus (the apostate) 132, 133
Antiochus II Theos 143
Antiochus III 138
Antiochus IV Epiphanes 128-130.
Antoninus Pius 147
Apamea 132, 134
Aphrodisias 61, 97, 121, 126
Apollo 92
Apollonia 150
apostles 121
Aquila and Priscilla 175
archisynagogus 123, 134
archon 188, 190
Argos 84
Asia Minor 124, 128, 138
    Christian presence in 126
Asterius 42-4
atheism 7
Athens 120, 124, 158
Augustine 159, 162
Augustus 7, 122, 145, 175, 183
Ausonius 159

Babylonia 138
baptism 41, 44, 119

Barnabas 47
Beroea 157
Beth She'arim 134
Bithynia 183
Bosporan Kingdom 112-6

Caesarea 120-1
Caligula 7-8, 131-2, 154, 171
calumnia 9
Capitolina 123
Chaldaeans 29
Chrestus 174, 176, 178, 180-81
Christian mission 126
Chrysostom 133, 135
Circumcision 13, 32, 119
    as a symbolic act 16
    and Jerusalem church 12
    as a synonym 11
    as initiation 32
    burden of 15
    exemption from 13
    of Timothy 12-14, 17
    relation to salvation 16
    circus factions 131
Claudius 29, 132, 142, 171-75, 177,
    179
Clearchus 138
Clemens 8, 123
Clement of Alexandria 14, 44
Coele-Syria 138
Coelicolae 115-6
Cohors Italica 121
Constantine 114, 133
Corinth 12, 84, 120, 174
Cornelius 11, 121, 123, 125
Cornelius Hispalus 29
Council of Constantinople 44
Council of Nicaea 101
Covenant 15
Cretans 199
Crete 87

cult
    building 54
    foreign 32
    of Bacchanalia 32
    of Dionysos 90, 100
    of Isis 32
    of Mithra 32
    of Most High God 106
    of Roman emperors 108
    of Sabazios 89, 92
    of Sabazius 32
    of Serapis 107
    of the Jewish God 32
    of the Most High God 84, 108
    of Zeus 84
    official Roman 121
    Sabazios 88
    under Jewish influence 106
cupiditas 9
Cybele 86
Cyril of Alexandria 59, 102

Dacia 85, 86
Daphne 133-5
Delos 57, 86, 97
Demetrius 130
Didymus the Blind 41
Dio Cassius 123, 171, 174, 176-7, 181
Diogenes 44, 46
Dionysus 32, 99
Divus Augustus 7
Domitian 4-5, 8-9, 123
Donatists 103
Dura Europos 57

Egypt 85, 132
Elche 57
Ephesian
    citizenship 143
    documents 145
    inscriptions 146
    Jews 146
Ephesus 144, 146
    and Temple tax 145
Epictetus 119
Erasmus 199
Eustathios 61

Flaccus 145, 168

Flavia Domitilla 5, 123
Flavius Clemens 5, 7, 36, 123
flood legend 151
Fulvia 30, 33

Gaius (emperor) see *Caligula*
Gaius Caesennius Paetus 133
Gaius Fannius 144
Gaius Norbanus Flaccus 146
Galatians 12, 37
Gentiles
    altars 30
    and the Sabbath 28
    Christians 13, 15, 121
    conflicts with 145
    conversion of 24, 26, 30
    in inscriptions 59
    mission to 52, 124, 143
    status of 11
    sympathetic 12, 56, 119,
        120, 125, 135
    taxing of 6
    worshippers 124
gerousiarches 134
Gnaeus Pompeius Collega 133
God-fearers 37, 47-8, 52, 113-24,
        121, 135
    Cornelius 11, 121
    'disappearance' of 125
    as a technical term 55, 56
    Gentile 37, 65
    in inscriptions 53, 58, 64
    Jewish attitude towards 126
    Justus 12
    mission to 125
    opposition to Christianity 122
    reception of Christianity 120
    significance in Acts 120, 126
gods, pagan 121
grammateus 190
Gregory of Nazianzus 101, 116
Gregory of Nyssa 101
gymnasiarchs 129

Halicarnassus 141
Heaven-fearers 120
Helios 92
Hermogenes 151
Hermonassa 115

Hermophilos 61
Herodas 151
Hippolytus 114
Holy Scriptures 15
Holy Spirit 121
Hypsistarii 101, 116
Hypsistarioi 115
Hyrcanus 144

Iconium 2
initiation of the proselytes 119
inscriptions
    Aphrodisias 25
    Jewish 25
    ossuary 44, 45
    proselyte 25
    women in 25
intermarriage 17
Izates 36

Jerome 14
Jerusalem 13, 43, 44
    Council 13, 15
    Temple 143, 171
Jesus 39, 178, 181
Jewish
    'charter' 139
    apostates 10
    atheism 7-9, 123
    cemeteries 182
    Christian families 13
    Christians 15, 121
    communities 2, 11, 15, 121, 123,
    125, 133, 140-1, 143, 171, 181, 185,
    192
    Greece 154
    court of law 134
    custom 28
    estimate of population 23
    ethnic identity 17
    ethnic origin 6
    ethnic self-definition 10
    expulsion 168
    God 3
    hospital 134
    identification 6
    identity 2, 3, 12
    imposters 30
    increase in population 24

law 15, 31, 52
leaders 39
life 9
literature 32, 119
manner of life 8
mission 20, 22-4, 28, 36-7, 48
mission to God-fearers 125
missionary activity 28
missionary zeal 21, 27
nation 11
opposition to Christian mission
125
Patriarchate 21
piety 121
pogrom 131-3
population in Syria 128
privileges 130, 138
propaganda 32
prophets 48
proselyte status in community 26
proselytes 24, 46
proselytism 8, 36
proselytizing activity 27, 46
proselytizing zeal 37
relations with Gentiles 2, 12
religious identity 11
religious self-definition 10, 12
rights 139, 142, 171
rituals 28, 31, 99
slaves 169
superstition 31
symbols—lulabs 59
sympathizers 3, 8, 21, 30, 49, 52-
53, 64, 124
tax 4, 9, 10, 145
tax exemptions 138
tax-evaders 9
tensions with Gentiles 130
victory 33
war against Rome 3
world 17
Jews
    and Roman citizenship 128, 144
    Antiochene 128
    banishment of 31
    Cicero's attitude to 168
    comparison with 27
    ethnic 6, 10

expulsion of 3, 29-31, 123, 171, 176
in Miletus 149
in Rome 168, 170, 182
military service 31
punishment of 29
status of 139
warning to 172
Jonathan 130
Josephus 36, 38-93, 119, 123, 128, 133--5, 138
Judaism
adherents of 5
converts to 3
fashionable 123
in the Second Temple Period 20, 23
Judaizers 118
Judea 121
Julia Severa 123
Julius Antonius 146
Julius Caesar 170
Justin 40, 45

lamps 29
lex maiestatis 8
Libanius 133
lineage
matrilineal 15-16
literary devices 121
Lucius Antonius 144
Lucius Lentulus Crus 144
Luke
as an historian 2
as historian 52, 124
as theologian 52
theological scheme 125
Lydia 11-12, 138

Maccabean period 10
Macedonia 85
Malalas 131-34
Manichaeans 103
manumission 31, 109, 154
Marcus Agrippa 146
Maria of Cassobela 44
martyrdom 123
Mary of Cassobela 42
matrilineal principle 17

Melanchthon 199
Mesopotamia 138
Messalians 102, 115-16
Miletus 64-65, 148, 158
Mishnah 26, 120
mission to the Gentiles 121-22
Mithridates 145
Most High God 110, 113-16, 155
(see also Theos Hypsistos)
cult of 84
dedications to 87, 106
epigraphic evidence 85
in inscriptions 96
in patristic literature 101
priest of 101
worship of 111
Mysia 183
Mytilene 87

Nero 123, 181
Nerva 3, 4, 5, 6, 9
Nicolas of Antioch 49, 135

Origen 14
Orosius 175-76, 180
Ostia 57

pagan writers 9
Palestine 10, 12, 17, 59, 181
environs of 21
Palestinian
agenda 17
background 2
Jews 17
Pan 94, 95
patron 26
Paul 12, 42, 47-48, 98, 122, 124
teaching of 13
conversion of 121
Paulus Orosius 172
Pergamene decree 140
Peter 43, 121
Pharisaism
converts to 38
Pharisees 39
Philadelphia 85
Philip 121
Philippi 2, 98, 100, 120

Philo 20, 24-25, 30, 33, 38, 40, 94, 98,
    119, 154, 171, 177
Phineas 132
Phoenicia 59, 183, 184
Phoenicians 158
Phrygia 57, 85, 138
Pisidian Antioch 120, 122-26
Pliny 114
Plutarch 99
polytheism 121
Pontus 42
Poppaea Sabina 123
prayer-house 96, 109, 114ff.
priest of the imperial cult 123
Principate 6
Priscillianists 103
proselytes 5, 23, 32, 119, 123-24, 135
    Christian 40, 46
    meaning of 22
    Paul, a noble 42
    semi-proselyte 52
    youngest 25
    ambigious status of 26
    and Pharisees 37
    as Gentile Christians 40
    as mediators 53
    assumptions about 21
    attitude to 33
    Christian 44, 46
    freed slaves 26
    Gentile 39, 41
    in inscriptions 25, 59, 60
    in literary sources 32
    in the New Testament 24
    Pharisaic 38
    population changes 23
    Roman 26
    women 25, 26
Proseuche 114ff
    (see also 'Prayer house')
public ceremonies 123
Publius Servilius Galba 148

rabbinic law 17
Rabbis 36
Roman
    apotheosis 8
    aristocracy 5, 8, 9
    army 144

    authorities 3, 9, 31, 140
    authority 31
    citizens 6
    citizenship 144, 169, 170
    emperors 61
    Empire 93
    gods 3, 6
    identity 32
    law 7, 17, 26, 103
    legislators 102
    literature 27
    officials 142
    onomastics 92
    Paul as a citizen 16
    Republican period 6
    Senate 144-45
    soldiers 16
    state 3, 4, 6, 10
    traditional virtues and beliefs 31
    treason law 6

Sabazius Jupiter
    cult of 29
Sabbath 8, 28, 47, 101, 144
Sabbistes 114
Sardinia 31
Sardis 54, 57, 62-63, 138, 141
Sarra from Cyrene 26
Sejanus 171
Seleucus I Nicator 128-29
Seneca 28
Septuagint 33, 38, 86, 96, 98, 109, 201
Serdica 88
Sertorius 145
Sidon 132
Silas 84, 124
Stephen 42
Stobi 57
Suetonius 174-77, 179-81
synagogue 12, 42-43, 47-48, 54-55, 57,
    61-63, 97, 101, 110, 133-5, 141, 143,
    146, 149, 170, 182, 184
    administration of 191
    business 186
    Corinthian 162
    Graeco-Jewish 186
    Jewish 157, 191
    of the Agrippesians 183
    of the Augustans 170

of the Augustesians 183
of the Calcaresians 183
of the Campesians 183
of Elaea 183
of the Hebrews 183
of the Herodians 185
of the Siburesians 184
of the Tripolitans 184
of the Vernaclesians 185
of the Volumnesians 185
officials of 186, 187, 190-1
Roman 170, 182, 185-6
structural diversity 188
structure of 192
worship 186
syncretism 29
definition of 198-99, 200
Hellenistic 201
heuristic model 203
history of use 199
Jewish-pagan 86
Syria 128, 130, 132

Tacitus 2, 179, 181
Talmud 184
Tanais 54, 87, 108, 110-12
Temple 61, 119, 132
Temple contributions 119
Temple tax 10, 145, 182
Tertullian 14
Thea Hypsiste 93
Theos Hypsistos 85-86, 88, 92-95, 98-
100, 115
Theosebeis 115
Thessalonica 120, 124, 156
Thrace 85-6
Thyateira 87
Tiberius 7
Timothy 12-3
as a Gentile 14
as Jewish 16
circumcision of 14-7
ethnicity of 14
Titus (in the NT) 12, 13
Titus (emperor) 130, 133
Titus Ampius Balbus 144
Torah 37-38, 53
Trachinitis 59
Trajan 9

Tralles 123
Turronii 123
Tyre 131

Valerius Maximus 29
Vespasian 10, 132, 134, 140

women 122-24
Damascenes 124

Zeus 87, 93-94, 99-100, 150
Zeus Hypsistos 85-88, 94
Zeuxis 138

THE BOOK OF
ACTS
IN ITS FIRST
CENTURY SETTING

Bruce W. Winter, *series editor*

THIS WIDE-RANGING SIX-VOLUME
series presents the results of interdisci-
plinary research between New Testament,
Jewish, and classical scholarship. Working
to place the Book of Acts within its first-
century setting, well-known historians and
biblical scholars from Australia, the United
States, Canada, Russia, Germany, France,
Israel, New Zealand, and the United Kingdom have collaborated here to provide a
stimulating new study that replaces older
studies on Acts, including aspects of *The
Beginnings of Christianity.*

Starting with the understanding that the
Book of Acts is rooted within the setting of
the peoples and cultures of the Mediterranean in the first century A.D., this compre-
hensive series provides a multifaceted
approach to the Acts of the Apostles in its
literary, regional, cultural, ideological, and
theological contexts.

The composition of Acts is discussed
beside the writing of ancient literary mono-
graphs and intellectual biographies. Recent
epigraphic and papyrological discoveries
also help illumine the text of Acts. Archaeological fieldwork, especially in Greece and
Asia Minor, has yielded valuable information about the local setting of Acts and the
religious life of urban communities in the
Roman Empire. These volumes draw on the
best of this research to elucidate the Book of
Acts against the background of activity in
which early Christianity was born.